# HANDBOOK OF THE WORLD'S RELIGIONS

# HANDBOOK OF THE WORLD'S RELIGIONS

Edited by
A. M. Zehavi

Franklin Watts, Inc.
New York
1973

# CONTENTS

# INTRODUCTION

The purpose of this *Handbook* is to facilitate access to basic information about the organized religions of the world. A handbook, as the name implies, obviates searching through five or twenty volumes for essential facts and concepts. This one volume presents the casual reader with a concise introduction to the subject, and to the student it offers details. The former will be satisfied with the table of contents as his guide; the latter will be aided by the comprehensive index.

The *Handbook* follows this format:

The first five chapters are each devoted to a different religion, the order determined by the number of adherents in North America as estimated in almanacs. A general discussion of the religion introduces the chapter, which is then divided into categories: major denominations, sects, and orders; foremost personalities; and a listing of appropriate terms. In some instances the terms have additionally warranted separate categories of holidays and sacred literature. ("Terms" include those dealing with doctrine, rites, and religious history. Terms having a primarily nationalistic significance have been avoided, but the line is not always easily drawn between religious history and nationalistic history.) Each category is arranged alphabetically.

The sixth chapter treats smaller organized religions. The last chapter may be read as foreword as well as afterword; it contains two essays on religion in general, followed by a list of terms that enhance a broader understanding of the subject.

Any work on religion seems almost by nature provocative, and even the question of what constitutes basic information will cause disagreement. Because this *Handbook* does not attempt to be encyclopedic, choices had to be made—and no slights are intended through inclusions, omissions, and length of entries. The development and peculiarities of each religion preclude comparison of the contents of similar categories; topic entries must be viewed only in relation to the religion concerned. Disputing particulars probably reflects a more intimate or comprehensive knowledge of a certain religion than a handbook intends to provide, and the reader is thereupon invited to turn to other chapters to learn about other religions in which he may be less knowledgeable.

Buddhist monks sit before holy images in the Shwe Dagon Pagoda in Rangoon, Burma. In some Oriental countries, it is common for young men to spend a period of time as Buddhist monks.

A Moroccan Muslim studies the Koran, the holy scripture of Islam.

Hindus bathing in the Ganges River of India. To Hindus, the Ganges is a sacred river whose waters cleanse, purify, and cure.

An Israel rabbi blows the ram's horn, or shofar. This is part of services on the day of the New Year and the Day of Atonement.

A Catholic priest prays as he holds up one of the consecrated hosts to be distributed to communicants in a New York church.

*Rapho-Guillumette*

A minister reads a passage from the Bible to his congregation in a Methodist church in Anchorage, Alaska.

*Monkmeyer Press Photo Service*

*George J. Adams*

# HANDBOOK OF THE WORLD'S RELIGIONS

"Christ Preaching," an etching by Rembrandt.

*The British Museum*

# 1 · CHRISTIANITY

**CHRISTIANITY** [krĭs-chē-ăn′ə-tē], the historic religion derived from the teaching and life of Jesus Christ. It was founded and grew up amid the vigorous currents and crosscurrents of religious thought and practice in the Greco-Roman world of the 1st century A.D. Arising as a sect within Judaism, it had behind it a long and complex religious development that culminated in the Hebrew prophetic movement and the deeply laid hope of the coming of the Messiah (the "anointed one"), who would establish the Kingdom of God on earth.

**Judaic Roots.** The prophets, more clearly than any other group of religious men in Israel, had seen the working out of the divine purpose of Yahweh, the God of Israel, in and through the history of their nation. They looked back on all that had happened and found in it His guiding hand, perceiving Him to be the sovereign Creator and Ruler of the universe, controlling its history and ordering the course of events in accordance with His will and for His own ends. After the Babylonian Exile in the 6th century B.C., Messianic aspirations occupied an increasingly prominent place in Judaism, especially at and after the time of the Maccabean Revolt (167 B.C.). Speculations concerning a divine intervention and an approaching Day of the Lord became rife—as hopes of deliverance were raised only to be dashed to pieces, as one catastrophe followed another, until in 63 B.C. the Jewish community in Palestine was incorporated into the Roman province of Syria.

**The Messiahship of Jesus.** It was in the capacity of this long-expected Messiah that Jesus of Nazareth gathered round Him a small band of followers after He had undergone a profound spiritual experience, and when at about 30 years of age He was baptized in the River Jordan by John the Baptist, the herald of His movement (Mark 1:1–11). According to the tradition compiled by various people from different sources and written down (c.65–90 A.D.) in the form of the Synoptic Gospels, Jesus was born of a Virgin Mother, Mary, betrothed to His foster father, Joseph, who was of Davidic descent (Matt. 1:6ff.; Luke 1:13ff.; 2:17). Jesus' conception of the Messiahship, however, was very different from that commonly held by the Jewish religious and political parties—the Pharisees, the Sadducees, the Herodians, and the Zealots. Indeed, at the beginning of His public ministry in Galilee He had not openly disclosed His identity; and even the disciples He had gathered round Him were very puzzled about His claims, until at Caesarea Philippi Peter explicitly declared that He was in fact the Christ (Mark 4:41; 8:29ff.; Matt. 16:16ff.). In the meantime He had secured a considerable amount of popular support through His remarkable healing powers; and on one occasion it is recorded that the people tried to make Him a King (John 6:15). This He steadfastly refused to countenance, because He had no intention of becoming the leader of a Messianic insurrection.

He had been anointed by the Spirit of the Lord to

"preach good tidings to the poor, to proclaim release to captives and recovering of sight to the blind, to set at liberty them that were bruised, to proclaim the acceptable year of the Lord" (Luke 4:18f.), thereby connecting His conception of the Messiahship with that of the Suffering Servant of Yahweh foretold by the Deutero-Isaiah at the end of the Exile (Isa. 61:1–3; 52:7ff.; 53). His mission was to bring salvation through suffering (Mark 8:31ff.; Matt. 16:21ff.), rather than to be a greater David or the spectacular Son of Man coming in power and glory to deliver the nation from the Roman yoke. While it would seem that He accepted the Jewish apocalyptic notions of a new age to be established by the appearance of the Messiah in the clouds of heaven (Mark 13; 14:62; 24; 26:64), the eschatological "sayings" attributed to Him in the Gospel narratives doubtless were influenced by the apocalyptic conceptions of a "Parousia," or Second Coming of Christ, current in Judeo-Christian circles before and immediately after the fall of Jerusalem in 70 A.D. (I Thess. 4:15ff.; 5:1ff.; II Thess. 2:2; II Pet. 3:7ff.; Rev. 14:15ff.; 21).

The Early Church was, in fact, obsessed by the idea of the imminence of this catastrophic event. Thus there was a tendency in compiling the records to interpret what Jesus had predicted—about the destruction of the Temple, and the tribulation in Judea at the time of the fall of Jerusalem, and the signs in the heavens—as a prelude to an apocalyptic Day of Judgment in terms of a current belief concerning the advent of the Son of Man. This is most apparent in the latest book to be admitted into the New Testament Canon, the so-called Revelation of St. John the Divine, or the Apocalypse, which is pure apocalyptic, compiled apparently at the end of the 1st century A.D., when persecution of the Church was rife under the Emperor Domitian. But while there is good reason to think that Jesus expected the Kingdom to be established immediately, and His followers at first were convinced that it might happen at any moment, the prevailing Christian tradition has been against speculation as to its time and manner (Mark 13:32), coupled with the certainty of a final General Judgment at the end of the present order in time.

The greatest enigma, however, for His disciples was the idea of a suffering Messiah (Mark 8:31ff.; Matt. 16:21ff.; Luke 17:25; 22:48,69; 24:7ff.; 12:49ff.; 13:31ff.). This was completely foreign to the Jewish conception of Messiahship. Nevertheless, once the crucifixion and its Easter sequel became accomplished facts, the implications of the Isaianic Suffering-Servant prophecies were recognized. Then the unique Christian interpretation of the office was formulated—largely under the influence of St. Paul—and proclaimed as the Gospel of Salvation for all mankind, irrespective of nationality, social status, or religious antecedents (Col. 3:11). The functions attributed to the Davidic King and then invested with apocalyptic glory in the Son of Man became transfigured with suffering in the person of the defeated yet victorious Saviour of mankind who had applied the figure of the Suffering Servant of Yahweh to Himself, not only in what He said about Himself and His mission, but supremely in laying down His life in an act of self-offering, humiliation, and complete surrender to the will and purpose of His heavenly Father. Thereby He demonstrated that "greater love" which was at the heart of the Gospel of Redemption which His duly commissioned apostles and their successors proclaimed to Jews and Gentiles alike.

**The Apostolic Church.** It was this conception of the reconciliation of God and man that differentiated Christianity from the Judaism in which it had its origin. The death and resurrection of its Founder, regarded as the Incarnate Lord from heaven, the only begotten Son of God, risen, ascended, and glorified, were the fundamental facts on which the Christian faith was established and propagated, first in Jewry and then in the Greco-Roman world at large. Having received a special outpouring of the divine afflatus in the descent of the Holy Ghost at the Feast of Pentecost immediately after the Ascension, the apostles went forth to make known far and wide the mystery of Redemption that had been revealed to them. To this end Christ is represented as bestowing upon them power and authority to become His agents in the dispensation of His divine grace within the Church which He had founded and endowed with the Holy Spirit to be the New Israel (Matt. 28:18ff.; Acts 2; Col. 1:24; I Cor. 12:27; Eph. 2:20–22).

The accession of Saul of Tarsus to the apostolic Nazoraean company unquestionably was the most significant event in the opening phase of the movement. Born and bred of Jewish stock in the Hellenistic environment of Cilicia, Saul, a Roman citizen, had been brought up in a cosmopolitan milieu before going to Jerusalem to be trained in the rabbinical school of Gamaliel, then the leading teacher of the Pharisees. There he himself became a fanatical "Pharisee of the Pharisees," engaging in a vigorous campaign to exterminate the Nazoraean heresy, until the position was reversed after his encounter with the risen and ascended Jesus on the road to Damascus (Acts 9:1–9). Although it is not easy to determine what exactly were his relations with the Church at Jerusalem, it is clear that he became the spearhead of the Christian missionary enterprise in the principal cities of Asia Minor, Macedonia, and Greece not later than 60 A.D., and established local ecclesiae (churches) wherever he went. St. Peter was the outstanding figure among the Twelve Apostles in the Jewish Christian community (Gal. 1:13ff., 17; 2:11–21; Acts 9:11–22); though it was James, the so-called Lord's brother (perhaps a cousin of Jesus), who presided over the Council of Jerusalem when the enforcement of the rite of circumcision on Gentile converts had become a matter of acute controversy (Acts 15:5ff.).

As the situation is presented in the Gospels and the Acts of the Apostles, the original 11 disciples and Matthias, who took the 12th place vacated by Judas Iscariot, constituted the nucleus of the Apostolic Church, having been the closest companions of Jesus during His lifetime, the witnesses of His resurrection, and His appointed representatives to carry on His mission in the world. Therefore, they exercised apostolic jurisdiction over the entire movement (Matt. 28:18–20; John 20:21; Acts 1:21–26; Mark 3:14; Luke 4:13–20). Among them St. Peter, the "rock-man" (Cephas), was the predominant personality, even though James, the Lord's brother, presided over the mother church at Jerusalem. Whether or not a special commission was given to St. Peter, the "Prince of the Apostles," when he acknowledged the Messiahship of

Jesus at Caesarea Philippi as the Matthaean logion seems to suggest (Matt. 16:17–19), St. Peter apparently occupied much the same position in the Jerusalem church as St. Paul subsequently claimed to fulfill among the Gentile Christians (Gal. 2). But St. Paul was in a different category from the Twelve, being a later convert and having persecuted the movement with, on his own admission, the same ardor as he eventually propagated it. He claimed, however, to have received a special commission from the risen Christ who appeared to him as "one born out of due time" and who had "labored more abundantly than them all" (I Cor. 15:8–10). To what extent there was a fundamental theological divergence between the Pauline and Jerusalem sections of the Church is difficult to determine, since most of the literature that has been handed down to us has come either from Pauline sources or from those compiled after the Pauline tradition was firmly established. The common foundation of the faith, nevertheless, was the Resurrection, and its worship was the Breaking of the Bread, or the Eucharist, as the perpetual memorial, or anamnesis, of the sacrifice of the Cross; for as often as the bread was broken and the cup drunk, the death of the Lord for the remission of sins was shown forth (Luke 22:19; Matt. 26:28).

**The Eucharist.** During his lifetime, Jesus had been in the habit of assembling the disciples for a common meal, *Chaburah*, to discuss the Messianic mission in its various aspects; and the stories of the miraculous feeding of large multitudes may have been connected with these ritual gatherings (John 6, where the feeding of the 5,000 is a prelude to the Johannine Eucharistic discourse). This practice reached its climax when on the same night in which He was betrayed—now commonly called Maundy, or Holy, Thursday—Jesus collected His disciples together in an upper room in Jerusalem, possibly in the house of John Mark, for what was to be the last supper He would have with them while He was still in the flesh. Whether or not it was actually the Passover or a *Chaburah* is still uncertain. The three Synoptic Gospels are all agreed that it was on "the first day of unleavened bread when they sacrificed the Passover" that it occurred (Mark 14:1,22; Matt. 26:17; Luke 22:7); but the Fourth Gospel maintains that it took place "before the feast of the Passover" (John 13:1ff.), and that the bodies were taken down from the crosses about the time the Paschal lambs were killed at sunset on the following day, which was the Preparation before the feast (John 19:31ff.). If this is correct, the Last Supper must have been a ritual meal (*Chaburah*) in preparation for the coming festival.

Expert opinion is still divided about these mutually exclusive chronologies and, in spite of ingenious attempts to reconcile them, the discrepancies in the records of the ordinance remain. What is clear, however, is that the ever-memorable gathering was held at the Passover season—within a few hours of the betrayal, passion, and crucifixion of Christ—and that at it He identified the bread and wine that He blessed and distributed among the apostles with His body that was about to be broken and His blood that was about to be poured out sacrificially to seal the New Covenant He was establishing in the New Israel (Mark 14:24; I Cor. 10:1–5; 11:23ff.). This, at any rate, is the way in which those events were regarded by the apostolic

"The Three Crosses,"
by Rembrandt.

company, who from the beginning were in the habit of meeting together in one another's houses on the first day of the week—sacred to the memory of the Resurrection —to have a common meal, at which the rite instituted at the Last Supper was performed (Acts 2:42,46; 20:7).

This practice, however, led to abuses—including drunkenness, gluttony, and heresies—which were condemned in no uncertain terms by St. Paul in his first letter to the Christian community at Corinth, written (c.55 A.D.) some 20 years after the Crucifixion. To rectify this unedifying state of affairs, St. Paul sought to restore the Eucharistic Rite to its pristine character by separating it from the social meal. To do this, he recalled its sacred nature, the intention of the Lord that it be the perpetual memorial before God of the death of Christ, enacted under the very shadow of the passion, and ordained by Christ to be the central act of Christian worship, taking the place of the Passover in the Jewish Dispensation, with Christ Himself as the Paschal Lamb (I Cor. 11:23–29). By His death, resurrection, and ascension, Christ had wrought a deliverance immeasurably greater than that effected by the Exodus of the Hebrews from bondage in Egypt, which the Passover commemorated; and it was the anamnesis of this all-sufficient sacrifice that was made in the Eucharistic oblation in the New Israel. Therefore, around it a mystical theology was gradually formulated in the Apostolic Church, centered in the Breaking of the Bread, as the weekly *Chaburah*, interpreted in this manner.

As the movement spread in the Greco-Roman world, and as converts were made outside Jewish circles, it was on the death and resurrection of Christ as Redeemer, conceived in terms of the mystery cultus prevalent in the Empire at the beginning of the new era, that attention was focused. St. Paul, however, took most of his illustrations from the Old Testament; and the Christian liturgy at first developed along the lines of the synagogue pattern—opening with the reading of Scripture and prayers and concluding with the dismissal of those who were preparing for baptism (the catechumens). After their departure, the most solemn part of the service, called the *Missa fidelium*, or Mass of the Faithful, began.

When the Agape, or common meal, was separated from the Eucharist, the synagogue type of service was confined to the preliminary part of the rite. The sacrament itself, the *Missa fidelium*, opened with the placing of the bread and wine on the altar at the offertory, followed by their consecration in commemoration of the passion and death of Christ, the symbolic breaking of the Host (the Fraction) and its comixture in the chalice, the kiss of peace, the Communion of the clergy and congregation, and the dismissal by the deacon with the words, "*Ite missa est*," a formula that led to the Eucharist being known as "the Mass" (*missa*).

To what extent St. Paul had been influenced by the Greco-Oriental mystery thought and practice current in Cilicia it is difficult to say. He regarded baptism as burial with Christ unto death and a rising again in newness of life as a reborn creature animated by a new life-principle —"walking not after the flesh but after the Spirit" (Rom. 6:3–5; 8:4; II Cor. 5:17; Col. 2:12). This was definitely a mystery interpretation of initiation; but so far as is known,

initiates in the pagan cults (those of Isis, Osiris, Serapis, Attis and Cybele, and Mithra) were neither baptized in the name of the saviour-god or goddess, nor were they the recipients of a pneumatic gift as a result of a ritual of lustration. For St. Paul incorporation into the person of Christ through the operation of the Holy Spirit was the central feature of the redemptive process—with the newborn initiate passing from death to life by a mystical experience and a conscious act of self-renouncing trust rather than by an elaborate series of initiation ceremonies. In short, Christianity was itself the mystery religion par excellence—the culmination of the age-long quest for resurrection and newness of life, expressed in mystery language and thought, but shorn of its magical content and polytheistic mythology. As Dean W. R. Inge pointed out, "If Christ had not instituted Baptism and the Eucharist, the Church would have been compelled to invent them if she were ever to prevail in the Empire" (*Contentio Veritatis*, 1916, p. 279), so deeply rooted in the Gentile mind was the cultus of which these rites were an integral part. It was not difficult to spiritualize the ancient symbolism in terms of the King and Saviour of mankind laying down His life in voluntary self-oblation, and expressing the death and resurrection theme liturgically in the myth and ritual pattern so long centered in the worship of the divine kingship in the Near East and the Greco-Roman world.

**The Sacred Ministry.** It was along these lines that the liturgy took shape in Christianity when the Church broke away from its Jewish moorings and entered the larger stream of Greco-Roman culture. At first the celebrant was the Bishop (an Anglicized designation for the Greek *episcopos*, "overseer") who occupied the position vacated by the apostles. He was assisted by the presbyters, an ambiguous name which came to include both "elder" and "priest" (*sacerdos*) when it was applied in the 2d century to a separate order particularly connected with the Eucharistic oblation. As the faith spread and local churches were placed under the care of presbyters, they, acting as deputies of the Bishops under whom they served, were given the right to consecrate the sacred Elements and eventually to exercise the priestly power of absolution. Episcopal functions (especially ordination and confirmation) remained with the Bishops and, by the middle of the 2d century, the principal centers appear to have had their diocesans. In each province the Bishop of the chief city was known as the "metropolitan" and had authority over the rest of the episcopate in the area.

**The Papacy and the Medieval Church.** When Christianity became the official religion of the Empire in the 4th century, the Bishops of Rome, Alexandria, and Antioch had jurisdiction, respectively, over Italy, Egypt and Libya, and Asia Minor, and this included the right of consecrating metropolitans. Their pre-eminence was recognized at the Council of Nicaea in 325, and to them were added those of Jerusalem and Constantinople at the Council of Chalcedon in 451. These five prelates, to signify their superior authority, were in the 9th century entitled "Patriarchs." Among them the supremacy and universal jurisdiction of the occupant of the Holy See (Rome) was widely recognized in Western Christendom from very early times. Not only was Rome the ancient capital of the Empire, but, in an age when relics were thought to bestow peculiar sanctity on those who housed them, it also claimed to possess the mortal remains of the Apostles St. Peter and St. Paul. Moreover, it was contended that, as the successor of St. Peter, the Bishop of Rome inherited the primacy believed to have been conferred by Christ on the "Prince of the Apostles" (Matt. 16:18f.; Luke 22:32; John 21:15–17). The independence of the Eastern provinces, however, in matters of faith and jurisdiction was steadfastly maintained. Eventually, this prolonged controversy ended in the Great Schism between East and West in 1054, when the Patriarch of Constantinople was excommunicated by Pope Leo IX. In the West the Papacy remained the unifying center with the Pope and the Emperor wielding the "two swords" of spiritual and temporal power. In the 11th and 12th centuries, Papal supremacy under St. Gregory VII (Hildebrand), Innocent III, and Boniface VIII unquestionably consolidated Western Europe until the disastrous Western Schism, with rival Popes at Rome and Avignon between 1378 and 1417, immeasurably weakened the institution.

By this time many abuses and anomalies were crying for rectification, and even the intellectual vigor of Scholasticism, which, following the foundation of the universities, constituted the crowning achievement of the 13th century, was on the wane. Led by Duns Scotus, the Franciscan opposition to St. Thomas Aquinas and the Aristotelian Dominican school became a potent factor in the rapid decline of Scholasticism in the 14th century. The finishing touches were supplied by the Renaissance, after the fall of Constantinople to the Muslims in 1453, with its secularizing influence and bid for freedom from ecclesiastical control. The Popes became the most ardent patrons of the arts and of the revival of classical culture, more intent on making Rome the most splendid city in the world than on remedying the defects of the Church under their jurisdiction.

**The Reformation.** The stage was set, therefore, for drastic reform. Indeed, voices demanding reform already had been raised in England by Wycliffe (1329–84) and in Bohemia by Hus (1369–1415); it only remained for Luther in 1517 to break out in open revolt against the sale of indulgences preached by Tetzel, and to proclaim the doctrine of "justification by faith" as the basis of salvation, against the medieval system of "good works" and the "treasury of merits," for the curtain to rise on the drama of the Reformation. From Germany the movement spread to Central Europe where, under the influence of Zwingli (1484–1531) in Zurich, and Calvin (1509–64) in Geneva, it acquired a more radical character. The apostolic succession of Bishops, priests, and deacons, as well as the universal jurisdiction of the Papacy, was abandoned, as was the doctrine of the real presence in the Eucharist and the sacrifice of the Mass. The Bible became the sole basis of belief, the religious orders were dissolved, liturgical worship ceased, and in an iconoclastic destruction of altars, reredoses, statues, and shrines, churches and cathedrals suffered irreparable damage. In Switzerland a theocracy was established by Calvin on the basis of his doctrine of the predestination of the elect believers, set forth in his *Institutes* in 1536.

In England the Reformation took a different turn because it arose as a result of a political quarrel between Henry VIII and the Papacy when the King failed to secure the nullification of his marriage to Catherine of Aragon. He had himself strenuously opposed Luther, thereby acquiring and retaining the title "Defender of the Faith"; and following the breach with Rome in 1533, apart from the repudiation of the jurisdiction of the Holy See and the rapacious dissolution of the monasteries, very little change was made in doctrine and practice until after his death in 1547. In the short reign of Edward VI, Protestant influences from the Continent were strongly felt, and subsequently when the return to the Papal allegiance in the interlude of Mary Tudor ceased on the accession of Elizabeth I in 1559, a gallant attempt was made to arrive at a settlement of the complex situation that had arisen, by establishing a national church which would embrace all the various factions in the country. But it failed to satisfy either the "recusant" Roman Catholics or the Calvinistic Puritans, as being a via media neither genuinely Catholic nor properly Protestant. So, after the restoration of the monarchy in 1660, the Anglican Establishment, claiming to be both Catholic and Reformed, was reinstated with its apostolic ministry, sacraments, historic creeds, liturgy, and offices based on their ancient Catholic prototypes but combined with a freer use of Scripture in public worship, the substitution of the vernacular for Latin, a very considerable latitude in doctrinal interpretation and ceremonial procedure, and Thirty-nine Articles of dogmatic tenets rather heavily weighted on the Protestant side.

In the meantime a Catholic Counter Reformation had made a serious effort to remedy many of the abuses of the Renaissance period, and from the protracted deliberations of the Council of Trent, between 1545 and 1563, definitions of the cardinal doctrines of the faith emerged. While these did not satisfy the Protestant demands, they gave the Papacy and the newly formed religious orders (among them the Jesuits, Capuchins, and Oratorians) a firmer basis on which to proceed with their new missionary enterprise in America and the East, and a new apostolic zeal was displayed in Western Europe by such outstanding figures as St. Ignatius Loyola, St. Francis Xavier, St. Francis de Sales, St. Charles Borromeo, and the Spanish mystics St. Teresa of Ávila and St. John of the Cross.

**Christianity the Heir of the Ages.** The disruption of the unity of Christianity in the 11th and 16th centuries was a major disaster, resulting in the unedifying spectacle of a Catholic Church divided at the center and with a ring of warring Protestant sects on its periphery. The seriousness of the situation has now become widely recognized, and has given rise to various attempts to heal the breaches, of which the Ecumenical Movement is an outstanding example. Nevertheless, the disruptions represent to some extent the product and expression of the all-embracing nature of Christianity itself as the heir of the ages. Basing its theology in the beginning on the ethical monotheism of the Hebrew prophets and the Messianic eschatology of Hellenistic Judaism, brought into relation with a highly spiritualized reinterpretation of the death and resurrection sacred drama so fundamental in Greco-Oriental mystery religions from time before memory, and reassembled around the unique personality of Christ the King, it "became all things to all men, that it might by all means save some." It met its own day and generation on their own ground, and spoke to them in their own language, interpreting and presenting its faith and worship in their own idiom. Thus, it fulfilled the spiritual demands of the era in which it emerged and made it its own, Christ having come "in the fullness of time," when "Greek conquered Jew, and Jew conquered Greek, and the world inherited the legacy of their struggle through Roman hands."

By the Incarnation of the Divine on the plane of history, a genuinely new revelation of faith and practice had been brought into being. But, as in the case of every emergence in the evolutionary process, it merged out of that which already existed, as had life, reflective thought and self-consciousness, appearing as mutations and creative occurrences, changing what had already existed rather than being merely resultants of previous conditions. So Christianity succeeded where its predecessors and competitors had failed, because it was at once a uniquely new movement in the history of religion, and yet a product and fulfillment of all that had gone before, meeting the deepest needs of men in every age. It was not so much what Jesus said as what He was and did that caused Him to be proclaimed the supreme disclosure of God to man, entirely different from all other religious founders, teachers, sages, prophets, and mystics. It is not that God was disclosed alone in Christ, but that in Him He was incarnate supremely, completely, and uniquely. "God, who at sundry times and in divers manners spake in time past unto the fathers by the prophets hath in these last days spoken unto us by His Son, whom He hath appointed heir of all things, by whom also He made the worlds" (Heb. 1:1,2).

## Denominations

**ANGLICANISM** [ăng′glə-kən-ĭz-əm], word, first used in the early 19th century, to describe the spirit or the teaching, not only of the Church of England but of the several Episcopal churches in communion with the Church of England. In addition to the Episcopal Church of Scotland and the Protestant Episcopal Church of the U.S.A., the churches in the old English colonies, which had once been subject to the bishops of the Church of England, found it desirable to become independent Episcopal churches as the colonies turned into self-governing dominions within the British Commonwealth. Other churches also included are the Nippon Sei Kokwai in Japan, and Episcopal churches in Korea, China, Madagascar, the Middle East, and South America. Of all these only the Church of England is now legally established.

These churches share (1) an episcopal ministry, with the Archbishop of Canterbury as an acknowledged president; (2) meetings of bishops, normally every ten years, called Lambeth Conferences (the first held in 1867), which have no formal constitutional authority but much informal prestige in guiding the constituent churches; (3) the use, though with manifold local variations, of a form of the English *Book of Common Prayer;* (4) complete intercommunion with each other and, subject to the approval of the local bishops, interchange of ministry. The Anglican Communion is also in communion with the Church of Sweden and the Old Catholic Church of Germany and the Netherlands.

Since 1800 the Established Church in England has widened its terms of comprehension so as to include at the one end members who are in sympathy with Methodists and Presbyterians, and at the other, members who are in sympathy with Roman Catholics. To some extent this breadth is reflected in the constituent churches of the Anglican Communion, so that, for example, the Church of South Africa tends to be "high church," while the Church of Ireland tends to be "low church." But within this breadth, excluding a few extremists at either end, it is possible to discern certain common principles.

First, Anglicanism is Protestant, in that it rejects the claims of the Pope, does not subscribe to Roman Catholic doctrines officially enunciated since the Reformation, especially the doctrines of the Immaculate Conception and of the Assumption of the Blessed Virgin Mary, and holds to the Reformation belief that "all things necessary for salvation may be found in Scripture." Secondly, it is Catholic in its allegiance to the Scripture and to the apostolic teaching of the undivided Church of antiquity. The liturgy of the *Book of Common Prayer* (1662) is used almost nowhere in the Anglican Communion without variation, but its historical and austere tradition of restrained piety has marked and guided all Anglican worship and devotion.

Since 1864 the Anglican Communion has allowed great liberty in matters of religious profession, and has normally refused to condemn formally, or to expel, persons whom an earlier age would have thought to have trespassed beyond the limits of sound Scriptural and Catholic doctrine. This liberty arises partly from the necessity of comprehending in one church the modern divergencies between high and low churchmen; partly from the legal difficulties which the English Establishment puts in the way of narrow or rigid interpretations of faith; and partly from a strong belief, inherited from Richard Hooker and other divines of the English Reformation, in the proper place of reason in religion—a belief which has made Anglicans reluctant to hamper sincere inquirers, for instance, amidst the complexities of modern Biblical studies.

Though many Anglicans do not regard the resulting breadth of faith and practice in the Anglican churches as good, because it leads to troublesome varieties in worship between dioceses and parishes, they claim that it proves that many of the divisions between other communions are unnecessary, since the Anglican churches contain such divergent groups as Anglo-Catholics and Evangelicals within the same fold.

**BAPTISTS,** members of one of the largest and most distinctive Protestant denominations.

**Origins.** Baptists trace their history as a Protestant denomination to a 17th-century congregation of English Puritan separatists who had taken refuge in Holland. In 1609 the pastor, John Smyth, a former Anglican clergyman, became convinced that only adult believers should be baptized. Consequently he baptized himself and then a group of his believing followers. Smyth soon left the church he had founded, but under the leadership of Thomas Helwys the congregation returned to England, becoming the first permanent Baptist church on English soil. Other congregations were soon started. There were some influences from continental Anabaptism, but the Baptists stemmed directly from Calvinist Puritanism. The first English Baptists were moderate Calvinists, however. They believed in a "general" atonement: that Christ died for all men; hence they were called "General Baptists."

About 30 years later, probably in 1638, another Baptist group arose. These Baptists split off from a Puritan Independent congregation. They were more strictly Calvinistic than the first group. They believed in a "particular" atonement: that Christ died only for the elect; consequently, they were called "Particular Baptists." The Particular Baptists soon adopted the practice of baptism by immersion, a practice later followed by all Baptists. The Particular Baptists became the larger and stronger Baptist body in England.

**Principles.** Since their early history, there has always been a wide range of belief and practice among Baptists. A few main points of emphasis, often called Baptist principles, distinguish them. First, Baptists stress the authority of the Bible. They seek to follow the New Testament as their only guide in matters of faith and practice. Some hold to conservative theories of the Bible as being verbally inspired by God throughout, while others understand the Bible in the light of historical and critical study. All stress the centrality of the Scriptures in matters of doctrine and polity.

Second, Baptists practice baptism of believers only, insisting that the one to be baptized be mature enough to confess belief in salvation through personal faith in Jesus Christ. Some Baptist churches receive members by letter of transfer from other evangelical churches which practice infant baptism; but these churches themselves baptize only believers. The mode of baptism is normally immersion, on the basis of New Testament evidence.

Third, Baptists believe in a "gathered" church. They organize their churches congregationally, with each church independent of all others. They affirm that Christ is the true head of each local church, which is therefore autonomous under Him. But they also affirm the associational principle, by which the independent congregations of similar faith and order form associations and national conventions for mutual support and inspiration, and for missionary and evangelistic co-operation. Baptists seek to order their church democratically at all levels.

Fourth, Baptists have put considerable emphasis on the Reformation doctrine of "the priesthood of all believers." They have given prominent place to laymen and laywomen in the life of the church. Though they generally ordain as ministers only those who have experienced a spiritual call to the ministry, they do not regard ministers as forming a priestly caste or order. They ordain women as ministers.

Fifth, Baptists believe strongly in religious liberty and in the separation of church and state. Insisting that churches should be under the authority of the Bible only, they resist any kind of governmental control of churches,

*Ewing Galloway*

The First Baptist Meeting House in Providence, R.I., was built in 1775. The spire is of a later date.

and in the struggle for religious liberty they have taken a leading role.

**Baptists in North America.** Baptist beginnings in America date from about 1639, when churches were founded in Providence and Newport, Rhode Island, the former with the help of Roger Williams, and the latter under the leadership of John Clarke. These were originally Particular Baptist churches. Soon General Baptist churches were also formed, but as in England, the Particular Baptists were the stronger. The organization of the Philadelphia Baptist Association in 1707 greatly furthered their cause. At its peak, in the middle of the 18th century, the influence of the Philadelphia Association extended northward as far as Rhode Island, and southward into South Carolina. Many new associations were formed along the lines of the Philadelphia Association.

Baptists were greatly influenced by the spread of revivalism during the Great Awakening of the 18th century. In general, they became less Calvinistic and more evangelistic and pietistic in this period. In New England, many former Congregationalists became Separate Baptists during the Awakening. They spread to the South, chiefly through the influence of Shubal Stearns, who settled at Sandy Creek, N.C., in 1755. Within three years he had gathered many converts, organized several churches, and set up the Sandy Creek Association, the boundaries of which extended into Virginia and South Carolina. In 1787 the Separates merged with the Regular, or Calvinistic, Baptists. With their congregational order and intense piety, Baptists proved to be admirably adapted to the western frontier, and spread rapidly in the expanding West.

Baptists in the United States achieved a form of over-all national organization in 1814 through establishing the General Missionary Convention of the Baptist Denomination in the United States for Foreign Missions. The American Baptist Publication Society was founded in 1824, and the American Baptist Home Mission Society in 1832. But in 1845, the national unity that had been achieved was broken by the slavery issue, as Baptists in the South withdrew from these societies to found the Southern Baptist Convention. Baptists in the North continued the societies, reorganizing them in 1907 as the Northern (later American) Baptist Convention. Many Negroes are Baptists, grouped mostly in the two large National Baptist Conventions. By 1960, there were about 22,500,000 Baptists in the United States, in 27 bodies, the largest being the Southern Baptist Convention (nearly 9,500,000 members), the National Baptist Convention, Inc. (about 5,000,000), the National Baptist Convention (over 2,500,000), and the American Baptist Convention (approximately 1,500,000).

The three Baptist conventions in Canada came together for fellowship and the promotion of common interests in 1944 in the Baptist Federation of Canada. The two Baptist universities with theological departments are McMaster, in Hamilton, and Acadia, in Wolfville. There are over 1,200 Baptist churches and missions in Canada, and over 500,000 people classified in the Canadian census figures as Baptists. In 1905, the Baptist World Alliance was formed, bringing together in a co-operative fellowship Baptists from around the world.

**CALVINISM** [kăl'vĭn-ĭz-əm], type of Protestant theology stemming from the teaching of John Calvin. Calvinism has often been regarded as the chief feature of churches specifically called "Reformed," and thus distinguished from those known as Lutheran and Anglican. To a lesser extent, Calvinism is associated also with a system of morals and with a form of church-state relation.

**Theology.** Outlined fully in his *Institutes of the Christian Religion*, Calvin's theological system is firmly based on the infinite sovereignty of God. What God does is good, simply because He does it. In creating the world, He was displaying His own glorious attributes. God "fore-ordains whatsoever cometh to pass," and His eternal plan cannot be thwarted by any effort of man, whose chief end is to glorify his Maker. In stark contrast to God's transcendent majesty, man is utterly helpless. Made originally in God's image, he was dispossessed of goodness and freedom through Adam's sin, which infected humanity with "an hereditary corruption and depravity," leaving man free to sin, but not to do good. God has, however, chosen (elected) some for salvation through the atoning work of Christ. When God chooses a man, moreover, His grace is irresistible, His hold permanent; he who is elect will persevere in goodness to the end.

This was no new theology; Augustine of Hippo and Martin Luther had expressed similar views. What was new in Calvin was his carefully worked-out assertion of double predestination—that while God elected some to salvation, He elected others to damnation. For man to try to understand or question this divine mystery is blasphemy. "Shall not the judge of all the earth do right?" The five main points outlined by Calvinism are usually listed as particular predestination, limited atonement, irresistible grace, total depravity, and perseverance of the saints. These were the points relentlessly pressed and further defined in the Canons of the Synod of Dort in 1618–19, when a minority party holding the views of Jacobus Arminius tried unsuccessfully to soften the rigors of Calvinism.

The Bible is the sole authority in faith and morals; its writers verbally inspired, "the sure and authentic amanuenses of the Holy Spirit." No man could say, however, with complete certainty of another that he was of the elect, for even in the church wheat and tares grew together. One's own election is confirmed by an inner witness, and this "testimony of the Spirit" came to play a distinctive part in Calvin's theology. He never doubted his own election and God's call to interpret His Word; hence his inflexibility in the face of opposition. All parts of the Bible are equally true, but Calvin went to the Old Testament more often than to the New, and stressed God's sovereignty and His judgment upon sinners more than God's love and self-revelation in Jesus Christ.

Baptism and the Lord's Supper are the only two sacraments. By the first is signified initiation into the church; by the second Christ is truly exhibited and His sacrifice remembered through the medium of the symbolic bread and wine.

**Ethics.** Only a certain type of conduct is worthy of man made in the image of God; redemption should transform morality. The new life does not excuse man from moral effort (a common objection advanced against Calvinism); it calls him rather to labor with untiring zeal for the glory of God and in the service of men. Calvin never taught that only the elect could be moral; what he did say was that morality was unable to save a man. Good works apart from God are useless, but they could be a sign that God had saved one. Such works took three main forms: preaching to others; keeping the Ten Commandments and forcing others to keep them; and serving God in one's vocation.

**Politics.** The state is inferior to the church, which guards the Word of God. In the church there was democracy, not because all men are free and equal, but because under Adam's curse all are equally unfree. The powers that be, though ordained of God, are to be resisted if they defy God (though Calvin does not specify how this is to be done). While choosing those best qualified to govern, Calvin does not restrict political authority to the elect. This was not possible in any case, for we do not know who are elect; furthermore, even the natural man has a capacity for political morality.

In Calvin's political theory Anabaptism was condemned, for it held that the Christian is not a citizen in an earthly state, and that he has nothing to do with the civil government. Oddly enough, with a much more formidable adversary, Roman Catholicism, Calvinism shared two beliefs—that submission to the church is necessary for salvation and that no toleration in religion could be permitted.

**Influence.** Calvinism, being generally more democratic at a time when democratic ideas were in the air, soon outstripped Lutheranism. It emphasized communal responsibility, giving scope to all men to share in local and national affairs, and encouraged the spread of education. It taught the worth of labor, raised the status of the laborer, and is echoed in the Declaration of Rights. Inevitably modified through the years, Calvinism has shaped more minds and reached more lands than any other Reformed creed. It strengthened the French and Dutch Protestants and the Scottish Covenanters in resisting secular interference with their form of worship. It molded the Puritanism of the Old World, and gave backbone to that of the New when the Pilgrim Fathers went out like Abraham of old to settle in an unfamiliar land at God's call.

Calvinism—logical, Biblical, authoritarian—subdued the excesses which the heady wine of newly found religious freedom might have provoked, and organized a system which stood firm against the inevitable counterattack from Rome. In the formation of successive Confessions its influence has been immeasurable. No one who reads the Westminster Confession of Faith or the Thirty-nine Articles of Anglicanism is likely to deny it.

**CHRISTIAN CHURCHES (DISCIPLES OF CHRIST) INTERNATIONAL CONVENTION,** a Protestant denomination growing out of the work of Barton W. Stone (1772–1844), Thomas Campbell (1763–1854), and his son Alexander Campbell (1788–1866). Stone was a revivalist who broke away from Presbyterianism in 1803 to form churches which claimed no other name than "Christian." Thomas Campbell departed from a very conservative Presbyterian body shortly after his arrival in the United States from Ireland, and organized his followers into The Christian Association of Washington, (Pa.) in 1809, in an effort to restore the primitive apostolic pattern of faith. Alexander Campbell became the most prominent leader in this new movement, which for some years identified itself with the Baptists, adopting the baptism of believers by immersion. But the distinctive emphasis on restoration and unity led to the severing of this connection, and in 1832 most of the followers of Campbell and Stone merged to form the Christian Churches, or Disciples of Christ.

Christian Churches are congregationally organized. Disciples like to think of themselves as a brotherhood rather than as a church or denomination. Their free patterns of worship focus on the ordinance of communion, observed weekly. Their attitude toward theology has been expressed historically in three familiar slogans: "Where the Scriptures speak, we speak; where the Scriptures are silent, we are silent." "In faith unity, in opinions liberty, in all things charity." "No creed but Christ, no book but the Bible, no law but love, no name but the divine."

Most Disciples would agree that the acknowledgment of Jesus Christ as Lord and Saviour is the sole affirmation of faith necessary to the fellowship of Christians, that the New Testament is the primary source of knowledge concerning the will of God and His revelation in Christ and that Christian unity will come about by the restoration of

New Testament Christianity. Christian Churches are missionary-minded and are deeply interested in the ecumenical movement.

In the late 19th century a rift appeared in the denomination between those who were concerned to relate the Disciples' heritage to the larger Protestant world and those who resisted this and opposed the "unscriptural innovations" of musical instruments in worship and the development of missionary societies. By 1906 two distinct groups existed: the Churches of Christ (q.v.) and the Christian Churches or Disciples of Christ.

The main bond of unity among the latter is the International Convention, an annual gathering of representatives from the congregations, begun in 1917, with a continuing board of directors and headquarters in Indianapolis. The Christian Churches act together in the fields of home and foreign missions, Christian education, social action, and evangelism, chiefly through the United Christian Missionary Society, formed through the merger of previous societies in 1920. In the early 1960's there were about 8,000 Christian Churches, with about 1,800,000 members, located predominantly in the Midwest and Southwest.

**CHRISTIAN METHODIST EPISCOPAL CHURCH.** At the close of the Civil War there were more than 250,000 Negro members in the Methodist Episcopal Church, South. They had long been dissatisfied with the restrictions and humiliations of segregated church life. In 1866, one-year after the war, they petitioned the General Conference of the Methodist Episcopal Church, South, to be set aside in a church of their own. Four years later the Conference voted that the petition of the Negro members should be granted. In Dec., 1870, the Colored Methodist Episcopal Church was organized in Jackson, Tenn. Two Negro bishops were elected, Henry Mills and Richard H. Vanderhorst. This church, like the other Negro bodies, grew rapidly. In 1956 the word "Colored" in its name was changed to "Christian."

The Christian Methodist Episcopal church in 1961 had 2,523 churches, 444,493 members, 2,025 Sunday schools with an enrollment of 115,424. There were 1,792 active pastors. This church has played an important part in Negro educational development. It operates four senior colleges, a seminary, and other schools. It maintains a foreign mission program. John Wesley Gilbert, a highly educated teacher and minister, served as a missionary to Africa, and established the church there.

**CHRISTIAN REFORMED CHURCH,** American Protestant denomination founded in 1857 by the secession of a conservative Calvinistic group from the (Dutch) Reformed Church in America. The church maintains Calvin College and Seminary in Grand Rapids, Mich., and conducts an aggressive missionary program. In the late 1960's membership of the Christian Reformed Church totaled about 270,000 in some 625 churches.

**CHRISTIAN SCIENCE,** a religion founded in the United States in 1879, now a world-wide denomination with approximately 3,300 churches in 45 countries. It is an interpretation of Biblical Christianity emphasizing that the mission of Jesus Christ was a unity of words and works. The full statement of Christian Science is contained in the denominational textbook, *Science and Health with Key to the Scriptures*, by Mary Baker Eddy, who was the founder of the church organization as well as the discoverer of the religious system.

Christian Scientists believe that the works of Jesus and his apostles are closely related to his teachings. They consider these works an essential part of his revelation of the constant presence of the divine Father's love for His creation. Christ Jesus is accepted as the Saviour, or mediator between God and men, raising mankind from sin and limited views of all things to the awareness of God as infinitely good and as truly supreme in His creation.

The Mother Church, The First Church of Christ, Scientist, in Boston. The original building (*right*) was dedicated in 1895. The larger domed extension was dedicated in 1906. (FIRST CHURCH OF CHRIST, SCIENTIST)

Prayer in Christian Science is understood as the means of bringing mankind into communion with God, who is defined in *Science and Health* (p. 465) as "incorporeal, divine, supreme, infinite Mind, Spirit, Soul, Principle, Life, Truth, Love." The natural result of this deepened understanding of God is seen as healing, both moral and physical. Christian Scientists rely radically upon prayer for solving problems of human experience. They believe that whatever is evil, finite, mortal, and material must yield to the illumined understanding of God, Spirit, and of man as His spiritual image and likeness. Prayer is therefore described by them as "knowing the truth," in accordance with Jesus' words, "Ye shall know the truth, and the truth shall make you free."

The Christian Science church organization took its permanent form in 1892. It is comprised today of The Mother Church, The First Church of Christ, Scientist, in Boston, its branch churches, and some 250 affiliated college and university organizations. The denomination is governed by the Church Manual administered by a Board of Directors of five members. Branch churches are democratically self-governed.

Each branch church maintains a Sunday School for pupils up to the age of 20. Lessons are based upon the Bible and *Science and Health with Key to the Scriptures*. Individual churches also maintain Christian Science Reading Rooms, where the Bible, the Christian Science textbook, and Christian Science literature may be studied or obtained.

Christian Science is a religion which has no clergy. Church services and church government are conducted by lay members. Sunday services include hymns, a solo, silent prayer, and responsive readings of Scriptural verses. The reading of the lesson-sermon, consisting of correlated selections from the Bible and *Science and Health*, by the first and second readers takes the place of a pastoral sermon. The references for the lesson-sermon are published in the *Christian Science Quarterly*, and the Sunday service is uniform in all Christian Science churches. Wednesday evening meetings follow a similar order of service, except that time is reserved for spontaneous testimonies of healing and regeneration through prayer by members of the congregation.

Among the publications of the Christian Science Church are *The Christian Science Journal*, a monthly magazine containing articles on Christian Science, verified testimonies of healing, and a listing of churches, reading rooms, and Christian Science practitioners; the *Christian Science Sentinel*, a weekly magazine; and *The Herald of Christian Science*, in numerous foreign-language editions. *The Christian Science Monitor*, an international daily newspaper which has won wide recognition for its journalistic ethics in reporting world events, is the most well-known Church publication.

**CHURCHES OF CHRIST,** group of autonomous churches which have separated from the Christian Churches, or Disciples of Christ. They look upon such leaders as Alexander Campbell and Barton W. Stone as restorers of the primitive New Testament pattern for the church. Believing that the Christian Churches were moving away from a rigorous New Testament Christianity through such things as the use of the organ in public worship and the utilization of Sunday schools and missionary societies, the Churches of Christ requested to be separately listed in the federal religious census of 1906. Churches of Christ regard Jesus Christ as the founder, head, and saviour of the church. They contend that the Word of God is the seed of the church and that, when the Word is preached without any admixture of human opinions, it will produce Christians, or a church of Christ. These churches hold to a strict congregational independency, and have no general organization or missionary societies, though they do considerable overseas work. In the early 1960's they reported nearly 18,000 churches with some 2,000,000 members. They are strongest in the South and Southwest.

**CONGREGATIONAL CHRISTIAN CHURCHES,** an American religious denomination formed by the union of the Congregational and the Christian Churches in 1931. Until recently it has been generally held that the founder of Congregationalism was the English Separatist, Robert Browne (1550–1633). His *Treatise of Reformation Without Tarrying for Any* (1582) declared that the true church was a self-governing local body of believers gathered together by voluntary consent. Today it is widely believed that, though Browne was the father of Separatism, modern Congregationalism stems more from Henry Jacob (1563–1624), an English Puritan Independent who developed the position of nonseparatist Congregationalism. He gathered a Congregational church at Southwark, England, in 1616. His aim was not to separate from the Church of England, but to show how it could be reordered into a nationwide system of autonomous congregations in association with

The Congregational Church, in Windsor, Vt., built in 1789.
(AUBREY P. JANION—MONKMEYER)

each other. In North America, elements of both Separatist and Independent Congregationalism were represented at Plymouth, but in Massachusetts Bay the leaders were Independents, who established their churches by law.

Congregational principles affirm that the true visible church is manifest in a local congregation rather than in larger units, that the church is composed of voluntary believers who covenant together, and that Jesus Christ is the supreme head and the living center of each congregation. Congregations are held to be independent under Him, but are under obligation to associate together for common service to Christ and for mutual support.

Congregationalists were excluded from the Church of England by 1662, and became a separate denomination, a "free church" in the Reformed or Calvinist tradition. In the American colonies, Congregational churches multiplied during the great Puritan migration of the 1630's, and became established by law in Massachusetts, Connecticut, and New Hampshire. They formed one of the strongest religious bodies in the colonies, and were the last to be disestablished. Traditionally staunchly Calvinistic in theology, in the early 19th century many Congregationalists went over to Unitarianism, and in the later 19th century, the whole denomination moved largely in a liberal direction, being in the forefront of the social-gospel movement.

The Christian Churches arose during the 19th century through the union of groups of Virginia Methodists, Vermont Baptists, and Kentucky Presbyterians—all of whom preferred simply the name "Christian." In 1931 the Christian General Convention and the Congregational National Council (formed 1871) united as the General Council of the Congregational Christian Churches. Later union negotiations with the Evangelical and Reformed Church were begun, and in 1957, after long legal and theological controversy, the two bodies agreed to form the United Church of Christ. The full implementing of the union was delayed for some years by legal action; during this period the Congregational Christian Churches, about 5,500 in number with 1,400,000 members, continued until the ratification of a constitution for the United Church (1961).

**CONGREGATIONALISM** [kŏng-grə-gā'shən-əl-ĭz-əm], a democratic form of church order based on the autonomy of each local congregation and the belief that a church is composed of Christians joined together for worship, fellowship, and service. All members have equal rights, are "priests unto God," and are part of the Church Universal, of which Christ is the sole Head.

Modern Congregationalism began with the Reformation. Martin Luther reiterated the priesthood of all believers, and the Anabaptists asserted that the secular power has no authority in spiritual matters—principles which became explicit in Congregationalism. A further strand stems from the secret meetings held during the persecutions of Mary Tudor's reign in England, when worshipers experienced that reality of Christian fellowship familiar in the Apostolic Age. Often called Separatists, they opposed Queen Elizabeth's claim to be supreme governor of

Church as well as state, and her design for religious uniformity. They established four or five congregations in London between 1567 and 1581. Their principles were formulated by Robert Browne, who held that the kingdom of God "was not to be begun by whole parishes, but rather of the worthiest, were they never so few." For circulating Browne's books, men were put to death in 1583.

Persecution having its inevitable result, Brownists increased all over England. Suppressed for a time at home, they reappeared in Holland and in New England, where they contributed significantly in both religion and politics. As Independents they formed the backbone of Cromwell's troops. Like all Nonconformists, they were suppressed by Charles II's Act of Uniformity (1662) and sanctioned by William III's Toleration Act (1689), and later were the object of public opposition and, sometimes, of mob violence under the strongly Anglican Queen Anne. Nevertheless, they grew in numbers and influence and, being excluded from the ancient universities (a prohibition which lasted till 1871), set up Dissenting academies which showed a fine educational record. In New England, Congregationalism established colleges—notably Harvard and Yale—but thereafter tended to reverse the original principle by stressing good works as a means of producing religious experience. The movement was galvanized by the 18th-century Great Awakening in New England and the Evangelical Revival in England. Congregationalists were chiefly responsible for the founding of the London Missionary Society in 1795.

In America, the years 1800–50 saw missionary expansion in close collaboration with Presbyterians; in England and Wales a chief feature was the establishment in 1832 of the Congregational Union, with similar unions following in Scotland and Ireland. The Union could merely advise, since it had no legislative powers. In 1833 it issued a Declaration of Faith, in which the moderate Calvinism which paralleled the prevailing beliefs in America was propounded. This was no official definitive creed, the acceptance of which was a test of Communion. The only qualification for membership in the body of Christ was that the applicant should have felt the power of personal religion.

Congregationalism is ecumenical in tendency. In 1931 American Congregationalists formed the majority group in establishing the Congregational Christian Churches. Later negotiations with the Evangelical and Reformed Church led to a General Synod of the United Church of Christ in 1957, aimed at merging the two bodies. Congregationalism's world membership is about 2,350,000.

**COPTIC** [kŏp'tĭk] **CHURCH,** the Christian church of Egypt. The name means "Egyptian." The Coptic Church came into existence after the Council of Chalcedon (451), and was centered in Alexandria. Alexandria had long been a cradle of Christian learning and spirituality. Tradition holds that St. Mark was the founder of the church there. In 451 the Patriarch of Alexandria, Dioscorus (d.454), was condemned for his Monophysitism, and since then the church has been separated from the Eastern Orthodox Church.

Throughout their history the Christian Copts were severely persecuted, especially by the Persians (613–28), by the Arabs, who conquered Egypt in 639, and by the Turks, who came in 1517. Today less than 10% of the Egyptians are Christians. Beset by overwhelming obstacles, the Coptic Christians have striven since 639 to preserve their distinctive traditions. In their doctrinal teachings they have remained Monophysite (the belief that Christ had only a divine nature instead of both a human and divine). They believe in the Trinity and accept the seven sacraments, although baptism performed by a layman is not valid. They use a modified form of the Greek liturgy of Alexandria, in the Coptic language. Once the language of Egypt, Coptic has been preserved only in liturgical books since the Arab conquest.

The Coptic calendar year has 12 equal months of 30 days each, the remaining five or six days forming a "little month." The calendar is reckoned from 284, the "Era of the Martyrs."

The head of the church is a Patriarch, with the title, "the most Holy Father, Patriarch of Alexandria, of all Egypt, of Nubia, Ethiopia, the Pentapolis and all the countries evangelized by St. Mark." Since the 11th century the Patriarchal See has been in Cairo. There are about 900,000 members of the church. In the 18th century a uniat Coptic church, in communion with Rome, was established, and it has about 75,000 members.

**DOMINICANS,** popular name of the men and women of the religious order which takes its inspiration from St. Dominic. It has three main branches: the first order of St. Dominic known formally as the Order of Friars Preachers (O.P.); the second order of St. Dominic made up of cloistered nuns; the third order of St. Dominic, composed of Third Order Regulars, who are sisters living in convents and engaged in apostolic works, and Third Order Seculars, who are lay men and women.

**The Order of Friars Preachers** arose from an apostolic enterprise in Languedoc, France, against the Albigensian heresy. Dominic was in Rome in 1204 offering to undertake missionary activity among the Tatars, but Pope Innocent III sent him to combat the Albigensians of Languedoc instead. The task called for intensive preaching, and because the monks assigned to the work found that they were not properly prepared or disposed for such apostolic endeavors, the work floundered. On Nov. 17, 1206, Pope Innocent III ordered the papal legates to exert their power to further apostolic preaching by men suited to the task. This was not the formal founding of the order, but it made the founding of an order of Mendicant Preachers possible and assured such an order of ecclesiastical approval. After laboring for eight years without canonical status, Dominic and his preachers were finally, in 1215, appointed the official preachers of the diocese of Toulouse, and the first house was opened there on Apr. 25. The group lived under the rule of St. Augustine with additional provisions, since technically there was no rule of St. Dominic, and received the papal approbation of Honorius III on Dec. 22, 1216. In this same year

*Jean Marquis*

A Dominican friar in the Convent Sainte-Marie de la Tourette, Eveux-sur-Arbresle, France. The Dominicans became known as the "Black Friars" because of the long black mantle usually worn over the white habit seen in the picture above.

the customary practices were written down in the *Consuetudines*, which form the first part of the constitutions of the order. Members take vows of poverty, chastity, and obedience; observe perpetual abstinence; fast from Sept. 14 to Easter, and on all Fridays of the year; chant Divine Office, but simply, without pomp; and wear a white tunic with a black cloak, whence their title "Black Friars." In May of 1220 the General Chapter of Bologna drew up the constitutions of the order, which were revised by St. Raymond of Pennafort in 1239, and have remained virtually the same since.

The ascetic elements are joined to a vocation which is primarily apostolic and clerical. The preachers are clerics, not monks, but their clericalism is subordinated to their mission of saving souls by being "champions of the Faith" and "lights of the world." Their motto is "Truth." The intellectual element of a Dominican vocation is seen in the list of illustrious scholars, artists, and mystics who were Dominicans: St. Thomas Aquinas, St. Albert the Great (Albertus Magnus), St. Vincent Ferrer, John (Meister) Eckhart, John Tauler, Thomas Cajetan, John of St. Thomas, Fra Angelico, and Fra Bartolommeo. By their vocation to defend and extend the truth, the preachers were bound to make a twofold contribution to the intellectual history of the church. They have a continuous record of constructive work admired and assimilated by the church, but they have an equally uninterrupted record of theological controversy, especially with the Jesuits and Franciscans. Far from being a source of scandal, this fact redounds to the credit of all concerned and evidences the wealth of Christian inspiration and Dominican vocation.

**The Second Order of St. Dominic** dates from the first years of Dominic's apostolate in Languedoc. A house was founded at Prouille in 1206 for the women who had been converted from Albigensianism. From 1212 the house took on the appearance of a monastery of the cloistered

religious. In 1219 Dominic was asked by Pope Honorius III to reform some convents in Rome. He began the reform at the Monastery of St. Sixtus where the nuns were regrouped in 1221, along with some of the religious from Prouille. The rule of the second order is substantially the same as that of the first order, with proper modifications, and was declared final in 1259. The second order grew so fast that the first order asked on several occasions (1239, 1246, 1252) to be relieved of the burden of caring for them, which in each instance was granted temporarily (and partially). But finally, on Feb. 5, 1267, Pope Clement IV returned the second order monasteries to the permanent jurisdiction of the first order. Normally under pontifical cloister, the task of these nuns is continual penance and prayer for the success of all priestly activity and especially of their Dominican brothers.

**The Third Order of St. Dominic** is divided into regulars, who are sisters engaged actively in apostolic labors such as teaching and nursing and seculars, who are lay men and women, following a rule in their spiritual lives. St. Dominic himself did not write the rule for the tertiaries, but a group of pious laymen attracted by the Friars attached themselves to the order and asked for special spiritual direction. In reply to this request, Munio of Zamora wrote a rule for the Brothers and Sisters of Penitence of St. Dominic, their official title, in 1285. The rule is based on a similar rule of the Brothers of Penitence founded by St. Francis. The canonical existence of the Dominican tertiaries was given by Pope Honorius IV on Jan. 28, 1286.

**DUTCH REFORMED CHURCH,** a Protestant church of the subdivision classed as "Reformed." At the Reformation the initial influence of Ulrich Zwingli in the Netherlands soon gave way to a thoroughgoing Calvinism. Despite a challenge at the Synod of Dort (1618–19), this was the national creed till the 19th century. The liberal policies of William I's reign (1815–40) led eventually to a series of schisms which left Holland with three Reformed churches, each claiming to be the true custodian of Reformed Christianity. In 1848 the original church was disestablished, though the state still subsidizes this and most other Dutch churches.

In its four ecclesiastical courts—consistory, classis, provincial synod, and general synod—and in doctrine the Dutch Reformed Church closely resembles the Scottish and American Presbyterian churches. In Holland itself it has a membership of 3½ million, or 35% of the population. Immigrant Dutchmen established their church in America, and in South Africa, where it is the dominant church.

**EASTERN ORTHODOX CHURCH,** sometimes called the Eastern Church, comprising several self-governing, independent Christian churches situated in countries which once belonged to the Byzantine Empire or were evangelized by the Byzantine Church. These churches are united in doctrine and worship, and claim that they are the true church founded by Christ and His apostles. Their source of faith is holy tradition, of which the Scriptures are a part, and they accept seven ecumenical councils. The Fourth Council at Chalcedon divided them from the Monophysite churches, and the Great Schism of 1054 separated them from the Western Church.

The Orthodox Church embraces the four ancient patriarchates of Constantinople (100,000 members), Alexandria (200,000), Antioch (300,000) and Jerusalem (35,000); the churches of the Soviet Union (50,000,000), Rumania (14,000,000), Bulgaria (6,000,000), Serbia (7,500,000), and Greece (7,500,000); the independent churches in Georgian S.S.R., Cyprus, Poland, Czechoslovakia, and Finland; and others scattered throughout the world. The total membership is about 150,000,000. Each church elects its own Patriarch. The Ecumenical Patriarch of Constantinople holds "precedence of honor" and has jurisdiction over some churches (Finland, Czechoslovakia) and some dioceses in diaspora.

**ENGLAND, CHURCH OF,** the church established by law in England. Establishment denotes the following: (1) the King or Queen must be a member of the Church of England or abdicate; (2) the 26 senior Bishops sit and vote in the House of Lords; (3) the Archbishop of Canterbury has the right to crown the sovereign; (4) the supreme court in ecclesiastical cases is a crown court (and therefore secular), the judicial committee of the Privy Council; (5) the King or Queen nominates the Bishops for election, but in practice may only make the nomination on the advice of the Prime Minister; (6) any substantial change in the law of the church requires an act of Parliament; and (7) the parson, or priest, of the parish, feels a certain responsibility toward the whole population of the parish and not only to the confirmed members of the Church of England.

Establishment formerly meant more than this. Prior to 1868, dissenters were taxed for the upkeep of parish churches and, till 1836, had to be married in the parish church. Before 1828 dissenters could not sit as members of Parliament if they were Protestant, and not until 1829 if Roman Catholic; and prior to 1836 dissenters could not take a degree at a university. However, all these inequalities were removed during the 19th century. In the countries of the British Isles where the Church of England is a minority, it was disestablished: in Ireland in 1869, in Wales in 1920.

At present, approximately three-fourths of the English population is baptized in the Church of England, and approximately one-half of the total number of marriages are performed in the established church. The question of disestablishment has hardly been alive in England during the 20th century, though the relations between church and state give rise to epidemic discomfort—especially among churchmen who are concerned about the due independence of the church.

The official formularies of the Church of England are the Thirty-nine Articles of 1571, and the Book of Common Prayer of 1662. Although it was Henry VIII who broke with the Roman See, Protestant ideas came in under his son Edward VI. Queen Mary, who succeeded Edward, carried England back into the Roman obedience, and it was not until the reign of Queen Elizabeth I that religion was settled in a Protestant but moderate frame. It is clear that the Thirty-nine Articles were intended as the basis of a Protestant church. But they were framed widely, and within limits allowed more liberty of opinion than many of the Reformation confessions. And as time went on, a greater breadth of interpretation became customary. The original form of subscription to the Thirty-nine Articles exacted from the clergy was rigorous and detailed. But since the Clerical Subscription Act of 1865 the assent required has often been so general that it does not commit the subscriber to the truth of every phrase of the articles.

The Elizabethan Prayer Book of 1559 was an adaptation of the vernacular Prayer Book of 1552, created by the liturgical genius of Thomas Cranmer, but with small modifications designed to make it more palatable to conservatives. After the rule of Cromwell and the restoration of Charles II, this was readopted in 1662, with a few more modifications in a conservative direction. It is a liturgy of the Swiss Reformed tradition rather than the Lutheran, but having an atmosphere of liturgical tradition, and at some important points of the services retaining ancient formulas of which the Swiss reformers disapproved.

In particular, Queen Elizabeth's government took great care that the new Protestant Archbishop of Canterbury, Matthew Parker, should be consecrated by other Bishops in the old way. Hence the "apostolic succession" of the historic episcopate was retained. Though from the begin-

Canterbury Cathedral in 1961 as Michael Ramsey was enthroned as the 100th Archbishop of Canterbury. (PICTORIAL PARADE, INC.)

ning of Elizabeth's reign there was a group of recusants who refused to conform on the ground that Catholicism must mean obedience to Rome, many conservatives felt able to use this liturgy with a clear conscience. When historical circumstances strengthened the conservative element in the Church of England, the church could find room for a wider variety of faith and practice than could be found probably anywhere else in Christendom. By the 19th century it included Calvinists at one end and Anglo-Catholics at the other.

The Reformation, while it made important changes in the doctrine and liturgy of the church, made fewer changes in the constitution, apart from the abolition of papal jurisdiction. The old assemblies of the clergy, the Convocations of Canterbury and York, continued, though they were effectively suppressed between 1717 and 1852. Since 1919, in association with a house of laity, they have been able to prepare ecclesiastical bills for Parliament; and these bills do not require Parliamentary debate unless they affect existing acts of Parliament. The old system of appointment to parishes by some lay patrons continues, and there are very few parishes in the Church of England where the congregation may select its minister. Many of the more important parish churches are medieval structures, and the cathedrals retain their medieval constitution of a dean and canons. Thus English churchmen possess a sense of historical continuity going back to the foundation of Christianity in England, and look back upon the Venerable Bede and Anglo-Saxon saints with as much affection as they do upon the men of the Reformation. The strength of this historical sense is probably unique in Protestantism.

During the 18th and 19th centuries a devoted missionary endeavor carried the Anglican Church into the English dominions and beyond their borders, so that by 1867 the Church of England found itself the mother of a wider federation of Episcopal churches.

The Church of England has commanded the loyalty of many members because it has offered in worship a reformed Catholicism—faithful to the Bible, recognizing the insights of the Reformation, condemning the excesses of medieval Christianity, yet attempting to be Catholic in its austere traditions of ancient piety, and in its allegiance to the doctrines of the early, undivided Church. Its Elizabethan theorist, Richard Hooker, stood for the rightful place of reason in religious thought; and this tradition of reasonableness and learning has been marked among the English clergy.

In the period from 1660 to 1830 the church made signal contributions to science and philosophy, as well as to theology, and sometimes pursued learning almost at the expense of pastoral care. Consequently it was able, more easily than some churches, to make the needful adjustments before the new challenges of history and science in the age of Darwin. Especially since 1864, it has permitted a wide variety of opinion in doctrine and practice; and although these have been regretted at times as conducive to the development of ecclesiastical parties they have also been welcomed as a sign of a truly "Catholic" or "ecumenical" attitude.

**EVANGELICAL AND REFORMED CHURCH,** a union of the Evangelical Synod of North America and the Reformed Church in the United States, officially constituted in 1934 in Cleveland, Ohio. The members of the German Evangelical Church Society of the West (founded 1840), which later became the Evangelical Synod, came largely from the predominantly Lutheran sections of northern, central, and eastern Germany. The German Reformed Church, which in 1869 became the Reformed Church of the United States, was organized as an independent body in 1792. Its congregations, many of which dated back to the early 18th century and which had worked together in a coetus under Dutch Reformed auspices, were at first chiefly made up of immigrants of Reformed (Calvinist) background in western Germany. In 1922 definite steps toward the union of the two bodies were taken, and a plan of union was approved ten years later. At the time of union the total membership was 629,787; by mid-century it had increased to 735,941. In 1957 the Evangelical and Reformed Church entered into a union agreement with the Congregational Christian Churches which was ratified in 1961, forming the United Church of Christ.

**FRANCISCANS** [frăn-sĭs'kənz], popular name of the men and women of the numerous religious orders who follow some form of the rule of St. Francis of Assisi—specifically: the first order of St. Francis, the mendicant Friars Minor; the second order, known as the Poor Clares; and the third order, divided into third order regulars and the tertiaries, known as Brothers and Sisters of Penance.

The first order of St. Francis was officially recognized by Pope Innocent III on Apr. 16, 1209, after about a year of unofficial existence. The rule of 1209 (the *Primitiva*) is not extant, but consisted of little more than some Gospel passages with comments by St. Francis. The order met yearly in a general chapter, and statutes were added from experience, and approved by the Holy See as circumstances dictated. Later Francis found that this rather simple organizational procedure was inadequate, so he wrote a detailed rule (*Regula prima*) in 1220. It proved to be too severe for the brethren, so was revised in 1223 (*Regula secunda*), and received papal approval on Nov. 29. The ideal of poverty, not only of the individual but even of the order itself, is set forth in this rule, and it was the source of controversy and division even while Francis lived. After his death, on Oct. 3, 1226, the difficulties of observance became even more pressing and eventually culminated in the division of the order.

St. Francis' final work, his *Testament*, repeated his teaching about absolute poverty and literal obedience to the rule and refusal of all privileges. It was thought by some to supersede the rule of 1223, since it was written in 1226. But Pope Gregory IX determined that the *Testament* did not have the force of law, in his bull *Quo elongati*, of Sept. 28, 1230. Yet some Franciscans still felt bound in conscience to follow the *Testament* rigorously. A compromise whereby third parties held goods for the order was put into practice, but was thought by many to make a fiction of absolute poverty. The general chapter of Metz, in 1254, found the order divided into those who wanted to return to the primitive ideals of St. Francis, called Spirituals, and those called Conventuals, who saw the necessity for the order becoming more clerical, in order to fulfill its obligations of preaching and missionary activity. This deep division within the order determined its subsequent history. In 1257 St. Bonaventure became master general. He accepted the duties thrust on the order by the needs of the church and endorsed the practice of engaging in intellectual pursuits, having larger monasteries, and preserving some privileges. Accused of laxity by the Spirituals, he drew up the Constitutions of Narbonne in 1260, which served as a model for future constitutions and aimed at insuring the unity of the order. The tensions between the Spirituals and Conventuals increased, but in 1317 Pope John XXII denied permission to separate, and on Dec. 8, 1322, he restored all property to the order, literally ending the ideal of absolute poverty and thus increasing the tension in the order. Those wishing for reform and a return to the original observance of the rule increased in number from 1367 on and were called Observants. Finally Pope Martin V, in the bull *Ad statum*, of Aug. 23, 1430, gave the Conventuals permission to hold property in common; and this ended all hope of a union of the order along lines of the original observance. A permanent division of the order was inevitable, especially since no masters general from 1443 to 1517 were Observants.

Under the auspices of Pope Leo X, a general chapter was called in 1517, in which all the reformed communities were unified under the Observants, henceforth called Order of Friars Minor (O.F.M.); and the other communities were joined under the Conventuals, henceforth called Order of Friars Minor Conventual (O.F.M. Conv.). In 1525 there was a split among the Observants, and the third part of the Franciscan first order came into existence, the order of Friars Minor Capuchin (O.F.M. Cap.), known simply as Capuchins.

Despite the long history of tension and division, it must be remembered that all the members of the three branches of the Franciscan first order are true sons of St. Francis, since each branch is the result of an unbroken continuity starting with their holy founder. The reason for all these divisions was not any real difference in the understanding of the ideals of St. Francis, but rather derived from the differences which arose when holy men had to make prudential judgments as to how practically to live this ideal in an ever changing world. The glorious contributions of each branch give glowing testimony to the validity of each such judgment.

The tertiaries of St. Francis, known officially as Brothers and Sisters of Penance, trace their existence back to St. Francis himself. They were established in 1221, and their rule consists of three chapters, which give in detail the manner of life and the works required of members, most of whom are laymen and laywomen living in the world. There are some 3,500,000 Franciscan tertiaries in the world.

**FRIENDS, SOCIETY OF,** commonly called Quakers, the most significant of the new religious movements arising on Puritan soil during the period of the civil wars in England. The founder was George Fox, who came to an illuminating conviction that every man receives from God a divine Inner Light, which if followed can lead to spiritual truth. Fox began his stormy public ministry in 1647 and soon attracted a few followers. The Friends believed that the Scriptures were a true Word of God, but that revelation was not confined to them. They rejected the Calvinistic concept of man's total depravity, insisting that there is a seed of God in every soul. The central principle of the Quaker movement was belief in the inwardly present and creative work of God's Spirit operating in man. Emphasizing the inward nature of religion, the Friends reacted against outward ceremonies. They did not observe the sacraments, objected to established churches and professional ministries, and refused to take oaths or use "artificial" titles. They put great stress on economy and simplicity. They believed that war was unlawful for Christians. Rigorous and intense, they grew by accession from various other Puritan and separatist bodies. The first Quaker community was gathered in Preston Patrick in northern England by 1652.

The new faith was soon carried by enthusiastic adherents throughout the British Isles, to the Continent, and to America (1656). The movement met with persecution during the Cromwellian and Restoration periods; thousands were imprisoned, and in Massachusetts four were hanged. Tendencies toward extravagance in the society caused an internal system of discipline and order to be worked out in the 1660's. Monthly meetings were instituted to watch over the life and conduct of Friends in local areas, and quarterly and yearly meetings, culminating in the London yearly meeting, provided some over-all coherence for the society. The stabilization of the movement was greatly aided by the work of "public Friends," or traveling Quaker "ministers," who journeyed from meeting to meeting and from continent to continent. An able theological apologist for the movement was Robert Barclay (1648–90), who wrote *An Apology for the True Christian Divinity* (1678).

The colonies of Rhode Island, New Jersey, and especially Pennsylvania, which was founded by an eminent convert to Quakerism, provided refuges in which the Friends could flourish in peace. The Toleration Act of 1689 brought freedom of worship and relief from the more pressing disabilities. By 1700 there were about 50,000 Friends in the British Isles and 40,000 more in North America.

Quaker life of the 18th century was marked by the growth of mystical quietism in religious thought and practice and by the flowering of a notable humanitarian spirit. A distinctive Quaker culture developed during that century, especially in America. Following a tradition of opposition to slavery, they established the first U.S. antislavery society in 1775, and were important members of Abolitionist societies and the Underground Railroad.

In the 19th century the Quakers were torn by tension and declined somewhat in influence. In general, the conflict was between "evangelical" Quakers, who put considerable stress on correct doctrine, and "mystical" Quakers, whose theological views were somewhat liberal in tone. In England only small schisms resulted from the tension, but in the United States the society divided into two main parts, an evangelical wing influenced by an English Quaker, Joseph John Gurney, and a liberal wing following Elias Hicks, a Long Islander. Other schisms followed the major split. Some Quakers adopted the pastoral system and became more like the traditional denominations.

The 20th century has seen both a renewed interest in social questions on the part of the Friends and the development of forces making for Quaker unity. These are illustrated in the forming of the American Friends Service Committee with the support of many Quaker bodies during World War I. Under the chairmanship of Rufus Jones, the Quaker witness against war was continued, and a ministry of service was extended to victims of war and disaster. An All-Friends Conference was held in London in 1920, and in 1937 the Friends World Committee for Consultation, representing 45 Quaker groups in 24 countries, was organized. *The World Christian Handbook* (1957) reports that there are about 150,000 members of Quaker societies in the world, four-fifths of them in the United States. Many Quaker bodies participate in world, national, and local councils of churches.

**GREEK CHURCH,** independent national church of modern Greece, one of the Eastern Orthodox churches.

**History.** Its historical development may be divided into four periods. The first embraces the time from St. Paul's mission until Constantine the Great. St. Paul preached the Christian message in Greece and established several churches there. At the beginning of the Christian era, the church of Greece, then called Achaea, was an independent diocese, with Corinth as its center.

The second period began under Constantine the Great, when Greece, as part of the prefecture of Illyria, came under the ecclesiastical jurisdiction of the Roman patriarchate. This lasted until 733, when Leo III of the Eastern Roman Empire placed the church under the jurisdiction of the patriarchate of Constantinople.

Throughout the third period (733–1833) the church in Greece was dependent upon Constantinople and shared in the destiny of this patriarchate. It suffered much under Turkish rule.

The modern era opened with the Greek war of independence against the Turks (1821–28) and the proclamation of a Greek independent state and self-governing church in Greece in 1833. Constantinople, however, did not recognize the Greek church as independent until 1850.

**Organization.** The Greek Church consists of 81 small dioceses with about 7,500,000 members. The governing body of the church is the assembly of all the Bishops, who in Greece bear the title of Metropolitans. They meet every three years. The presiding Bishop is "the Blessed Archbishop of Athens and all Greece," who possesses "primacy of honor" among the Bishops. The assembly is responsible for discipline and teaching in the church and the church's relations with other religious bodies.

Church affairs are administered by a permanent synod, composed of twelve Bishops with the Archbishop of Athens presiding. Every Bishop in turn serves for a year on this body, and the Archbishop is a permanent member. A representative of the government attends the meeting of this synod as an observer. The board is responsible for the election of new Bishops, and the Archbishop is elected by the assembly of Bishops.

**Zoe Movement.** One of the most outstanding features of the modern church is its mission inside Greece, carried on by several organizations. The most significant movement is the Brotherhood of Theologians, Zoe ("life"). Its 130 members, laymen and priests, direct an extensive program of religious education, preaching, and publication of religious literature and teaching. They lead a semimonastic life, without taking permanent vows. Most members are graduates of the theological faculties of the universities in Athens and Salonika.

**Doctrine and Worship.** The doctrines of the Trinity (that one God exists in three persons, Father, Son, and Holy Spirit) and the Incarnation (that God became man, that Jesus is the incarnate Son of God) and the teaching that the Holy Spirit proceeds from the Father only (the Filioque being rejected), that the Virgin Mary is the God-bearer (Theotokos, "Mother of God"), and that the church was founded by the Lord Himself are fundamental beliefs of the church in Greece, as well as of the other Eastern Orthodox churches.

The Greek Church, like other Orthodox churches, venerates saints and icons. The divine liturgy is the center of worship, and theology is inseparable from worship. Like all Eastern Orthodox churches, the Greek Church recognizes seven sacraments (baptism, chrism, Eucharist, orders, matrimony, penance, and unction). The Byzantine liturgical chant, which is enharmonic and rhythmic, is used in the services. There are eight modes, or tones. Traditionally the singing is unaccompanied. Its liturgical language, Greek, is also used in the Patriarchate of Constantinople and the churches of Cyprus and Sinai, and is used together with Arabic in the Patriarchates of Alexandria and Jerusalem. Greek is also used in the Greek Church of North and South America, which has over 1,000,000 members, is headed by an Archbishop, and is under the jurisdiction of the Patriarchate of Constantinople. The Church of Greece is in communion with other Eastern Orthodox churches.

**JEHOVAH'S WITNESSES,** a movement begun in 1872 by Charles Taze Russell at Pittsburgh, Pa. His preaching of "no-hell" and the imminent end of the age attracted multitudes. Its chief corporate controlling body is the Watch Tower Bible and Tract Society. Under "Judge" J. F. Rutherford, Russell's successor, the movement took the name Jehovah's Witnesses in 1931. N. H. Knorr, succeeding Rutherford at his death, solidified and strengthened the movement and extended it throughout the world. Bitterly persecuted at times because of their refusal to salute the flag and in many cases to serve in the armed forces, Jehovah's Witnesses have vigorously defended their cause and have won notable victories for civil rights, not only for themselves but for all other religious faiths.

Their chief doctrinal emphasis is on the imminent end of the age, when Christ will come to power and, after the fateful battle of Armageddon, set up the rule of God on earth. The imminence of this event lends urgency to their task of "witnessing" to it by word of mouth and through distributing their literature.

**JESUITS,** common name for the Society of Jesus, an association of clerks regular, founded by St. Ignatius Loyola in 1534, in France. It is dedicated to the greater service and glory of God through the close imitation of Jesus Christ by working for the salvation and sanctification of souls. It was approved by Pope Paul III in 1540. Besides the three usual vows of poverty, chastity, and obedience, the professed of the order take a fourth vow of obedience to the Pope, which obliges them to go to any part of the world and engage in any kind of work His Holiness many appoint.

The Society originated during Ignatius' student days at Paris, where he gathered a group of young men about him, and imbued them with his ideals of a life of poverty and chastity and the spiritual service of their neighbors. Their group labors began in Venice, where all of them except Peter Favre, already a priest, were ordained to the priesthood. In Rome their apostolic efforts were so successful that they decided to organize themselves into a permanent body. They elected Ignatius as their head and delegated him to expand the brief formula of their Institute, which had been submitted to Paul III. Ignatius dedicated the next 10 years to drawing up these detailed Constitutions, which were approved by Julius III in 1550. These Constitutions described in detail the purpose of the order and the means by which it proposed to attain its goals.

The almost unlimited field of activity envisaged by St. Ignatius led him to introduce a number of novel changes in the religious life: the individual recitation of the divine office instead of choir, the giving up of a distinctive dress, and the practical fusion of contemplative prayer with apostolic activity. Other distinctive changes in the Constitutions were, for example, the election of a General superior for life, and the dropping of the chapter, strictly so called. A congregation of procurators meets every three years in Rome to determine whether there is reason, because of conditions within or without the Society, for calling a General Chapter, which otherwise would meet only on the death of the General to choose a successor.

Novices must undergo a probation of two years, at the end of which they pronounce perpetual but simple vows. After the completion of his studies and ordination to the priesthood, the young priest goes through another year of ascetical training, after which in due time he is admitted to his final vows.

From the outset the Society was active in foreign missions. Before the death of Ignatius, Jesuits were established in the Far East, Ethiopia, Brazil, the Congo, and Morocco; and Francis Xavier was preparing for his mission to China when he died in 1553.

From the beginning the Jesuits were also keenly interested in doctrinal matters and were active in stamping out heresy. Peter Favre (1506–46), accompanying Pedro Ortiz, the ambassador of Charles V, took part in the Diet of Ratisbon (1541), where Catholic and Protestant theologians tried unsuccessfully to resolve their doctrinal disagreements. At the same time Peter Canisius waged the battle of the church, almost singlehandedly, against heresy at Cologne, Ingolstadt, Worms, Spires, Augsburg, in the Rhineland, Bavaria, the Tyrol, and even as far as Vienna and Bohemia. Cathedrals and universities, bishops and princes, cities of the Holy Roman Empire, even church councils vied for the services of this man, who came to be called the "hammer of heretics." The Pope, Paul III, named two Jesuits as theologians of the Holy See: Diego Laynez (1512–65) and Alfonso Salmeron (1515–85).

Because of this deep interest in Christian doctrine, the Society from the start was vitally concerned with education. In 1537 Simon Rodrigues (d.1579) was instrumental in re-establishing at Coimbra, Portugal, a university which had been founded in 1290 at Lisbon, and before Ignatius' death, in 1556, colleges were established at Messina, Sicily, and at Gandia, Spain; and the German and Roman colleges were founded in Rome. At the time of Ignatius' death, the order was conducting 30 colleges, and 17 years later, in 1573, the first Jesuit college in the New World, St. Ildefonse, was established in Mexico City—63 years before the founding of Harvard.

The second period in the history of the Society of Jesus was between the death of St. Ignatius and the suppression of the order by Clement XIV on July 21, 1773. The growth of the Jesuits in membership and influence during this period was phenomenal. In 1556 there were about 1,000 members in 11 provinces; in 1749 on the eve of the suppression of the order in Portugal, the Society numbered 22,589 members, of whom 11,293 were priests, distributed through 39 provinces, and the Jesuits had 669 colleges, 176 seminaries, and 273 missions abroad. Historians now generally concede that the papal suppression was decreed as a prudential measure by the Pope, yielding to the pressure brought by the Bourbon courts of France, Spain, and Naples, and the Marquês de Pombal of Portugal, supported by the Jansenists and extreme Gallicans in France.

Since its restoration in 1814, the society has grown appreciably, in spite of frequent national suppressions in France, Spain, and Italy, when its schools have been closed, its property confiscated, and its members driven into exile. At the beginning of 1960 the Society had 34,687 members, 3,818 of whom were in foreign missions. Throughout the world the Society directs 5,211 educational institutions, including 341 seminaries (Jesuit and non-Jesuit), of which the largest is the Gregorian University in Rome, with an international enrollment of 2,552. Jesuits are also in charge of the Istituto Biblico in Rome.

The Society of Jesus is especially active in two other fields: the publication of periodical literature and the conducting of retreats. The order publishes 1,320 periodicals, of which 130 are scholarly or scientific, 200 are devotional, 45 are on missions, and 150 are on devotions to the Sacred Heart of Jesus. In one year the Jesuits conducted 19,483 closed retreats, ranging from 3 to 30 days, for some 969,356 participants. The Society operates 174 retreat houses with an average yearly attendance of 2,000 retreatants at each house. Of these retreat houses 32 are in the United States.

The Society in the United States has 7,978 members, with 1,180 in foreign missions, and conducts 41 high schools, with a student body of 25,235, and 28 colleges and universities, with 97,183 students. American Jesuits conduct 13 law schools and five of the six Catholic medical schools in the country. Jesuits have charge of 123 parishes in the United States, including 16 missions among the American Indians. They operate nine radio stations throughout the world, one program in St. Louis, the Sacred Heart, serving 1,300 stations.

*Lutheran Church in America*

Services at the Lutheran convention which marked the merging of the American Evangelical, Augustana, Finnish Evangelical, and the United Lutheran churches into the Lutheran Church in America.

**LUTHERANISM** [lōo'thər-ən-ĭz-əm], form of Protestanism deriving from the teaching of Martin Luther (1483–1546). Lutheran churches are spread throughout the world, but they are strongest in Germany, the Scandinavian countries, and the United States. The great majority of them (61) are confederated in the Lutheran World Federation, founded in 1947 in Lund, Sweden. Their distinctive mark is loyalty to their own historic creeds. All Lutheran churches adhere to the Augsburg Confession and Luther's catechisms, and most of them attribute authority to the Book of Concord.

However, in organization and polity, these churches display a great variety. Those of Sweden, Norway, and Denmark are national churches. Those of Germany are territorial churches (until 1918 they were at the same time state churches). Others, mainly those in North America, are free churches. Most are governed by synods, some by bishops (in Scandinavia and parts of Germany), and a few take pride in being congregationalist in polity. In Denmark, Sweden, Norway, and Finland 95% to 98% of the people are members of the Lutheran Church; but in Great Britain, France, Spain, Italy, and many other countries the Lutherans represent very small minorities. The Lutheran churches in western and southeastern Europe, South America, and Australia owe their origin almost exclusively to German colonizers and immigrants. Those in the United States and Canada were founded by Germans and Scandinavians.

The Lutheran churches of Germany and the United States have long been engaged in foreign missionary work in Africa and the Far East. As a result Lutheranism is strongly represented among the so-called younger churches. Only a few of these are comparatively large: those in the Malagasy Republic and Tanganyika in Africa and that of Andhra in India. The strongest is the Protestant Christian Batak Church in northern Sumatra, with nearly 700,000 members, which became an independent church in 1942 and joined the Lutheran World Federation in 1952.

In the United States, Lutheranism began with the founding of the Evangelical Lutheran Ministerium of Pennsylvania by H. M. Mühlenberg in 1748. In the course of its expansion paralleling the growth of the American nation, it assumed a great diversification, due chiefly to the transplantation of the numerous European Lutheran traditions to the New World. However, since the end of World War I, efforts for unification have determined its course. In 1918 the United Lutheran Church came into being as the result of the union of the old Lutheran synods in the eastern and southern states. In 1962 this church united with the strong Augustana Lutheran Church (Swedish) and two smaller bodies as the Lutheran Church in America. Meanwhile, in 1960, the American Lutheran Church was formed by the union of the Ohio, Buffalo, and Iowa synods (chiefly German), united since 1930, and the large Evangelical Lutheran Church (Norwegian).

In the United States the Lutheran churches with the most exclusive creed are represented by the Evangelical Lutheran Synodical Conference in North America (founded, 1872), of which the Lutheran Church—Missouri Synod is the strongest and most influential member. They have declined membership in the Lutheran World Federation, have refused to co-operate with the other Lutheran bodies in America, and have denied them even pulpit and altar fellowship, in the interest of strict adherence to the unaltered Augsburg Confession. They are distinguished by their energetic activity in home and foreign missions and by their cultivation of an educational system which includes parochial schools.

As a Protestant tradition, Lutheranism is marked chiefly by its dependence upon the work of Martin Luther. This dependence, however, is of a special kind. Luther did not want his followers to call themselves by his name. "Who am I," he said, "that anybody should call himself by my insignificant name! I do not want to be anybody's master, for only one is our master, even Jesus Christ." The reason why this wish was not fulfilled was, and still is, that his followers adopted his conception of the person and work of Christ in terms of the doctrine of justification by faith (the "material principle" of the Reformation) and his emphasis upon the authority of Scripture alone (the "formal principle" of the Reformation). Though they never ceased to honor him, they refused to regard him as a church founder, church father, or saint. Hence they coupled their dependence upon him with loyalty to other traditions. Philipp Melanchthon has become almost as important in Lutheranism as Luther, not so much because of his authorship of the Augsburg Confession as because of the influence of his *Loci communes* (Basic Concepts) upon theological thought. For more than a century after the Reformation it was he rather than Luther who determined the character of Lutheran orthodoxy.

In connection with the emphasis upon the real presence of Christ in the Lord's Supper (in, with, and under the bread and wine) as it was implied in Luther's doctrine of the ubiquity of Christ, Lutheran theology, as well as piety, has always been marked by a sense of the indwelling of God in all life and of the nearness of Christ, the incarnate God, to all men of faith. Thus Lutherans tend to identify religious faith with trust in the divine love and providence.

**MENNONITES** [měn′ən-īts], followers of Menno Simons, who reorganized the Dutch Anabaptists after 1536, and settled them in remote rural regions in closely knit, autonomous communities. Faithfully adhering to the principles of their forefathers, the Mennonites practice adult believers' baptism, observe a strict Biblicist piety, reject the oath and the use of violence, and strongly advocate the separation of church and state. They have found it necessary, however, to agree to compromises in connection with such matters of civil obedience as the payment of taxes, recognition of police power, and compulsory education; but they have consistently refused to render military service and to participate in war. After the middle of the 19th century, when their pacifism became unpopular, they were forced to leave their homes in Germany, Switzerland, and Austria, and many of them resettled in Russia and the United States. Since the rise of Bolshevism, most of those who settled in Russia have migrated to the United States, Canada, Paraguay, and Uruguay.

**METHODISM** [měth′ə-dĭz-əm], form of Protestantism deriving from the Wesleyan revivals in England in the 18th century. The term Methodist was originally a derisive epithet leveled at a small band of Oxford scholars, including George Whitefield (1714–70), Charles Wesley (1707–88), and John Wesley (1703–91), because of their strict regularity in study and worship. The eventual leader of

the group, John Wesley, while at a Moravian meeting in Aldersgate Street, London, on May 24, 1738, came forcefully to know and experience for himself that man as sinner is justified before God by faith alone. This date has traditionally marked the beginning of Methodism, as John Wesley and others of the Oxford band forthwith began preaching their new understanding of faith regularly to "classes" of interested members of the Anglican Church.

Methodist doctrine did not differ from that of the Church of England, and the Methodists considered themselves to be faithful members of the Established Church. Moreover, when they preached that man could know and experience the saving grace of God through faith in Christ, such faith producing inward and outward holiness of life, they were stressing what was already part of the Reformation heritage of the Anglican Church. However, the Methodist emphasis upon the possibility of everyone's knowing this "experientially" came as good news to great multitudes of people, often disruptively. This circumstance resulted in the closing of many Church of England pulpits to the Wesleyan preachers. The Methodists turned to preaching in the fields and at the mine pits, with the result that many unchurched and spiritually indifferent persons became members of the Methodist societies. The formation of societies into "circuits" regularly visited by itinerant ministers, many of whom were lay preachers, spread Methodism rapidly across Great Britain. On the local level, "local preachers" pursued regular occupations but devoted spare time to shepherding societies toward inward and outward holiness, between the regular visits of the full-time "traveling preacher." Conversion experience and Christian perfection were emphasized. The latter, often a matter of debate, was interpreted by John Wesley to mean "simplicity of intention and purity of affection," a matter of intention and disposition, not of achievement.

In 1741 Methodism's only major doctrinal division occurred. George Whitefield, one of the great preachers of all time, held to a Calvinistic interpretation of redemption, contending that God in His inscrutable wisdom had elected certain of mankind to salvation and others to damnation. John Wesley opposed this view of the Calvinistic Methodists by insisting that Christ had died for all men and that any and all of mankind could, through God's grace, by an act of will, trust God and expect more of God's grace to be forthcoming. Wesley's position, called Evangelical Arminianism, has influenced most of subsequent Methodist theology. While Methodism has not put great stress on theology, it has taken as normative in its doctrinal position John Wesley's *Notes on the New Testament*, his *Standard Sermons*, and the Wesleyan hymns. Of these last, Charles Wesley wrote over 6,500. Singing became one of the marks of a Methodist meeting, and the hymn one of the major vehicles of Methodist belief.

By 1766 British Methodism had expanded to 19,753 members, and in America two immigrant Irish local preachers, Robert Strawbridge (d.1781), in Maryland, and Philip Embury (1729–75), in New York, had established the first Methodist societies. The date and location of the earliest Methodist society in the United States is a matter of debate. The evidence points only to near contemporary foundings in Pipe Creek, Md., and New York City.

Wesley, learning of the American effort, sent English

Exterior and interior views of St. George's Methodist Church, in Philadelphia, Pa. The church has been in continuous use since it was purchased as an unfinished building in 1769.

preachers to help establish the societies. Their mission prospered, and in 1773 the first American Methodist conference was held in Philadelphia, with 10 traveling preachers present. By this time there were 1,160 American Methodists, over half of them in Maryland and Virginia, where the Church of England was strongest.

At the outbreak of the American Revolution the English Methodist preachers, with the exception of Francis Asbury (1745–1816), along with most of the Anglican clergy, returned to England. Work in America fell to native lay preachers, such as William Watters, Freeborn Garrettson, and Jesse Lee, due to whose diligence there were 15,000 Methodists in America by the end of the Revolution. But since Methodists were still members of the Church of England, the departure of the Anglican clergy left them without ordained ministers and without sacraments. In this dilemma some of the Methodist preachers in Virginia in 1779 threatened to withdraw from the Anglican Church and form a separate church, ordaining one another. Francis Asbury, aided by Freeborn Garrettson and William Watters, managed to prevent division until word came from John Wesley. When Thomas Coke (1747–1814) arrived in America in 1784 as John Wesley's representative, with plans for a new church, he conferred with the American preachers, and they determined to set up a separate episcopal church.

Freeborn Garrettson was sent to summon the preachers to the so-called Christmas Conference at Baltimore, Dec. 24, 1784, and here the Methodist Episcopal Church was organized. Coke and Asbury were elected joint superintendents (later called bishops), and several of the preachers were elected and ordained deacons and elders. The conference adopted a *Discipline* based on Wesley's *Large Minutes* and a *Sunday Service* which was an abbreviated form of the *Book of Common Prayer*, with 25 Articles of Religion derived from the Anglican Church's 39 Articles. The circuit rider on horseback, preaching the new understanding of experiential faith extemporaneously, organized Methodist societies into circuits as he followed the American frontier west. With Bishop Asbury setting the example, itinerants carried Methodist belief and practice the length and breadth of the country.

In both Great Britain and America, Methodism grew rapidly, but not without many divisions, primarily on matters of polity. In America concern over the power given to bishops, coupled with the desire for lay representation,

eventually caused the establishment of the Methodist Protestant Church in 1830. Slavery also divided American Methodism. It had been outlawed in the Methodist Church, but by 1840 the abolition issue had become so intense that a rule was passed prohibiting discussion of the subject in conference. When Bishop James Andrew, in 1844, inadvertently became a slave owner and was unable to rid himself of his slaves, it created a difficulty which led to the separation of the Southern churches and the organization of the Methodist Episcopal Church, South, in 1845.

After long effort, in 1939, the three largest Methodist denominations in America, the Methodist Episcopal Church, the Methodist Episcopal Church, South, and the Methodist Protestant Church, met at a conference in Kansas City, Mo., and united to form the Methodist Church. This unity movement continued and in 1968 the Methodist Church and the Evangelical United Brethren Church merged to form the United Methodist Church. This church, the second-largest Protestant denomination in America, made up of over 11,000,000 members, is part of the World Methodist Conference, comprising Methodist churches throughout the world.

**MORAVIANS or MORAVIAN BRETHREN,** also called Herrnhuters, Protestant Pietist church group, first organized from remnants of the Bohemian Brethren by Christian David (d.1751) on the estate of Count N. L. von Zinzendorf near Berthelsdorf in Upper Lusatia. There the Brethren, who were soon joined by other Moravian refugees, as well as by Pietists who found themselves attracted to them, established (June 17, 1722) the "colony," or separate society, which, under the name of "Herrnhut" (the Lord's Protection), became the headquarters of their church. They developed their own Christocentric forms of piety, worship, and church polity (1727) and remained autonomous. But under the leadership of Zinzendorf, whose influence shaped their common life, they attached themselves to Lutheranism and adopted the Augsburg Confession. They believe themselves organically connected with the Bohemian Brethren by episcopal succession; but their bishops exercise no episcopal authority except that of ordination. As the church spread throughout Germany, and then to England and North America, it gradually became organized in independent synods, which, however, co-operated closely with each other.

A distinctive trait of the Moravians is their ardent missionary zeal. As early as 1732, two of the Brethren were sent to the Negro slaves on the island of St. Thomas, and shortly thereafter, others went to the Eskimos in Greenland.

Their chief concern at home and abroad is the cultivation of the community life of each local congregation under the lordship of Christ. All members are divided into choirs, according to age, sex, and family status, each choir having a separate leader. They attach great importance to the discipline of daily common prayer and frequent worship and are noted for their music.

**MORMONS,** popular name for members of the Church of Jesus Christ of Latter-day Saints. The church was founded at Fayette, N.Y., in 1830 by a young farmer, Joseph Smith, known to Mormons as "the prophet." They claim he discovered by divine revelation certain long-buried "golden plates," which he miraculously translated and published as the *Book of Mormon.* Led by the prophet, the Mormons migrated to Kirtland, Ohio, where they established a community and built the first Mormon temple. Persecution led to another westward migration to Independence, Mo. Prosperous there, but soon resented by neighbors, they were bitterly persecuted and finally were driven from that state into Illinois, where they built in the swamplands along the Mississippi the city of Nauvoo, and commenced the building of another temple. In four years Nauvoo became the largest city in Illinois, with a population of some 20,000. The church grew rapidly, many converts coming from the eastern states and from Europe, where active missionary work was being carried on. In Nauvoo new conflicts between Mormons and their neighbors developed, and Joseph Smith, as mayor of Nauvoo, was arrested and lodged in the Carthage, Ill., jail, where a mob broke in and shot him and his brother Hyrum on June 27, 1844.

Brigham Young was selected as Smith's successor. After failing to bring peace between Mormons and their neighbors, he resolved to lead the community westward to a new home where its members could practice their beliefs. The story of the westward Mormon migration is a true American epic. They established and built a Mormon empire in the Great Salt Lake Basin, from which it spread into neighboring areas, becoming one of the great religio-socio-economic experiments of American history. Utah became first a territory and finally a state in 1896, six years after the leaders of the Mormon Church had formally agreed to abandon the practice of polygamy.

A basic doctrine of the Mormons is their belief in continuous revelation: that God has revealed Himself in the Bible, in the *Book of Mormon,* and in two later books of revelations to Joseph Smith, *Doctrine and Covenants* and *The Pearl of Great Price;* and that He continues to reveal Himself through the channel of the proper Church leadership. The formal "Articles of Faith" of the Mormons are Christian in concept, but among their distinctive beliefs are those regarding baptism for the dead, by proxy, and marriage for eternity, when properly performed in a temple. Salvation is essentially universal, but there are degrees or levels of salvation: telestial, terrestrial, and celestial. The Mormons believe "in the same organization that existed in the Primitive Church, namely: apostles, prophets, pastors, teachers, evangelists" with the First Presidency as the highest authority, then the Council of the Twelve, then the Presiding Quorum of Seventy. There are no professional clergy. The entire church is divided into "stakes of Zion" and "wards." Mormons are very missionary-minded, and thousands of young men and young women serve for a period of two to three years as missionaries at their own or their parents' expense. Emphasis is placed upon both temporal and spiritual salvation. The church is supported financially through a system of "tithes" and voluntary "offerings." Through a cooperative welfare work program, an ample supply of goods is produced and stored to sustain those who suffer misfortune or economic hardship. The Mormons, with headquarters in Salt Lake City, number over 2,000,000. They have adherents in every U.S. state and in most foreign countries.

**PENTECOSTAL CHURCHES,** a group of independent religious bodies originating in the United States in the early part of the 20th century, as a late outgrowth of the post-Civil War holiness movement in the Methodist Church. The name derives from their doctrine that all Christians are to reproduce the experience of the original disciples on the first day of Pentecost following Christ's ascension, as recorded in Acts 2:1-4. This involves being baptized in the Holy Ghost, "speaking with tongues," and faith healing. Apparent manifestations of these phenomena in some Pentecostal meetings in Los Angeles in 1906 attracted wide attention, and the movement spread rapidly.

The largest Pentecostal groups are to be found in the United States and Canada, the Scandinavian countries, and Brazil. There is also a sizable following in Great Britain. The largest Pentecostal organization is the Assemblies of God, with over 8,000 churches and 500,000 members in 70 countries.

**PRESBYTERIANISM** [prĕz-bə-tēr′ē-ən-ĭz-əm], name used primarily to describe the system of church government found in that branch of Protestantism known as "Reformed." Its main features are the right of every member to share in the government of the local church, which is exercised through elected or approved elders; a single order in the Christian ministry, in which all ministers are of equal status; and the governing of the national church through a graded arrangement of ecclesiastical courts composed of equal numbers of ministers and laymen.

Presbyterianism is associated also with a system of theology usually described as Calvinistic. The significance of this association is reflected in the great creedal statements Presbyterianism has produced. These include the Helvetic Confessions of 1536 and 1566; the Scots Confessions of 1560 and 1581; the Canons of the Synod of Dort, 1619; and the fullest expression of English-speaking Presbyterianism, the Westminster Confession of Faith, 1647. However, since Calvinistic theology is found also in the Thirty-nine Articles of the Anglican Church, and to some extent in Congregationalist and Baptist churches, it is the ecclesiastical polity which is the most distinctive characteristic of Presbyterianism. Presbyterianism is also frequently connected with a simple form of public worship, and (especially in Scotland) with an inflexible Sabbatarianism, which lays great emphasis on the binding nature of the Mosaic law.

The name "Presbyterian" was applied to the Church of Scotland to distinguish it from the Church of England, since both were Reformed, in the Continental sense, with regard to theology. The issue between them after the union of the crowns in 1603 was largely one of polity. The Church of Scotland was presbyterian in government, like the Continental Reformed churches, while the Church of England was episcopal, like the Lutheran churches of Scandinavia. On the Continent the historic and distinctive name of the Calvinistic churches is Reformed rather than Presbyterian, because there they are to be distinguished, not from some Episcopal Reformed church, but from the Roman Catholic Church, on the one hand, and from the Lutheran churches on the other.

**History and Expansion.** As a system of church government in the modern age, Presbyterianism derives from John Calvin, who based his concept of ecclesiastical polity on the position and function of the presbyter in the New Testament church. Calvin's doctrine was methodically expounded in his *Institutes of the Christian Religion* (1536), and his polity was first put into practice in Geneva. But it was in Paris that the first national synod (1559) adopted a constitution which laid the foundation for the church courts which Presbyterianism now knows as Kirk Session, Presbytery, Synod, and General Assembly.

In Scotland this form of church government was adopted in all significant particulars as the national establishment in 1560, following the reformation of the Scottish Church by John Knox; and its foundations were strengthened by Knox's successor, Andrew Melville. Except for the century of struggle against episcopacy during the Stuart Dynasty, the dominance of Presbyterianism in Scotland has not been threatened. The conduct of the church service in certain areas has varied remarkably little in the intervening four centuries. Scottish Presbyterians now number some 1,500,000.

In England, Presbyterianism has for the most part received the pointedly frigid welcome which has been the lot of episcopacy in Scotland and can claim now only about 70,000 members. This stands in marked contrast to the church's flourishing condition in the adjacent, much smaller countries of Wales (155,000) and Northern Ireland (130,000).

Presbyterianism came to America mainly through settlers from Northern Ireland and Scotland. Today it is one of the great ecclesiastical bodies in the United States, where the various Presbyterian branches total more than 4,500,000 members. In Canada the different Presbyterian streams were combined into a single church in 1875, and the majority 50 years later joined the Congregationalists and Methodists in forming the United Church of Canada, which is basically Presbyterian in polity. A minority continued as the Presbyterian Church of Canada, and now numbers some 185,000. Presbyterianism is found in some strength also in Australia (105,000) and in New Zealand (70,000).

**Modern Trends.** During the past 80 years the influence of Biblical criticism has induced most Presbyterian bodies in varying degree to modify their view of Scriptural authority and their earlier rigid adherence to the Westminster Confession of Faith. (A notable exception is the Free Presbyterian Church, strong in the western seaboard of Scotland, which will not yield an inch to what it regards as the blighting influence of modern scholarship.) Evident also is an increased interest in liturgy, as seen in the number of Presbyterian books of common order.

Other features of modern Presbyterianism include the policy on the missionary front of encouraging the establishment of indigenous churches (particularly in Africa), an increasing concern in social and welfare matters, and an influential role in the rise and growth of the ecumenical movement.

**PROTESTANT EPISCOPAL CHURCH,** religious denomination in the United States stemming historically from the Church of England. During colonial times the Anglican Church planted and nurtured its first parishes, ordained its clergy, and imparted to it the basic patterns of its doctrine and worship. After the Revolution, at a convention of clergy and lay representatives meeting in Philadelphia (Oct., 1789), these parishes, taking the name "Protestant Episcopal," became a self-governing federation of dioceses (each diocese at that time being coterminous with a state), adhering to a common national church constitution and a common ritual of worship in a revised *Book of Common Prayer*.

The church had already obtained the episcopate by the consecration of Samuel Seabury of Connecticut by bishops of the Episcopal Church of Scotland on Nov. 14, 1784, and of William White of Pennsylvania and Samuel Provoost of New York by bishops of the Church of England on Feb. 4, 1787. With all other Anglican churches, with which it shares intercommunion, the Episcopal Church affirms the Bible to be the final authority of all necessary doctrine. The church adheres to the historic Apostles' and Nicene creeds, admits baptism and the Eucharist to be the only two necessary sacraments, and maintains the episcopate as a witness of the unbroken succession of the church's ministry since apostolic times.

The Protestant Episcopal Church has about 7,000 churches and a membership of over 3,000,000 in 90 or more dioceses. The church is governed by a triennial General Convention, consisting of a House of Bishops and a House of Deputies (clerical and lay). Its ranking officer is a Presiding Bishop, who is also the president of its National Council, which carries on the missionary work of the church. The headquarters are in New York.

**PROTESTANTISM,** the system of Christian doctrine and practice which grew out of the Reformation (q.v.) in the 16th century. The term is derived from the formal *Protestation* presented at the Second Diet of Speyer, in 1529, by those members of the three estates of the Holy Roman Empire (clergy, nobility, and *bourgeoisie*) who were in sympathy with the cause of Martin Luther. It was a protest against the decision of the majority of the Diet to repeal a unanimous vote of the first Diet of Speyer, in 1526, which had allowed the provisional establishment of territorial churches independent of Rome. The followers of the Reformation came to be called Protestants because they identified themselves with this formal *Protestation.*

Generally speaking, all Christians who object to the Roman Catholic form of Christianity on the basis of the teachings of the Reformers are considered Protestant. They include principally the following: Lutherans, Calvinists, Anglicans, and Mennonites, who broke with the Church of Rome in the 16th century; the so-called nonconformist groups that broke off from the Church of England—the Baptists, Congregationalists, and Quakers in the 17th century, and the Methodists in the 18th; the various evangelical churches formed in the United States in the 19th century as offshoots of the major Protestant denominations; and the so-called "younger churches" which have been organized in the 20th century as a result of Protestant missionary enterprise in various countries.

It is not easy to give a characterization of Protestantism which fits all these groups. The Protestant churches have responded very freely to the environment in which they were formed. Actually a variety of doctrines, polities, and moral requirements constituted Protestantism from the beginning, because the major Protestant churches organized during the 16th century were territorial or national churches.

Moreover, the inner character of Protestantism has undergone several profound changes, partly under the impact of the power inherent in the Protestant interpretation of the Gospel, and partly in response to the encounter of Protestant teachings with modern science and philosophy. Historians, therefore, distinguish between "Old Protestantism" and "New Protestantism." Old Protestantism comprises also those churches and movements which rely on creeds and confessions of faith formulated at the time of the Reformation or Counter Reformation. This phase of Protestantism is marked by the endeavor to make all religious life conform to doctrinal standards. New Protestantism is represented by those Protestant churches, chiefly in the United States, which came into being under the impact of the freedom of religion guaranteed in the U.S. Constitution and its Amendments. "Modern Protestantism," as distinguished from New Protestantism, is seen in those forms and systems of theological thought in which the Christian religion is interpreted so as to do justice to the new insights of modern philosophy, history, and science, and the understanding of nature, man, and God which they have made possible.

But all the Protestant churches as such share certain historic tenets and attitudes:

(1) They regard the Bible as the word of God and the only source of revealed truth, as against the Catholic reliance upon tradition and the authority of the church. Conservative Protestants may hold to some doctrine of literal inspiration, but the more liberal accept the general conclusions of historical criticism. All, however, as Protestants, regard the Bible as the sole repository of the teaching of Christ and His apostles, and as the only authentic record of their lives.

(2) Protestants also hold to the principle of "private judgment" in the interpretation of Scripture, as against the Catholic dogma that only the church can interpret the Bible authoritatively. It is this combination of considering the Bible as divine revelation, plus the reliance upon the voice of personal conscience in its interpretation, that is responsible for the divisive tendency in earlier Protestantism. One cannot disregard what he considers to be the word of God. Nor can any Biblical teaching be a matter of indifference, about which there can be an easy attitude of toleration. But Biblical passages sometimes appear to conflict, and the particular interpretation depends upon which verse or passage is taken as the "key": hence the forming of separate denominations over such relatively minor questions as the mode of baptism and the organization of the church.

(3) Protestants, as such, still subscribe to the principle involved in Luther's famous doctrine of "justification by faith," as against any reliance upon ceremonial observances as effective for salvation. Modern Protestants may have gotten away from a strictly legalistic conception of justification, and they may favor the liturgical enrichment of Protestant worship. But they do not believe that such observances are of vital significance compared to the individual's faith in God and the divine revelation in Christ.

(4) Protestants still subscribe, also, to Luther's doctrine of the "universal priesthood of believers." Fundamentally this is a protest against the Catholic dogma of two distinct classes of Christians—priests and laymen—and that only properly ordained priests can be the mediators of divine grace. Protestants believe that all Christians stand in the same relation to God through Christ and that every believer is responsible for the spiritual and bodily welfare of his fellowmen. All are called to God's special service, and through their various callings are required to render service to God and their fellowmen. This is the Protestant sense of *vocation,* where every activity of the consecrated Christian is as holy to God as that of cloistered monks.

(5) In line with this idea of the "universal priesthood of believers," all Protestants, as such, have a conception of the church which is profoundly different from that of Roman Catholics. According to Roman Catholic teaching, the church is the "mystical body of Christ." This means that in the sacraments, as they are administered by sacramental persons, the priests, the Incarnation of God in Christ is continued, and Christ's sacrifice for sin is continuously re-presented in the Mass. Thus the church must be seen as a sacramental-priestly institution mediating salvation to its faithful adherents. The adherents belong to the church, but apart from the sacramental priesthood there is no true church.

In Protestantism, however, the church is simply the "fellowship of believers" or "the people of God." The church may still be thought of as the "mystical body of Christ," not in the sense of an institution mediating salvation to its adherents through the recurring presentation of Christ's sacrifice, but, as St. Teresa expressed the thought, in the sense that each Christian is the hands and feet and voice of Christ ministering to the needs of his fellows in the world.

Thus from the beginning Protestantism has stressed the prophetic conception of the church and its ministry as distinguished from the priestly. Following the teaching of the Epistle to the Hebrews and the Gospel of John, Protestants consider Christ as the high priest of the church and the Lamb of God offered once in sacrifice for the sins of the world. The sacrifice cannot be repeated, and needs no re-presentation. Therefore, Protestants consider the ministers of the church as "ministers of the word," who, like the prophets of old, call God's people to serve Him in righteousness in all the vocations of life. Religion, then, from the standpoint of Protestantism, is not something removed from ordinary life, but a transforming power to permeate every aspect of daily living, not just for "the religious" who by special vows are removed from the world, but for all believers who live and work daily in the world.

As modern Biblical and historical scholarship has made its impact upon Protestant thought, a new tendency has appeared in Protestantism. The old tendency toward divisiveness has been supplanted by a new spirit of toleration. This is based, not upon an attitude of indifference to essentials, but upon a new sense of discrimination with regard to what is essential. It has expressed itself in the new Ecumenical Movement that has grown up in the 20th century and has resulted not only in such national organizations as the Federal Council of Churches in the United States (now supplanted by the National Council of Churches), but also by such international organizations as the World Conferences on Faith and Order, the Universal Christian Council on Life and Work, and the International Missionary Council, all combined now in the World Council of Churches. That this new ecumenical spirit is not limited to the forming of agencies merely for deliberation and social enterprises, however, is shown by such organic mergers of particular denominations in the United States as those between the Congregational and Christian Churches, and the Evangelical and Reformed, now further consolidated into the United Church of Christ, and the merger in Canada of most of the Congregationalists, all the Methodists, and a majority of the Presbyterians to form the United Church of Canada.

**REFORMED CHURCH, THE,** one of the two major divisions of Protestantism stemming from the Reformation. The name signifies that it was the Catholic Church reformed according to the pattern of doctrine and polity in the New Testament. The Reformed Church was to Switzerland, broadly speaking, what the Lutheran Church was to Germany. In 1529 at the famous Marburg colloquy the breach between Lutheran and Reformed became irreparable when Luther and the Swiss leader Zwingli disagreed on the doctrine of the sacraments.

Ulrich Zwingli, Martin Bucer, Heinrich Bullinger, and John Oecolampadius were among those early leaders in Switzerland who steered the Reformation through a bitter civil war against the Roman Catholic cantons. But it was John Calvin who molded and developed the Reformed Church and gave it an international influence. Having gained control of Geneva, Calvin welcomed foreign refugees, maintained his interest in them when they returned to their own countries, and was regarded by John Knox and others as a true father in God. His *Institutes of the Christian Religion* (1536) was adopted as the authoritative doctrinal confession of the Reformed faith, of which another influential statement, drawn up in Germany, was the Heidelberg Catechism (1563).

From Switzerland the Reformed Church soon spread into the Netherlands, France, parts of Germany, Hungary, Czechoslovakia, and other countries. Generally the term "Reformed" was retained, and to it was added the name of the local country. In Scotland, however, the Reformed Church was styled "Presbyterian," after the form of government found in all the Continental churches of this tradition, to distinguish it from the Reformed Church of England, which was "Episcopal." In France, the Calvinistic Protestants were called Huguenots.

Even after immigration to the New World, each of the various national types of Reformed faith maintained its separate existence. In 1628 the Dutch Reformed Church was officially established in New Amsterdam (New York) by settlers from Holland. Emigrants from Germany and Switzerland founded German Reformed churches on the Eastern seaboard, and these united in 1863 to form a single church. Various other mergers have since been effected in the United States within the Reformed family.

The Church of Scotland and smaller Scottish Presbyterian bodies also established themselves throughout North America. In Canada many of them are now identified with the United Church (whose polity is a modified Presbyterianism). In the United States, consequent on a 1958 merger, most Presbyterians are members of the United Presbyterian Church in the United States of America.

In varying degree one can still trace in all the different sections of the Reformed Church the essential doctrine and polity formulated four centuries ago by John Calvin. Nevertheless the American churches have developed in their own way, exhibiting particularly a greater tolerance and a willingness to co-operate with other Christians. A further distinctive mark, one common to the whole Reformed group, is an extensive and well-organized foreign mission program. The Reformed churches belong to the World Presbyterian Alliance, a nonlegislative international body which represents some 80 churches and 45,000,000 persons throughout the world.

**ROMAN CATHOLIC CHURCH.** There are two equally valid definitions of the Catholic Church, comparable to the twofold nature of Jesus Christ, its founder, who was both human and divine. One definition stresses the visible aspect of the church as a juridical institution. The other stresses its internal qualities as a spiritual entity, whose cohesive force is the invisible grace of God. An adequate understanding of Roman Catholicism covers both viewpoints.

**Juridical Institution.** The clearest exponent of the church as a visible institution was St. Robert Bellarmine (1542–1621), Jesuit cardinal. To meet the Protestant reformers' challenge of a new concept of the Christian Church as a purely spiritual society, composed of all the believers, or all the just, or all the predestined, he defined the Catholic Church as "the assembly of men, bound together by the profession of the same Christian faith, and by the communion of the same sacraments, under the rule of legitimate pastors, and in particular of the one Vicar of Christ on earth, the Roman Pontiff." The purpose of this definition is mainly functional, to determine who are members of the Catholic Church and who are not.

There are three conditions for membership. Since profession of faith is the first requisite, only those who accept all that the church infallibly proposes for belief actually belong to the Catholic Church. They may not be aware of the whole body of required doctrine, or they may be subjectively mistaken in their understanding of what is taught, but they do not deliberately reject any fundamental dogma, such as belief in Christ's divinity or in the Mass, which they know is part of the church's official teaching.

Sharing in the use of the same sacraments is the second essential. Baptism, the first sacrament, is the indispensable "door of the church." The baptism must be administered with water and in the name of the Trinity. The other six sacraments—confirmation, the Eucharist, penance, holy orders, matrimony, and extreme unction—need not all be received by any one person (and seldom are), but as occasion demands they may not be excluded. Thus confirmation is normally received in early childhood in order to strengthen one's profession of faith. The Eucharist, which is Christ under the appearances of bread and wine, must be received at least annually and is recommended daily.

Penance or confession is also an annual duty for the remission of grave sins. Holy orders are conferred on qualified candidates who as priests have power to offer the sacrifice of the Mass and give absolution from sin. Matrimony is contracted as a lifelong means of grace for husband and wife. Extreme unction is administered to a person in danger of death to prepare him for the journey into eternity.

Up to this point, other Christians participate to some extent in the conditions set forth. For example, the Eastern Orthodox and Episcopalians believe in the historic episcopate and in the Real Presence in the Eucharist. But the third element, obedience to the Roman pontiff as vicar of Christ, is uniquely Catholic, and in fact explains the term "Roman" added to "Catholic Church" in popular terminology.

In accepting papal authority, the Catholic Church understands that the Roman pontiff has more than just the highest office of inspection as a kind of superintendent or director. He is believed to have received from Christ full and supreme power of jurisdiction over the universal church, not only in matters of faith and morals, but also in those things which relate to the discipline and government of the church throughout the world. The Pope, therefore, is held to possess not merely the principal part but the fullness of this supreme power. His authority is held to be not merely occasional or delegated, but ordinary and immediate, both over each and all the churches, and over each and all the pastors of the faithful.

In the foregoing concept of the church, the external phase is emphasized in order to clarify the church's visibility and therefore perceptibility to the senses. As explained by Bellarmine, the church is a definite society, not of angels or of spirits but of men. It must therefore be bound together by external and visible signs. It would not be a society unless those who belong to it could recognize each other as members, by the three elements of a common profession of faith, communion of the same sacraments, and obedience to one visible head.

**Mystical Body of Christ.** There is another aspect of the church, more profound than the juridical one developed by Bellarmine, and universally accepted in Catholic theology. For the church is not only a visible organization with discernible members, an external ritual, and a code of laws, but also a spiritual organism whose character was

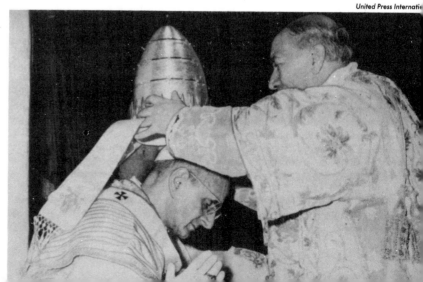

United Press Internatio

The coronation of Pope Paul VI. The Pope, formerly Giovanni Battista Cardinal Montini, received the papal Crown from Alfredo Cardinal Ottaviani on June 30, 1963, in St. Peter's Square, Vatican City.

first delineated in the Gospels and developed by St. Paul into a whole system of faith.

In the words of Pius XII, "If we would define and describe the true Church of Jesus Christ—which is the one, holy, Catholic, apostolic Roman Church—we shall find nothing more noble, more sublime, or more divine than the expression 'the Mystical Body of Jesus Christ'—an expression that flows spontaneously from the repeated teaching of the sacred Scriptures and the holy Fathers." As in the preceding analysis of the church as a juridical institution, so in the mystical body three basic elements are discernible, considering the church as a body, as the body of Christ, and as His mystical body.

The term "body" when referring to the church derives its meaning from the analogy used by St. Paul when he says to Christians, "you are the Body of Christ, member for member" (I Cor. 12:27) and when he calls Christ "the Head of His Body, the Church" (Col. 1:18). If the church is a body, it must be perceptible to the senses, since the essence of a body as distinct from spirit is precisely its perceptibility.

Corollary to being a body, the church must have a multiplicity of discernible members, because, along with perceptibility, the possession of parts is an essential feature of anything bodily. Yet the parts of a human body are not merely aggregated but intimately united to form a single substance. Moreover, the various organs differ in their purpose and nobility, and are closely integrated to collaborate for the benefit and partake in the sufferings of the whole being.

In like manner members of the Catholic Church are linked together in such a way as to help one another. And just as a natural body is formed of different organs with different functions arranged in due order, so the church is bound together by the combination of structurally united parts, and has a variety of members that are reciprocally dependent. This interdependence is manifested in the hierarchy, with its graded levels of orders and jurisdiction, of superiors and subjects, beginning with the sovereign pontiff and terminating in the simple laity.

The body which St. Paul identifies with the church is a living reality, and like every organism requires suitable means to enter into life, to grow and mature and prosper according to its nature. Similarly in the Catholic Church the sacraments are divinely instituted means of grace to souls from birth to death, that is, from baptism to extreme unction—with sacramental energy available for every need and circumstance of human life.

Going a step further, the Roman Catholic Church regards itself as the body of Christ. He bears a relation to the body so intimate that St. Augustine often equates the two and, as in the phrase "Christ preaches Christ," practically identifies the Saviour with the society which He founded.

Christ was the originator of the church by His preaching, by His choice of the apostles to carry on His work, by His death on the cross when He merited the graces to be channeled through the mystical body, and by His sending of the Holy Spirit, who descended on Pentecost ar d thus converted the first contingent of several thousand members to His cause.

But Christ's relation to the church is not only historical. It is not only that He began a religious society and then left its government entirely to someone else. He rules the church from within by supernatural means that are permanent, constantly active within the members, and so inexpressibly personal that His own divine spirit is the soul of the mystical body.

This government by Christ does not give the church two independent heads. As Pius XII explained, Peter and his successors, the Popes, are only Christ's vicars, "so that there is only one chief Head of this Body, namely Christ, who never ceases Himself to guide the Church invisibly, though at the same time He rules it visibly, through him who is His representative on earth."

Finally, the term "mystical" describes the nature of the union between Christ and the members of the church and among the members themselves. It is immeasurably nobler than the common will that constitutes other societies, and at the same time it does not form one substance, as in the union of body and soul, or one person, as in the union of the humanity and divinity of Christ.

It is called mystical because it is a mystery, which God revealed to be true, but whose inner essence must be accepted on faith and without full comprehension by the mind. The end or purpose of the church is not temporal or earthly, as in other societies, but heavenly and eternal. Its spiritual bond is the will of God. Incorporation in the church effects a profound internal change in the members. The whole reality which appears to be only another human organization is actually of a higher order of being, called supernatural because beyond the capacities of nature and leading to the destiny of seeing God in the beatific vision after death.

Moreover the Roman Catholic Church is said to be the *mystical* body of Christ because it is sacramental. The Greek word for sacrament is *mysterion*. Broadly speaking, anything spiritual transmitted through external signs partakes of the nature of a sacrament. In this sense the church is the great sacrament of the new law, instituted by Christ for the communication of invisible grace to the world. Accordingly not only those who profess the Catholic religion but all human beings are beneficiaries. For although by definition the only actual members of the church are baptized persons who profess Catholic doctrine under obedience to the Pope, the whole of mankind receives grace from Christ, through the mystical body, in the measure of each person's faith and his fidelity to the will of God.

**RUSSIAN CHURCH,** the Eastern Orthodox church of Russia. According to tradition, Christianity was preached in Russia by the apostle Andrew in the 1st century; but the historical records are much later. There were certainly Christians in Kiev in the 9th century, though the great advance came in the 10th. Prince Vladimir of Kiev was baptized in 988. Mass baptism of his people followed in 989. According to legend, the prince had sent envoys to various countries in search of the true religion. Those sent to Constantinople were impressed by the beauty of the divine liturgy in St. Sophia, so the new church was headed by a Greek metropolitan in Kiev, who was under the jurisdiction of the Patriarch of Constantinople.

As a result of the work on Slavonic begun by Sts. Cyril and Methodius in the 9th century, the Russians received Christianity in their own language. Monastic life was organized on the pattern of Mount Athos, but a native school of iconography developed. Church art and architecture reached a high point between the 12th and 14th centuries.

After the Mongols took Kiev in 1240, the metropolitan see was transferred to Moscow in 1328, and St. Sergius of Radonezh (1314–92), the first Russian mystic, inspired the national opposition which saved Russia from the Tatars in 1380. Then, with the fall of Constantinople to the Turks in 1453, Moscow became the most important center of Eastern Christianity, the "third Rome," according to some theorists of the period.

The 16th century was marked by prolonged conflict between the followers of St. Nil Sorsky (d.1508), who advocated poverty and contemplation and opposed religious persecution, and those of St. Joseph of Volotsk (d.1515), who supported church ownership of property, closer ties between church and state, and persecution of heretics. When the "Josephite" party eventually prevailed, the church's wealth and political influence increased, and in 1589 Metropolitan Job of Moscow was elevated to the rank of patriarch, and the Russian Church became independent.

In the 17th century Western religious penetration was countered by Metropolitan Pyotr Mogila's (1596–1647) system of theological training. But schism resulting from the reforms of Patriarch Nikon (1605–81) sapped the strength of the church and prepared the ground for the events of Peter the Great's reign (1689–1725). In 1721 Peter abolished the patriarchate, replacing it by the Holy Synod, whose members were nominated by the Tsar. St. Tikhon of Zadonsk (1724–83) and St. Seraphim of Sarov (1759–1833), however, revived the spiritual life of the church in the latter part of the 18th century. In the 19th century Aleksei Stepanovich Khomyakov (1804–60) and Vladimir Soloviev (1853–1900), lay theologians, contributed to a revival of spiritual life. Monasticism and missionary activity began to flourish again, and Russian missions were established in Siberia, Alaska, and Japan.

During the Revolution, in Aug., 1917, at the All-Russian Council, the patriarchate was restored, and Tikhon (1865–1925) was elected Patriarch. After his death, the Soviet government forbade the election of a new patriarch and the church was severely persecuted. But in 1943 Metropolitan Sergei (1861–1944) was elected Patriarch. He was succeeded by Metropolitan Aleksei of Leningrad and Novgorod.

The church is governed by the Holy Synod, under the presidency of the patriarch. There are no reliable statistics of church membership in Russia, but there are about 3,000,000 members of the Russian Church outside Russia. In America there are three separate jurisdictions of the Russian Church, all of which hold the same doctrines and use the same liturgy. The largest is the Russian Orthodox Greek Catholic Church of America, with about 850,000 members, under the independent Metropolitan of America and Canada. There is also the Russian Orthodox Church Outside Russia, the metropolitan of which has been in New York since 1950. In addition, there is a group

of parishes directly under the jurisdiction of the Patriarch of Moscow.

The Russian Church is the largest of the Eastern Orthodox churches and is united with the others in faith and worship. Orthodoxy is translated in Slavic as *pravoslavie* (true glorifying, true worship).

**SALVATION** [săl-vā′shən] **ARMY,** international religious and social welfare organization founded in 1865 as the Christian Mission, by William and Catherine Booth, in East London, England. The name Salvation Army was adopted in 1878 when a military organization and terminology, uniforms, and martial music were found effective in attracting neglected slum dwellers. With a fundamentally Protestant evangelical ministry, combined with social welfare services for all persons, regardless of race, color, religion, or depth of depravity, the "Church for the Churchless" spread throughout the British Isles and around the world. Active in more than 80 countries and colonies, the Salvation Army is strongest today in Great Britain, the United States, Scandinavia, and Australia. International headquarters are in London.

**In the United States.** The Salvation Army began in the United States in 1880 and won recognition for its success in bringing religion to city slums and for its work with American forces during World War I. Its program of social activities includes homes and hospitals for unwed mothers, shelters and rehabilitation centers for homeless men and women, youth programs, prison work, and emergency disaster services. The Salvation Army in the United States is organized into four territories, each with a headquarters, a training college, and its own edition of the official weekly publication, *The War Cry*. National headquarters are in New York City.

**In Canada.** The Canadian Salvation Army was started by two English immigrants, Jack Addie and Joe Ludgate, at London, Ontario, in 1882. From the start welfare work was concurrent with religious. Its homes, shelters, hospitals, clinics, centers, stores, and various counseling, educational, and emergency services operate from over 1,450 centers. Canadian national headquarters are in Toronto, where the Canadian edition of *The War Cry* is published.

**SEVENTH-DAY ADVENTISTS,** largest of the Adventist groups growing out of the work of William Miller, father of American Adventism. Its distinctive features are its recognition of the inspired prophetess Ellen Harmon (later Mrs. James White) as virtual founder, and its observance of Saturday rather than Sunday as the Sabbath. Otherwise it is orthodox Protestant and evangelical, baptizes by immersion, and is organized and operates on a modified congregational basis.

**UNIAT** [ū′nē-ăt] **CHURCHES,** in general, those branches of Eastern Christian churches which are in communion with Rome. Their principal features are such privileges as a distinctive ritual and liturgical language, and, with notable exceptions, baptism by immersion, a married clergy,

## RITES OF THE UNIAT CHURCHES

| Ethnic Group | Locality | Liturgical Language | Date of Schism | Date of Reunion |
|---|---|---|---|---|
| **ALEXANDRIAN RITE** | | | | |
| Copts | Egypt | Coptic; Arabic | 451 | 1741 |
| Ethiopians | Ethiopia | Geez | 550 | 1839 |
| **ANTIOCHENE RITE** | | | | |
| Malankarese | India | Syriac; Malayalam | 1653 | 1930 |
| Maronites | Syria; U.S.A. | Syriac | — | 1182 |
| Syrians | Syria; Iraq; U.S.A. | Syriac; Arabic | 543 | 1656 |
| **ARMENIAN RITE** | | | | |
| Armenians | Syria; Near East; U.S.A. | Classical Armenian | 525 | 1198; 1742 |
| **BYZANTINE RITE** | | | | |
| Bulgars | Bulgaria | Old Church Slavonic | 1054 | 1860 |
| Greeks | Greece; Turkey | Greek | 1054 | 1860 |
| Hungarians | Hungary | Magyar | 1054 | 1595 |
| Italo-Greek-Albanians | Italy; U.S.A. | Greek | Never separated | |
| Melchites | Syria; Egypt; U.S.A. | Arabic | 1054 | 1439; 1724 |
| Rumanians | Rumania; U.S.A. | Rumanian | 1054 | 1701 |
| Russians (in Poland) | Poland | Old Church Slavonic | 19th cent. | 1920 |
| Russians (elsewhere) | Europe; U.S.A. | Old Church Slavonic | 1054 | 1905 |
| Ruthenians | Europe; U.S.A. | Old Church Slavonic | 1054; 1200 | 1595; 1652; 1905 |
| Yugoslavs | Yugoslavia | Old Church Slavonic | 1054 | 1611 |
| **CHALDAEAN RITE** | | | | |
| Chaldaeans | Asia Minor; U.S.A. | Syriac | 431 | 1551 |
| Malabarese | India | Syriac | — | before 1599 |

leavened bread for the Eucharist, and the receiving of Communion by the laity under both bread and wine. The simplest classification of the Uniats is according to their respective rites, namely, Alexandrian, Antiochene, Armenian, Byzantine, and Chaldaean. Each rite is practiced in one or more churches, which differ in name and administrative organization, though all are finally subject to the Roman see. Their total world membership is about 10,000,000.

The following table indicates ethnic group, locality where mainly found, liturgical language, date or dates of schism of original church, and date or dates of Catholic reunion.

There are nine Eastern rite Uniat churches in the United States, among which the Byzantine comprises 80% of the total 700,000 church membership. These are mostly Italo-Greeks, Melchites, Rumanians, and Russians. The Ruthenians, with almost 500,000 adherents, are the largest group of Eastern rite Catholics in America. Smaller in number are the Maronites, Syrians, Armenians, and Chaldaeans in the United States. All five Eastern rite Uniat bishops in the United States at present belong to the Ruthenian group, divided into two coextensive jurisdictions: the archeparchy (archdiocese) of Philadelphia, together with the eparchy of Stamford, Conn., and the exarchate of Pittsburgh. All other rites in the country are under the authority of the local Roman rite bishop. In Canada the Ruthenians are also in the majority. They have a metropolitan province with headquarters in Winnipeg and suffragan sees in Edmonton, Toronto, and Saskatoon.

The most recent reunion of Eastern Christians with Rome on a large scale was that of the Syrian Jacobites of the Malabar Coast in India, under Mar Ivanios in 1930. To distinguish themselves from the Malabarese who remained Jacobites, they called their rite Malankarese. They currently number over 100,000, with 200 priests in two dioceses. In 1946 the Uniats of the Ukraine (about 5,000,-000) and in 1948 those of Rumania (1,500,000) were forcibly separated by the Communists from the Roman Catholic Church and joined to the Russian and Rumanian Orthodox churches. The change was effected by arresting the entire Catholic hierarchy and offering the clergy a choice between imprisonment (or death) and separation from Rome.

**UNITARIANISM** [ū-nə-târ'ē-ən-ĭz-əm], theological doctrine that emphasizes belief in the unity of God and in the normal humanity of Christ, opposing doctrines of the Trinity and of the eternal deity of Christ. Positions suggestive of later Unitarian thought were sometimes advanced by Arians and Pelagians in the early Christian centuries. An antitrinitarian movement, known as Socinianism, after its most influential thinker, Faustus Socinus, developed in Poland in the late 16th century and spread to Transylvania in the 17th. A related Unitarian movement split off from the Reformed Church in Transylvania in 1568 and continues to the present.

In England, Unitarian tendencies in thought appeared sporadically from the time of the Reformation. But an organized movement first appeared when an Anglican clergyman, Theophilus Lindsey (1723–1808), founded a Unitarian church in London. Joseph Priestley (1733–1804), a dissenting minister and a famous scientist, became the most conspicuous early figure in the new church. In 1825 the British and Foreign Unitarian Association was formed, and James Martineau (1805–1900) was the dominant influence in Unitarian thought in the 19th century.

Unitarianism in America arose indigenously in the late 18th century. The first specifically Unitarian church appeared when the oldest Episcopal church in New England, King's Chapel in Boston, adopted the Unitarian position in 1785, under the leadership of James Freeman. By the turn of the century many New England Congregational leaders had quietly adopted a liberal, antitrinitarian theological position, and in 1805 they succeeded in having Henry Ware seated as professor of divinity at Harvard. Ten years later the controversy between liberal and orthodox Congregationalists broke out into the open. William Ellery Channing emerged as the main leader of the Unitarian party in his famous Baltimore sermon of 1819 on Unitarian Christianity, and in 1825 the American Unitarian Association was formed. More than a third of the Congregational churches joined the new denomination.

For a time it seemed as though Unitarianism might spread widely across the nation. But a resurgent evangelicalism, under the leadership of such men as Lyman Beecher (1775–1863), checked it and kept it largely centered in eastern New England, though it later developed strong churches in the West. Channing was essentially a rational supernaturalist in theology, believing in the authority of the Bible, though not finding it to support the Trinitarian position. But Unitarian leaders, such as Theodore Parker (1810–60), with more radical theological opinions soon appeared.

Contemporary Unitarianism in America is congregational in organization, puts great stress on religious and doctrinal freedom, and contains many different strands of religious thought, including nontheistic humanism. In 1961 the American Unitarian Association united with the Universalist Church of America to form the Unitarian Universalist Association.

**UNITED CHURCH OF CANADA,** largest Protestant communion in Canada. It was formed in 1925 by union of the Methodist, Presbyterian, and Congregational churches. The merger followed 20 years of conversations and brought together all Methodists and Congregationalists, about 80% of the Presbyterians, and a number of local union or community churches. By merger on Jan. 1, 1968, the United Church further added the Canada Conference of the Evangelical United Brethren to its fold. The adult membership of the United Church has grown from 610,000 in 1925 to more than 1,000,000. There are 5,200 local churches, served by some 3,500 ministers. The annual budget exceeds $60,000,000, of which more than $13,000,000 goes to overseas and home missions and benevolence programs. The church is organized into 100 presbyteries and 11 conferences; the biennial General Council is its highest governing body. National headquarters are in Toronto, Ont.

**UNITED CHURCH OF CHRIST,** name of the church formed by the union of the Congregational Christian Churches and the Evangelical and Reformed Church (qq.v.) in 1957. The full implementing of the union was delayed, but in 1961 the overwhelming majority of the churches of both groups formally ratified a constitution, and the merging of the denominational agencies, with headquarters in New York, was consummated.

# Personalities

**APOSTLE** [ə-pŏs′əl], one "sent out" on behalf of somebody to perform a service for him. According to ancient Jewish teaching, "the one whom a man sends is the equivalent of himself." The name is mainly used to describe the 12 disciples (Peter, Andrew, James, John, Philip, Bartholomew, Matthew, Thomas, James the son of Alphaeus, Thaddaeus, Simon the Cananaean, and Judas Iscariot, with Matthias replacing Judas), together with Paul, Barnabas, James (the brother of Jesus), and others who saw the risen Jesus and were sent out as His missionaries (I Cor. 9:1; Gal. 1:11–17). They performed the unique task of witnessing to Christ's resurrection, and formed the human foundation of the Church. They also acted as church leaders and helped to choose and appoint other leaders (Acts 6:1-6).

**AQUINAS** [ə-kwī′nəs], **ST. THOMAS** (1225–74), commonly regarded as the greatest philosopher and theologian of the Middle Ages. Born in Roccasecca, Italy, he received his early education from the Benedictine monks at Monte Cassino. Later he studied at the University of Naples, where he was so deeply impressed by the life of the Dominican monks that he joined the Dominican order in 1244, despite violent family opposition. In 1245 he went to Paris, where, under St. Albertus Magnus, he first became acquainted with the philosophy of Aristotle. There in 1252, after a sojourn in Cologne, he began teaching.

The philosophical and theological spirit then prevalent was Augustinian, with strong Platonic tendencies. Despite this, and despite the fact that Aristotle (known largely through Arab commentators) was held suspect as a pagan, Thomas developed a philosophy that was Aristotelian in inspiration, rather than Augustinian.

To his first teaching period in Paris (1252–59) belong his commentaries on the *Sentences* of Peter Lombard and on the *De Trinitate* and *De Hebdomadibus* of Boethius, as well as his more independent work, *De Veritate* (On Truth).

In 1259 Thomas left Paris, and until 1269 he taught as a member of the theological faculties attached at that time to the papal courts. It was while he was at Orvieto with Pope Urban IV that he met the famous Flemish translator William of Moerbeke, whom he encouraged to go to Greece to find early manuscripts of Aristotle and to make new, more accurate translations of his treatises than were then available.

During this period he also began his two greatest works, the *Summa Contra Gentiles* and the *Summa Theologica*. The first was for use by Spanish priests in controversies with Islam; the second was to be a general summary of Christian theology for teaching purposes.

In 1269 Thomas returned to Paris and resumed the teaching post he had given up 10 years earlier. To the period 1269–72 belong his commentaries on Aristotle's *De Anima, Physics,* and *Metaphysics,* as well as other works of lesser importance. In 1272 he was sent to Naples to organize a theological faculty in the university there. Two years later, while on his way to attend the ecumenical council at Lyons, he fell ill, and on Mar. 7, 1274, he died in the Cistercian abbey at Fossanova, between Rome and Naples.

The works of St. Thomas, constituting 34 volumes in one well-known edition, have had a profound influence on Western thought. For almost 700 years, they have been studied in Catholic seminaries and universities, and many Protestant and Jewish scholars, as well, have been strongly influenced by them. In the 20th century his philosophical genius has been recognized by thinkers as diverse as Henri Bergson, Etienne Gilson, Martin Heidegger, and Edmund Husserl.

Rejecting the Augustinian theory of divine illumination as the source of abstract knowledge, Thomas insisted that all human knowledge is ultimately derived through the senses. In his theory, the intellect transforms sense perception into knowledge through the process of abstraction. But since mental concepts are derived from what is perceptible, the intellect is kept in constant contact with concrete reality.

In the great medieval controversy between Nominalists and Realists, St. Thomas represented a position sometimes called Moderate Realism, opposed to the Nominalism of Roscellinus, but not going to the extremes of the Realism of William of Champeaux. Thus Thomas rejected St. Anselm's "ontological" argument for the existence of God, because he insisted that any valid proof for the existence of God must be based, not upon an abstract idea, but upon concrete evidence manifested in the universe.

Like Aristotle, Thomas held that both matter and form are immanent principles of material reality, and he contended that whatever is limited and finite is a composite of its essence and its act of existence. Only in God are essence and existence identical.

Unlike St. Augustine and other fathers of the early Church who held that human government was the result of original sin, Thomas maintained that society was natural to man and necessary for his normal development, and that government was necessary to the maintenance of society. His treatise on law, found in the *Summa Theo-*

New York Public Library—Picture Collection
Fresco of St. Thomas Aquinas by Fra Angelico, in Florence.

*logica,* has long been regarded as a classic by legal philosophers of all persuasions.

General councils of the Roman Catholic Church, from Lyons (1274) to the Vatican Council (1869), have frequently drawn from his theological writings for precise formulations of traditional Christian beliefs. He was canonized in 1323, declared a "Doctor of the Church" by Pope Pius V in 1567, and has been frequently called "The Angelic Doctor" and "Prince of Scholastics."

**AUGUSTINE** [ô′gəs-tēn, ô-gŭs′tĭn], **ST.** (354–430), Christian philosopher and theologian. Bishop of Hippo, in North Africa near Carthage, he was the greatest of the Latin Church Fathers, and his teaching has been a dominant influence in subsequent Christian thought. Born at Tagaste, a small town in North Africa, he was raised as a Christian by his saintly mother, Monica. At the age of 16, however, he left home to study humanities at Carthage, and soon adopted the riotous manner of living common in that ancient city.

His own inner turmoil led him eventually to the teaching of the Manichaeans, who maintained that there are two ultimate principles: one good (God or Ormuzd); one evil (Ahriman); and that the eternal strife between them is reflected in our world, where matter, created by Ahriman, and spirit, created by God, are locked in continuous struggle. Failing to establish a school first at Tagaste and then at Carthage, he left Africa for Italy, and in 384, while a teacher of rhetoric at Milan, he met St. Ambrose, bishop of the city, who urged him to return to the faith of his childhood.

Augustine's return to Christianity was preceded by a philosophical acceptance of certain Platonic principles which freed him from Manichaeanism. The moving story of his final conversion is told in the 8th book of his *Confessions.* On Holy Saturday of 387, Augustine was formally received into the Church by Ambrose. His mother Monica, who had come to Italy, died at Ostia on their return to Africa. Despite his protests of unworthiness, Augustine was chosen for the priesthood by the bishop of Hippo, and he himself later became bishop of that see in 396, dying there in the late summer of 430, as the Vandals laid siege to the city.

Augustine's philosophy is Neoplatonic in inspiration. He had fallen under the spell of Plotinus (205–70) prior to his conversion, and certain permanent elements in his thought, such as the role of the divine ideas in human knowledge, must be attributed to Plotinus' influence. According to Augustine, the eternal truths as they are in God somehow supply light to the human mind, enabling it to understand the characteristics of changelessness and necessity in true judgments and moral standards. The same Platonic influence appears in Augustine's commentaries on Sacred Scripture, for he often distinguishes between the literal meaning and the "spiritual" meaning—the latter being a hidden supernatural truth mystically signified by the words of the text. To the problem of evil, Augustine applies similar Platonic principles. All things are created

by God; hence they must be good. They may be used for an evil purpose, but they have no evil in themselves. What is said to be bad about them is merely a defect of goodness. Hence evil has no intrinsic reality and no meaning apart from its relation to a good. The ascending degrees of goodness found in creatures are ultimately found united in the supreme good, which is God.

The concept of the relationship between Church and State as outlined in Augustine's *City of God* shaped the medieval political structure, from which many of our modern laws are derived. In his struggle against Pelagius, who contended that man can attain salvation without divine assistance, Augustine insisted upon the necessity of God's special grace.

In some respects Augustine's later works seem to echo his early Manichaean pessimism, for in them he writes as though the vast majority of men are doomed to damnation. But it must be remembered that these works were written when the Roman Empire was crumbling and morality was at a low ebb. Beneath his apparent pessimism lay a firm belief in a God who loves all men and desires their salvation.

Protestant and Catholic theologians are similarly indebted to Augustine for his speculations on the nature of the Trinity, contained in his *De Trinitate.* The first seven books give Scriptural evidence for the existence of the Trinity; the last eight contain speculative reflections on its nature.

Augustine's philosophy of history is contained in *The City of God.* Here he answers those pagans who accused Christianity of being responsible for the fall of Rome by showing that the new faith includes and transcends all the values of the ancient pagan culture. Like Plato, Augustine contends that there can be no city at all without justice. The perfect city is the spiritual city of all who practice the justice of Christ, who is its Head.

The *Enchiridion,* written nine years before his death, is a short statement of Augustine's beliefs, and is unrivaled in depth and clarity in Christian literature.

**CALVIN** [kăl′vĭn], **JOHN** (1509–64), French reformer and theologian. Born in Noyon in Picardy, Calvin was intended for an ecclesiastical career and from 1523 was, for five years, a theological student at Paris, where he displayed exceptional ability. Then his father, a man of some standing, quarreled with the local ecclesiastical authority and ordered John, who was not in any case sure of his priestly vocation, to turn to law. This he studied first at Orléans, then at Bourges, during which time he met and was greatly influenced by Protestants, notably by Melchior Wolmar. A restraining influence having departed with his father's death in 1531, Calvin broke with the Roman Church in 1533, after a conversion experience in which he believed himself called to restore the Church to its original purity.

Having suffered in some undefined way from the persecution of the French Protestants by Francis I, Calvin, in Jan., 1535, settled at Basel to lead the life of a scholar. His greatest work, *The Institutes of the Christian Religion,*

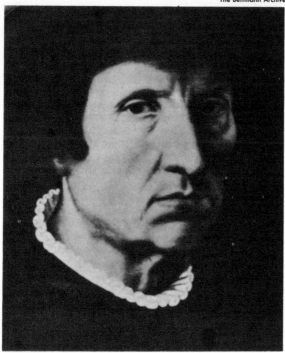

Painting of John Calvin, French reformer, by Hans Holbein.

even for purely religious offenses. Adultery, blasphemy, and heresy were punishable by death.

This inflexible system was not maintained without the exercise of force. Opponents were exiled, or executed as was the Unitarian Michael Servetus. Calvin had earlier been responsible for a sentence of perpetual banishment passed on the Anabaptists. By 1555 all resistance had crumbled; Calvin and Calvinism had won, and now controlled both the ecclesiastical and the civil government.

**Calvin's Influence and Character.** Calvin made Geneva the focal point of Reformed teaching and brought order into civil affairs, but he bludgeoned the people into conformity and upheld an intolerance in religious matters which ironically had much in common with the old Church. He preached regularly, was responsible for introducing congregational singing into the Reformed Church services in Geneva, and gave lectures which attracted students from near and far. He wrote Biblical commentaries still regarded as classics, and in 1559 founded the Academy of Geneva to continue his teaching.

But Calvin's influence was not limited to Geneva. He was a lifelong champion of the French Huguenots; lectured the Protector Somerset on the changes he would like to see in England, and welcomed later Protestant refugees escaping from persecution under the Catholic Mary Tudor; trained John Knox for his impending leadership of the Reformed cause in Scotland; and counseled and encouraged Protestants in Italy, Hungary, and Poland.

Judged by modern standards Calvin can be condemned at many points, but in rendering a verdict one must take into account the religious temperature of the age, see that no incident is wrested out of context, and remember that men are often kinder than their creeds. Calvin's own life was simple and austere, "easy to calumniate, but difficult to imitate." Joseph Ernest Renan, no friend of the orthodox, regarded him as "the most Christian man of his generation." Calvin believed that virtue should be practiced for its own sake, regardless of future rewards and punishments. In the pursuit of goodness he did not spare himself and all he had; he left only $170 when he died.

appeared in Mar., 1536, in Latin. His studious inclinations were disrupted when, on a visit to Geneva in July, 1536, he reluctantly yielded to the importunities of Guillaume Farel and became his coadjutor in organizing the Reformation in that somewhat turbulent city.

**Geneva and Strasbourg—1536–1541.** Calvin was appointed preacher and professor of theology in Geneva. Reintroducing a practice of the early Church, he excluded the unworthy from Communion, and proposed other radical reforms. These met with fierce opposition, as did his refusal to follow in some practices the lead of the powerful city of Bern. The upshot was the expulsion of Calvin and Farel in Apr., 1538.

For the next three years Calvin was in Strasbourg, ministering to the French congregation and lecturing in the theological school. There he became a close friend of Martin Bucer, whose influence is visible from this time, and of Philip Melanchthon; published a commentary on Romans (1539); dealt effectively with a letter addressed by Cardinal Sadoleto to Geneva, pleading for the city's return to the Roman obedience; attended various Reformed conferences; and married (1540) a widow who died nine years later. No child of the union survived.

**Calvin's Control of Geneva from 1541.** His supporters having gained the upper hand in Geneva, Calvin returned in Sept., 1541, was welcomed by the city fathers, and given a house, a salary of 500 florins, 12 measures of wheat, and two tubs of wine. There ensued the establishment of a regime with a strong Old Testament emphasis. A series of ordinances placed the ecclesiastical government in the hands of four classes: pastors, doctors, elders, and deacons. These were assisted by a supreme council, which under Calvin had far-reaching powers over the private lives of citizens. Severe penalties were devised,

**GREEK FATHERS, THE.** The classic Christian doctrines about God and the Person of Jesus Christ in terms of the Trinity and Incarnation, respectively, were chiefly molded and given an orthodox precision of definition by the Greek theologians of the Church from the 2d to the 8th centuries. The challenge to this task was set for them from two directions: the attack of pagan intellectuals upon the apparent irrationality of the apostles' testimony about Jesus; and the emergence within the Church itself of interpretations of Jesus, whether by way of denying His divine origin in the Godhead or conversely His complete humanity and historical reality. Two convenient tools lay to hand for the accomplishment of the Greek Fathers' task, both of which were employed with acumen, subtlety, and discrimination: an allegorical method of interpreting the text of the Bible, and the vocabulary and dialectic finesse of Greek philosophy, especially Platonism.

The initial attempts to formulate a systematic Christian

theology, philosophically grounded, were made by the 2d-century Apologists (q.v.) and Irenaeus, an Asian who was Bishop of Lyons. Their formulations were given a cosmological frame of reference in the Alexandrian Fathers of the 3d century: Clement, Origen, and Dionysius. The creeds of the ecumenical councils of the 4th and 5th centuries served as foci of orthodox exposition of the faith in the work of Athanasius, the Cappadocians, and the two Cyrils, of Jerusalem and Alexandria, and in the less allegorical exegetes of the Antiochene school, John Chrysostom and Theodore of Mopsuestia. The last phase of ancient Greek theology witnessed the mystical speculation of Pseudo-Dionysius the Areopagite and Maximus the Confessor and the scholastic synthesis of John of Damascus (died c.749).

**JESUS CHRIST** (c.4 B.C.–c.30 A.D.), founder of the Christian religion and, according to Christian teachings, the Son of God. The name Jesus is the Greek form of the Hebrew name *Joshua*, which means "Yahweh is salvation." Christ comes from *Christos*, which is the Greek form of the Hebrew *Messiah*, or "Lord's annointed."

Our knowledge of the life and teaching of Jesus comes almost exclusively from the New Testament. According to two of the Gospels (Mathew and Luke), Jesus was born of a virgin named Mary, who was betrothed to a man named Joseph, a descendant of King David, and the birth took place in Bethlehem of Judaea before the death of Herod the Great, which occurred in 4 B.C.

After Jesus' circumcision and presentation in the Temple in Jerusalem (Luke 2:21–39), Joseph and Mary went to Nazareth of Galilee, where Jesus grew up. Nothing is known of His youth and early manhood except that when He was 12 He accompanied His parents to Jerusalem to the feast of the Passover (Luke 2:41–50), as the stories of His boyhood in the earlier known of the two Gospels of Thomas are all apocryphal.

*National Gallery of Art, Mellon Collection*

A detail from "The Adoration of the Magi" (c.1482), by Sandro Botticelli, shows the three kings worshiping the infant Jesus.

**Jesus' Ministry.** In the 15th year of the reign of Tiberius Caesar (Luke 3:1), which would be during the year 28 A.D., Jesus' cousin John the Baptist came into the wilderness of Judaea preaching repentance and baptizing penitents in the Jordan River. Here Jesus Himself was baptized (Mark 1:9–11), and immediately afterward withdrew into the wilderness for 40 days, in what is called His temptation. During this period of solitude, He evidently determined the character of His ministry, deciding that instead of trying to satisfy men's physical needs, or appeal to their love of the sensational, or seek worldly power to control their lives, He would devote His life to teaching.

And this He did for almost three years, most of the time

*Alinari—Art Reference Bureau*

"Christ in the Garden of Gethsemane," a panel from an altarpiece painted between 1308 and 1311 by the Sienese artist Duccio di Buoninsegna. In the center, Christ addresses Peter, James, and John. At right, Christ prays as an angel extends to Him a chalice, which is symbolic of His destiny.

"The Crucifixion," a fresco in the Arena Chapel in Padua, was painted by Giotto (c.1305). Mary Magdalene weeps at the foot of The Cross. Mary the Mother of Christ is supported by disciples at left. At right, Roman soldiers haggle for Christ's garment. The air is filled with grieving angels, some extending vessels to receive blood from Christ's wounds.

in Galilee, with occasional visits to Jerusalem at the time of the feasts, sometimes passing through Samaria, at other times going down through Perea on the eastern side of the Jordan, sometimes staying in Judaea and preaching there. The geographic scope of His ministry was very limited. So far as the record indicates, He was never outside Palestine.

According to the Gospels, He went about doing good, healing the sick, opening the eyes of the blind, causing the deaf to hear, the dumb to speak, the lame to walk, and even raising the dead (Matt. 11:5). When the multitudes were without food, twice He fed them with a few small loaves and fishes. Early in His ministry, when the wine ran out at a marriage in Cana of Galilee, He turned water into wine. He cast the devils out of demoniacs; He quieted a storm on the Sea of Galilee; He walked on the water. But He was no mere wonder worker, and there is no indication that He ever performed any miracle just to show His power. Even the relief of human need and suffering was not the main purpose of His mission. If it had been, there would have been no such lasting effects from His life and ministry as there were. In the three years of His ministry He did not heal all the sick of the world, or even all the sick of Palestine. And those who were healed would be sick again, and other sick and suffering people would follow them in the long chain of generations. Even those whom He raised from the dead —the widow's son, Jaïrus' daughter, Lazarus—would all die again, and did, long since.

The main purpose of Jesus' ministry was to preach the good news of God and His kingdom and to teach men about God and their relation to Him. Mark says (1:14, 15), "Jesus came into Galilee, preaching the gospel of the kingdom of God, and saying, The time is fulfilled, and the kingdom of God is at hand: repent ye, and be-

lieve the gospel." A little later Mark reports (1:35-39), "And in the morning, rising up a great while before day, he went out, and departed into a solitary place, and there prayed. And Simon and they that were with him followed after him. And when they had found him, they said unto him, All men seek for thee. And he said unto them, Let us go into the next towns, that I may preach there also: for therefore came I forth. And he preached in their synagogues throughout all Galilee, and cast out devils."

To help with His ministry Jesus gathered about Him a small band of disciples. Some of them had been disciples of John the Baptist—these Jesus had met just after His own baptism (John 1:35-51). There were three of them to start with, Andrew, Peter, and one other, whose name is not given, and they were joined by two more, Philip and Nathanael, evidently all Galileans like Jesus Himself. And apparently they went back to Galilee with Jesus. So later, when Jesus came to Simon Peter, Andrew, James, and John and asked them to leave their nets and follow Him, He came to them as no stranger. There is no indication that He had ever had any previous contact with Matthew, or Levi, the publican; but we cannot be sure of this. Eventually He chose 12 to be with Him and to go out and preach on His behalf: Simon Peter, James, John, Andrew, Philip, Bartholomew (who may be the same as Nathanael), Matthew, Thomas, James the son of Alphaeus, Thaddaeus or Judas, Simon the Canaanean, and Judas Iscariot (Mark 3:13-19; Luke 6:12-19). These were evidently the inner circle of His followers, for later He sent out 70, in pairs, to heal and teach (Luke 10:1-24); and on one of His preaching tours certain women accompanied Him, among whom Mary Magdalene, Joanna the wife of Chuza, Herod's steward, and Susanna are specified by name (Luke 8:1–3). Then there was the little household in Bethany that He visited, Martha and Mary and their brother Lazarus (Luke 10:38–42; John 11:1–46). It was this Mary of Bethany who anointed Him with the precious ointment, in preparation, as He said, for his burial (John 12:1–8). These were His closest friends, all of them humble people, most of them from Galilee. There were not many of the rich and powerful among His followers. Zacchaeus was rich; but he was a publican and despised. Two of the Sanhedrin, however, were numbered among His secret admirers and friends: Nicodemus, who came to Him by night in the early days of His ministry in Jerusalem (John 2:23–3:21), and Joseph of Arimathea, who had not agreed with His condemnation, and who buried Jesus in his own sepulcher, with the help of Nicodemus (John 19:38–42).

**Jesus' Teaching.** Most of Jesus' teaching was in parables, simple stories from everyday life to illustrate some particular truth about the kingdom of God: the sower whose seed was the word; the tares that are permitted to grow with the wheat until the harvest; the grain of mustard seed which becomes a tree; the leaven that permeates the whole measure of the meal; the treasure hid in the field; the merchantman seeking goodly pearls; the fishing net that gathers of every kind (Matt. 13:1–53). These were some of the stories that Jesus told. And there were many others: the Good Samaritan who had compassion on the man who had fallen among thieves (Luke 10:25–37); the Prodigal Son who took his journey into a far country, and there wasted his substance in riotous living, and who,

"The Resurrection of Christ" (c.1465), by Piero della Francesca. Guards sleep beside the tomb, unaware that Christ has risen.

*Alinari—Art Reference Bureau*

when he began to be in such dire want that "he would fain have filled his belly with the husks that the swine did eat," came to himself and arose and came to his father, who, when he was yet a great way off, saw him, "and had compassion, and ran, and fell on his neck, and kissed him" (Luke 15:11–32).

There was no formal presentation of a system of doctrine. The Sermon on the Mount (Matt. 5–7), which includes the Beatitudes (Matt. 5:1-12), the Lord's Prayer (Matt. 6:9–13), the Golden Rule (Matt. 7:12), and other well-known teachings of Jesus, is the longest of His discourses. But one of His most profound statements was that to the woman of Samaria at Jacob's well, in Sychar, to whom He said, "God is a Spirit: and they that worship him must worship him in spirit and in truth" (John 4:24). This is the background for the 6th chapter of Matthew, with its teaching of the fatherhood of God, of our dependence on His bounty, and the necessity of our seeking first His kingdom and His righteousness.

**Jesus' Messiahship.** Jesus' disciples, of course, thought He was the Messiah, and they expected Him eventually to throw off the Roman yoke and establish an earthly kingdom. But that was not His idea of messiahship, and He had no intention of setting up an earthly kingdom. As He said to Pilate, "My kingdom is not of this world. . . . Thou sayest that I am a king. To this end was I born, and for this cause came I into the world, that I should bear witness unto the truth" (John 18:36, 37). Earlier He had said to those who believed in Him, "If ye continue in my word, then are ye my disciples indeed; And ye shall know the truth, and the truth shall make you free" (John 8:31, 32). This was the real freedom, the freedom of the spirit that came from the knowledge of the truth. That is what Jesus had meant when He said, "It is the spirit that quickeneth; the flesh profiteth nothing: the words that I speak unto you, they are spirit, and they are life" (John 6:63).

**Jesus' Enemies.** According to Jesus, the good life was not a matter of blindly obeying a multitude of rules; it was a matter of understanding the principles of right conduct and ordering one's life accordingly. That was what brought Him into conflict with the Pharisees. He did not obey the strict law of the Sabbath; He healed on the Sabbath, and His disciples plucked the ears of grain and ate them on the Sabbath; because, He said, "The sabbath was made for man, and not man for the sabbath" (Mark 2:27).

All through His ministry He was at enmity with the scribes and the Pharisees, the legalists; and the antagonism grew so bitter between them that the time came when the Pharisees would have liked to do away with Him. But they were not the party in power.

It was when Jesus drove the money-changers from the temple (Mark 11:15–19) and defied the priests that He was in danger; for they were the party in power.

Jesus knew what was in store for Him (Mark 10:32–34). On the first day of that last week as He rode into Jerusalem the multitude "took branches of palm trees, and went forth to meet him, and cried, Hosanna: Blessed is the King of Israel that cometh in the name of the Lord" (John 12: 13). It was the fulfillment of an old prophecy of Zechariah (9:9), but it only served to arouse the fear and further antagonism of the national leaders.

All that week He taught in the temple. Finally the Pharisees and their erstwhile enemies the Herodians united against Him, and trying to catch Him in His words they asked Him: "Is it lawful to give tribute unto Caesar, or not?" If He said yes, they could impugn His Jewish patriotism and turn the multitude against Him; if He said no, He would be in trouble with the Roman authorities. When He requested them to show Him the tribute money, and then asked them, "Whose is this image and superscription?" they had to say, "Caesar's." "Then saith he unto them, Render therefore unto Caesar the things which are Caesar's; and unto God the things that are God's" (Matt. 22:15–22). "And they could not take hold of his words before the people: and they marvelled at his answer, and held their peace" (Luke 20:26); but their hatred of Him was only increased.

Finally Judas Iscariot, one of Jesus' 12 disciples, went to the chief priests and bargained for Jesus' betrayal for 30 pieces of silver, since the priests were afraid to arrest Him publicly for fear of arousing a tumult.

Things moved rapidly from then on. That Thursday evening Jesus had the Last Supper with His disciples, in the upper room where He instituted the sacrament of the Lord's Supper, to be a memorial of His death. Later He went into the Garden of Gethsemane with His disciples, and there Judas betrayed Him to the soldiers of the high priest, and they took Him away to Annas and Caiaphas; and Peter, warming himself at the fire in the court of the high priest's house, denied Jesus thrice, as Jesus had said he would. Early the next morning they bound Jesus and took Him to Pilate, the Roman governor, who, when he found that Jesus was a Galilean, sent Him to Herod, who had jurisdiction over Galilee and who was in Jerusalem at the time. When Herod sent Him back to Pilate, Pilate tried to release Him, but the Jewish authorities demanded that Jesus be crucified and that Pilate release unto them Barabbas, a famous insurrectionist who was imprisoned there at the time. And in the end Pilate acceded to their wishes, released Barabbas, and turned Jesus over to the soldiers to be crucified.

**Crucifixion and Burial.** The soldiers, mocking Him, put a purple robe on Him, and a crown of thorns, and led Him away to Golgotha, or Calvary, a hill outside the walls, to crucify Him with two thieves. And Pilate wrote a superscription in Hebrew and Latin and Greek, which was put on His cross: JESUS OF NAZARETH, THE KING OF THE JEWS. Three hours later He was dead.

Joseph of Arimathea asked His body of Pilate, and he and Nicodemus buried Jesus in Joseph's tomb in the Garden of Gethsemane. That was the end, presumably, of Jesus of Nazareth.

**Resurrection and Ascension.** But two days later, early in the morning on the first day of the week, Mary Magdalene and some others, coming to the tomb with spices, found it empty. According to the Gospels, Jesus had risen from the dead, and for the next 40 days His disciples saw Him and talked with Him on various occasions (Mark 16: 1–18; Matt. 28:1–20; Luke 24:1–49; John 20:1—21:33). Then at the end of this period, according to the record, Jesus took His disciples to a place near Bethany, and there He blessed them and was carried up into heaven (Mark 16:19; Luke 24:50, 51; Acts 1:9–11).

**The Divinity of Christ.** The disciples, downcast by the Crucifixion, had their faith restored by the Resurrection, and were convinced that Jesus was indeed the Messiah, as Peter had said earlier (Mark 8:29). But according to the Fourth Gospel, Jesus had also proclaimed Himself to be the Son of God (John 9:35–37), and so His disciples and friends regarded Him (John 11:27). But there is no theological explanation of His relation to the Father in the New Testament, nor any specific doctrine of the relation of His human and divine natures. The doctrine of the Trinity is implied in the baptismal formula at the end of the Gospel of Matthew (28:19), but it was the Greek Fathers who formulated the doctrine of the Incarnation as the explanation of Christ's divinity. The problems of the relation of Christ to the Father and of Christ's two natures were not resolved until the councils of Nicaea (325) and Chalcedon (521), respectively.

**KNOX, JOHN** (c.1513–1572), Scottish reformer. Born in Haddington and apparently educated at Glasgow University, Knox was ordained priest about 1539. Nevertheless he is found six years later as bodyguard to the reformer George Wishart, after whose execution he became successively tutor, minister in St. Andrews, galley-slave in French bondage, and chaplain to Edward VI of England. Edward offered him the bishopric of Rochester, but Knox declined. On Mary Tudor's accession in England Knox went into exile, first in Frankfurt am Main, then in Calvin's Geneva.

**The Reformation Leader.** He came home briefly in Aug., 1555, and through his preaching many were won to the Reformed faith in still-Catholic Scotland. Condemned to death in his absence, he returned finally in May, 1559, and the Queen Regent proclaimed him an outlaw. His presence was soon felt. When the cause seemed lost because of French intervention and the fickleness of the new English Queen Elizabeth (who disliked Knox for writing against women rulers), Knox in a memorable sermon put new life into his flagging supporters. Victory for the Reformation was secured in July, 1560; the Auld Alliance with France was revoked; and Scots for the first time in their history cheered the appearance of an English army which had come to help the Protestants.

**The Writer and Administrator.** Knox and five others soon produced first the *Scots Confession of Faith* (which remained authoritative till superseded in 1647 by the *Westminster Confession*), then the *First Book of Discipline*. The latter aimed at uniformity in doctrine, sacraments, election and sustenance of the ministry, ecclesiastical discipline, the support of the poor, the equality of all men before God, and the advancement of education. Knox produced also the *Book of Common Order*.

But his dream that the revenues of the old Church would pass to the ministers, the schools, and the poor was rudely shattered by politicians and self-seekers less disinterested than he. Two-thirds of the revenues in fact remained in the hands of the former owners; the remaining one-third was to go partly to the Reformed clergy, partly to the crown. "Two parts freely given to the Devil," commented Knox, "and the third part divided betwixt God and the Devil."

The *Scots Confession* and the *First Book of Discipline*, following the Genevan model, had assumed church and state to be two parts of a Christian commonwealth. This may have been the case in Calvin's Geneva, but it was far otherwise in a land where the new order had to be hammered out against the opposition of the 19-year-old Mary, Queen of Scots, a Catholic.

**The Man and His Achievements.** There was little originality in the Scottish Reformation; Knox belonged to the second generation of reformers. His great merit lay, rather, in the thoroughness with which he grasped current ideas, in the way he influenced the imagination of the Scots with those ideas, and in the framework he established to further them.

No true appreciation of John Knox is possible without reference to his turbulent age, when war, waged in the name of God, was staining with blood the hands of men throughout Europe. Admitting his vehemence, Knox said: "To me it is enough to say that black is not white, and man's tyranny and foolishness is not God's perfect ordinance." He was blamed for making use of worldly allies; defamed by some who knew him only as the man who made a queen weep; and often remembered rather as an iconoclast than as a builder.

After becoming sole minister of St. Giles', Edinburgh, he preached twice every Sunday and three times during the week, sometimes to thousands. His life was often in danger. He was shot at, ambushes were laid for him, and, as he said in 1559, "I have need of a good and assured horse." Yet he laid the Scottish Reformation on a solid foundation: he recounts the story in his *History*. He had few of the qualifications generally looked for in a leader: an apostate priest of undistinguished appearance and obscure origin, without a university degree; a man lacking tact and diplomacy, to whom compromise was anathema; a humble man, concerned never to go where God had not summoned; yet he felt himself called to fight, not for fleeting things, but for the everlasting truth of God.

He died in St. Andrews on Nov. 24, 1572. At Knox's funeral the Regent Morton, no friend of ministers, spoke his epitaph: "Here lies one who neither flattered nor favoured any flesh."

**LATIN FATHERS,** the great Latin-speaking theologians of the early Church in the West. The earliest was Tertullian of Carthage (c.160–c.220). His masterful works on doctrinal, apologetic, ethical, and cultic subjects gave the Latin churches a basic theological vocabulary and many of their primary doctrinal formulae. Later Latin Fathers of the 3d century elaborated and refined Tertullian's teaching—notably Novatian of Rome, and the North Africans Minucius Felix, Cyprian, Arnobius, and Lactantius. Creedal orthodoxy in the 4th and 5th centuries found its principal Latin defenders in Hilary of Poitiers, Ambrose of Milan, and Pope Leo the Great of Rome. In the same period tower the figures of Jerome, translator and exegete of the Bible and champion of monasticism, and Augustine of Hippo, whose works treat the whole range of Christian

theology and philosophy. The last Latin Father, Pope Gregory the Great (d.604), popularized the Augustinian synthesis and gave definitive shape to the Roman liturgy.

With the exception of Augustine, the Latin Fathers were less philosophically minded than the Greek Fathers. But Stoicism, as interpreted by Cicero, had considerable influence upon Tertullian, Minucius Felix, Lactantius, and Ambrose, whereas Augustine, though he valued Cicero highly, was a thoroughgoing Platonist. Because of the rhetorical emphasis of Latin education, the Latin Fathers, unlike their Greek counterparts, were generally literary stylists of considerable distinction.

**LUTHER** [lo͞o'thər], **MARTIN** (1483–1546), German Protestant reformer. Born in Eisleben, in central Germany, he was the son of a Saxon peasant who ultimately became an economically successful mine owner. Luther received his early education at the Latin schools in Mansfeld (1488–97), Magdeburg (1497), and Eisenach (1498–1501). In May, 1501, he entered the University of Erfurt, and in the fall of 1502 received his B.A. degree. After obtaining the degree of M.A. in 1505, he matriculated in the faculty of law. But on July 17, 1505, he presented himself at the gate of the cloister of the Augustinian hermits in Erfurt, asking to be admitted. This sudden decision had been induced by a frightening experience 14 days earlier while he was walking from Mansfeld to Erfurt during a thunderstorm. Thrown off his feet by a stroke of lightning, he had uttered the vow "Help, St. Anne! I want to become a monk!" which he felt morally bound to keep.

He said later that he had decided to become a monk "in order to get a merciful God"—that is, to obtain assurance of salvation by submitting to the discipline of the monastic rule. On completing the novitiate, he was assigned to theological study, and in 1507 was ordained a priest. After a trip to Rome (1510–11) in connection with an appeal for monastic reform to the highest Augustinian authorities, he was permanently transferred to Wittenberg, where the Augustinian monks were in charge of theological education.

Encouraged by his superior and friend, Johann Staupitz, he gradually acquired a position of influence both as a monk and as an academic theologian. In 1512 he was appointed subprior and director of studies, and in 1515 district vicar to supervise 11 smaller monasteries. On Oct. 18, 1512, he attained the highest academic dignity, the doctorate in theology. Shortly afterward he was installed as professor of Biblical theology in the University of Wittenberg—a position he held for the rest of his life.

He rapidly became famous as an interpreter of the Bible, and students flocked to Wittenberg to hear him. His teaching was unusual, not only because he had broken with the traditional theological curriculum by substituting Biblical theology for the older systems of the schoolmen, but chiefly because he was imbued with a spiritual power derived from his own inner struggle for salvation. In the context of the theology in which he had been trained, and in connection with the monastic piety which he pursued with rigorous passion, he had come to the painful conclusion that man could never obtain righteousness by his own moral and religious efforts, but only by God's promise and gift. He achieved a fresh understanding of the Pauline doctrine of justification and interpreted the whole Bible in its light. He became severely critical of scholastic theology, because he felt that its basic Aristotelian orientation made it unable to interpret the Gospel correctly. The performance of good works, he began to teach, was not the condition but the fruit of salvation: "Good works do not make a man good, but a good man does good works." A man becomes righteous not by relying on what he is and has from himself, but by trustfully depending on God's promise of forgiveness given in Jesus Christ.

Substituting for a priest in the town church of Wittenberg, Luther had come in touch with the common people and was greatly troubled by their reliance on indulgences. He felt that this attitude represented a concern for security rather than readiness for repentance. He also felt that it tended to deform true religion by expressing a selfish search for salvation rather than a love for God and one's neighbor.

On Oct. 31, 1517, he nailed the 95 theses, or statements, on the power of indulgences to the door of the castle church in Wittenberg. He hoped they would become the subject of academic discussion and that the doctrine on indulgences would be clarified and the abuses in its practice corrected. But in view of the fact that the Papacy was encouraging the sale of indulgences to obtain funds for the rebuilding of St. Peter's Church in Rome, a criticism of indulgences could easily be interpreted as an assault upon papal authority. And he was soon attacked for having done just that. He was denounced in Rome, and an ecclesiastical trial was opened against him, because he was suspected of heresy. Compelled to defend himself, he was led to examine the basis of authority on which he relied.

In the first days of Oct., 1518, he appeared in Augsburg before the papal legate Cardinal Cajetanus. Believing that he was not being refuted, he refused to recant, and in order to escape arrest fled from Augsburg and appealed to a general council.

In an academic disputation in July, 1519, at Leipzig, with Johann Eck of Ingolstadt, who was to be his lifelong opponent, Luther discussed the authority of the Papacy. He was forced to acknowledge that church councils had erred, that the Papacy had made mistakes, and that the only supreme authority in Christendom was the Bible as the Word of God. In the course of further studies he concluded that the Papacy was antichrist, that it embodied the power of the devil who by posing as the vicar of Christ was undermining the church by preventing the Gospel from taking a free course among men.

**Excommunication.** Now the die was cast. On June 15, 1520, the Pope issued the bull *Exsurge Domine*, in which several statements of Luther were condemned and he was threatened with excommunication unless he recanted. Luther, who in the meantime had found a wide following, called for the reformation of the church. During 1520 he published a quick succession of tracts in which he stated his basic principles. In his *Manifest to the German Nobility on the Improvement of the Christian Estate*, he

The Bettmann Archive

Martin Luther, after a painting by Lucas Cranach the Elder.

assailed the Papacy and the hierarchic leadership of the church and called upon the princes to initiate a reformation. In *The Babylonish Captivity of the Church*, he attacked Roman Catholic sacramentalism and demanded the reduction of the sacraments to two, namely, baptism and the Lord's Supper. In *The Freedom of the Christian Man*, he characterized the nature of the Christian life simply as faith and love.

Ecclesiastical and secular authorities began to follow the papal order that his books be burned. In reply, on Nov. 10, 1520, he publicly burned a copy of the papal bull, together with several representative Roman Catholic writings. On Jan. 2, 1521, the Pope excommunicated him.

Because the newly elected Holy Roman Emperor Charles V had promised not to condemn a German subject unless he had been given a hearing, Luther was ordered to present himself at the Diet of Worms. On Apr. 18, 1521, standing before the Emperor, the German princes, and the papal representatives, he again refused to recant. He declared that his conscience was bound to the Word of God and that unless he was shown that his teachings were not Biblical, he would not change them. "Here I stand," he concluded, "I can do no other."

A few weeks later the imperial ban was imposed upon him. By the authority of church and state he was now an outcast. But neither Pope nor Emperor could execute this sentence. They could not prevent Luther from gaining more and more followers, nor could they prevent Roman Catholic practices being abolished in many places under the influence of evangelical preaching.

In order to protect Luther, his prince, Duke Frederick the Wise of Saxony, had him hidden in one of his castles, the Wartburg. During the 10 months of his stay there, Luther kept busy as a religious and theological pamphleteer. But his chief accomplishment was the translation of the New Testament into German (published Sept., 1522). In 1534 he completed the translation of the Old Testament. He kept working on his German Bible until the end of his life. It was his most important literary work, and has not been superseded even today.

**The Reformation.** His friends in Wittenberg proceeded to institute the reformation of the church. The Augustinian monastery was dissolved, the Mass was abolished. When iconoclastic riots broke out, Luther decided to return to Wittenberg. Preaching on eight successive days early in Mar., 1522, he restored order and stopped the innovations. He objected to the introduction of the Reformation either by coercive legalism or by revolution. "The Word must do it," he said. (One must note that, according to his understanding, the Word was ineffective apart from faith.) It was therefore inevitable that he opposed the radical reformation advocated in Saxony by his former followers, Andreas Karlstadt and Thomas Münzer. Luther accused both of arbitrariness, which he said was the consequence of their reliance upon the free working of the Spirit and their neglect of the Biblical word. Münzer founded and led dedicated Christian congregations, for whom he prepared entirely new evangelical orders of worship and church constitutions. He believed that in order to fulfill God's design for church and world, the use of violence might be necessary. This horrified Luther.

When in the spring of 1525 the German Peasants' Revolt reached Saxony, Münzer joined the rebels and fought and died with them. But Luther opposed them passionately. In his eyes revolution was rebellion against God, a worse evil than tyranny.

After the princes had put down the revolt in a blood bath, the character of the Reformation changed. Luther lost the support of the common people. His earlier hope that a change in the faith and order of the church could be effected under the Word of God by the action of the Christian congregations could no longer be realized. Henceforth the reformation of the church in most German lands was introduced from the top downward.

**Character and Achievements.** Luther was no organizer or administrator. He left the actual institution of the Reformation to others. In Saxony, where the church had been reformed since 1526 under the leadership of the territorial ruler, Melanchthon and Bugenhagen supervised and organized the new order. But its character was determined by Luther's interpretation of the Gospel and the power of his genius, both coming to full expression in the *Small* and *Large Catechisms* (1529). They were his chief specific contribution to the life of the new churches.

Luther served mainly as a teacher and preacher. Throughout his life he combined the responsibilities of a professor of the Bible with those of a pulpit leader of the common people. In both capacities he was extraordinarily influential, despite the fact that in later life he was often handicapped by sickness. Moreover, he was sought after for advice and counsel by people of all walks of life. He received an incessant stream of visitors and carried on a voluminous correspondence with friends and strangers.

His main concern was always the right interpretation of the Gospel. This kept him involved in many conflicts. On the one hand, he fought against Roman Catholicism. On the other, he found it necessary to set his teaching apart from that of other Reformers who, though they owed their evangelical position to him, drew conclusions either in doctrine or in practice which he judged to be too radical.

Until the end of his life he was engaged in conflicts with the Papacy. Even in 1545, one year before his death, he published a tract entitled *Of the Papacy at Rome, Founded by the Devil.* He believed that the Roman Catholic Church distorted the authority of the Bible by adding that of human traditions to it. For a similar reason he consistently criticized Erasmus and his humanistic program. He suspected that Erasmus meant to live by his creative human iniative as well as by the grace of God. His major theological work, *On the Bondage of the Will* (1525), was a forceful rejection of this humanistic view. He declined to make common cause with certain adherents of the Reformation because they appeared to him to subtract from the authority of the Word. Zwingli's symbolic interpretation of Christ's presence in the Lord's Supper was irreconcilable, Luther believed, with the Biblical affirmation of the Real Presence in the sacrament. And the Anabaptists' refusal to make common cause with the churches of the Reformation was derived, he suspected, from their attributing more authority to their own spiritual insight than to the Word of God.

Some of Luther's judgments were one-sided and extreme. He tended toward excesses in verbal expression, especially when he gave vent to his deepest disagreements with others. But actually he was not a harsh or violent person. He was a man of religious genius, deeply sensitive to all things of the spirit and able to articulate what they meant to him. He had not planned the Reformation and did not become its spiritual leader by his own choosing. Considering the role he was forced to play, he once compared himself to a horse with blinkers that was being led not knowing where.

In his private life he was a charming, thoughtful friend and companion. Hence it is not surprising that he was remembered by his followers and admirers not only as a reformer but also as a father surrounded by his family. In 1525 he married Katharina von Bora, a former nun, and they lived for more than 20 years in a happy marriage, she and three of their six children surviving Luther. On Feb. 18, 1546, he died of heart failure in Eisleben, where he had gone to arbitrate a conflict between the counts of Mansfeld.

**NIKON** [nyē′kən] (1605–81), Patriarch of the Russian Church who reformed its religious books and liturgical practices. Of peasant origin, Nikon was first a secular priest, then became a monk and eventually hegumenos of a small northern monastery. After Tsar Alexis befriended him, he became Metropolitan of Novgorod in 1648, and in 1652 was elected Patriarch of Moscow. In 1653 he began to revise Russian ritual and liturgical books to accord in all respects with those in use in the Greek Church. The sign of the cross was to be made with three fingers instead of two, in accordance with the Greek custom. He used to say, "I am Russian, but my faith is Greek."

Nikon's reforms met fierce opposition from a group led by Archpriest Avvakum. These "Old Believers" defended the Council of 1551, which had proclaimed the Russian Church superior to other Eastern Churches. Nikon aimed to bring the Russian Church closer to other Orthodox churches. After losing the confidence of the Tsar, Nikon retired to a monastery, leaving the church without a patriarch for nine years. In 1666–67, a Church Council in Moscow condemned and exiled Nikon but accepted his reforms, excommunicated Avvakum and the Old Believers, and repudiated the Council of 1551.

**PAUL, ST.,** originally named Saul. Paulus, a Roman surname meaning "little," may first have been his nickname. It is not known when Paul was born. If he called himself "the aged" (*presbutēs*, Philemon 9), he was past 60 when he wrote, and so was born about when Jesus was; but he may have said "ambassador" (*presbeutēs*) with no implications of age. He was "a Jew, born at Tarsus in Cilicia" (Acts 22:3). Growing up outside Palestine, and using Greek rather than Aramaic, such Jews absorbed much from their pagan environment. Paul's own thinking was colored by his non-Jewish contacts. Still, he was raised an orthodox Jew and was ever proud that he was "taught according to the perfect manner of the law of the fathers" (Acts 22:3; Phil. 3:5). Through his father he inherited Roman citizenship (Acts 22:25–28), but how his father got it we are not told.

**Paul's Conversion.** Sent early to Jerusalem, Paul studied under Gamaliel (Acts 22:3) and became a zealous Pharisee. Intense and proud, he drove himself hard in whatever he thought his duty. He could express both great love and great hatred, but he had little sense of humor and cannot have been an easy man to work with. He may have belonged to the Sanhedrin, a council of Jewish leaders that had legal authority in and near Jerusalem but whose prestige extended wherever Jews lived. Under Sanhedrin auspices he used threats, imprisonment, and murder to stamp out the young Christian movement (Acts 9:1f.; 22:4f.; 26:9–11; I Cor. 15:9). On the way to Damascus, in pursuit of this enterprise, he was converted to Christianity (Acts 9:1–19; 22:5–16; 26:11–20). Although the accounts in Acts vary somewhat, they are agreed that Paul saw a brilliant flash and heard a voice say "Saul, Saul, why persecutest thou me? . . . I am Jesus whom thou persecutest." Jesus told him to proceed to Damascus for instructions. Thereafter he was to proclaim the Gospel. The experience left Paul physically blind, and his companions led him into the city. After three days Ananias, a Christian of Damascus, visited him. His sight was restored, and he was baptized.

Acts 9:9–30 has it that Paul began immediately to preach his new faith, that thereupon Jews sought to kill him, and that he escaped to Jerusalem, where he joined the church leaders. But Paul says he did *not* go to Jerusalem then, but repaired to Arabia, returned to Damascus, and only after three years made contact with the Jerusalem apostles (Gal. 1:15–19). Although Luke appears mistaken here, the rest of his chronology fits fairly closely with Paul's own recollections.

Some time later Paul revisited Tarsus, then went with Barnabas to Antioch. The Antioch church was raising funds for famine relief, and Paul and Barnabas were dispatched to Jerusalem with the gifts.

**The First Missionary Journey.** They returned to Antioch (Acts 12:25–13:1; Gal. 1:18) and later left on what is called Paul's "first missionary journey" (Acts 13:2–14:28). With John Mark as assistant, they preached in synagogues throughout Cyprus, thence crossed over to Perga on the mainland. Mark now deserted them, perhaps because Paul intended to preach to non-Jews. From Perga they went to Pisidian Antioch. Finding many Jews extremely antagonistic, Paul began work with Gentiles and succeeded in establishing a church. He and Barnabas then continued to Iconium, Lystra, and Derbe, towns on a commercial road through southern Asia Minor in the Roman province of Galatia. It was probably to these parishes that Paul later addressed his *Epistle to the Galatians*.

From Derbe they returned to Antioch in Syria. Meanwhile reports had reached Jerusalem that Gentiles were coming into the church on equality with Jews. Yet, Jewish Christians believed, Jesus Himself was a thoroughgoing Jew who insisted that every "jot and tittle" of the Mosaic law was binding, that Pharisaic rules must be obeyed, and that He and His followers were sent "only to the lost sheep of the house of Israel" (Matt.5:17–19; 10:5f.; 15:24; 23:2f.). Indeed, the Christian claim was that Jesus fulfilled the Jewish Scriptures. To most Jewish Christians, then, it was unthinkable that one could accept the Messiah while avoiding Judaism, circumcision, and the ceremonial law.

Advocates of this view are termed "Judaizers." Other leaders besides Paul opposed them, but it was Paul whose deeper understanding set Christianity's future course. His keen, cultured mind saw in Christianity implications that escaped other, "unlearned and ignorant" apostles (Acts 4:13). Trained in Biblical exegesis, Paul could argue persuasively that the Scriptures supported his wider universalism. A third, less exalted motivation was Paul's own ineffectiveness when preaching to Jews. No doubt his repeated failures where other apostles succeeded led him to try more promising fields.

**Doctrine of Justification.** Yet more impelling than any

of these factors was Paul's doctrine of *Justification.* As a Jew he had sought security through obedience to Moses' law. Even afterward, he called this law "holy, righteous and good," the true revelation of the divine will. But man does not obey God's will. In particular, the law says "Thou shalt not covet," and this demand for purity of *inward desire* is violated by every one, every day. So the law, divine as it is, cannot make us good, nor can it forgive us when we sin. In a word, the law cannot "justify." Unless God intervenes and provides some other means to forgiveness and strength, man is doomed (Rom. 7). Just this justification, this forgiveness and moral strength, Paul found in Christ.

Here Paul drew an analogy from pagan mystery cults. Devotees of the latter sought by various rites (baptisms, sacred meals) to merge themselves into the life of one of the gods, and thereby to share in the god's own immortality and divinity. The Christian, says Paul, interlocks his life with Christ's, "dies" to the old, and "rises" to the new. He is then secure in the knowledge of God's forgiveness. Temptation is easier to cope with. Death, though still a physical fact, loses its fearfulness and must soon disappear entirely.

Therefore, when one joins himself to Christ, one accomplishes all that the law had aimed at, one fulfills the law in fact, and belongs more truly to Israel than does any non-Christian Jew who continues to break the law.

A delegation came to Antioch from Jerusalem, insisting that Gentile converts be circumcised. So serious was the resulting variance that Paul, Barnabas, and a few others went to meet with the apostles in Jerusalem.

**Second Missionary Journey.** On the eve of a second missionary journey (Acts 15:40–18:22) Paul and Barnabas quarreled. Their quarrel turned on the Jewish-Gentile problem and on Mark's previous desertion. Barnabas and Mark went again to Cyprus. Paul and Silas went to Derbe by way of Cilicia and then to Lystra, where they picked up Timothy. After visiting churches organized on the previous tour, they moved on to Troas. Here Acts switches to the first person plural, "we," perhaps because Luke now joined the band of missionaries. At Troas Paul dreamed of a man summoning him to "come over into Macedonia, and help us." Persuaded that he must go into Europe, he crossed to Philippi and thence to Thessalonica and Beroea, establishing parishes in each town.

His usual method was to speak in the synagogue, then to welcome inquirers to his own lodgings, and then, when opposition mounted, to withdraw his adherents to the home of some newly won convert. From the group thus formed he chose leaders to carry on after he left.

At Beroea hostility became so dangerous that Paul departed for Athens. His famous address on Mars Hill (Acts 17:22–31) failed to convince his Athenian listeners. Deeply disappointed, he sent Timothy back to Thessalonica while he and Silas went on to Corinth. Here he met Priscilla and Aquila, Jews recently banished from Rome, and joined them at the trade of tentmaking. Timothy returned with good news from Macedonia. For 18 months Paul and his friends now labored to found a parish at Corinth. This was a large commercial port, notorious for its vice. The Corinthian congregation included people of every conceivable background. Jewish opposition again

The apostle St. Paul, painted by El Greco.

developed. Paul was brought before Gallio, who had come as proconsul in 52 A.D. Although Gallio dismissed the charges, Paul thought it best to go back to Syrian Antioch. En route his group stopped at Ephesus, and Priscilla and Aquila remained there. After the briefest stay in Antioch, Paul started on his third missionary journey (Acts 18:23–21:17).

Meanwhile Apollos, a Jew of Alexandria, had come to Ephesus. A member, apparently, of a sect of John the Baptist, Apollos knew some facts about Jesus, but not the claim that He was the Messiah. Now, under Priscilla's and Aquila's guidance, Apollos became a Christian. Soon he departed for Corinth, where he became a powerful church leader.

Priscilla and Aquila seem not to have baptized Apollos, evidently thinking John's baptism sufficient. This would have accorded with the practice of other Jewish Christians. But Paul, on returning to Ephesus, did rebaptize some converts from John's movement (Acts 19:1–7). Paul never belonged to that movement, and his estimate of John plainly differed from that of the Jerusalem apostles.

**In Peril at Ephesus.** Though Ephesus was the most important cultural center in Asia Minor, and though Paul's second stay there lasted three years, Acts says little about it. Perhaps Paul had a terrifying experience there, and Luke, who usually plays down Roman cruelties, glossed it over.

Paul himself wrote from Ephesus that he was "in peril every hour," "a spectacle to the world," like one "sentenced to death." There were "many adversaries." He even "fought with wild beasts at Ephesus," though it is not certain that he meant this literally. It was illegal to throw a Roman citizen into the arena, but Paul's captors did not always know his status. "We were so utterly, unbearably crushed that we despaired of life itself" (I Cor.

4:9; 15:30,32; 16:9, II Cor. 1:8f.). Further, in three letters written from a prison (Philippians, Colossians, Philemon) Paul mentions people with him—Aristarchus, Onesimus, Timothy, and Tychicus—all of whom lived and worked around Ephesus. In these same letters Paul hopes soon to be released and to visit the Lycus valley and Philippi (Philemon 22; Phil. 1:26f.; 2:12–24). Such things would be reasonable if Paul were writing from an Ephesian jail. The evidence, however, is short of proof.

The stay at Ephesus was interrupted by a further visit to Corinth. Some at Corinth were rejecting Paul's leadership, preferring Apollos or Peter. Paul, uncertain of his reception, took the indirect route through Troas and Macedonia. He was met on the way by Titus, who brought encouraging reports from Corinth (II Cor. 7: 5–7), so he hastened on and spent the winter there. Paul's Corinthian letters deal with this trouble.

All this time Paul was raising a collection for the church at Jerusalem. He hoped to take the funds there and then move on to Rome. Quitting Corinth, he stopped briefly at Miletus, where he met a delegation from the church of Ephesus. Their sorrowful leave-taking is described in Acts 20:17–38. Accompanied by Luke and others, he sailed for Tyre and then Caesarea. At both places he was warned of serious danger at Jerusalem, but he would not halt his journey.

**Paul's Arrest, Imprisonment, and Martyrdom.** Arriving at Jerusalem, he reported to the leaders there and handed over the collection. He was told that his attitude toward the law was widely suspect, and he was advised to prove his Jewish loyalty by joining with some other men in purification rites in the Temple. He agreed to do so. At the Temple, however, a report got about that Paul had taken an uncircumcised Gentile into the area set apart for Jews. A riot started and Paul was nearly killed, but was rescued by a Roman officer. The officer allowed Paul to speak to the crowd, but his words inflamed them the more. So Paul was put in protective custody and, upon word of further plots to kill him, was sent under guard to Caesarea, the seat of Felix, the Roman governor of Palestine. Though Felix quickly saw that Paul was innocent of any crime, he kept him jailed, perhaps hoping for a bribe. After two years Felix was replaced by Festus. Paul, despairing of justice in Palestine, finally exerted his right as a Roman citizen and appealed to Caesar. He was then told that, had he not so appealed, he would have been released. Now, however, he would have to go in bonds to Rome.

Luke and other friends were allowed to go with him. The ship, carrying numerous prisoners, was wrecked near Malta, and the group had to winter there. Paul's courage and good spirits, through all this, won the commendation of his Roman guard, and he was treated leniently. Finally, in the spring, they reached Italy. He was met on the Appian Way by Christians who had heard of his coming but knew little of the circumstances. At Rome he remained under house arrest but was allowed visitors. Once more he had difficulties with fellow Jewish Christians. Once more he declared that Christianity must be taken to Gentiles.

The Book of Acts closes with the statement that Paul spent two years in Rome. If he was then executed, Luke perhaps could not bring himself to describe the tragedy. Or perhaps Acts was written before Paul's case was set-tled. A third possibility is that "two whole years" means the legal time limit, after which he was released without a hearing. Clement, Bishop of Rome, wrote in 96 A.D. that Paul had traveled "to the extreme limits of the west." That can hardly mean Rome itself and suggests that Paul was indeed set free and went to Spain as he had intended to do (Rom. 15:24). From I and II Timothy it would appear that he then revisited churches in the east, went back to Rome, and was arrested again, and that this time his case went against him.

Whether on his first hearing in Rome, or on a later one, in the end Paul was martyred. As a citizen, he would not be crucified but beheaded. If this occurred at the end of his first Roman imprisonment, it was probably during the Neronian persecution of 64 A.D. If there was a second Roman trial, Paul died about 67 A.D.

**Three Major Problems.** From Paul's letters it seems that three widely different problems nagged him all through his ministry. One was his "thorn in the flesh" (II Cor. 12: 7), a physical disability of some sort. Paul often had ecstatic visions (Acts 16:9; 18:9ff.; 22:17–21; 26:13–19; II Cor. 12:1–5) and it is sometimes supposed that he had epilepsy. More likely, he had an embarrassing disease of the eyes. After his conversion "he was three days without sight," and when he regained his vision "there fell from his eyes as it had been scales" (Acts 9:9,18). He says he has to write with large letters (Gal. 6:11) and that, confronted with his trying "bodily ailment," the Galatians would, if possible, have plucked out their own eyes and given them to him (Gal. 4:15).

Another problem was that his right to the title apostle was challenged by many Christian leaders, on the grounds that he had not known Jesus as the Twelve had and that the Twelve had not commissioned him. Paul recognized that his commission came "not from man" but insisted that he had met Jesus Himself, and was personally ordained by Him. Also, said Paul, the success of his ministry proved his apostleship. The strain between Paul and some of his predecessors is particularly noticeable in Galatians and I Corinthians.

Paul's third major problem was Docetic Gnosticism, a heresy that flowered in the 2d century but was already rife in Paul's day. It held that Christ only *seemed* (Gr. *dokeo*, "I seem") to be incarnate and that man is saved by a special wisdom (*sophia*) and knowledge (*gnosis*). Many Gnostics thought moral behavior and chastity unnecessary. Paul meets the problem, notably, in I Corinthians, Galatians, and Colossians.

**PHOTIUS** [fō'shəs] (c.810–895), Patriarch of Constantinople (857–67; 877–86) and theologian of the Eastern Church. He opposed the prerogatives claimed by the Roman see and advocated equality among the ancient patriarchates. An influential, learned layman, Photius was elevated to the patriarchate within six days, replacing the deposed Patriarch Ignatius. Pope Nicholas I considered Photius noncanonical, and in 863 excommunicated him and recognized Ignatius as legitimate. In 867 Photius convened a synod which answered the Pope by condemning him personally and denouncing Latin missionary activity in Bulgaria and the use of *filioque* ("and the Son") in the Nicene Creed. That year Photius was deposed by Emperor Basil (867–88), who took the throne after assassinating Michael III, and Patriarch Ignatius was reinstalled. A new council at Constantinople (869–70), attended by legates of Pope Hadrian, confirmed the excommunication of Photius. When Ignatius died, Photius became Patriarch again and was recognized by Pope John VIII. At the Photian Council of 879–80, the decisions of 869–70 were repudiated. But Photius was deposed for the second time by Emperor Leo VI and died in exile.

He was the author of three important works: the *Treatise on the Holy Spirit*; *Bibliotheca*, a summary of 280 books he had read, many of which are now lost; and the *Amphilochia*, a collection of theological essays. He was canonized in the Eastern Church.

**VIRGIN MARY, BLESSED,** the mother of Jesus, also known in the Christian tradition as the Mother of God, the Mother of Christ, and the Blessed Virgin. She is first mentioned in the Scriptures as "a virgin betrothed to a man named Joseph" (Luke 1:27) and the recipient of an "angelic revelation" specifying her maternal role in God's plan of salvation. Through "the power of the Most High" (Luke 1:35) she will conceive a son to be named Jesus (Matt. 1:21) who "shall be great and shall be called the Son of the Most High" (Luke 1:32), heir through "the Lord God" of "the throne of David his father," and he shall be "king over the house of Jacob forever" (Luke 1:32), and "shall be called the Son of God" (Luke 1:35). His birth from the virgin Mary fulfills a prophecy of Isaias (7:14), which Matthew (1:23) records as follows: "Behold, the virgin shall be with child, and shall bring forth a son, and they shall call his name Emmanuel; which is interpreted, 'God with us.'"

Thus, in the Gospels of Matthew and Luke, representing the thought of the primitive Church, Mary appears as the Virgin mother of Jesus, the Christ, the Son of David and the Son of God. According to this ancient Christian preaching, Mary's role in salvation history is determined by the prophecies of the Old Testament. Shortly after this "angelic revelation" the visit of Mary to her kinswoman, Elizabeth, the mother of John the Baptist, is described by Luke (1:39–45). Greeted with the salutation, "Blessed art thou among women" (Luke 1:42), she replies to Elizabeth in a highly religious canticle (the Magnificat—Luke 1:46–55) in praise of God's mercy, power, and fidelity. The birth of Jesus occurred in Bethlehem, the royal city of David, whither Mary and Joseph had gone to be enrolled in the imperial census (Luke 2:1–2). When the shepherds (Luke 2:8–20) and the Magi (Matt. 2:1–12) appeared at Bethlehem to adore the child Jesus, Mary was present. After the circumcision and the presentation of Jesus in the temple (Luke 2:21–38), Mary fled with him and Joseph into Egypt to escape the wrath of Herod (Matt. 2:13–15); and later, when the danger had passed, she returned to Nazareth. Thus the infancy narratives clearly place Mary in a Messianic context (of prophecy fulfillment). At the

beginning of the public career of Jesus, she was also associated with him, for example, at the marriage feast in Cana (John 2:1–5). Later, she stood at the foot of the Cross and was presented by her dying son to the care of St. John (John 19:26–27). After the Ascension she was found united in mind and prayer with the Apostles (Acts 1:14). With this reference Mary disappears from Scripture.

In the doctrinal history (the Greek and Latin Fathers) of the early Church, Mary is represented as the Virgin Mother of God and the "new Eve" in parallel with Christ, "the new Adam." Her divine maternity is her supreme prerogative, the root of all the others. Though at first this doctrine is not prominent in the sources (largely because the liturgy stressed the humanity of Christ, the Mediator and Priest), later, under the stimulus of the Christological controversies, theologians turned more directly to Mary and her relation to Christ. But apart from theology, the art, liturgy, and devotion of the early Christians witness the truth that Mary, as Mother of God, enjoyed more than an ordinary place in the primitive Church.

The Christian Gnostics (for example, Docetists), who negated the reality of the human body of Christ, denied in consequence the maternity of Mary. Later, the Adoptionists (c.200) were led to the same denial though for different reasons. They maintained that Christ was not the true Son of God at the moment of His conception but much later, at His baptism, for example, when the power of God came down upon Him and dwelt in Him as in a temple. Paul of Samosata (c.270), allied to this tradition, flatly denied on the basis of his Trinitarian theology that Mary was the mother of the Logos (God). According to him, she begot Jesus, a man equal to us, though better in every respect, the Son of God indeed, but not the Logos who is from the Father alone. Arius (d.336) logically denied the divine maternity of Mary, because he refused to admit that the Logos was the divine Son of God.

In the school of Antioch (in the late 4th century) theology began to focus more closely on the place of Mary in Christology. The Antiocheans, rationalistic, historically minded, humanistic theologians, tended, against the Apollinarists (4th-century theologians who falsely explained the humanity of Christ), to stress the perfect completeness of the human side of Christ. They claimed for Christ not only two perfect natures (human and divine) but two perfect persons (human and divine). Thus Diodorus of Tarsus (d. about 390) distinguished in Christ the Son of God (Logos) and the Son of David (the man). The first is eternal and from the Father; the second, temporal and from Mary. The former dwells in the latter as a god in a temple. Mary, therefore, is only the mother of Jesus, the temple of the indwelling Logos. She is not God's mother.

The thought of Diodorus greatly influenced Theodore of Mopsuestia (d.428), and through him Nestorius (d.452) of Constantinople, who denied the divine maternity of Mary. Though the precise nature of his Christology is obscure, through the loss of almost all his works, it seems that he distinguished in Christ the perfectly human and perfectly divine, so that there were in Christ two distinct natures and two distinct persons (human and divine). Mary is *Christotokos* (mother of the human person, Christ), not *Theotokos* (mother of the divine person, Logos). Nestorius could not see the possibility of predicating contingencies of the transcendent God. Nor could he grasp the full significance of the hypostatic union in which two complete, perfect, distinct natures (divine and human) are substantially united in one person (the Logos) so intimately and personally that properties of each nature can be predicated of the person to whom the natures belong.

Against Nestorius, Cyril of Alexandria (d.444) urged this doctrine, and insisted that Mary is the true Mother of God, because she generated that human nature which is hypostatically united to the person of the Logos. It was a development of the patristic dictum that God became man without ceasing to be God. At the third ecumenical council, at Ephesus in 431, Mary was declared solemnly to be *Theotokos*, a truth which the whole Church joyously accepted. From this moment can be traced that surge of Marian piety which reached unexcelled heights in the medieval Church and is still alive today.

The doctrine of the virginity of Mary, which is rooted in Scripture (Matt. 1:23), was understood by the Church from a very early date in a total sense: integrity of body (as material element) and of mind (as formal element) "before, during, and after the birth of Christ." The earliest ecclesiastical documents (for example, the Creeds) speak of Mary as the ever Virgin Mother of the Son of God made man. And this dogma, universally accepted by the early Church (save for Jovinianus and Helvidius) has a continuing tradition in Catholicism.

Closely related to the doctrine of the divine maternity is the dogma of the Immaculate Conception: Mary's singular preservation from original sin from the first moment of her conception, through the grace of God and the merits of Christ. The dogma itself can be regarded as contained implicitly in Scripture (Mother of God) and in tradition (Mary, the "new Eve"). In the history of salvation her role is parallel, though subordinate, to that of Christ. Her freedom from sin is analogous to His. At no moment of her existence was she under the dominion of sin. Though the medieval schoolmen (for instance, St. Thomas Aquinas) experienced difficulty in understanding the possibility of the doctrine, in view of the universality of original sin, it was from their circle in the person of the Franciscan Duns Scotus (d.1308) that the theology of the Immaculate Conception emerged. Through the perfect mediatorship of Christ, Mary was conceived in grace; through His merits she was preserved (rather than liberated) from original sin. On Dec. 8, 1854, Pius IX in the bull *Ineffabilis Deus* solemnly defined the Immaculate Conception as a part of the Catholic faith.

The dogma of the Assumption may be considered as springing from the doctrine of Mary's sinlessness and her role as the "new Eve." After her earthly life (the question of her bodily death left undecided) Mary passed, body and soul, into heavenly glory through the power of God. This doctrine can be conceived as a fuller expression and development of the prerogatives of Mary (Mother of God, the "new Eve," the Immaculately Conceived, "full of grace") contained in Scripture and tradition. It is further confirmed by the ancient liturgy and Marian piety of the Church. On Nov. 1, 1950, Pius XII, in the apostolic constitution *Munificentissimus Deus*, defined the Assumption as Catholic dogma.

Current interest in Mariology centers on the doctrines of Mediatrix: that every grace granted through the merits of Christ is also somehow granted through the intercession of Mary; and Coredemptrix: that Mary is in some way the cause of our redemption in a position subordinate to and secondary to Christ the Redeemer.

**WESLEY, JOHN** (1703–91), English evangelical preacher and founder of Methodism. Born in Epworth, Lincolnshire, England, he was the 15th child of Samuel Wesley, rector of Epworth, and his wife Susanna. After graduation in 1724 from Christ Church, Oxford, he was ordained in the Church of England and in 1726 became a fellow of Lincoln College, Oxford, as Greek lecturer and moderator. While at Oxford, he joined a group of students who, because of their regularity in study and worship, were derisively called "Methodists." Organized by his brother Charles Wesley, the group included George Whitefield and James Hervey, but it soon recognized John Wesley as its leader. In 1735 Wesley accepted an invitation by Governor James Oglethorpe to preach to the colonists of Georgia, but discouraged with his efforts there, he returned to England in 1737. Peter Boehler, a Moravian Pietist preacher, exerted a profound influence on Wesley's understanding of the Christian life, and in 1738 Wesley visited the Moravian colony at Herrnhut, in Saxony.

Wesley's discouragement with his own life and ministry continued, however, until his "evangelical conversion" on May 24, 1738. He records in his *Journal*, "In the evening, I went very unwillingly to a chapel in Aldersgate Street, where one was reading Luther's preface to the Epistle to the Romans. About a quarter before nine, while he was describing the change which God works in the heart through faith in Christ, I felt my heart strangely warmed." This experience so affected Wesley that he subsequently dated events in his life as before or after his conversion. Thereafter he began to preach with new confidence that God's grace was in and for all men, and that all who accepted it, freely offered, would experience its saving power. This emphasis, coupled with stress on the necessity of practicing holiness in daily life, powerfully influenced persons in every social class across the nation and began the Wesleyan Revival. The movement transformed the social, ethical, and political life of the British Isles and America.

Accused of being an "enthusiast," Wesley eventually found the pulpits of the Church of England closed to him, but, following the example of George Whitefield, he preached in the open fields. Thousands who came under the impact of his sermons were organized into societies for their spiritual edification and were encouraged to attend the Church of England regularly. But the growing Methodist movement had its own preaching services and produced many effective lay preachers, who traveled about in regular order among the Methodist Societies. John Wesley himself had no permanent residence, but rode 40 to 60 mi. a day, 5,000 mi. a year, preaching as many as 16 sermons a week.

George Whitefield's insistence on the doctrines of predestination and election ran counter to Wesley's theologi-

John Wesley, the founder of Methodism, as portrayed by George Romney. The painting is in the Philadelphia Museum of Art.

he was buried at City Road Chapel in the vestments of an Anglican priest.

cal position, often called Evangelical Arminianism, after the Dutch theologian Jacobus Arminius (1560–1609). Wesley insisted that Christ died for all men, as against Whitefield's Calvinistic doctrine of limited atonement, so the two men, while remaining close friends, pursued their different ministries.

By 1784 the gradual separation of the Methodist Societies from the Church of England was furthered by the Deed of Declaration, which placed the Methodist organization on a legal basis. This breach was widened also by Wesley's decision to ordain Richard Whatcoat and Thomas Vasey as elders for the administration of the Sacraments to the brethren in America. Thomas Coke, already a priest in the Church of England, was set apart as superintendent of the American movement, with authority to ordain Francis Asbury as joint superintendent with him. Charles Wesley was horrified that his brother should countenance anything other than episcopal ordination. But John Wesley, knowing the need of the Methodists in America, which was bereft of Church of England clergy because of the American Revolution, justified his action by saying that he understood himself to be a Scriptural *episcopos*, and claimed as a presbyter, from the evidences of Scripture and the early Church, the right to ordain other presbyters with authority to administer the Sacraments. This use of Scripture to justify his action was usual with Wesley and was born of a lifelong study of the Bible. He called himself a man of one book.

Wesley's writings were numerous and varied, and included biographies, histories, grammars, hymns, dictionaries, sermons, and pamphlets on ethics, logic, medicine, and politics, as well as other writings. In 1780 he began the publication of *The Arminian Magazine,* and from 1735 to 1790 he kept his truly remarkable *Journal.*

His marriage in 1750 to Mary Vazeille, a widow, was unhappy, and subsequently she left him. Wesley never separated from the Church of England, and after his death

## Terms

**ABBEY,** canonical dwelling, enjoying autonomy, governed by an abbot, and housing at least 12 monks. The great abbeys of Europe grew out of the caves, abandoned tombs, and mud huts of the hermits, first established in the desert by St. Anthony of Egypt (3d–4th centuries). The founders of the earliest monasteries were the hermits who attracted disciples, their huts clustering around that of the solitary. St. Pachomius (c.290–346) introduced a simple order by laying out these huts in rows and erecting community buildings surrounded by a wall. He also devised a single, self-contained building, with cells for the monks, as a novitiate community life before attempting the hermitical. Eventually the conventual life superseded the hermitical. Its adoption by St. Benedict (6th century) and the spread of monasticism under the influence of his rule standardized the housing of the monks by standardizing their life. At first the Roman villa, its buildings arranged around a quadrangle, was adapted to monastic life, the form varying with local conditions and customs. The initial buildings included oratory, dormitory, refectory, kitchens, infirmary, and conference room. As the monks also worked the fields, cultivated the arts, and plied various trades, barns, stables, and workshops were added. The large abbeys became self-contained cities. The abbeys became extremely beautiful and imposing structures, passing from the architecture of the Roman basilica through Romanesque to Gothic. Each bore the place name of its location, whether in the wilderness or in the city; some also bore the name of the founder or of a saint whose relics were there.

**AGAPE** [ăg'ə-pē], (Gr., "love," hence the common designation "love feast"), name given to the fellowship meals of the early Christians. The Church took over the custom from the noncultic meals of religious associations among the Jews; but gentile converts were also familiar with similar practices in Greco-Roman paganism. In the earliest days of the Church, the common meal was a regular part of the celebration of the Eucharist, and it is not clear how Christians distinguished the sacramental from the nonsacramental aspects of the observance. By the middle of the 2d century, however, such meals had been separated from the Eucharist and their observance made optional.

Usually provided by a wealthier member, the agape served primarily as a charity to the poor, especially to widows. By the 4th century, frequent disorders of behavior led to its gradual suppression. A special form of agape was the memorial banquet on the anniversary of a deceased member. Some of the oldest Christian paintings in the catacombs are of these funerary feasts.

**APOLOGETICS** [ə-pŏl-ə-jĕt'ĭks], that branch of theology which deals with the relation between Christian and non-Christian thought. The latter may be the thought of those whose religious views are different from those of Christians, members of other religions, agnostics, or atheists. Or it may be the thought of those whose main intellectual in-

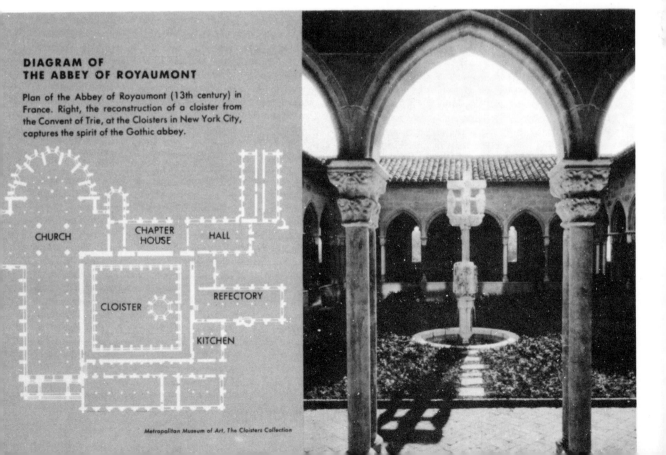

**DIAGRAM OF
THE ABBEY OF ROYAUMONT**

Plan of the Abbey of Royaumont (13th century) in France. Right, the reconstruction of a cloister from the Convent of Trie, at the Cloisters in New York City, captures the spirit of the Gothic abbey.

CHURCH    CHAPTER HOUSE    HALL

CLOISTER

REFECTORY

KITCHEN

*Metropolitan Museum of Art, The Cloisters Collection*

terest is not religious but whose doctrines have a bearing on Christianity: for example, philosophers and scientists.

Since the religious and nonreligious alternatives to Christianity change, as do science and philosophy, the task of apologetics must always be undertaken afresh. The apologist tends to concentrate on those aspects of Christianity that at the moment are either being attacked or provide material for a counterattack, rather than to attempt to give a balanced, over-all picture of Christianity. Hence Karl Barth, the famous reformed theologian, has suggested that apologetics be dropped, on the ground that it takes unbelief too seriously. In reply, it might be argued that apologetics is (1) simply evangelism in the form of preaching the Gospel to intellectuals in their own language, and (2) a necessity, in that no one can keep his science, philosophy, and religion in watertight compartments.

The mark of a good apologist is the ability to state Christianity in the thought forms of his time without losing sight of its distinctive character. Thus, Justin Martyr, one of the earliest Christian apologists, maintained both that philosophers like Plato and Heraclitus shared in the Divine Logos or reason, which was a key idea in contemporary Stoic philosophy, and also that the Logos had been manifested fully only in Christ. Similarly, St. Thomas Aquinas, in an age when Christians were afraid of revived Aristotelianism, showed that a doctrine of God could be expressed in terms of Aristotelian thought forms and yet leave a vital place for the revelation of God in Christ.

In the 20th century the work of apologetics has become more complex, owing to vast developments in all branches of science. Perhaps Karl Heim, the well-known Lutheran theologian, has shown himself most conversant with the quantum theory and the theory of relativity, and their destructive effect on the absolutes of an earlier physics. Heim's view that the self stands at the intersection of three "spaces," the space of material objects, the I-thou space, and the suprapolar space of God, seems to throw light on such factors as miracle, the omnipresence and transcendence of God, and the fact that He is not found in the field investigated by natural science.

Among other writers, Paul Tillich has done much to keep Christian thought in touch with both depth psychology and art. I.T. Ramsey has opened up discussion with the logical analysts. Rudolf Bultmann states Christianity in terms of existential analysis, in the conviction that this does not involve a surrender of faith but rather the appreciation that it is a decision between genuine possibilities of human existence.

Also important, though not strictly a Christian theologian, is Karl Jaspers, who finds modern science to have its foundation in the religion of the Bible, with its demand for truth in the inward parts.

**APOSTLES' CREED,** traditional baptismal formula of the Western Church, which can be traced back to the "Old Roman Symbol" of the mid-2d century. Like other ancient creeds, it consists of two elements: a brief expansion of the threefold divine name, "Father, Son, and Holy Spirit," and a longer summary of the saving events of the life of Christ, sometimes called the kerygma. While the material can be found in the New Testament and early writers, the actual ascription to the Apostles is a later development. In the Byzantine period the Nicene Creed Superseded the Old Roman Symbol at Rome itself, but the Apostles' Creed, with local variants, prevailed in the rest of the Latin Church. The standard form is one used in France in the 9th century, and from there introduced into Rome some time after 850. In interrogative form it is still the baptismal formula of the Roman Catholic Church, and it is also used in various devotions, such as the Rosary. Anglicans and Lutherans retain its use at Baptism, and also employ it in public worship. Most other Protestants recognize it as a valuable statement of the historic Christian faith, and there is a growing trend toward its liturgical use in several denominations.

**APOSTOLIC SUCCESSION,** a doctrine held by the Eastern, Roman Catholic, and Anglican churches concerning the origin, continuation, and authority of bishops and other ordained ministers. According to this belief, the apostles of Christ ordained the first bishops of the churches they founded in the Roman world and entrusted to them the rule and discipline of these churches, the guardianship of the faith as preached by the apostles, and the power to transmit this same governance and teaching to those whom they should ordain to follow them in office, in an unbroken succession until the end of the world. A valid ministry in the Church, therefore, can only be exercised by persons ordained by bishops in this succession. The doctrine was rejected by most Protestants at the Reformation, on the grounds that such a succession lacks sufficient historical evidence in the 1st-century Church, and that its necessity is not verifiable in Scripture.

The earliest affirmation of apostolic succession occurs in I Clement (c.95), a letter of the Roman Church to the Church in Corinth. Irenaeus, Bishop of Lyons (c.190), gave the doctrine its definitive formulation, as a counterattack of the Catholic Church against the claims of Gnostic heretics that their teachings descended by a "secret tradition" from the apostles. In Irenaeus, emphasis lay upon the bishop's authority, by virtue of his succession from the apostles, to witness to the true apostolic faith. Later, in the writings of St. Augustine (d.430)—after the Church had experienced schisms among bishops who held essentially the same faith—an added significance was given to the manner of episcopal ordination, and the transmission of sacerdotal and sacramental grace through the laying on of hands. Thus a bishop could claim a share in apostolic succession by virtue of a valid ordination, whether or not he ever exercised episcopal jurisdiction in the Church.

**ARCHBISHOP,** ecclesiastical title used by the Roman Catholic Church in its Latin and Oriental rites, by the Greek Orthodox churches, and by the Anglican Church. In some instances it signifies an administrative jurisdiction somewhat wider than that of a bishop, and in this sense the term "metropolitan" is often used as a synonym. This is especially true in the Greek Orthodox churches where, along with the national synod, the archbishop governs the national church. In the Roman Catholic and Anglican communities, archiepiscopal authority is considerably less. Here the title is sometimes honorary and personal. In strict usage, however, it does convey a distinct administrative jurisdiction, as defined in canon law. In the Anglican and Roman Catholic churches, an archbishop presides over an ecclesiastical province, and he exercises two sets of functions. Over his own archdiocese he enjoys all the ordinary authority of a bishop. In regard to the simple dioceses within his province, however, he exercises supervision over the bishops, who are known in Roman Catholic terminology as his suffragans. He has the right to summon them to a diocesan council, to insist on their residence within their diocese, and to compel them to provide for the education of their clergy.

Today archbishops do not impose sanctions against lax bishops, but they see to it that this is done by others. Among the prerogatives of an archbishop are taking precedence over bishops at public ceremonies, wearing the pallium, and having a cross carried immediately before him in processions. The historical origin of the office of archbishop is obscure, but it is generally agreed that it developed out of the special prerogatives that belonged to the ancient metropolitans. These were the bishops of the chief cities of the Roman civil provinces, whose pre-eminence was acknowledged in councils of the 4th century.

**ARCHDIOCESE,** ecclesiastical administrative unit directly under the jurisdiction of an archbishop. The archdiocese is a subdivision of an ecclesiastical province, which normally includes, in addition, a varying number of dioceses under their own bishops. It is located around the most important political or economic center, or simply the most populous city, within the province. Sometimes, as with Canterbury, the city's civil greatness has declined, but it remains an archdiocese because of tradition. In very unusual cases, the archdiocese is coterminous with the province, as with some small Italian archdioceses. Archdioceses are the present-day counterpart to the metropolitanates of Christian antiquity.

**ARIANISM,** early Christian heresy, propounded by Arius, which denied the full divinity of Christ and was condemned at the Council of Nicaea (325 A.D.). The Council of Nicaea was followed by a long period of confusion. Many, not prepared for the new definition of the Son as consubstantial (*homöousios*) with the Father, supported the Arians, who broke into several sections, some maintaining the extreme position of Arius, that Christ as the Son of God was not eternal but was created by the Father, others compromising between the extreme Arian position and the Nicene by declaring the Son to be "like the Father" (*homoios*), or even "like in substance" (*homoiousios*). Arian leaders, who were often willing to accept imperial domination of the Church, grew in favor during the last years of Constantine and the reign of Constantius (337–361). By 360 Constantius had expelled the non-Arian bishops, and the Arian Creed of the Council of Ariminum was the official faith of the empire. But when deprived of imperial support Arianism rapidly declined, and the effort of the eastern emperor Valens (365–378) to revive it was only partially successful. The victory of the Nicene party was recognized by Emperor Theodosius in 379 and sealed by the Council of Constantinople in 381. But Arianism survived as the faith of the Goths, to whom Bishop Ulfilas had taken it under Constantius, and of other Germanic invaders. Most of the Arian kingdoms fell in the mid-6th century; the Visigoths in Spain were united with the Catholic Church and accepted the Nicene Creed in 589; and the Lombards a few years later. Arianism was revived by some English theologians in the 17th and early 18th centuries as a step toward Unitarianism.

**ATONEMENT** [ə-ton'mənt], a cardinal doctrine of the Christian faith which concerns the means and conditions through which reconciliation of man to God is accomplished. At the time the Bible was translated into English, this word was pronounced at-one-ment, and referred to the restoration of the union lost through man's sin.

The need for such reconciliation is presupposed in the Old Testament conception of God's holiness and righteousness, before which nothing impure or sinful can be presented. Atonement occurs in the Old Testament through a sacrificial system in which uncleanness is purged by the shedding of blood. Some prophets insisted that without repentance and ethical responsibility, the offering of sacrifice for sins was futile. The church remembered Jesus after the pattern of Isaiah's concept of the suffering servant as one who gave himself for the sins of many.

In the history of Christian thought, several interpretations of the atonement came to be formulated. In general the Church fathers viewed the death of Christ as a ransom paid by God to the devil for the souls of fallen men. St. Anselm instead proposed that the death of Christ must be understood as a satisfaction paid not to the devil but to God for the sins of man which had offended God. Since the sins are infinite, the retribution can only be made by God himself. So God becomes man, in Jesus, in order to make a full satisfaction for human sin through his vicarious death. According to Abelard, the effectiveness of Christ's atonement comes essentially through its exemplary character, since it evokes in the believer a similar response of love.

**AUGSBURG CONFESSION,** the authoritative Lutheran statement of faith. It was first presented by the evangelical-Lutheran Estates of Germany to Emperor Charles V at the diet of Augsburg, on June 25, 1530. On convening the diet, Charles V had indicated his desire to effect a reconciliation between the Roman Catholic Church and the Lutherans and he, therefore, requested the latter to submit a defense of their cause.

Under the leadership of the Elector of Saxony, the Lutherans hoped at first to justify their demand for a reformation of the church by relying on several earlier statements of faith (The Articles of Visitation, 1527; the Schwabach Articles, 1529); but because of sharp attacks upon them by John Eck and other Roman Catholics, they found it necessary to prepare a new statement.

Outlawed by the Edict of Worms in 1521, Luther could not be present at Augsburg, so his friend and colleague Philip Melanchthon served as the theological spokesman of the Lutheran party. It was he who composed the new confession. Hoping for the restoration of religious peace, he was as conciliatory as possible, stating what he believed was the universal Christian faith and avoiding a repetition of Protestant criticisms of the Roman Catholic Church.

The Augsburg Confession consists of 28 articles, of which the first 21 deal with doctrines of faith, while the last seven defend the abolition of what the Lutherans regarded as Catholic abuses.

The Confession was rejected, on the basis of a *Confutation* written on Imperial command by Roman Catholic theologians. Melanchthon replied to these criticisms in a detailed defense of the Augsburg Confession. In this *Apology*, he dealt specifically with the chief Roman Catholic teachings. It, too, is one of the main credal statements of Lutheranism.

**BAPTISM,** application of water to a person as an initiatory rite of membership in the Christian Church. It is accounted a major sacrament, and is generally considered necessary to salvation. Its authority rests upon a command of the risen Christ (Matt. 28:19), and also upon Christ's example in receiving baptism from John the Baptist (Matt. 3:13–17). It developed from the ancient Jewish custom of baptizing Gentile converts.

The original mode of baptism was by immersion of the entire body in water, but a widely accepted method since the 2d century has been baptism by affusion. Before baptism a mature candidate must make a formal renunciation of his sins and a confession of his faith in Christ, and in administering the sacrament the minister pronounces over the candidate the name of the Trinity. In most churches the children of believing parents may be baptized in infancy; but since the Reformation, Protestant Christians of the Anabaptist tradition have rejected the baptism of infants as unwarranted by the teaching of the New Testament.

**BEATIFICATION** [bē-ăt-ə-fǐ-kā′shən], the name given in the Roman Catholic Church to an act or decree issued after a process of inquiry by which public religious veneration may be paid to some deceased person who testified to his faith by a martyr's death, or whose life manifested Christian virtue in a special or "heroic" way. The man or woman so honored is thereafter given the title "Blessed."

Beatification must be distinguished in Catholic writings from canonization. Beatification is a preparatory, or provisional, judgment, by which public veneration is permitted—usually in a very restricted area (as within a certain country, or a certain diocese, or to the houses of a religious order of which the person was a member). Canonization is a final decree, by which public veneration is prescribed throughout the whole Church. While the judgment affirmed in the decree of beatification is of its nature subject to revision, the judgment affirmed in the decree of canonization is irreversible and must be accepted by all members of the Church.

Originally, and up to the 11th century, the outcome of spontaneous popular veneration or of the actions of local bishops, beatification was gradually reserved to the popes, and is now decreed at the end of the elaborate procedure set down in the Code of Canon Law.

**BEATITUDES** [bē-ăt′ə-tūdz], **THE,** those sayings, pronouncing certain classes of people "blessed" or "happy," with which Jesus' Sermon on the Mount (q.v.) opens. In Matthew (5:3–10) there are eight beatitudes; in Luke (6:20–23) there are four, followed by four corresponding woes. The classes of people thus congratulated by Jesus in both accounts are the poor ("in spirit," says Matthew), the mourners, those who hunger ("for righteousness," says Matthew), and those who are persecuted for Christ's sake (or, adds Matthew, "for righteousness' sake"). To these Matthew's version adds the meek, the merciful, the pure in heart, and the peacemakers. Appropriate spiritual rewards are attached to each beatitude. The contrast with the reasons for which people normally receive the congratulations of their fellow men is impressive, but these beatitudes show who are promoted to high honor in the kingdom of God. Jesus pronounced other beatitudes, including a final one on those "that have not seen, and yet have believed" (John 20:29).

**BISHOP,** title bestowed in certain Christian churches on ecclesiastics who have special spiritual functions or who supervise church affairs. Derived from the Greek *episkopos* ("overseer"), the term originally designated those who exercised authority in the various early Christian communities. After the Reformation, the notion of the bishopric or episcopate held by the Protestants who retained the title (Lutherans, Methodists, and Moravians, for example) diverged from the "catholic" notion, held, with variations, by Roman Catholics, Orthodox and other churches of the Near East, and Anglicans (Episcopalians).

In general, the Protestant bishop possesses no special permanent priestly power or power of Orders (for confirming, ordaining priests, or consecrating other bishops) which sets him at the summit of a clerical group within the community. His teaching power is limited by principles of individual interpretations of the Scriptures, and his power of ruling and directing conceded by the community is limited largely to administrative functions and is subject to review according to the democratic structure of the churches themselves. In the "catholic" concept, the priestly powers, as well as the powers of teaching and ruling, belong to the bishops as successors of the Apostles, and thus derive immediately from the permanent institution of Christ.

**BREVIARY** [brē'vē-ĕr-ē, brĕv'ē-ĕr-ē], the liturgical book used in the singing or recitation of the Divine Office, the official prayer of the Roman Catholic Church offered by all who are in major orders (subdeacons or higher) and by members of most religious orders and congregations.

During the early Middle Ages, the Office was sung only in choir, and several books of readings and chants were used. By the 13th century, however, all clerics in major orders, even if unable to attend choir, had the duty of private recitation. Hence, there was need for a single book comprising all the necessary readings. Though the earliest examples date from the 10th century, the prototype of the modern Breviary was compiled at Rome at the beginning of the 13th century. The name, originally designating a single sheet of directions for the choral performance of a day's Office, was afterward applied to the book, which was to some extent an abbreviation of the choral Office.

In the course of the centuries, the Breviary has undergone several important revisions, notably those of 1535, 1568, 1913, and 1961. The latest Breviary is published in two volumes: one for winter and spring, the other for summer and autumn. In addition to the Psalms, each volume contains four main sections: the Bible passages for each day, the readings and prayers for each saint's day, and the "Common of the Saints." In this last section, the "Common of a Martyr," for example, contains the passages generally read on the feast of any martyr; and there is a similar common for confessors, virgins, widows, among others.

In its annual cycle, the Breviary focuses by turns on the various mysteries of the Christian year, beginning with Advent and Christmas. Simultaneously, the feasts of the saints are celebrated almost daily. Each day's Office is divided into eight parts or hours: matins, lauds, prime, terce, sext, nones, vespers, and compline.

**CANONIZATION,** a juridical process of the Roman Catholic Church whereby special honors are decreed to a deceased member of the Church by reason of holiness of life and the practice of heroic virtue. The decree of canonization declares the person to be a saint and to be worthy of veneration as a special friend of God whose intercession before the throne of God is efficacious in attaining divine assistance. The decree does not explicitly state that the canonized person is in heaven with God, but that the person practiced Christian living to an eminent degree.

There are three lengthy and formal stages through which the investigation must proceed, requiring sometimes as much as 50 years. When a petition for canonization is sent to the Congregation of Rites in Rome, a promoter of the cause, called the solicitor, is appointed to gather information regarding the character of the person in question, his reputation for holiness, and the miracles that have been worked through his intercession. The results of these investigations, together with a report on his writings, are sent to the tribunal of the Congregation of Rites. If the tribunal passes favorable judgment, then the person is raised to the rank of venerable servant of God and his cause proceeds to the next step in the process.

In this stage a more intensive investigation is made concerning his sanctity, the quality of his virtues, and the miracles worked by his intercession. Besides the promoter of the cause, there is the office of the promoter of the faith, the "Devil's Advocate," to find weaknesses in the case presented. If the judges of the tribunal decide that the objections of the promoter of the faith have been satisfactorily answered, then the Holy Father elevates the venerable servant of God to the ranks of the Blessed in a solemn ceremony at St. Peter's. This second step is known as beatification.

The process of canonization, the final step, consists of an investigation of the miracles worked in behalf of the intercession of the Blessed since his beatification. If the alleged miracles are proved to be genuine, then the Holy Father elevates the Blessed to the rank of the Saints and commands all Catholics to venerate him as such.

**CANON LAW** may be defined as a code or body of laws, established, proposed, or accepted by legitimate ecclesiastical authority. Here the term is restricted to the laws of the Roman Catholic Church. By this code of laws the duties of the members of the Church are defined, the Church herself is preserved and directed, and the members themselves are guided to their eternal salvation. The majority of the Church's laws emanate directly from her in virtue of God-given authority. Some laws, however, are of immediate divine origin. These are proposed as such by the Church and often fortified with an ecclesiastical penalty. Some civil laws have in time been accepted into Church law. This is called "canonization" of civil law. Moreover, in time some customs of peoples have been accepted and given the force of law.

Church law has been variously designated: Sacred or Ecclesiastical by reason of its authority, subject-matter, and final purpose; Pontifical to distinguish it from civil law. Ordinarily, however, Church law has been called "Canon Law." The word "canon" is of Greek origin and originally meant an architect's measuring rod; later the word was used to indicate a norm of religious action.

Since the councils of the Church of the 4th century the term "Canon Law" has been used to signify the complexity of Church law.

From apostolic times Popes and councils issued disciplinary decrees. In time private collections of these decrees abounded. In the 12th century a Camaldolese monk named Gratian collected the accumulated legislation into an unofficial work called *Decree of Gratian*. At pontifical request St. Raymond of Pennafort, O.P., issued the first official collection called *Decretals of Gregory IX* in the 13th century. In the 16th century John Chapuis made a further compilation called *Corpus Juris Canonici*. A new codification of Church law, started under Pope St. Pius X in 1904, was finished and promulgated on May 27, 1917, under the title *Code of Canon Law*.

The Code, which went into effect May 19, 1918, retains the previous legislation for the most part. The new compilation is divided into five books: General Norms; Laws for Persons; Legislation for Things, v.g. for Sacred Times and Places; Procedural Law; Ecclesiastical Penalties. The Code affects in general only Latin Catholics. Oriental Catholics follow their own law. A Code for the Oriental Church has been partially issued. A Code Commission has been established to decide doubtful points of Code law.

**CARDINAL,** the title given to a member of the senate of the Roman Pontiff. The task of a Cardinal is to advise the Pope and assist him in the work of administering the Roman Catholic Church. According to the new Code of Canon Law in 1917, Cardinals should be "remarkable for their doctrine, piety, and prudence in the handling of affairs."

No age limit is set by the Code, but minimum age for ordination to the priesthood is 24. For a bishop it is 30.

A Cardinal has many privileges: he may hear confessions or preach all over the world without further authorization. He may celebrate Mass wherever he pleases. For over 300 years Cardinals have had the title of "Eminence." The Congress of Vienna in 1815 recognized a Cardinal as having the rank of a royal prince.

**The College of Cardinals,** the senate of the Pope, was formed originally from the important clergy of Rome and its neighborhood. Hence, even today the rank of a Cardinal is in accord with the title to which he is elevated. The title of one of the small dioceses around Rome makes the elect a Cardinal-Bishop. The title of an important Roman Church makes him a Cardinal-Priest. The title of one of the seven ancient Roman districts makes him a Cardinal-Deacon. Actually, the vast majority of the College of Cardinals are bishops, and all, of course, are priests. The number of the College of Cardinals was limited to 70 by Sixtus V in 1586, but John XXIII raised this. Since the College of Cardinals is the Pope's senate, a number of Cardinals must live in Rome. But today the college has representatives serving as Archbishops of important sees on every continent and in most of the large, and many of the small, countries throughout the world.

The duty of the College of Cardinals is to assist the Pope in the administration of the Church. The Cardinals must meet with the Pope in secret, semipublic, or public consistory to give him their advice—advice the Pope is by no means obliged to follow. At one time the Consistory was more important, but today the Cardinals do a great deal of their administrative work in the Congregations. A Cardinal is at the head of every Congregation, most of the Offices, and two of the Courts of the Roman Curia.

When a Pope dies, the Cardinals direct the administration of the Church until a new Pope is elected; but their supervision is strictly limited by regulations established by St. Pius X and Pius XII. Then the Cardinals must perform perhaps their most important duty, that of electing the new Pope.

**CATECHISM** [kăt′ə-kĭz-əm] (from Gr. *Katēchein*, "to teach by word of mouth"), a manual of religious instruction usually in question and answer form. The first manual resembling a modern catechism was used by Alcuin (735–804), an English theologian and scholar, although catechetical writings go back to the early patristic age and were already well developed in the *Catecheses* of St. Cyril of Jerusalem (313–86). The content and format of the standard Catholic catechisms date from the Middle Ages, when special attention was paid to instructing young children in the rudiments of Christian doctrine.

During the Counter Reformation St. Peter Canisius (1521–97) wrote three catechisms for different age and maturity levels which became the norm for subsequent catechetical literature. By decree of the Council of Trent (1545–63), the Roman Catechism was published as a reference source for priests and teachers of religion.

In the United States, the Baltimore Catechism is the most authoritative. First issued in 1885 and often re-edited under the direction of the American Catholic hierarchy, it is now the basic compendium of doctrine for catechetical instruction.

The most famous Protestant catechisms were Luther's two, a larger one for adults and a smaller for children. In England a synod of Calvinist divines published the Westminster Catechism in 1647: the Longer Catechism, which is little used, and the famous Shorter Catechism, still used by Presbyterians and others in the Calvinist tradition.

**CATHEDRAL** [kə-thē′drəl], the principal church of a diocese where the Archbishop or Bishop has his headquarters. It is not size or architecture that makes a church a cathedral, but the fact that the throne of the Bishop is there. From the beginning the "pastor" of the cathedral was, by canon law, the Bishop who was aided by the cathedral canons in the administration of the ecclesiastical property and pastoral functions. As the diocese grew and the Bishop was forced to spend more time away from the cathedral residence on diocesan business, the local canons assumed more of the administration of the cathedral. Eventually the Bishop's residence became separated from the cathedral, and he came there only to officiate at the more solemn functions.

In the Anglican communion the chief official is the dean, who, together with the canons, constitutes the governing body of the cathedral. The dean is appointed by the Crown. The Bishop has no authority in his own cathedral, but is received there as a guest by the dean and canons, and may be invited to preach.

In the Roman Catholic Church the cathedral is administered by the rector and the clergy, all of whom are appointed by the Bishop of the diocese, except in places where cathedral chapters have been erected. The trustees and chief administrators of the diocese generally reside at the cathedral. In some dioceses the cathedral also serves as a parish church, ministering to the faithful who live in the neighborhood. This has been a secondary function since the 12th century, when local parishes branched off from the cathedral, and ecclesiastical government became more complex.

While the more important aspect of the cathedral has been its connection with church administration, it is the architectural splendor of cathedrals that has made them the object of popular interest.

### Architecture

Writings of the early Church Fathers and other documents prove that hundreds, even thousands, of churches had arisen throughout the pagan world before the time of Constantine. One of the finest, the Cathedral of Tyre, erected shortly after 300, but now entirely lost, is described as a magnificent basilica, a type of church already hallowed by long tradition. In plan, the typical early basilican cathedral was an oblong rectangular structure, its entrance to the west, its sanctuary opposite and to the east, so that the officiating priest, standing before the altar with his back toward the congregation, might face in the direction of Jerusalem. This traditional east-west orientation is followed in almost all cathedrals.

The basilica was fronted on its narrower, western end by a cloistered court (atrium), at whose open center often stood a fountain for ceremonial ablutions. The eastern arcade of this court, which actually adjoined the church, was incorporated in the latter's façade to serve as a vestibule (narthex), from which opened three or more doors to the interior. The body of the basilica was divided by ranges of columns into a long central area, called the nave, and two (sometimes four) flanking aisles. Above the inner ranges of columns, which bordered the nave to left and right, walls were raised, each pierced by a row of lofty windows, to form a clerestory. The windows, overlooking the sloping roofs of the aisles, gave light and air to the nave. The aisles, lighted by windows in the outer walls of the church, were roofed in wood, which was also used for the high, double-pitched roof of the central nave.

Across the eastern, or upper, end of the nave, and at right angles to it, extended the transept, which rose as high as the nave and was lighted by the clerestory. The area where nave and transept intersect is called the crossing. From the eastern wall beyond the crossing projected the sanctuary apse, normally semicircular in plan. The floor area within and in front of the apse was generally raised three or more steps to form the bema, a broad platform divided from the transept by the chancel rail. At

A. Devaney

St. Patrick's cathedral in New York City is a foremost example of the Gothic church architecture which was prevalent in the United States during the 19th century.

the middle of the bema stood the altar, its religious and artistic significance enhanced by a graceful architectural canopy (ciborium, or baldachin).

Unlike the pagan temple, whose exterior was richly adorned with marble columns and sculpture, the outside of the early cathedral was left plain and bare. Its interior, however, gleamed with costly marbles, a gilded ceiling, and colorful mosaics, where, on a background of deep and flashing blue, appeared the august form of Christ enthroned, surrounded by His apostles.

Constantine's most famous church, Old St. Peter's (4th century), built on the scheme just described, established the basilica as the basic form of cathedral design. It should be mentioned that the Pope's title of Bishop of Rome derives from the Church of St. John Lateran, and that St. Peter's is not technically a cathedral; it is, however, generally considered the "Papal cathedral." Later modifications of church architecture, such as a wider lateral extension of the transepts and the introduction of a choir extending eastward from crossing to sanctuary, gave to the over-all plan the shape of a Latin cross. This scheme

*Silberstein—Monkmeyer*

Salisbury Cathedral, England, on the Avon River. The main structure was built during the 13th century. The spire, the highest in England, was added in the 14th century.

Construction of the New Coventry Cathedral, England, was completed in 1962. It was built on the site of the old cathedral which was almost completely destroyed by bombs in World War II. Remains of part of the old cathedral can be seen to the rear.

The word cathedral stems from the Greek *cathedra*, meaning a seat or throne. Thus, it is the presence of the throne of a bishop that distinguishes a cathedral from a church.

*Camera Press—Pix*

*Max Tatch—Black Star*

*French Embassy Press and Information Division*

The Cathedral of Notre Dame, Amiens, France. It was begun in 1220; the spire is 16th century.

Santa Maria del Fiore, Florence, Italy, was begun in 1296 and completed in 1461.

has since generally prevailed, not only in medieval but also in modern cathedrals.

### Role of the Cathedral

Throughout the Middle Ages and Renaissance, and even, occasionally, in modern times, cathedrals have played a leading role in the life of city and nation, their creation engaging the devoted efforts of hundreds of artists and builders, their construction usually going forward from generation to generation. In ages when books were rare, and few could read, they served, moreover, as an important medium of religious and popular education, taking the place of such modern institutions as schools, libraries, museums, and concert halls.

Rich mosaics in the Constantinian and Byzantine eras, frescoes and sculpture in those of Romanesque date, sculpture and stained-glass in the Gothic period, and again frescoes and sculpture during the Renaissance, gave vivid and often beautiful visual form to Bible stories. The depicted scenes and incidents were used, not for mere decoration, but rather for their inspirational and didactic impact. They range from the creation and fall of man, and his instruction by the early Hebrew prophets, to his redemption through the life, teachings, crucifixion, and resurrection of Christ, and they conclude with the Last Judgment, its terrors and rewards as foretold in the Book of Revelation.

The pictorial rendering of this rich and varied lore is always simple and direct, beautifully adapted to instruct and inspire a largely illiterate people. Its climax came in the great cathedrals of Romanesque and Gothic Europe, where, to scenes of the lives and martyrdom of countless saints and prophets, was added, symbolically, the teaching of Christian morals. Thus were inculcated the Seven Virtues, the four called cardinal (prudence, fortitude, temperance, and justice), the three called theological (faith, hope, and charity). Each was opposed by its corresponding vice—the cardinal virtues by folly, cowardice, intemperance, and injustice; the theological by idolatry, despair, and avarice. For warning and encouragement, the moral is pointed in every case, often by crude and realistic representations of the rewards or punishments to be expected for the particular virtue or vice.

Likewise summarized in these great cathedrals were all the energies of mankind, symbolically represented through the Seven Liberal Arts and the Sciences, and in a fascinating sort of calendar, the so-called Labors of the Months, each of which is grouped under its appropriate Zodiac emblem. Magnificent series of the Arts and Sciences, the Labors and Zodiac, plus graphic scenes from the lives of patriarchs, apostles, saints, and martyrs, are beautifully carved on many European cathedrals, particularly on the façade of Amiens and about the portals of Chartres and Reims, all in France.

By its mass and its lofty dome or towers, the cathedral was generally the most conspicuous landmark of its city. Usually it was situated on a commanding site, rising centrally from a cluster of lower secular structures. Almost invariably it served as a vital center, not only for the religious, intellectual, and artistic life of the diocese, but also for political activities of urban and even national scope. The Cathedral of Hagia Sophia in Constantinople (Istanbul), the imperial church of the Byzantine Emperors, was thus often the scene of decisive events in Byzantine history. The original St. Peter's in Rome witnessed the coronation of Charlemagne (800) as Emperor of the Holy Roman Empire. The Gothic Cathedral of Reims (begun 1211), the traditional coronation church of France, saw its most stirring and memorable ceremony in July, 1429, when Charles VII was crowned King in the presence of Joan of Arc, who, by her inspired leadership of his troops against the English invaders, had made the coronation possible. The Cathedral of the Annunciation (1484–89), which stands in the Kremlin in Moscow, served for centuries as the coronation church of the Russian Tsars. And on Dec. 2, 1804, in the famous Notre Dame of Paris, Napoleon took the imperial crown from the hands of Pope Pius VII, and set it on his own head.

Since almost every cathedral, beginning with the open atrium before Old St. Peter's, was fronted on the west by a parvis, or broad plaza, the latter became the preferred assembly area for all sorts of popular activities. These ranged from weekly markets, gay patriotic celebrations, and solemn religious pageants, to annual fairs, political rallies, horse races, public executions, and still more turbulent demonstrations. These sometimes culminated in wild riots, bringing indiscriminate slaughter, and destructive attacks on the cathedral itself. During the French Revolution (1789–99), the downtrodden people of France turned their wrath against the cathedral—too often identified in their minds with a rich and aristocratic Bishop. Many cathedrals throughout the land were burned and pillaged. Their priceless stained-glass windows were shattered, their statues thrown down and smashed, their delicate relief sculptures scarred and battered. Worst sufferers in this holocaust were Notre Dame in Paris and the cathedrals of Reims and Amiens.

### Notable Cathedrals

Since cathedral architecture involves the architectural history of all Christian lands for a span of 16 centuries and comprises thousands of monuments in a bewildering variety of styles, the discussion that follows is necessarily highly selective, intended merely to indicate a few of the most important and interesting cathedrals.

From among the earliest mentioned above, Hagia Sophia, at İstanbul, still ranks as a supreme masterpiece of world architecture. Built 532–37 for the Byzantine Emperor Justinian, its spacious nave is covered by a lofty dome 184 ft. high, the massive vaults of its aisles and galleries rest upon giant columns of green marble and purple porphyry, and all interior surfaces are sheathed with colored marbles and flashing gold mosaic. Almost equally famous and resplendent, St. Mark's in Venice, the main structure of which was rebuilt (1042–71) in a later Byzantine mode, has one dome over the crossing and four others grouped about it. After the year 1000 had safely passed—feared by many as destined to bring the end of the world—the great age of cathedrals began with massive Romanesque churches, such as those in Mainz, Germany (rebuilding begun 1036), Pisa, Italy (11th century) and its famous Leaning Tower, and Périgueux, France (1047–1120), which was modeled on St. Mark's, but built of stone instead of brick.

With the rise of the Gothic style, based on the pointed

arch and a daring new system of ribbed-vault construction, the climax was reached in France. There, surpassing Chartres, Amiens, and Reims in height, the vaults of Beauvais (13th–16th centuries) attained a height of 158 ft., as yet unequaled in any later cathedral. Although English Gothic derived from France, appearing first in the choir of Canterbury, whose present structure dates from the 11th to 16th centuries, the style evolved independently and produced distinctive national features: notably, two successive transepts and choirs, the easternmost terminating in a rectangular sanctuary, as, for example, in the cathedrals of Lincoln (rebuilt late 11th–13th centuries) and Salisbury (1220–66). Both the Germanic Cologne (begun 1248) and Spanish León (13th century) cathedrals were inspired by Amiens. But the huge Milan structure (begun 1385), the second-largest medieval cathedral, is as typically Italian with its massive marble walls as is that of Florence (1296–1461) with its towering dome.

Although fewer cathedrals arose in the Renaissance, and fewer still in modern times, St. Peter's in Rome surpasses all others in size and magnificence. Begun before 1500 on the site of the old Constantinian basilica, it grew slowly, until Michelangelo marked it with his powerful genius during the middle years of the century, when he designed its tremendous dome (404 ft. high, with a 137-ft. interior diameter). Other famous Renaissance cathedrals are St. Paul's, in London, built 1675–1710 by Sir Christopher Wren; those of Granada (16th century) and Valladolid (begun 1585) in Spain, and a few, on Spanish models, in Latin America. The earliest cathedrals in the United States are those of New Orleans (finished 1794) and Baltimore (1805–21). St. Patrick's, built 1858–79 in New York City, is the largest Roman Catholic church in the country. It follows a modified Gothic style, as do two Episcopal cathedrals, New York's St. John the Divine, begun 1892 and still unfinished, and St. Peter and St. Paul, in Washington, D.C., which is also incomplete. During World War II the 14th-century Gothic cathedral of Coventry, England, was almost totally destroyed by bombing. A new cathedral, built in a modern architectural style and physically linked to the old tower and chapter house, was consecrated in 1962.

**CHURCH,** term derived from the German *Kirche* and ultimately from the Greek *kyriakon*, "something belonging to the Lord." Scriptural equivalents in the Old Testament are *qahal*, "the entire religious community of the people of Israel," and *edah*, "a congregation of believers." Greek synonyms for these terms in the Septuagint are *ekklesia* and *synagoge*, respectively. In the New Testament the first means the assembly of people called together by God, as illustrated in the text of St. Matthew's Gospel (16:18), where Christ promised Peter that "on this rock I will build my Church (*ekklesia*)." Christian tradition has since canonized the terminology by reserving *ekklesia* for the society of Christ's followers and *synagoge* for the gathering of the Jews.

In Catholic theology, the classic definition of the Church is that of St. Robert Bellarmine (1542–1621). "The one and true Church," he said, "is the assembly of men, bound together by the profession of the same Christian faith, and by the communion of the same sacraments, under the rule of legitimate pastors, and in particular of the one Vicar of Christ on earth, the Roman Pontiff."

The Eastern Orthodox Church redefines the Church by excluding submission to Roman authority as necessary for actual membership in the Christian communion. In general, Protestants agree that the Papal primacy is not essential, but beyond that they hold various different opinions about the nature of the Church. Some hold that the Church is essentially visible and should be one throughout the world, but that the corruptions which entered Christianity allow a breach in this visible unity and the secession of national churches, as in England. Others say that the Church is substantially invisible, that membership arises from faith and justification (Luther) or from predestination to glory (Calvin), but that according to needs and circumstances, visible unity is desirable and should be striven for on the local, national, and even world scale. This view gives impetus to national churches and those in the Free Church tradition. A few, like the Quakers, are willing to dispense with marks of external unity in favor of fidelity to the Inner Light which illumines each person individually.

Pope Pius XII, in the middle of the 20th century, defined the Church on earth as the Mystical Body of Christ, according to the teaching of St. Paul that the faithful followers of Christ are joined together in a mysterious union, of which Christ Himself is the invisible Head and His indwelling Spirit is the animating principle.

**CLERGY** [*klûr'jē*], term generally applied to ministers of religion, be they Christian or otherwise. The word "clergy" is derived from "cleric," which meant a person who was admitted to the ranks of the ecclesiastical hierarchy of the early Christian Church. This hierarchy consisted of eight grades of ascending order. The first four, called minor orders, consisted of lector, or reader; porter, or doorkeeper; exorcist, or expeller of demons; and acolyte, or altar-server. The second group, major orders, consisted of subdeacon, deacon, priest, and bishop. Minor orders were preceded by a rite called tonsure in which a circular area of hair was removed from the head to indicate that the candidate was casting his lot with the Lord. Anyone receiving the tonsure was considered a cleric. The clerical state was considered a state apart from the laity and was granted special privileges, consisting mainly in exemption from public burdens, both as to person and possessions, and in immunity from lay jurisdiction in both civil and criminal matters.

Today the minor orders, subdiaconate, and diaconate are preparatory stages to the priesthood, and are not to be considered permanent states; but in the early Church this was not so. Division of the clergy was not an arbitrary one, but was based on the growing needs of the young Christian community in administrative and liturgical areas. The origin of grades goes back to apostolic times, when the Apostles (Acts 6), overburdened with the complex duties of the ministry, appointed seven deacons, among whom was St. Stephen, to assist them in ecclesiastical functions. It was the function of the minor clergy to instruct the faithful, to assist at liturgical services, and to take care of such duties as the maintenance of churches and cemeteries. With the passing of time many of these duties were absorbed by the clergy in higher orders, and chanting and serving at the altar was done by the laity. Since the 16th century the function of the minor clergy has been very limited, but in the Roman Catholic Church one must pass through the lower orders before being ordained to the priesthood.

The chief duty of the priest is to assist the bishop in the apostolic mission of the Church. Only a priest can offer the holy sacrifice of the Mass, forgive sins, distribute holy communion, and baptize, though exceptions are admitted in the latter two. Thus it is the priestly office to make available to the faithful the sacramental graces of the Church. To the bishop, the successor of the Apostles, belongs the full priestly power of Christ. Besides the powers of the priesthood, the bishop also has the power to ordain other bishops and priests and administer the sacrament of confirmation. Thus, anyone who has received the tonsure, or belongs to any of the above grades, is accounted in the ranks of the clergy. However, by extension, the term is also employed in canon law for all to whom clerical privileges have been extended, such as members of religious orders: monks and nuns, and even lay brothers and novices. In England the term "clergyman" is still mainly restricted to the clergy of the Established Church.

**CONCORDAT** [kŏn-kôr′dăt], an agreement between the Pope as head of the Roman Catholic Church and any state or ruler. Concordats have the nature of treaties, in that the parties act as sovereigns dealing with their respective interests. Roman canonists disagree in regarding them either as true treaties or as mere concessions granted by the Pope. The subject of a concordat is the condition of the Church within a particular state. Such items as selection of Bishops, ecclesiastical funds and property, religious orders or associations, and general religious liberty are usually treated. About 170 concordats have been concluded since the 11th century.

**CONFESSION, AURICULAR** (Lat. *auricula*, the external ear), the private acknowledgment of sins to a priest in the Sacrament of Penance. In the early Christian Church, sinners were frequently held to public confession and to public penance by the Bishop and his council. Public confession usually took place on Ash Wednesday; public reconciliations on Holy Thursday. In the 5th century, however, Pope St. Leo the Great, approving continuation of private or auricular confession, condemned public confession. In 1215 the Fourth Lateran Council imposed upon Roman Catholics the duty of private confession at least once a year after reaching the age of reason.

In private confession, the penitent normally confesses his sins to a priest seated behind a screen in the confessional. Judging the gravity of the sins, the priest prescribes penance or restitution, and then in the name of the Trinity gives absolution. In the Latin Church the words of absolution are: "I absolve you from your sins in the name of the Father and of the Son and of the Holy Spirit. Amen." In order to receive this absolution, the penitent must be willing to do penance, be sorry for his sins as offenses against God, and be resolute against repeating them. Bound by the seal of confession, the priest, even if threatened with death, may never reveal the identity or the sins of the penitent.

Auricular confession is required only when it is possible. Persons too weak to confess are bound to confess serious sins committed since their last confession only when they have sufficiently recovered. When a priest is not available (as in an accident or during a battle), willingness to confess, together with sorrow for sin out of love of God, is considered sufficient for the forgiveness of sin. Forgotten sins are forgiven when other sins are acknowledged.

**CONFIRMATION,** initiatory rite in many Christian churches. It consists of a minister laying his hands on the head of a candidate, with prayer for the bestowal of the Holy Spirit, following the example of the apostles in the Book of Acts. In the ancient Church, it was normally administered by a Bishop immediately following baptism, and was associated with the anointing of the candidate with a blessed oil called chrism. In the Eastern churches, baptism and confirmation are still combined in a single rite, which may be performed by a priest, provided he use chrism blessed by a Bishop.

In the medieval Western Church confirmation became detached from baptism and was defined by Scholastic theologians as a distinct sacrament, its ministration normally reserved to a Bishop. At the Reformation, both Lutherans and Anglicans continued the custom, and made it a prerequisite for admission to Holy Communion. Only Bishops administer confirmation in Anglican and in Roman Catholic churches; but in Lutheran churches pastors may do so.

**CONSUBSTANTIATION** [kŏn-səb-stăn-shē-ā′shən], Lutheran doctrine concerning the relation of the body of Christ to the elements of bread and wine in the Communion service. Luther rejected the Roman Catholic view of Transubstantiation—according to which the substances of bread and wine at consecration pass into the substances of the body and blood of Christ, only the sensible properties, or "accidents," of the former remaining. In the Lutheran view, both the body of Christ and the elements exist together in the Sacrament. One analogy is the way in which both iron and fire remain when a poker is heated red hot. Another is the existence of the divine and human natures in Christ.

**CONVENT** [kŏn′vənt] (Lat. *convenire*, to come together), term originally applied to the residence of any group of religious—male or female—living the religious life according to a Rule. It had the same signification as the term "monastery," but is preferable to "monastery" to signify community life rather than the eremetical, which is implied in "monastery." Through popular but erroneous usage "convent" has become restricted to the residence of female religious and thereby synonymous with nunnery. Through a further popular restriction it is applied to the schools exclusively for girls which have been associated with convents from earliest times. The centuries-old policy of educating girls separately from boys, with the girls taught by female religious, has a history as old as the various orders of nuns dedicated to such work.

**COUNCILS, ECCLESIASTICAL,** church councils, whose prototype is the meeting of "the apostles and elders" at Jerusalem to settle the relation of Gentile converts to the Law of Moses (Acts 15:23). Councils of Bishops appear in the late 2d century, when a number were held to discuss the Easter Controversy and Montanism, and by 250 the council was a regular institution in areas where the episcopate was numerous. Such councils included the councils of Africa held under Cyprian, the councils of the Eastern Church at Antioch dealing with the heresy of Paul of Samosata, and the councils concerned with the problems produced by the aftermath of persecution. In order to guide his Church policy, Constantine as patron of the Church summoned the Western Council of Arles (314) and the first ecumenical council at Nicaea (325).

In the following centuries the church normally acted through provincial, plenary (from a group of provinces), and ecumenical (universal) councils. Their importance declined somewhat with the rise of the personal jurisdiction of the Patriarchs in the East and the Popes in the West. However, in early medieval Europe councils functioned as national legislative bodies for the Gallican, Spanish, and Anglo-Saxon churches. The proper members of councils are Bishops, but in this period it is often hard to distinguish between church councils with lay advisers and royal councils with ecclesiastical members.

Since the 11th century Roman canon law has held that provincial councils require papal approval, and that only the Pope can call plenary and ecumenical councils. However, the papal schism of 1378 was resolved by the irregularly summoned councils of Pisa (1409) and Constance (1414–17). Thereafter reformers often appealed to councils as the supreme authority in the Church until papal authority over Catholic councils was restored at the Council of Trent (1545–63). Since then Roman Catholic councils have met mainly to apply the decrees of Trent to local conditions or to organize new jurisdictions, for example, the 19th-century councils of Westminster for England and Baltimore for the United States. In the Church of England the convocations of Canterbury and York are derived from the medieval provincial councils.

**COUNCILS, ECUMENICAL,** Church councils which, either at the time or by subsequent recognition, have spoken for the whole Church. In Catholic theology their doctrinal

decisions are of infallible authority. The first four were the councils of Nicaea, Constantinople, Ephesus, and Chalcedon, which dealt with the Christological problems involved in the doctrine of the Incarnation. The fifth and sixth, Constantinople II (553) and III (680–81), further defined the theology of Chalcedon; the seventh, Nicaea II (787), upheld the use of images in divine worship in opposition to the iconoclasts. These seven are recognized by the Eastern Orthodox Church. The Roman Catholic Church acknowledges thirteen more: a number of medieval councils, mainly concerned with matters of discipline, and the modern councils of Trent (1545–63) and the Vatican (1869–70). In 1962 Pope John XXIII called the Second Vatican Council.

**COUNTER REFORMATION,** reform movement within the Roman Catholic Church during the 16th century, and the political action it engendered among some of the Catholic princes. The three sources of the Counter Reformation were (1) the Oratory of Divine Love, an informal sodality of pious, sincere Roman churchmen, founded in 1516; (2) the vigorous Spanish Church, which contributed many leading figures; and (3) the educational program of Christian humanism.

Pope Hadrian VI's brief reign (1522–23) witnessed the first serious but abortive efforts to reform the Papacy; under Paul III the task was taken up anew. In 1535 he appointed a commission of nine Cardinals, including Contarini, Sadoleto, and Caraffa, to study the situation. Their report, the *Consilium . . . de emendanda ecclesia* (*Advice on Reforming the Church*), contained a severe indictment of the Papacy and a constructive program— which Paul III began hesitatingly to apply—aimed at eliminating the administrative anarchy which had brought the Church to the brink of disaster. In 1542 Paul III organized the Roman Inquisition which, along with Paul IV's *Index of Forbidden Books* in 1559, slowed the spread of heresy in Italy. Subsequent Popes repressed luxury and extravagance, improved the personnel of the Curia, and brought back genuine spirituality to their office. Revisions of the Breviary, Missal, and Vulgate were prepared. Gregory XIII (1572–85) encouraged the founding of numerous seminaries. Outside Rome, Bishops such as Giborti of Verona, Borromeo of Milan, Du Prat of Clermont, and Hosius of Ermland (Poland), reformed their dioceses and were widely imitated.

Doctrinally, the Council of Trent (1545–63) marked the greatest work of the Counter Reformation. It clarified the Catholic position on all major points, so that thereafter the line was sharply drawn between Catholic and Protestant doctrine. The *Tridentine Catechism* brought its work to the level of the people, and ended the conciliatory efforts of Catholics such as Contarini, who had sought to reunite all Christians through colloquies and compromises. The disciplinary decrees of Trent, especially those on clerical education, put the Reform on an enduring basis.

New religious orders—Jesuits, Theatines, Barnabites, Oratorians, Somaschi, and Ursulines—and reformed branches of the older orders disseminated the Catholic revival. The Jesuits were particularly active and successful; their members ranged over the entire European continent, becoming especially influential through their numerous schools and their association with the ruling classes. The Capuchins were not far behind. These orders' zealous missionary enterprises in South America, India, Japan, and the Philippines also manifested the Counter Reformation on a world-wide scale.

A vast new literature of Catholic mysticism and devotion was produced by Teresa of Ávila, John of the Cross, Ignatius Loyola, Robert Parsons, Francis de Sales, Pierre de Bérulle, and others. In painting and sculpture, the Counter Reformation emphasized chaste, dignified subjects and treatment, combining didactic and inspirational purposes—exemplified by the works of Murillo, the four Carracci, and Callot. The Jesuit church of the Gesù in Rome established new architectural principles that later developed into the Baroque. Palestrina rejuvenated Church music, and the Oratorio appeared as an art form.

In the areas where religion and politics met, Philip II of Spain appeared the foremost champion of the Counter Reformation, since its cause coincided with his own political goals. His unsuccessful Armada, following Pius V's excommunication of Elizabeth and the execution of Mary Stuart, ruined the Catholic cause in England. He checked Protestantism in his Belgian lands, but not among the Dutch. The Spanish-Italian fleet inflicted a mortal defeat on the Turks at Lepanto in 1571. In France, the religious wars ended with a Catholic victory, although Henry IV tolerated the Huguenots (Edict of Nantes, 1598). Many portions of Switzerland and Germany returned to Catholicism, but Scandinavia remained Lutheran. Protestantism's progress in Austria, Hungary, and Poland was checked, largely through Jesuit efforts. By the Union of Brest-Litovsk, 1596, the Orthodox Ruthenians of Poland and Lithuania rejoined Rome and were allowed to retain their own rite.

**DEACON** (Gr. *diakonos*, "servant"), rank in the Christian ministry below that of presbyter or priest. Traditionally the office goes back to the ordination by the apostles of seven men in the Jerusalem Church to minister to the poor (Acts 6:1–6), principal among whom were Stephen and Philip. In the Roman Catholic, Eastern Orthodox, and Anglican churches the diaconate is the first of the holy orders, and in certain Protestant churches deacons are lay officers who help especially with finances and benevolences. In 1964–65, Vatican Council II voted to restore the permanent diaconate, whereby married men of mature age may be ordained and perform many of the functions of a priest.

**DIOCESE** [dī′ə-sēs] (Gr. *dioikesis*, "administrative district"), an ecclesiastical territory under a Bishop's jurisdiction. In the Eastern Roman Empire a diocese was a district subject to a city. Under Diocletian (reigned 284–305) the Empire was divided into four prefectures, which were subdivided into dioceses. In the 4th century the word was applied to the area within a Bishop's or Patri-

arch's jurisdiction. By the 5th century the territorial limits of dioceses conformed to the civil divisions of large towns and population centers. New ecclesiastical dioceses were often formed independent of papal authority. But since the 10th to 11th centuries the Roman Catholic Church has considered the creation of new dioceses a papal prerogative, and details of this work are handled by special congregations of the Roman Curia. Once established, the diocese is governed by the Bishop through his vicar-general, chancellor, synod, and cathedral chapter (or clerical consultors in the United States).

In churches of the Anglican Communion new dioceses are organized by the local clergy and laity, and are governed by the Bishop and diocesan convention of clerical and lay delegates. Ordinarily the diocese is named after the principal city or state of the area.

In Eastern Churches not affiliated with Rome the formation of dioceses belongs to the Patriarch and Archbishop, who appoint the Bishop and vicar-general.

**DISPENSATION** (Lat. *dispensatio*, "management"), in theology, a divinely appointed order or period of time in which men are considered subject to a specific revelation of God's will, as the Jewish Dispensation and the Christian Dispensation.

In the Roman Catholic Church, dispensation is an act of competent ecclesiastical authority by which a church law is suspended, relaxed, or deprived of its penal effect in a special case. Dispensation from laws, even of general councils, was granted by early Christian Bishops; but since Innocent III (d.1216) the Roman Catholic Church has claimed this power for the Pope alone. The power to dispense from certain ecclesiastical laws is delegated by the Pope or is possessed by Bishops and pastors by reason of their office. However, some ecclesiastical laws, such as the celibacy of the Western clergy and certain matrimonial impediments are rarely, if ever, dispensed. The Pope has no authority to dispense from provisions of the divine law, but he can dispense from a personal obligation to God incurred by an individual of his own free will, as in an oath.

In 1534 Henry VIII declared the Church of England independent of this papal jurisdiction. And so in the Anglican Communion all dispensing power belongs to the Bishop.

Among the Jews a dispensation is called "giving a *heter*" ("permission") to certain laws arising from custom or rabbinic precept.

**EASTER, or PASCHAL, CONTROVERSY,** argument in the early church as to whether the feast of redemption should be celebrated at the Jewish Passover (Gr. and Lat. *pascha*) or on the Sunday following, as the day of the Resurrection. By 180 A.D. the latter custom prevailed generally, but the churches of Asia Minor retained the Jewish date, the 14th of the lunar month, hence they were called Quartodecimans ("fourteeners"). Even at Rome, parishes of Asian Christians observed their own custom until Pope Victor I (189–198) demanded uniformity and threatened to excommunicate the churches of Asia. A number of councils supported the Roman custom, but Irenaeus and others urged Victor to take a more moderate course.

By 325 the Quartodeciman custom was extinct among orthodox Christians, and the Council of Nicaea fixed the rule still followed for the date of Easter: the Sunday after the first full moon of spring. Later controversies relate to details of calculation. In the early Middle Ages the Celtic churches used an older system, superseded elsewhere; and in modern times the Eastern churches retain the Julian calendar, which in the 20th century is 13 days behind, putting the first day of spring on Apr. 3 instead of Mar. 21.

**EASTERN ORTHODOX LITURGY,** central service of the Eastern rite, also called the Divine Liturgy, or Holy Eucharist (Thanksgiving). The term may apply generally to all church services. Divine liturgy commemorates the Last Supper and presents the life of Christ. Communion is in both bread and wine, for both priests and laymen, who also participate actively in the service.

The four liturgies in the Eastern Church are: the liturgy of St. John Chrysostom, the usual liturgy of the Eastern Church; the liturgy of St. Basil, used 10 times a year; the liturgy of the Presanctified Gifts, celebrated during Lent and the first three days of Holy Week; and the liturgy of St. James, used very rarely. The major parts of the liturgies of St. John Chrysostom and St. Basil are the preparation of the bread and wine, liturgy of the catechumens (learners), and liturgy of the faithful.

**EPISCOPATE** [ĭ-pĭs′kə-pĭt], **THE,** name for the office of Bishop in the Christian Church. In the New Testament the word Bishop (Gr. *episcopos*) means "overseer" and is used as equal to the word "presbyter." But within a very short time in Asia Minor, and probably elsewhere, the name became attached to the president of the council of presbyters who governed each local church. As the original apostles died, their function of witnessing to the events of the Gospel passed into the New Testament as its canon was formed. But confronted by controversies, the leaders of the churches attributed a unique importance to the Bishop as the guarantor of the authentic Gospel in his church, and finally, by 200 A.D., as the inheritor of apostolic authority. Ignatius of Antioch, soon after 100 A.D., shows the unique status of the Bishop in Asia Minor as the center of unity; Irenaeus of Lyons, around 180 A.D., writes of "apostolic succession" in the great Christian sees as the guarantee of truth and continuity; and Cyprian of Carthage, who died in 258, uses the words "bishop" and "apostle" as interchangeable.

Cyprian laid down the classic statement of the episcopal theory of the government of the Church by councils of Bishops. After the conversion of Constantine in 313 and the end of persecution, it became possible to hold councils

representative of the Church in the whole Roman Empire, and from the Council of Nicaea (325) onward, the council became the normal instrument of church government. Others besides Bishops were permitted to be present (presbyters, deacons, lay nobles) but essentially the councils were meetings of Bishops, each representative of his own see. Certain councils achieved, in subsequent thought, the special status of ecumenical. The Eastern Orthodox Church, which has maintained government by episcopal councils, recognizes seven ecumenical councils before the breach with the West. The Roman Catholic Church, disregarding the absence of the Eastern Orthodox, and later of Protestants, recognizes 21 ecumenical councils, the last two of which were held at the Vatican (1869–1870 and 1962–1965).

Among Protestants, certain churches at the Reformation retained the episcopal form of church government, but under the Catholic order a Bishop was brought into the succession by being consecrated by other Bishops, and this practice survived only in the churches of England and Sweden and, until 1884, Finland. In these churches and in the Roman Catholic and Eastern Orthodox churches the Bishop alone has the power to ordain priests and deacons, and in England and in the Roman Catholic Church the power of confirmation is restricted to him. In the Roman church the power of the Bishop has been effectively diminished, partly by the growth of papal jurisdiction and partly by the existence of exempt bodies within his diocese. In England the Bishop's prestige is very great, but his effective power is closely limited by the independent status of his clergy and by the nature of the legal establishment. The office is much valued in the Church of England, however, especially as a sign of Christian continuity through the centuries.

**EUCHARIST** [ū′kə-rĭst], one of the two principal sacramental rites of the Christian churches, the other being baptism. The term is Greek, meaning "thanksgiving," and was used by the early Christians. Eastern Orthodox Christians refer to it as the Divine Liturgy. Among Roman Catholics it is generally called the Mass or Blessed Sacrament; among Protestants, the Lord's Supper or Holy Communion. Participation in the rite has, from the beginning of Christianity, been confined solely to baptized members of the church; and exclusion from the Eucharist, called excommunication, is the severest discipline with which the church may punish offending members.

The institution of this rite by Jesus Christ at the Last Supper with His disciples, on the night before His Crucifixion, is recounted in the Gospels and by St. Paul in I Corinthians 11:23–26. Because of the variant chronologies of the Gospels, it is disputed whether the Last Supper was a Jewish Passover meal or not. But the distinctive elements of the Christian rite, as defined by the words and actions of Christ, consist of bread and a cup of wine, which are blessed by a prayer of thanksgiving, then shared in common as sacred food and drink by all the disciples present. In ministering the blessed bread and wine, Christ identified them with His Body a •d Blood which were broken and shed upon the Cross for th salvation of mankind. And in and through these elements He promised to be present with those who believe in Him and renew this act "in remembrance" of Him as an earnest of fellowship with Him in the Kingdom of God. It is part of the New Testament witness to the Resurrection that the risen Christ made Himself known to the disciples in the "breaking of the Bread."

Thus from the first Easter Day the Eucharist has been a unique and distinctive action of the Church's corporate life, and its celebration a characteristic observance of Sundays and other holy days. In the apostolic age, the Eucharist was usually combined with a simple meal called the agape and prefaced with devotions of song, Scripture reading, prayer, and preaching of both formal and informal character. By the middle of the 2d century, however, it had become restricted to a purely ceremonial meal, and its devotional introduction formalized into a sequence of Scripture lessons, psalmody, preaching, and intercessory prayer much after the order of Jewish synagogue worship. All church members were expected to participate in it every Sunday, even at the risk of their lives during times of persecution. Those who were physically prevented from attendance shared in the "reserved" species of consecrated bread and wine taken to them from the church assembly by the deacons. The Bishop was normally the officiant, but in his absence a presbyter could preside in his place.

During the 4th and 5th centuries, after the freedom of the church from persecution, the Eucharistic celebration took on a more elaborate ceremonial, musical, and artistic splendor, and the liturgies began to crystallize, first in the East, then in the West, into their classic forms under leadership of the great metropolitan sees. The East Syrian liturgy of Edessa was adopted by the Nestorian Christians, and the liturgy of Alexandria has been preserved among the Coptic and Ethiopic Monophysites. The Antiochean tradition was developed at Constantinople in the Liturgies of St. Basil and St. John Chrysostom and became the rite of all Eastern Orthodox Churches. A variant of it is used by the Church of Armenia. In the West, two types of Latin liturgy developed: the Gallican, employed not only in Gaul, but in North Italy (Ambrosian rite), Spain (Mozarabic rite), and Celtic lands; and the Roman, to which the liturgy of North Africa was related. After Charlemagne, the Roman rite became predominant in medieval Western Churches. The liturgies of the Eucharist produced by the Protestant Reformers of the 16th century were all based upon the Roman Mass—those of the Lutherans and the Church of England being conservative revisions, those of the Reformed churches of Calvin and Zwingli more radical adaptations.

The Reformation era witnessed much controversy concerning the doctrine of the Eucharist, especially as regards the Real Presence of Christ in the consecrated bread and wine and the propriety of applying sacrificial concepts to the consecrated species. The divisions then created still remain as a major obstacle to the reunion of Christian churches. All parties appealed to the New Testament and the teaching of the early Church Fathers. Protestant theologians did not agree among themselves, but all were unanimous in rejecting the medieval scholastic interpretation of the Real Presence in terms of transubstantiation, which in the 13th century was proclaimed a dogma by the Roman see. They also rejected the doctrine that the sacrifice of Christ was mystically re-presented in the Eucharist as a propitiation for sin of the living and the dead. In general, the Reformers believed in a "spiritual" rather than a "substantial" Presence of Christ in the Eucharist, and a memorial rather than a re-presentational relation to the sacrifice of Christ on Calvary. The differences were primarily due to varying philosophical presuppositions, as well as disagreements in the method of interpreting the Scriptures.

**EVANGELICALISM** [ē-văn-jĕl′ĭ-kəl-ĭz-əm], theological attitude of certain Reformation churches, especially the Lutheran, based on their appeal to the Gospel (Evangel) against the hierarchy of the medieval church. In England after the 18th century it was applied to those who, like Wesley, recalled the church to Gospel truths. Wesley's successors slowly separated from the Church of England; but many evangelicals remained within the established church and have profoundly influenced its life. Evangelicals were largely instrumental in abolishing slavery in the English dominions and in forwarding the missionary endeavors of the English church. In modern times they emphasize the literal inspiration of the Bible, the importance of preaching, and the need for personal conversion.

**EVANGELISM** [ĭ-văn′jəl-ĭz-əm], term which in its broadest sense covers any activity designed to spread the Evangel, or the Gospel, the "Good News" of Jesus Christ. Although popularly applied to revivals, emotional services conducted by itinerant preachers, a distinction is sometimes drawn between revivals, which seek to reawaken lapsed or indifferent Christians, and evangelism, which reaches out to those who have not previously heard the Gospel. The church today makes use of many modern methods of evangelism: visitation by laymen to unchurched homes, radio and television services, newspaper advertising, direct mail messages, and rural and industrial evangelism.

**EXCOMMUNICATION** literally means "exclusion from communion with the faithful." Such exclusion is mentioned in the New Testament (I Cor. 16:22) and it is the oldest penalty in the Roman Catholic Church. In the canon law of the Roman Catholic Church excommunication is a species of church penalty called a censure. A censure is an ecclesiastical penalty whereby a baptized person who has committed a serious sin punishable by a penalty and who scorns church authority, is deprived of certain spiritual goods until he repents and is absolved. Censures are intended to effect the conversion of the culprit. Censures are: interdicts, suspensions, and excommunication. Abortion, for example, is punished by excommunication.

The excommunicated person, while cut off from communion with the faithful, does not cease to be a Christian. He is, however, deprived of the rights and the privileges that a member of the church possesses, until he repents and is absolved. He has no right to attend divine services, but may listen to sermons. He may not receive the Sacraments while excommunicated. In certain instances he may not receive the sacraments or Christian burial. An excommunicated person does not share in the indulgences, suffrages, and public prayers of the church, but the faithful may pray for such a person privately. Many ecclesiastical acts are forbidden excommunicated persons.

**EXTREME UNCTION** (Lat. *unctio extrema*, "last anointing"), in the Roman Catholic and Eastern Orthodox churches the sacrament administered to those so ill as to be in danger of death. Such an anointing is prescribed in the Epistle of St. James (Jas. 5:14–16) as a means of raising up the sick man and freeing him from his sins. In the Roman Catholic Church, the priest administering the sacrament dips his thumb in blessed oil and makes a small sign of the cross on the eyes, ears, nose, lips, hands, and feet of the sick person, saying each time in Latin: "Through this holy anointing and by His most tender mercy may the Lord pardon whatever sins you have committed by your sight (hearing, smelling, taste and speech, and so forth)." Before and after these anointings, appropriate prayers are said for the spiritual and physical health of the suffering person. This sacrament is now called the anointing of the sick.

**GODFATHER,** male sponsor for a person receiving baptism. In infant baptism the godparent is a proxy for the child in pronouncing the promises of faith, and he assumes the responsibility of religious instruction, if the parents fail in this duty. In the Anglican Communion two of the three godparents must be of the same sex as the child. The Roman Catholic Church requires two godparents of different sex. In adult baptisms the godparents act as witnesses to the ceremony. The practice of sponsorship dates at least from the late 2d century.

**GOLDEN RULE,** teaching of Jesus, "All things whatsoever ye would that men should do to you, do ye even so to them" (Matt. 7:12), in which He summed up the Old Testament law and the teaching of the prophets.

**GREAT SCHISM** [sĭz′əm], **THE,** separation of the Latin and Greek Churches, resulting (1054) from progressive estrangement. The Greek-speaking East and the Latin West had been slowly drawing apart since the 3d century. Cultural diversity and historical evolution were reflected in their respective religious practices. Sharing a common faith, they nevertheless differed on such matters as the Filioque clause in the Nicene Creed, papal primacy, clerical celibacy, rules of fasting, and the kind of bread to be used in the Eucharist. In 1053 Patriarch Michael Cerularius of Constantinople instigated a literary attack on

Latin practices and also closed and desecrated Latin chapels in his city. Pope Leo IX sent Cardinal Humbert to Constantinople, but when Cerularius refused even to receive him, Humbert excommunicated the Patriarch, on July 16, 1054. Cerularius eventually won the support of the other Easterners, and by 1100 the schism was an accomplished fact. Although the schism persists, the mutual excommunications were removed in Dec., 1965.

**HOLY ORDERS,** in the Eastern Orthodox, Roman Catholic, and Anglican churches, the various ranks of ecclesiastical ministry; also, the indelible character or permanent sacramental power to exercise that ministry. The episcopate, priesthood, and diaconate are held to be of divine origin and are administered by the Bishop with the laying on of hands. The subdiaconate and minor orders are not generally considered part of the sacrament of holy orders. The validity of Anglican orders is disputed by the Roman Catholic and Eastern churches. Some churches avoid the term "holy orders" because it implies a hierarchical constitution within the church.

**ICON** [ī′kŏn], painted or sculpted image with extraordinary mystical or religious power attributed to it. The supernatural quality associated with an icon differentiates it from an ordinary religious image. Although veneration of icons is inimical to the Roman Catholic Church, they are an integral part of the worship of the Greek and Russian Orthodox churches. The architecture of Greek and Russian churches includes the iconostasis, designed to hold the icons, as an integral part of the building.

Most icons were painted on wooden panels by anonymous monks. They reached their first great importance in the 8th-century Byzantine Empire. The "iconoclastic" period, lasting a little over 100 years, prohibited production of icons in the Byzantine world. By the 10th century they were produced again and assumed an even greater importance throughout the Greek and Russian east. The Russian, Andrei Rubliev (1370–1430) stands out as one of the greatest icon painters of all times. The "Virgin of Vladimir" and Rubliev's "The Saviour," in Moscow are among the most famous and venerated of icons.

**ICONOCLASTIC** [ī-kŏn-ə-klăs′tĭk] **CONTROVERSY,** 8th- and 9th-century controversy concerning the use of icons in the Byzantine Church. In 726 Emperor Leo III of Byzantium ordered the destruction of all images on grounds of idolatry. Pope Gregory II objected, as did St. John of Damascus, the most eminent contemporary Greek theologian. Nevertheless, a synod of Eastern bishops in 754 pronounced the use of images heretical. Later, Empress Irene took the lead in convoking the 7th ecumenical council at Nicaea in 787, where the Greek bishops reversed themselves and authorized the veneration of images.

In 813 Emperor Leo V renewed the earlier prohibitions. Patriarch Nicephorus of Constantinople opposed him but was deposed. St. Theodore, abbot of the monastery of Studios in the capital, suffered exile for denouncing the Emperor's caesaro-papism. The Greek monks in general opposed iconoclasm, but the army and court circles upheld it. Finally, under Empress Theodora another Greek synod, in 843, again permitted images. With that, the controversy ended. During the Reformation in the 16th century, a new wave of iconoclasm erupted in some of the Protestant churches.

**IMMACULATE CONCEPTION,** Roman Catholic teaching which, according to the definition (1854) of Pope Pius IX, "maintains that the most blessed Virgin Mary, in the first instant of her conception, was, by the singular grace and privilege of Almighty God, through the foreseen merits of Christ Jesus the Saviour of mankind, preserved immune from all stain of original sin." The doctrine concerns Mary's conception in her mother's womb, and is not to be confused with the virginal conception and birth of Christ.

**INDEX OF FORBIDDEN BOOKS,** list of books banned by the Roman Catholic Church and requiring ecclesiastical permission to be read or retained. The first formal ecclesiastical condemnation of a book was made by the Council of Nicaea, when in 325 it condemned Arius and his work *Thalia*. On given occasions individual condemnations followed. However, the invention of printing made some sort of list necessary. The first "Index" appeared in the 16th century. Revised lists have since appeared. The latest edition of the Index was issued from the Vatican in 1948.

The Index is not, and was not meant to be, a catalog of all forbidden books of all times. Rather, it is a list of authors whose works the Church, on specific request, has examined and condemned. The Index lists the prohibited authors alphabetically according to categories, depending on whether one or other or all of an author's works are proscribed. The 1948 edition of the Index contains 4,126 prohibited books, 255 of which have been banned since 1900. Since the Index is not a complete list, Canon Law itself sets down various categories of forbidden books. With sufficient reason and adequate safeguards, permission can be obtained from ecclesiastical authorities to read many of these books. Penalties, including excommunication, are inflicted for violation of church law in the matter of forbidden books.

**INDULGENCE** (Lat. *indulgere*, "to be kind or merciful"), originally, term used in the Roman Empire to designate the remission by the emperor of tribute or punishment on certain occasions. In its technical Catholic sense it means "the remission before God of the temporal punishment due to sin even after its guilt has been forgiven, which (remission) ecclesiastical authority grants from the treasury of the Church" in behalf of her members.

From the beginning of the Church, Christians were convinced that they could aid one another by prayers, sufferings, and good works. In the early days of the Church sinners were not given absolution until they had performed a long penance. Hence they often appealed to the martyrs to intercede with the bishop to obtain their reconciliation with the Church and a shortening of their public penance. Later, penitents were given a penance to be performed after confession and absolution from the guilt of sin. This implied that though they were forgiven their sins and so freed from eternal punishment, they had still to do penance in terms of temporal punishment. When this penance was officially lessened by good works, pilgrimages, alms giving, or joining the Crusades, for instance, the reduction was called an indulgence. Thus Urban II in 1095 granted an indulgence for all who joined the First Crusade.

The theology of indulgences, elaborated in the 13th century, finds the reason for such practices in the infinite merits of Christ and, secondarily, those of the Blessed Virgin Mary and the saints, which the Church has at her disposal in a kind of spiritual treasury. Certain abuses crept into the practice of granting or gaining indulgences, however, which tended to obscure the correct doctrine. The Council of Trent (1562) and Pope Pius V (1567) eradicated these abuses by forbidding any monetary element in their concession.

An indulgence therefore is not an absolution from sin or its guilt; it is not a permission to commit sin or a pardon for future sins. It is simply a way of lessening the payment of the debt which the sinner owes to God, through the merits of Christ and the saints.

**INFALLIBILITY OF THE POPE,** Roman Catholic doctrine that the Pope, "when he teaches ex cathedra" (that is, from the chair of St. Peter, in a formal manner and with supreme authority as the Vicar of Christ and head of the Church), "possesses, by reason of the divine assistance promised to him in the blessed Peter, that infallibility with which the divine Redeemer wished His Church to be endowed in defining doctrine regarding faith and morals." What the Vatican Council thus formally defined in 1870 had been more or less explicitly a Catholic belief from apostolic times. History abounds in instances of recourse to the successors of Peter for surety of faith in doctrinal and moral decisions. Irenaeus proclaimed it at the end of the 2d century, and the Council of Chalcedon (451), on hearing Pope Leo the Great's definition of the Incarnation, exclaimed: "This is the faith of the Apostles. Peter has spoken through Leo." Papal infallibility, which is neither impeccability (sinlessness) nor inspiration on the part of the Pope and does not involve any new doctrine (revelation) or omniscience—that is, unerring knowledge on subjects other than faith and morals—is exercised only rarely and then under certain well-defined conditions which clearly indicate the Roman Pontiff is making solemn use of this prerogative of his office.

**INQUISITION** [ĭn-kwə-zĭsh'ən], **THE,** tribunal organized by the medieval church for the detection, punishment, and prevention of heresy. Primary responsibility lay with the individual bishops, although some Christian emperors took a hand.

Absence of any widespread heresy in the early Middle Ages obviated the need for such a program, but by the 11th century, the Albigensian, or Catharist, heresy appeared and raised pressing problems for both church and state. In 1022 King Robert of France, in the name of the public welfare, burned 13 heretics, and in 1051 and 1052 Emperor Henry III burned some in his domain; in other cases, lynch mobs dispatched those accused of heresy. The need became apparent for a more legal and humane method of dealing with heretics. Hence there gradually developed two types of formal courts: the episcopal and the monastic, or papal, inquisitions, both operating according to recognized, legally sanctioned techniques.

Two features characterized the Inquisition: the application by the state of physical or temporal punishment against those excommunicated by the church for heresy, and the particular method of conducting trials to determine who was a heretic. The early penalties for heresy show a predilection for the use of physical force; but there existed no real legal basis for this, nor were all the bishops convinced of its propriety. It was the civil rulers who gradually created the legal foundations for temporal punishments. Frederick Barbarossa's Verona decree of 1184 prescribed penalties of exile, confiscation of property, demolition of heretics' houses, infamy, and loss of various personal rights. Pedro II of Aragon decreed in 1197 death for heretics who did not leave his kingdom within a stated time. Emperor Frederick II enacted a series of measures between 1220 and 1239 which definitely established the death penalty for heresy in his domains. Canon law also became more specific on the issue: the Second, Third, and Fourth Lateran Councils enunciated increasingly detailed canons concerning heresy. Innocent III's Fourth Lateran Council, in 1215, imposed on secular rulers the obligation to "exterminate" heresy by suitable punishments and provided minute instructions for the bishops in determining guilt. This episcopal Inquisition, however, failed to check the Cathari, so Pope Gregory IX (reigned 1227–41) created the monastic, or papal, Inquisition.

The papal Inquisition operated through special agents, usually Dominican friars, but occasionally Franciscans also; the episcopal Inquisition employed local clergy. Their procedure was basically the same. The inquisitors announced their presence and summoned any heretics to recant. Those who voluntarily confessed within the allotted time received absolution and light penalties, such as prayers or good works. Those who were denounced by informers were placed on trial. Inquisition trials were secret, and the informers were seldom revealed. The inquisitors served as both prosecutors and judges, and the accused had no right to counsel or to call defense witnesses. In 1252 Pope Innocent IV authorized the use of torture to extract confessions.

When a prisoner was found guilty and abjured his heresy, he might still receive a light penance or a prison term. Those who refused to recant or to admit guilt after being convicted were handed over to the secular authorities to be burned at the stake. Relapsed heretics automatically suffered this fate. Canon law forbade the inquisitors themselves to execute anyone, but the same law compelled secular authorities to carry out these sentences. Inquisitors enjoyed a wide discretion in imposing sentence. The Dominican, Robert le Bougre, himself a former heretic, within one week judged and caused to be burned 183 people, although he was later imprisoned for life for his fanaticism. Bernard Gui was a more typical inquisitor: in 16 years, 1308–23, he found 930 people guilty; 89 of these were already dead, 42 were executed, 307 went to prison, and the remainder received lighter sentences. This happened in an area where the Cathari were especially numerous.

The methods of the Inquisition were entirely consonant with medieval practices in secular judicial affairs. Innocent III theorized that heresy was the equivalent of treason against God and should be dealt with as severely as treason against civil authorities. A source of abuse was the confiscation of heretics' property, which offered an incentive to unscrupulous rulers. It also explains the trials of dead men. Later extensions of the concept of heresy to include witchcraft and sorcery opened new fields for the Inquisition.

There was much variation from country to country in the use of the Inquisition, both episcopal and papal. In southern France, Savoy, and the Papal States, the papal Inquisition worked consistently. It was never established in England, it worked only intermittently in northern France and the Slavic countries, and only in 1372 did it take root in Germany. The episcopal Inquisition was even more intermittent. The burning of Joan of Arc by the Bishop of Beauvais shows the dangers of the local tribunal. Spain witnessed few trials until the 14th century, and the Inquisition established by King Ferdinand of Aragon in 1480 was essentially a national institution, beyond the control of bishops or Popes. During the 16th century, inquisitorial methods were applied by both Protestants and Catholics, until the spirit of toleration finally won general acceptance.

**LORD'S PRAYER, THE,** prayer which Jesus taught his disciples. It has been preserved in two forms, which can be distinguished more clearly in a later Bible translation like the Revised Standard Version than in the King James Version. The shorter form (Luke 11:2–4) is probably the one the disciples originally learned from Jesus. The longer form (Matt. 6:9–13) is perhaps an adaptation for church use, but if so, a very early one. Before the end of the 1st century A.D. the doxology "For thine is the kingdom . . ." was added, though it does not appear in the best texts even of Matthew's form. While the separate clauses can be paralleled in Jewish prayers, together they mirror Jesus' central teaching and comprehend all matters which can be taken to God in prayer—from God's eternal purpose to His people's daily bread.

**LITURGY** [lĭt'ər-jē] (Gr. *leitourgia*, "a public service"), in the Roman Catholic Church, the homage paid to God by the Church in union with Christ; in the Greek Church, specifically, the eucharistic sacrifice. The liturgy *in its essence* is a communal act of the church, though at times it is performed by a priest alone, acting officially for the church. Since the Roman Catholic Church is a hierarchical organization, its liturgy must be conducted by priests, who because of holy orders share in a special way in the priesthood of Christ. But the laity, who share in the same priesthood in a lesser way, take an active part by responding to the prayers, by singing at high Mass, and above all by uniting themselves inwardly to the liturgical act.

Concretely, liturgical actions are those set forth in the approved liturgical books such as the Missal and the Breviary. However, inclusion in the books is not of the essence, since the church offered public worship to God prior to their compilation. At the heart of the liturgy is the sacrifice of the Mass. In addition to this central act, the liturgy includes, for example, the administration of the sacraments and sacramentals, the recitation of the Breviary, and benediction.

In all these ceremonies, the twofold purpose is to pay homage to God and to bring God's grace to men. Christ Himself is considered the High Priest of the liturgy, inasmuch as "He lives on still to make intercession on our behalf" (Heb. 7:25); and for this reason most liturgical prayers end with the phrase, "Through Christ our Lord. Amen."

**MASS, THE,** principal order of public worship in the Roman Catholic Church. The word is derived from *missa*, as used in the late-Latin formulary at the end of public gatherings, *"ita missa est"* ("Go, it is the dismissal"). By the end of the 6th century, the word had become the official designation of the rite in the Western Church. The Orthodox, or Eastern, Church uses the Greek word "liturgy" (a public service) to designate its principal rite. In both traditions the terms designate the public celebration of the Lord's Supper.

The Mass originated in the words and acts of Christ at the Last Supper (Matt. 26:26–29; Mark 14:22–25; Luke 22:15–20; I Cor. 11:23–25). Like its prototype, the Mass signifies a complex of meanings through visible form. It is a memorial event, a communal meal, a gift or sacrifice, a ritual act, a celebration, a symbol. As a symbol, it invokes the mystery of the Resurrection as it was prefigured at the Last Supper. Thus, the Mass is a dramatic action that perpetuates Christ's reconciliation of man to God.

As a human institution, the Mass is Roman and Latin. It is important to realize what this means. Romans were a practical, dramatic, blunt people. Their language reflected these qualities. It was well suited to the government of an international state and to a universal church. However, unlike other cosmopolitan cities in the Imperial age—for example, Alexandria or Antioch—Rome had become a city of slaves and barbarians. The churches of the East were established among a literate public. The church of Rome was not.

By the end of the 3d century the Mass of the bishops of Rome had begun to be the normative rite in the Western Church. This was due more to the bishop's success as a public figure than to the popularity of the Church's teaching. During the Imperial decline the Church in Rome had become useful to public order. The Mass was popular, and public halls were filled. The bishop of Rome had authority, both within and without the Church.

In the ensuing century the Mass underwent further popularization. The traditional separation of the Christian service into a service of teaching (the "Mass of the Catechumens") and a service of communion (the "Mass of the Faithful") ceased sometime in the 4th century, when the distinction between the illiterate "student" and the illiterate "graduate" had become practically meaningless. In the same period the slow change from Greek to Latin, both of which were dying languages, was completed under Pope Damasus (366–384). By the time final shape was given to the Roman Mass under Pope Gelasius I (492–496), a church Latin—simple, intelligible, and beautiful—had taken shape as the language of the Mass.

The rite, meanwhile, had become a brief, concrete, and highly dramatic ritual composed of the following parts: entrance of the priest and his ministers as the congregation recited a psalm (the "Introit"); an invocation of Christ's mercy (the "Kyrie," the remaining Greek prayer); a prayer of petition for the assembly (the "Collect"); two or three Scripture readings followed by a homily or sermon; public recitation of the Nicene Creed (required after 325); the offering by the people of bread and wine; consecration of bread and wine (the "Canon," or criterion, of the Mass); Communion of the Faithful; prayer or prayers of thanksgiving; a benediction; and the dismissal.

In the 8th century the "Gloria" was attached to the "Kyrie," the "Sanctus" added during the consecration, and the "Agnus Dei" incorporated in the Communion of the Faithful. The Mass also was divided into the "Ordinary" and the "Propers," the first consisting of permanent elements, the second of variable elements—prayers and biblical readings related to the "seasons," or periods separated by the Church's principal feasts.

By the 9th century the Roman Mass had become universal in Western Europe, mainly because of Charlemagne's desire to impose uniformity of worship by way of the *Gregorian Sacramentary*, a codification of the Roman ritual. The obvious sorts of abuse set in. For example, ecclesiastics and rulers used the Roman distinction between sung and said ("high" and "low") Masses, not to elevate feast days but to promote themselves. Courts, cathedrals, abbeys, and city churches began a tradition of smothering the Mass in opulence and pageantry. The "Low Mass" became a hurriedly muttered exercise, the "High Mass" a grand spectacle. The *Roman Missal* of Gregory VII (1073–85) attempted to correct these abuses by returning the Mass to Roman simplicity and strictness. But his reforms concentrated on matters of form—the very source of excess and error.

At the end of the Reformation the Council of Trent (1545) sought reforms along Gregorian lines. The Protestant revolt had proved that the people did not understand the Mass. The revised *Roman Missal* of Pius V

(1566–72) attempted, like its predecessor, to bring order to public worship, but it, too, failed to teach the Mass as a communal rather than a heirarchical rite.

In 1922 the *Congregation of Rites* (established in 1588 by Sixtus V to implement reform) published a decree encouraging a community, or dialogue, Mass. In 1943, Pius XII (1939–58), in the Encyclical *Mystici Corporis*, declared that it was the community, the mystical body of Christ, that defined the Church's character. In the reasoning of Pius, the Church is a living body by its very nature, in which no member, as no limb or vital organ, can act alone without the direction of its head, which is Christ. In *Mediator Dei* (1947), Pius described the Mass as the "public worship" of the Church in its essential, corporate act, the liturgy, by and through which all other expressions of the life of the church are secondary.

In 1963 Paul VI promulgated the *Constitution on the Sacred Liturgy*. Resulting from the second session of the Second Vatican Council, it declared the Roman Rite to be only one valid rite among many; duplications, confusions, and historical accretions were struck from the liturgy; Pius XII's desire to bring liturgical commonality out of variety was reaffirmed; clarity of teaching, including vernacular or local language, was encouraged; and promotion of local customary practices, which may not violate the canon of the Mass, was given support.

**MONASTERY** [mŏn′ə-stĕr-ē], dwelling place of at least 12 monks or nuns. Originally the term designated the cave, hut, or abandoned tomb which constituted the shelter of a hermit, but as the eremitical life gave way to the cenobitic, the term came to designate the dwelling of a congregation of monks or nuns bound by vow to a fixed rule of life. Strictly speaking such a residence should be called a convent, though that term is now commonly restricted to the dwelling place of nuns. Aiming at self-sufficiency, the monastery usually contains the land, buildings, and areas necessary for the different activities of monastic life. For the physical needs of its occupants it provides kitchens, refectory, dormitory or cells; for the spiritual life it includes church or oratory, chapter house, cloister, and library; and since the monks or nuns combine the practical with the contemplative life, it provides the requisite workshops, storerooms, or barns. Although the term properly applies only to the residence of those who bind themselves to the monastic life in its entirety, it is sometimes used for the dwelling of those embracing a semimonastic way of life, such as friars, canons regular, or regular clerics.

**MONASTICISM** [mə-năs′tə-sĭz-əm] **or MONACHISM** [mŏn′-ək-ĭz-əm] (from Gr. *monos*, "alone"), originally the way of life of a hermit, one living in austere seclusion from the world. Such a mode of life is found in many religious systems and among many races. In all its forms monasticism involves a withdrawal from the world to achieve through asceticism, or the exercises of self-abnegation, the contemplation or love necessary for full union with ultimate reality or God. It may be theologically or philosophically motivated; it may be theistic or nontheistic.

Christian monasticism appears as a spontaneous outgrowth of the Scriptural admonition "Love not the world, nor the things that are in the world. . . ." (I John 2:15–17). It arose as an attempt to escape the worldly and often sinful environment into which the Christian was born. By the 3d century it was already common for Christian men, and especially women, to seek seclusion in caves, huts, and abandoned tombs, living a life of chastity and extreme poverty, dedicated to prayer, meditation, and religious exercises. Their goal was the maximum love of God made possible by the renunciation of all worldly loves. At first without fixed rule or standard practice, such ascetics were governed by individual tastes or by the example of some noted hermit near whom they lived. His influence in this regard gave St. Anthony of Egypt the title "founder of Christian monachism."

In the 5th century, under the influence of St. Pachomius, this purely eremitic life gave way to the less austere semisolitary form which St. Pachomius intended as preparatory to the solitary, but which became the prototype of monasticism as now understood. A well-organized and highly developed rule was introduced, governing in detail all phases of monachal life. The freedom of individual practice was curtailed in favor of exercises in common. Prayer and meals became community functions. Physical labor replaced the leisure of the purely contemplative life. St. Basil carried the new concept of monasticism into Asia Minor, where it became the prototype of Greek and Slavic monasticism, and St. Athanasius carried it into the Mediterranean countries, where it passed quickly into western Europe.

In Italy, St. Benedict of Nursia experimented with both solitary and semisolitary ways of life before founding his celebrated abbey of Monte Cassino, where he wrote the rule which became the dominant monastic code of Europe for centuries. The new rule modified the extremes of desert practices by placing still greater emphasis on community life. To the vows of chastity and poverty was added the vow of obedience. Chastity, the precept of perfection, has never varied throughout the long history of monasticism, but the extent to which poverty has been practiced has varied widely. In Egypt it involved a poverty as absolute as possible; with St. Benedict the concept was moderated to one of severe austerity. Under the vow of obedience, law and order, binding upon superior and inferior alike, replaced former arbitrariness. Bound by the vow of stability, the monk became a corporate part of one religious community until death. Physical labor for its own sake was introduced as an intrinsic part of monastic life.

In Britain and Gaul, Benedictine monasticism came in conflict with the prevailing Celtic form. The origins of the latter are obscure, but its emphasis on physical austerities and the subordination of community life to individual freedom would seem to indicate that it derived from Egyptian and Syrian monasticism. Eventually Celtic monasticism yielded to the influence of the Benedictine.

The 10th century witnessed the culmination of the monastic system with the origin and development of religious orders, properly so called. The establishment of Cluny in 910 introduced the concept of closely knit institutions subordinate to a mother house, in place of the previous loose federations of autonomous abbeys. Despite the rise of orders such as the Carthusians and Camaldolese, which retained the earlier autonomous status, the subsequent development of Western monasticism moved in this direction.

The 11th century introduced a form of religious life frequently confused with the monastic, but marking an essential break with the monachal ideal. The Canons Regular of St. Augustine, professing to follow the pseudo "rule of St. Augustine," introduced the concept of a clerical life to which a community life was subjoined. In the monachal ideal the recitation in common of the Divine Office was the principal work of the monk, and to it all other work was subordinated. The break with the ideal was widened in the 13th century by the rise of the mendicant orders of St. Francis and St. Dominic. Created to fill a particular need of the times, these orders relaxed the vow of stability binding the friar to a particular house for life and permitted him to belong rather to a province or to the order itself.

The great wealth and power which the monastic orders acquired throughout Europe exposed the monks to corruption. Abuses of many kinds crept into the system, so that the Council of Trent found it necessary to curtail the power of abbots and abbeys and to enforce reform through return to more primitive standards. And the Protestant Reformation was responsible for bringing into existence other religious orders not monastic in character. Though living a community life, these regular clerics, such as the Jesuits and Passionists, devoted themselves primarily to some special work, such as teaching, preaching, or missionary endeavors, while the Redemptorists introduced the concept of a simple religious congregation.

The 18th and 19th centuries saw the decline of the monastic system throughout Europe, with the suppression or expulsion of the religious orders; but the 20th century has witnessed their revival, particularly in the New World.

**NICENE** [nī′sēn] **CREED,** the conciliar creed of the Council of Nicaea (325 A.D.). Based on an Eastern baptismal creed, it excluded Arianism by using the term *homoousios* ("of one substance," Lat. *consubstantialis*) of God the Son. The Muslim confession of faith is "God is God and Mohammed is the Apostle of God." The Jewish formula called the *Shema* ("Hear") is composed of several texts, beginning with Deut. 6:4, "Hear, O Israel, the Lord is our God, the Lord is one." To this Christians added the confession that "Jesus is Lord" (I Cor. 8:6, 12:3) and the baptismal formula, "in the Name of the Father and of the Son and of the Holy Ghost" (Matt. 28:19).

The oldest Christian creeds are brief expansions of this baptismal confession, which also provided the outline of instruction for converts. Western baptismal creeds are of the simple type represented by the Apostles' Creed; those of the Eastern Church are often more elaborate and theological. A second type is the conciliar, representing the faith as taught by the churches represented at a council. The original form ends abruptly with "and in the Holy Spirit," adding anathemas on Arian doctrines. With the defeat of Arianism it became the common creed of the Church, but for practical purposes needed further expansion. The form commonly used is connected, probably correctly, with the Council of Constantinople (381). It enlarges the section on the Spirit, thus incidentally repudiating Macedonianism, and omits the anathemas. This is the form used liturgically, except by the Armenians, who use the older form. At the union of the Visigothic Arians with the Catholic Church in Spain in 589 the word *filioque* ("and from the Son") was added with reference to the origin of the Spirit, to stress the equality of Father and Son. This addition came into general use in the West, and since the 9th century has been a point of distinction between the Greek and Latin churches.

**NUN,** member of a congregation of women leading a secluded religious life. By their solemn vows and stricter seclusion nuns are distinguished from sisters, whose simple vows permit them greater freedom in practical life, for example, in teaching and nursing. Convents for women were established early in the Christian Era and are believed to have preceded the monasteries for men.

**ORDO** [ôr′dō], (1) a small book published yearly by each diocese and religious order in the Roman Catholic Church, indicating the daily Mass and office proper to each locality. For example, if two feasts fall on the same day, the *Ordo* tells which one should take precedence. (2) Any one of a series of medieval books giving detailed directions for various liturgical functions at Rome and elsewhere. The *Ordines Romani*, recording ceremonies as performed from the 6th to the 15th century, are the source of such modern liturgical books as the *Roman Pontifical* and the *Ceremonial of Bishops*.

**ORIGINAL SIN,** in Christian theology, the sin or hereditary stain which is attached to and results from the origin of each man as a descendant of Adam. The doctrine that the effects of Adam's disobedience have passed to his posterity, so that all are by nature children of wrath (Eph. 2:3), that is, unreconciled to God and subject to the punishments imposed on the first man and woman, is implicit in the Old Testament (IV [II] Esdras 3:21, 22; 4:30; 7:48) and is most explicit in the writings of St. Paul (Rom. 5:12–21) and the early Fathers and councils. Properly speaking, original sin consists in the hereditary lack or privation of grace, charity, and justice (Rom. 5:17) needed to be in the friendship of God. Hence every descendant of Adam (apart from the Virgin Mary, and, *a fortiori*, the human nature of Christ) inherits this taint, which is removed only through the grace of Christ. Accompanying this lack are other effects: an inclination to evil on the part of the will and sense appetite, sufferings, and the penalty of death (Rom. 6:23).

**PAPACY** [pā'pə-sē], **THE,** rule of the Bishop of Rome, or Pope, as successor of St. Peter over the Catholic Church. The foundation of the Papacy is the primacy of Peter. That Peter was singled out for pre-eminence over the other apostles is clear from the Gospels. Peter is mentioned 195 times, while all the other apostles together are mentioned only 130 times. The name of St. John, the apostle most frequently mentioned after St. Peter, occurs only 29 times. The primacy of Peter is based chiefly on the following texts: Matt. 16:16–19, where Christ says that Peter is the rock on which He will build His Church; Luke 22:31, 32, where Christ says that Peter being confirmed will confirm the others; and John 21:15–17, where Christ tells Peter to feed His lambs and His sheep.

Peter also appears as the leader of the apostles in Acts, as, for example, when he presides at the selection of Matthias (1:15–22), takes the lead in explaining Christ's message at Pentecost (2:14–39), and insists on releasing the Gentiles from the obligation of circumcision (11:1–18).

That Peter eventually went to Rome and was martyred there is challenged by few scholars today. That he transmitted his authority as Vicar of Christ to his successors is, of course, challenged by many Protestants. The Catholic Church holds that since Christ intended His Church to go on to the end of the world, He also intended the authority He gave the apostles to be transmitted to their successors. Actually this transfer was accepted quite naturally in the Church.

It would be naïve to expect full-blown the elaborate governmental setup of the 20th century in the 1st, when the Church was inchoate and struggling for survival in the face of bitter persecution. The Church, as any living organism, was to grow and develop. Then, too, there is a lack of documents from this period, a lack due not only to time but to the persecutions. Still, what evidence there is of papal government is quite impressive. Bishops of Rome did act as if they had authority over the Church, as St. Clement in the 1st century, St. Victor in the 2d, and Dionysius in the 3d. Early Fathers of the Church, such as Ignatius of Antioch and Irenaeus, spoke of the Bishop of Rome as of someone special.

The letter of St. Clement, the 4th Pope, to the Corinthians in the year 95 or 96 is highly significant. Clement urged the Corinthians to stop rebelling against their pastors. His interference was accepted, his letter reverenced, and this at a time when the apostle St. John survived at Ephesus. Corinth, it must be remembered, was itself an apostolic church.

During the first centuries the Church suffered severe, even if intermittent, persecution, and many Popes died as martyrs. With the coming of peace under Constantine, new dangers assailed the Church. Heresy, or the denial of some truth revealed by Christ, had already troubled the Church, but it assumed new proportions after the emergence of the Church from the catacombs. Arians, Nestorians, and Monophysites tried to make their views prevail, but the waves of heresy broke on the rock of orthodoxy, which was the Papacy. Great councils condemned these heresies, and the Popes strongly backed the upholders of orthodoxy.

The Papacy survived the menace of persecuting emperors only to face the danger of being smothered by the oversolicitude of interfering emperors. Caesaropapism, or undue interference by emperors in ecclesiastical affairs, was a persistent threat. The collapse of imperial authority in the West helped the Popes, and even Justinian's reconquest of Italy did not permanently alter the trend toward papal independence. While emperors were having their troubles, great Popes like Celestine I (reigned 422–32), Leo I (440–61), Gelasius I (492–96), and Gregory I (590–604) safeguarded orthodoxy at home and stimulated mission activity abroad.

### Papal States

The decline of Byzantine power in Italy led gradually to the establishment of the Pope as a temporal sovereign. By the 8th century Italians had begun to look to the Popes for protection against the Lombards, and the Popes had begun to look to the Franks. Not only were the 8th-century emperors ineffective in restraining the Lombards, but they had become iconoclast heretics and, indeed, persecutors. Finally Pepin the Short, King of the Franks, in 756 gave the Popes the Italian lands he had won from the Lombards. The close connection between the Carolingians and the Papacy was cemented when Leo III (795–816) crowned Charlemagne Roman Emperor in 800.

Europe suffered cruelly during the terrible civil wars among the descendants of Charlemagne and the more terrible raids of the Vikings, Saracens, Avars, and Magyars; and the Papacy suffered, too. Saracen raiders sacked St. Peter's in 846, and in the general confusion the powerful family of Theophylactus practically controlled the Papacy —not to the Papacy's advantage. While not every man put on the papal throne by this house was unworthy, the reigns of Popes like John XII (955–63) and Benedict IX (1032–44; 1045; 1047) were a scandal.

By the middle of the 11th century the tide of reform ran strongly. A series of excellent and devout Popes, among whom St. Gregory VII (1073–85) was outstanding, led the way in a long and severe struggle against lay investiture and other abuses. But though the 11th century saw a great renovation in the Papacy, it also saw a sad breach between the Eastern Church and the See of Peter. This schism was made worse by the Fourth Crusade, and with the exception of short intervals of reunion in the 13th and 15th centuries has endured to the present.

During the high Middle Ages the Papacy became very influential. Popes called for crusades, rebuked and cowed powerful monarchs, and became feudal suzerains of kingdoms like England and Hungary. Still this power must not be exaggerated. The Papacy found itself involved in a long struggle with the Hohenstaufen Emperors which raged intermittently from the mid-12th century to the mid-13th. However necessary it may have been, the struggle was unfortunate because it took so much of the time, energy, and resources of excellent Popes.

In spite of politico-religious involvements, the high-medieval Papacy did not neglect its prime duty of spiritual leadership. The Popes strove to keep down abuses, safeguarded orthodoxy with a zeal which, if rough, was well meant, and encouraged great spiritual leaders like St. Francis and St. Dominic.

In the 14th century papal influence began to decline. The century started with French King Philip IV's suc-

## THE PAPACY

The baldachin, bronze canopy over the main altar of St. Peter's, by Giovanni Bernini. The Pope celebrates Mass at this altar.

Statue of St. Peter in the Vatican, believed to have been commissioned by Pope Leo I (r.440–61).

Art Reference Bureau

Brown Brothers

cessful defiance of Boniface VIII (1294–1303) and ended in the welter of the Great Western Schism. Clement V (1305–14) took up residence at Avignon, and there, with one short interval, the Popes remained until Gregory XI (1370–78) returned to Rome in 1377. The cardinals revolted against his successor, Urban VI (1378–89), and elected an antipope, Clement VII (1378–94). Europe was divided for years. And the confusion was worse confounded when, at the Council of Pisa in 1409, the cardinals of both claimants, Pope Gregory XII (1406–15) and the antipope Benedict XIII (1394–1423), abandoned them and elected a third claimant, the antipope Alexander V (1409–10). Alexander was succeeded by the antipope John XXIII (1410–15). The schism was finally ended at the Council of Constance in 1417 with the election of Martin V (1417–31).

### Conciliar Theory—Renaissance Papacy

The 15th-century Papacy had to contend with the rise of a theory that a general council was superior to the Pope. This theory, however natural in the stormy days of the Great Schism, was indefensible theologically and soon died out. The excesses of the Council of Basel in its opposition to papal authority helped to kill it.

By the time the conciliarists were weakening, the papal court had begun to be infected by the Renaissance atmosphere. Under Nicholas V (1447–55) humanists were drawn to the papal court, some of whom were scarcely

ornaments to an ecclesiastical body. Sixtus IV (1471–84) practiced the most unblushing nepotism, and the College of Cardinals deteriorated alarmingly. Popes like Innocent VIII (1484–92), Alexander VI (1492–1503), Julius II (1503–13), and Leo X (1513–21) seemed to be more Renaissance princes than spiritually minded priests.

### Protestant Revolt and Catholic Reformation

Leo X was Pope when Martin Luther first moved against the Church. Leo condemned Luther but did little to remedy evils which caused many to listen to Luther. Hadrian VI (1522–23) tried hard to correct abuses but died too soon. Clement VII (1523–34) did not have the necessary qualities of leadership. It was only with Paul III (1534–49) that a thoroughgoing reform was begun. Paul encouraged the already growing reform movement, approved the Society of Jesus, and called the great Council of Trent (1545–63). The Papacy now led the powerful reform movement known as the Catholic Reformation or Counter Reformation.

The 18th century saw the Papacy harassed by "enlightened" despots, Jansenists, Febronians, Gallicans, regalists, and others. Clement XIV (1769–74) was compelled by Bourbon pressure to suppress the Society of Jesus, and Pius VI (1775–99) was carried off a prisoner by French revolutionists. The 19th century saw a revival. Pius VII (1800–23) survived his imprisonment by Napoleon to return to Rome, receive back the Papal States, and restore the Society of Jesus. The 19th-century Papacy was troubled by the Roman question. Pius IX (1846–78) was driven out of Rome by radicals in 1848, and the neo-Guelph dream of a federated Italy under papal leadership died. Nationalists took most of the Papal States in 1860 and Rome in 1870. Pius IX became "the prisoner of the Vatican."

Although the Papacy lost temporal power, it gained spiritual prestige. The Vatican Council proclaimed the dogma of papal infallibility in 1870. Leo XIII (1878–1903) impressed the world with his great encyclicals, especially *Rerum novarum*. St. Pius X (1903–14) struck hard at modernism and encouraged frequent Holy Communion. Benedict XV (1914–22) preserved papal neutrality in World War I. Pius XI (1922–39) settled the Roman question and gave the world many enlightening encyclicals. Pius XII (1939–58) led the church through the bad days of World War II and the Nazi menace. He, too, wrote significant encyclicals. John XXIII (1958–63) won the confidence of many non-Catholics by his breadth of vision and in 1962 called the Second Vatican Council. His encyclicals *Mater et magistra* and *Pacem in terris* show a profound awareness of the world's needs. His death interrupted the work of the Second Vatican Council, but his successor, Paul VI (1963–    ), promptly reconvened it.

The Papacy has seen many vicissitudes from Peter to the present. Though there have been occasional periods of weakness, the Papacy throughout the centuries of its existence has given the Roman Catholic Church a unity and strength it could not have had otherwise.

**PAPAL BULLS** (Lat. *bulla*, "seal"), written mandates of the Pope, of a more serious order than papal briefs. In the 8th century Pope Hadrian I (772–95), if a letter attributed to him is genuine, ordered that a leaden seal be attached to papal documents to ensure their authenticity. Prior to the 13th century the word "bull" referred to this leaden seal. After that it came to be used for the document to which the seal was attached, and it was so used not only for papal documents but for imperial and royal ones as well. For example, the Golden Bull of Emperor Charles IV in 1356 regulated the imperial electors. Today, however, the term is used more specifically for papal documents.

**PAPAL ENCYCLICALS** [ĕn-sĭk′lĭ-kəlz], papal letters concerning important matters addressed to the faithful throughout the world, to "Patriarchs, Primates, Archbishops, Bishops, and other Local Ordinaries enjoying Peace and Union with the Apostolic See." They differ in form from bulls and briefs, and today are the Pope's usual means for instructing the faithful. For instance, Leo XIII in 1891 gave a clear and forceful exposition of Catholic social principles in his encyclical *Rerum novarum*; Pius XI updated this in 1931 by his encyclical *Quadragesimo anno*; and John XXIII in 1961 by his *Mater et magistra*. Other encyclicals have dealt with such matters as marriage and education.

**PAPAL SCHISM** [sĭz′əm], known also as the Great, or Western, Schism (1378–1417), conflict between rival candidates for the Papacy following the Avignon Exile (1309–77). On Apr. 8, 1378, the cardinals elected Archbishop Bartolomeo Prignano of Bari as Pope Urban VI (1378–89). During the conclave the Roman populace had created a tumult, demanding the election of a Roman or, at least, an Italian Pope. Within six months the cardinals grew tired of Urban VI, a tactless reformer, and seizing on the circumstances surrounding the conclave, declared his election invalid and elected Clement VII (1378–94). Urban refused to recognize his deposition, Clement moved to Avignon, and both sought support. Clement, a Frenchman, won the allegiance of France, Scotland, and Spain, but England, Italy, and eastern Europe acknowledged Urban. In each camp were men who were later canonized.

Urban died in 1389, and was succeeded by Boniface IX (1389–1404). In 1394 the theological faculty of the University of Paris suggested three ways of ending the schism: (1) the abdication of both competitors, (2) arbitration, (3) a general council. But neither Boniface nor Clement would resign. Shortly thereafter Clement died, and the Avignon cardinals elected the celebrated Spanish Cardinal Pedro de Luna as Benedict XIII (1394–1417). Again, in 1404, the doctors of the University of Paris urged both claimants to resign, but they declined. Shortly afterward Boniface died, and the Roman cardinals elected Innocent VII (1404–6). He died before any resolution of the schism could be effected and was succeeded by Gregory XII (1406–15).

In 1408 Benedict arranged to meet with Gregory, last of the four Popes of the Roman line, at Savona, to discuss arbitration. At the last minute Gregory backed down. Exasperated, Gregory's cardinals deserted him, joined Benedict's cardinals, and convoked the pseudo-Council of Pisa. Here in 1409 they proclaimed the deposition of both the Avignon and Roman Popes and elected Alexander V (1409–10), who soon died and was followed by John XXIII (1410–15). This merely established a third claimant, yet the final solution was indicated. In 1414 another council met at Constance (1414–18), and in 1417, after the condemnation of John XXIII, the resignation of Gregory XII, and the desertion of Benedict XIII by his principal followers, Martin V (1417–31) was elected Pope. The Great, or Western, Schism was ended. The Roman Popes are recognized as legitimate, the others as antipopes; the schism damaged papal prestige and gave rise to conciliarism.

**PATRIARCH** [pā′trē-ärk] (Gr., "ruler of a family or tribe"), highest rank in the hierarchy of the Eastern Orthodox Church, and second only to the Pope in churches in communion with Rome. Originally the only patriarchs were the five bishops who occupied the important sees of Rome, Constantinople, Alexandria, Antioch, and Jerusalem. Although their rights and duties were defined at Chalcedon (451), the title came into usage only in the 6th century.

Patriarchs exercise jurisdiction over an area consisting of several provinces. They convene synods and ordain bishops in their patriarchates. Metropolitans are subject to them. In the 6th century the Patriarch of Constantinople, John the Faster, assumed the title of Ecumenical Patriarch, which has been retained by his successors. They have "primacy of honor" but no jurisdictional authority over other Eastern patriarchs. The Pope is the only patriarch in the West, and in this role he deals only with members of the Latin rite.

**PENANCE** [pĕn'əns], (1) the virtue disposing a person to regret his sins as offenses against God and to resolve against sinning in the future; (2) any good work offered to God in reparation for sin; (3) in the Roman Catholic and Eastern churches, the sacrament in which a Christian receives pardon for his sins by means of confession, contrition, penance (sense 2), and priestly absolution. The power of imposing penance and remitting sins is based on the commission of Christ to the apostles: "Receive the Holy Spirit; whose sins you shall forgive, they are forgiven them; and whose sins you shall retain, they are retained" (John 20:22, 23).

In antiquity the sacrament was conferred only when necessary for the remission of such notorious sins as apostasy, homicide, or adultery; ordinarily a Christian could be admitted to penance but once in a lifetime. Moreover, until some time in the early Middle Ages the penance imposed was lengthy, severe, and public. Thereafter, under the influence of the Irish missionaries the practice of private confession, penance, and absolution gradually became common, until by the year 1000 such was the custom everywhere.

The fourth Lateran Council (1215) imposed the obligation of annual confession. In the 16th and 17th centuries modern confessional boxes came into use. These are enclosed on all sides, and a partition separates priest from penitent. The penitent tells his sins (frequently, in "confessions of devotion," slight sins only), accepts a penance to be performed later, and receives absolution if he is well disposed. In giving or refusing absolution, the priest acts as the minister of Christ, who ratifies the action of the priest according to His promise: "Amen I say to you, whatever you bind on earth shall be bound also in heaven; and whatever you loose on earth shall be loosed also in heaven" (Matt. 18:18).

**PRESBYTER** [prĕz'bə-tər] (Gr. presbýteros, "elder"); one of the two terms used in Apostolic times to designate those whom the Apostles empowered to minister spiritually to their Christian communities. St. Paul used "presbyter" interchangeably with episcopos, "overseer." The former became the word for "priest," the latter for "bishop." The process whereby the bishop came to be recognized as the highest office in the Church while the priest, or presbyter, was relegated to the second rank is not clear from the New Testament. Nor is precise infor-

mation available to explain the division of spiritual power between them. During the Reformation some Protestant communities, following John Calvin, eliminated the office of bishop entirely and used the word "presbyter" to designate the possessor of ecclesiastical jurisdiction in their congregations. In these Presbyterian churches, "presbyter" indicates either a teaching elder who is an ordained minister or a ruling elder who is a layman.

**PRIMATE** [prī'mĭt], presiding bishop of an ecclesiastical province, in ancient times used for an archbishop or metropolitan, sometimes restricted to a patriarch. In England the two archbishops of York and Canterbury were given curious forms of the title, York being "Primate of England" and Canterbury being "Primate of All England."

**PROCESSION,** ceremonial progress from one place to another. Christianity is similar to most other religions in occasionally providing an outlet for spiritual joy or sorrow in the form of a stately march accompanied by singing or chanting. Perhaps the oldest type is the funeral procession, in which the mourners follow the corpse to the church and cemetery. Appropriate processions are also held on special days of the Christian year.

Among Roman Catholics, the most familiar processions are those on Holy Thursday, Corpus Christi (Thursday after Trinity Sunday), and at the beginning and close of the Forty Hours' Devotion. In all of these the priest carries the Eucharist in the monstrance, and is accompanied through the church, and sometimes outside, by clergy and people singing hymns in honor of the Sacrament. Other processions are those of Candlemas Day (Feb. 2), Palm Sunday, the Greater Litanies (Apr. 25), and the Lesser Litanies (Monday, Tuesday, and Wednesday before Ascension Day). These last, the days of the Litanies, are also called Rogation Days (Lat. rogare, "to ask"), because on them it is customary for priest and people to march through the fields, chanting the Litany of the Saints as a petition to God for a bountiful harvest. In the Middle Ages processions symbolized the Christian's journey to his eternal home with God.

**PURGATORY** [pûr'gə-tôr-ē] (from Lat. purgare, "to cleanse"), in Roman Catholic doctrine, a middle state or condition between Heaven and Hell, in which the souls of those who die in the state of grace but are not completely free of venial sins or of temporal punishment due to sin are purified. The state lasts only until the final judgment. St. Augustine remarks in his City of God that there are many who have not so lived as to merit hell-fire, yet were not so virtuous as to obtain immediate entrance into Heaven. In the justice and mercy of God, they are subjected to further purgation, to "pay the last penny" (Matt. 5:25, 26, interpreted by early writers as referring to purgatory), and to "be saved, yet so as by fire" (I Cor. 3:10–15).

Ancient belief in purgatory is attested by the practice of prayers for the dead (II Macc. 12:43–46; II Tim. 1:18) in the liturgies, inscriptions in the catacombs, exhortations of early preachers to private prayers, as well as by the doctrinal statements of many Fathers. At the same time the precise nature of the sufferings of purgatory is not certain, though many, especially in the Latin Church, speak of a purging fire more severe than any suffering of this present life.

Certainly the greatest torment is the separation from God, since the soul is able to recognize more clearly than in this life the meaning of the beatific vision, and so suffers a great longing to see God face to face. This does not exclude, however, a certain joy and security in knowing that when the last vestiges of sin have been purged away the soul will come to a blessed eternity.

**REFORMATION.** On Oct. 31, 1517, an event occurred in a remote university town in the German state of Saxony that marked the start of the Protestant Reformation. That day Martin Luther, an Augustinian monk, and professor in the University of Wittenberg, posted on the door of the Castle Church of Wittenberg 95 theses for a disputation on the power and efficacy of indulgences. These theses, written in Latin, were soon translated into German and spread quickly throughout the country. Luther, who had no desire to break with the Church, soon became the rallying point for all who were dissatisfied with the papal church. This widespread discontent must not obscure the fact that Luther's protest, based upon his new understanding of the Gospel, was religious and theological rather than political.

### Background of the Reformation

This is not to deny that the situation in Europe was ripe for Luther. The medieval identification of society with Christendom, while never so complete as some have thought, had long been in process of dissolution. Scholastic theology had reached its zenith with Thomas Aquinas, and then a steady decline had set in. William of Occam and his disciples brought about the downfall of scholasticism by their denial that any theological doctrine could be proved philosophically. The battles between the different scholastic schools bored an age grown tired of theological subtleties. Contempt for scholasticism was greatest among the Renaissance humanists, who were thrilled by their rediscovery of classical culture and by their renewed sense of the dignity of man. It was not so much that the Renaissance was pagan in its spirit, as that the humanists were critical of many of the practices and teachings of the Church. Many of them, by their study of the literary sources of the early Church, sought to renew it. They spread the knowledge of Greek and Hebrew and prepared editions of the Church Fathers.

Jan Huss, an early advocate of religious reform. His views were condemned by the Council of Constance in 1414. (RELIGIOUS NEWS SERVICE)

The greatest achievement of Christian humanism was Erasmus' publication of his Greek New Testament.

There was widespread dissatisfaction with practical abuses in the Church at all levels. The lower clergy were criticized for being theologically ignorant and for not fulfilling properly their priestly duties. The higher clergy were also attacked for being as theologically ignorant as the lower clergy and for subordinating spiritual duties to political interests. They were accused of selling church offices and of being inattentive to their duties. The Renaissance Popes often acted more like Italian princes than the successors of Peter. Some were immoral and ostentatious in their living, politically ambitious, and concerned with their own fame and the well-being of their relatives. This is not to say that there were not good, and even saintly, men in the ranks of both the lower and higher clergy.

Another factor in late medieval Europe contributing to dissatisfaction with the Church was the rise of nationalism, as a result of which each nation reappraised its relations with the Papacy. The Pope's influence in the internal affairs of all nations, resulting from his prestigious position, the financial obligations due him from all the clergy, the international character of canon law, and the right of appeal to Rome were now regarded as unwarranted foreign interference.

The demand for reform in the Church was not pecu-

liar to the 16th century; attempts had been made in previous centuries to effect a thorough renewal of the
Church. Often these had been confined to individual
monasteries and dioceses. But more widespread movements such as those among the Franciscans and the
Brethren of the Common Life had not been lacking. Dissatisfaction with the Church's worldly character had also
found an outlet in various types of mysticism. But the
most important earlier advocate of theological reform
was John Wyclif. Wyclif at first was concerned with
such practical abuses as the Church's great wealth and
clerical interference in politics. Later he advocated a
strict predestinarianism, the authority of Scripture as the
only law of the Church, the priesthood of all believers;
and he attacked the mendicant orders, the authority of
the Pope, the doctrine of transubstantiation, and the
veneration of saints and relics. Wyclif's followers, the
Lollards, were initially successful in proclaiming his
views, but they met with increasing opposition after his
death, and were eventually suppressed.

Wyclif's ideas, however, spread to Bohemia, where
they were advanced by Jan Huss. By criticizing the German clergy who dominated the Church in Bohemia, Huss
became a national hero. As a result of his advocacy
of Wyclifite views, his condemnation of a papal indulgence, and his attacks on the clergy, he was excommunicated. At the Council of Constance (1414), Huss's views
were condemned and he was executed, but his movement was carried on by two factions, the conservative
Utraquists and the radical Taborites.

Another important factor in the situation was the conciliar movement, which arose as a result of the scandal
occasioned by the papal schism, whereby, beginning in
1378, there were two claimants to Peter's throne. The
conciliarists sought to end the schism and carry out a
moral and administrative reform of the Church. The
schism was finally ended by the Council of Constance,
but no basic reformation was accomplished. The council
decreed that the Pope should call periodic councils; but

succeeding Popes had no taste for this limitation of their
power, and the conciliar dream of legislative regulation
of the Papacy soon ended.

### Luther and the Reformation in Germany

Martin Luther was born on Nov. 10, 1483, in Eisleben,
Germany. While studying law at Erfurt, he suddenly
entered the Eremitical Order of St. Augustine. The motives behind this decision are not altogether clear, but it
is certain that Luther became a monk as a result of
a strong religious conviction. As a monk he sought the
assurance of his own personal salvation, and to this end
he was diligent in keeping the rule. But no matter how
diligently he kept the rule and confessed his sins, he still
believed himself to be a sinner in the presence of God.

Through his Biblical studies, Luther discovered the
answer to his spiritual longing. He decided that there
can be no human achievement of salvation, no claim
made by man on God as a result of his spiritual and
moral deeds. Pondering Romans 1:17, he came to understand that God's justice is not that "active justice with
which God is just and punishes the sinners and the unrighteous," but rather it is that "passive justice with
which the merciful God justifies us by faith." Through
faith in the promises of God as He has revealed them in
Christ, we are made righteous by God. This insight
spelled the rejection of all works-righteousness, of all
moralism; and it was the heart of Luther's faith.

On the basis of this faith, Luther instituted a reform of
theological studies at the University of Wittenberg. The
reform was marked by a vigorous attack upon scholastic
theology and by the advocacy of a theology based upon
Scripture and Augustine. But the opposition which this
stirred up among the theologians was pushed into the
background by the furor that Luther's attack on the traffic in indulgences aroused.

The indulgence issue grew out of a financial arrangement worked out by Albert of Brandenburg, Archbishop

"Luther and Melanchthon Trans-
lating the Bible," by Pierre An-
toine Labouchère depicts Martin
Luther (*seated, center*) and Philipp
Melanchthon (*right*) working on
Luther's great German translation
of the Scriptures, published in Wittenberg in 1534.

of Mainz, with Pope Leo X. Albert was to share with the Pope in the profits received from the indulgences sold in his lands. The official theology of the Church was clear as to the real significance of indulgences. Originally bound to the sacrament of penance, they were a remission of the temporal penalties assigned to forgiven sins, made possible by the superabundant merits of Christ and the saints, and their efficacy extended to purgatory. It was the sale of these merits for financial gain that Luther considered a scandalous abuse of the Church's authority, and it was against Johann Tetzel's preaching these indulgences in the lands adjacent to Wittenberg that Luther registered his protest. The revolutionary aspect of his theses was the expressed conviction that indulgences led to a false security and denied the true nature of the Christian life.

Publication of the theses made Luther the champion of German nationalists, humanists, and reformers of all complexions. But not all who read them were enthusiastic, particularly Albert and Tetzel's fellow Dominicans, who complained to Rome. But a source of support emerged which was to prove decisive for the whole course of the Reformation, namely, Frederick the Wise, Elector of Saxony. Frederick's motives for supporting Luther are not known, but it is virtually certain that without his strong support Luther's life would have ended as Huss's had.

That Luther was not compelled to go to Rome was also due to Leo X's readiness to subordinate spiritual interests to political concerns. The election of a new Holy Roman Emperor was imminent, and the Pope was strongly opposed to the election of Charles I of Spain. To prevent Charles from being elected, Leo courted the good will of Frederick the Wise and refused to move against Luther. He thereby forfeited his greatest opportunity to suppress Luther and contributed to the advance of the Reformation by giving it a respite from pressure. In the end, Leo's forbearance proved unsuccessful, for Charles was elected (as Charles V) anyway, in 1519.

On June 15, 1520, Leo X signed the bull *Exsurge domine*, which condemned Luther for heresy and demanded that he retract his heresies, on pain of excommunication. Luther showed his contempt for the bull by throwing it into a bonfire, and proceeded to publish his three great reformatory treatises: *An Appeal to the Christian Nobility of the German Nation*, *The Babylonian Captivity of the Church* and *The Freedom of the Christian Man*. The first was a bold appeal made to the temporal authorities to reform the Church and the entire national life. The second attacked the Roman Church's teachings regarding the sacraments. The third was an affirmation of the religious and ethical implications of Luther's understanding of the Gospel. In 1521 Leo issued his final bull of excommunication, *Decet pontificem romanum*.

Even after Luther's excommunication, however, Frederick insisted on a hearing before the imperial diet. Charles V, aware of the dangerous situation that could arise with the condemnation of Luther, and hardly in a position to defy the demand of the electors that Luther be heard, summoned him to the Diet of Worms in Apr., 1521. There, to the demand that he retract his writings, Luther gave his famous answer: "Unless I am convinced of error by the testimony of Scripture or by clear reason, . . . I cannot and will not recant anything, for it is neither safe nor right to act against one's conscience. God help me. Amen." The Emperor then issued the Edict of Worms, which accused Luther of heresy and disobedience to the temporal authorities and placed him under the imperial ban. The break with the Roman Church was complete. The ties were cut, not by Luther, but by the Church and the Emperor.

While Frederick kept Luther in hiding, reform in Wittenberg went forward under the vigorous and radical leadership of Andreas Karlstadt. The arrival of the Zwickau prophets, with their heavenly visions, Karlstadt's radical theological development, and the uproar caused by his reforms made the situation in Wittenberg critical. In these circumstances, Luther, against Frederick's will, returned and took charge. Luther's conservatism, by which he retained those practices that were a matter of indifference, was shown by his appearing in his monk's habit. Primacy was again given to the central themes of the authority of Scripture and justification by faith.

Karlstadt and the more radical Thomas Münzer appealed strongly to the peasants, who had long suffered under the burden of social injustices. But Luther distrusted social radicalism and objected vigorously to the theological peculiarities of these reformers. The outbreak of the Peasants' War in 1524, with its violent excesses and the involvement of these religious reformers in it, thoroughly alarmed Luther. His violent writing against the peasants and their brutal suppression by the German princes do not present a pretty picture. The unfortunate result was that the peasants were no longer spiritually drawn to Luther's theological and religious ideas, and he lost much popular support. From then on, Lutheranism was increasingly carried on the shoulders of the princes.

In 1525, Luther's decisive break with Erasmus occurred. The humanists who had at first enthusiastically supported Luther gradually began to lose interest when the full implications of his criticisms of the Church became apparent. Most of them sought to preserve the peace and unity of the Church. In 1524 Erasmus, under constant attack by conservative churchmen, wrote his *Diatribe Concerning Free Will*, in which he attacked Luther at a key point in his theology. Luther, who had long felt that the humanists were not motivated by the same religious interests as he, replied in his *The Bondage of the Will* (1525), a vigorous affirmation of his conviction that man is saved solely by faith and not by his own alleged merit.

During this time a controversy began between the Lutherans and the Swiss followers of Ulrich Zwingli over the Eucharist. Both rejected transubstantiation, but Luther insisted that there was a real bodily presence of Christ in the sacrament, while Zwingli maintained that the sacrament was merely symbolic. The Strassburg reformer, Martin Bucer, took a mediating position that Christ is spiritually present in the Eucharist.

The Lutheran ferment spread throughout Germany, but Lutheranism did not become the nation's sole religion because of the country's territorial divisions. Lutheranism flourished in those territories where the princes accepted Luther's message, while in other territories the princes maintained Catholicism. The Catholic and evangelical princes had already aligned themselves into opposing leagues when the "recess" of the Diet of Speyer in 1526 granted each prince the right to decide for himself in matters of religion. This decision permitted the evangelical princes to organize the Reformation within their territories, and the pattern of the Lutheran state church thereby emerged.

As Charles V's political situation improved, his desire to suppress Lutheranism increased. When the Diet met at Speyer in 1529, the recess was revoked. Against this action, the evangelical princes issued a vigorous *Protestation*. It was from this that the name "Protestant" derived.

At this crucial juncture the final split between the Lutheran and Zwinglian parties occurred. The Marburg Colloquy in 1529 was called in the hope of resolving the Eucharistic controversy so that a political confederation might be formed. The Lutherans opposed any political alliance with those who were not in confessional agreement with them. The norm of doctrine chosen was Luther's Schwabach Articles, which concluded by saying that the Church is composed of those who "hold, believe, and teach the above enumerated articles."

Charles V asked the evangelicals to present their views at the Diet in Augsburg in 1530. The Lutheran position was stated by Philipp Melanchthon in the Augsburg Confession, a conciliatory document which became the official doctrine of the Lutheran churches. Catholic theologians prepared a refutation, and their views were upheld by the Diet. The evangelicals were given a year to conform. In this dire situation the Lutheran princes formed a defensive alliance, the Schmalkaldic League. Fortunately for the Reformation, the Emperor's international situation prevented him from taking decisive action for over a decade, and during this period Protestantism conquered new territories. Charles did not move against the Protestants again until the 1540's. Believing sincerely in the unity of Christendom, Charles had long desired a council which might heal the schism in his lands, and after many years of ignoring his requests, Pope Paul III convened the Council of Trent in 1545.

In the meantime the Augsburg Interim and the Leipzig Interim, strongly Roman in character, governed the religious situation in Germany. But, in spite of this, the Protestant political position improved, and the pendulum swung against the Emperor. The Peace of Augsburg in 1555 ended the religious struggle by recognizing Protestantism and granting equal rights to both Lutherans and Catholics. The territorial princes were permitted to determine the religion of their territories by the principle *cujus regio, ejus religio* ("to whom the region, his the religion").

### The Reformation in Switzerland

The Reformation in Switzerland assumed a different character from that in Germany. In the Swiss cantons the tie between humanism and religious reform was much stronger than with Luther. Swiss nationalism and the special political character of the cantons were also strong factors in spreading Protestant ideas. The religious factor, however, was the most significant one in Switzerland, as in Germany. The evangelical conviction of the sole authority of the Word of God was as strongly held among the Swiss reformers as among the Lutherans, but with a noticeable difference in nuance. The Swiss em-

Culver Pictures, Inc.

John Calvin. His book *The Institutes of the Christian Religion* (1559) was one of the most important documents of the Reformation.

phasized the notion of law and Christian discipline, while the Lutherans stressed the doctrine of justification by faith.

These differences can be traced in part to the personal differences between Luther and Zwingli. Ulrich Zwingli was a humanist by temperament and intellectual outlook. The humanist battle cry, *ad fontes* ("back to the sources"), was his own, and it contains the key to his religious outlook. His rejection of many Catholic practices and his reforms were based on his reading of the sources of the Christian faith, the Bible and the Church Fathers. He had never known Luther's experience of the terrible reality of sin and the gracious mercy of God who justifies the sinner solely by faith, with the result that his religious outlook was more intellectual. In his own theology, Zwingli emphasized the divine will and the importance of the Christian's living in harmony with it. However, he learned much from Luther, even though he was often reticent about admitting it.

Zwingli's reforming work was carried out in Zurich, where he was the people's priest in the Münster chapter. Zwingli believed that only what is expressly authorized in Scripture is authoritative, and on this basis the Swiss reform was more radical than Luther's. It is indicative of the Swiss Reformation that ecclesiastical changes were instituted by the cantonal government and not by the Church.

The Swiss Reformation spread under leaders who were also humanistically oriented, as Johannes Oecolampadius of Basel. Zwingli's influence was also strong among the Strassburg reformers, Martin Bucer and Wolfgang Capito. Zwingli sought to spread his ideas through the formation of political alliances. This political activity led to his death on the battlefield of Kappel in 1531.

The leading figure in spreading the Reformation at this time in the French-speaking cantons was the fiery and courageous Guillaume Farel. Under his leadership, Geneva declared for the Reformation, largely for political reasons. The real triumph of evangelical Christianity in Geneva came later, with the work of John Calvin, who while passing through the city in 1536 was induced by Farel to remain and help him in his reformation of the city and canton.

Calvin was born in Noyon, France, on July 10, 1509, the year Luther began to lecture on the *Sentences* of Peter Lombard. He was a second-generation reformer, but his work and writings merit him the place next to Luther among the leaders of the Reformation. Calvin studied theology and law, and then came under the spell of humanistic interests. While still in his early 20's he experienced a religious conversion, the nature of which he characteristically never disclosed. His growing involvement in proclaiming the need for reform in the Church led to his flight from France to Basel. At the age of 26 he published the work which in its definitive edition of 1559 became the greatest systematic presentation of Christian doctrine produced during the Reformation: *The Institutes of the Christian Religion*. The *Institutes* is one of the few books that have noticeably affected the course of history. It served as the handbook of a courageous, industrious, and determined group, the Calvinists, who from Geneva spread through Western Europe and to other parts of the world.

Calvin had been strongly influenced by Luther, and he, also, stressed justification by faith and the authority of Scripture. But his own distinctive theme, *Soli Deo gloria* (the glory of God alone), was emphasized in conjunction with these other two. Men truly glorify God when they render Him complete obedience, and this obedience is the mark of the Christian. Herein was the source of Calvin's passionate concern for the law, which is the guide for the Christian life. But Calvin was not a legalist; he always spoke of the law and obedience in connection with God's gratuitous mercy. Calvin's famous doctrine of election—the belief that God chooses certain people for salvation—was for him a cause for comfort and thanksgiving, and not the fearsome and arbitrary thing it became among some of his later followers.

Calvin and Farel's program of reform in Geneva met with considerable opposition. This, coupled with Calvin's insistence on the freedom of the Church in spiritual matters, led to their banishment in 1538. But Calvin was again persuaded to abandon the life of study and writing that he yearned for, and he went to Strassburg to be pastor of a congregation of French refugees and lecture on theology. When he was recalled to Geneva in 1541, the liturgy which he introduced and the constitution he proposed for the Genevan Church, his *Ordonnances ec-clésiastiques*, reflected what he had learned from Bucer in Strassburg. However, Calvin's second sojourn in Geneva was not free from controversy either, and it was not until 1555 that he achieved his goal: the Church's freedom from governmental interference. Acting only in his capacity as a minister, Calvin dominated the life of Geneva.

### The Radical Reformation

Some of the early followers of Luther and Zwingli objected to the course the Reformation was taking and its progress. These men were more radical in their criticisms of the Church and in their interpretation of Christianity. They and their followers constituted what is commonly called the left wing of the Reformation. The name which has often been attached to these groups, that of Anabaptists, is really only applicable to a particular segment of them. Opposed by Catholics, Lutherans, and Zwinglians, these radical reformers were persecuted in virtually every part of Europe. Their history is a heroic tale of martyrdom and courage, and from their faith the modern world has derived such cherished convictions as religious liberty and the separation of church and state.

The dynamic character of the movement was exhibited first in Zurich, although radical reformers had appeared earlier in Wittenberg. Men like Balthasar Hübmaier, Conrad Grebel, Felix Manz, and Wilhelm Roubli were dissatisfied with the extent of the Reformation measures taken by Zwingli. In addition, they reached the conclusion that there was no scriptural justification for infant baptism. When some of them refused to have their babies baptized, the city council ordered a debate on the matter, and then decided to order the baptism of all infants. In 1525 the radicals went further and were themselves rebaptized. Denying the validity of infant baptism, they regarded baptism based on an adult confession of faith as the only true one. Their opponents then charged them with rebaptism, hence the name Anabaptist; on this basis they were persecuted.

The Anabaptists spread their views throughout Europe, especially among the peasants, who were disillusioned with Luther after his opposition to the Peasants' War and who had long nursed grievances against the Roman Church. Herein lay the great difference between the churches of the radical reformers and the churches of Rome, Wittenberg, and Zurich. The latter were part of the state, while the former were sectarian, and membership in them was regarded as hostility to the established order. This charge appeared substantiated by many of their convictions: pacifism, their refusal to participate in civil government and to take oaths, and their tendency to draw apart into conventicles. They defied the principle which almost all political leaders took for granted, namely, the necessity of religious uniformity within a given territory.

These radical reformers sought to restore Christianity to what they considered the integrity of the Apostolic church. They were pietistic, and their polity was congregational, based on the principle of voluntary association. The chief articles of faith of the Anabaptists and of many of the other groups as well are found in the Schleitheim Confession of 1527.

Many gifted and brilliant men were attracted to the left wing of the Reformation. Some, like Hans Denck, were highly spiritual mystics, who regarded the inner light as the source of their faith. Others, like Hans Hut, were extremely apocalyptic. The most famous of these was the fanatical Melchior Hoffmann, who proclaimed the imminent coming of the Last Judgment. Others by their attempts to secure the victory of their beliefs through violent means were atypical of the movement. Among these were Jan Matthys and Jan Bockelson, the leaders of the infamous Münster revolution. And some were intellectual radicals, such as Michael Servetus and Fausto Sozzini, known chiefly for their anti-Trinitarianism.

### The Reformation in England

The Reformation in England differed strikingly from the Reformation on the Continent. It was not primarily religious; rather, in its conception, and at every leading point, it was political. Religious elements were always subordinated to the interest of the state.

The root cause of the English Reformation lay in the desire of Henry VIII to divorce Catherine of Aragon. Henry had originally received a papal dispensation to marry her, since she had been his brother's widow. Catherine's failure to give him a son led Henry to believe that their marriage was contrary to God's will, and he sought an annulment. In this his desire to marry Anne Boleyn was not an inconsequential factor. The Pope was reticent for two reasons: first, he did not want to deny the validity of his earlier dispensation; and secondly, Catherine was the aunt of Charles V, under whose power the Pope was at the time.

Henry, who had earlier distinguished himself as a loyal son of the Church by his theological attack on Luther, sought by every means to obtain papal approval for the annulment. The Pope's refusal turned him into a resolute foe of the Papacy and made the English Reformation possible. With the aid of Parliament, which supported each of Henry's moves, the English Church was severed from Rome (1532–34) and reconstituted as the Church of England, with Henry as its "only supreme head on earth." The steps leading to the Supremacy Act of 1534 included the forbidding of the payment of annates to Rome, the agreement of convocation to make no new ecclesiastical laws without the King's permission, the banning of appeals to Rome, the declaration of divorce, the King's marriage to Anne Boleyn, the abjuring of papal supremacy by the convocation, and the transferral of papal powers to the King.

The two chief agents of Henry in carrying through this Reformation were Thomas Cromwell, the brilliant secular-minded royal official who dreamed of an English empire, and the equally brilliant Archbishop of Canterbury, Thomas Cranmer, who, while remaining a dutiful royal servant, increasingly sought to further the religious side of the Reformation.

Henry was intellectually and religiously committed to Catholic orthodoxy. He only permitted moderate concessions to Protestantism in the Ten Articles of 1536 because he needed German Protestant support. Later, to prove his orthodoxy, he had these articles revoked, and in 1539 Parliament passed the Statute of the Six Articles, which affirmed the doctrine of transubstantiation, permitted private masses, auricular confession, and the observance of vows of chastity and prohibited communion in both kinds and priestly marriage.

The Protestant party in England was distressed by this reversion to pre-Reformation doctrine and practice, and with the accession of the nine-year-old King Edward VI, in 1547, the Protestants took charge. The Six Articles were repealed, the cup was given to the laity, clerical marriages were permitted, images were taken from the churches, and church lands were confiscated. In 1549 Cranmer issued his first Book of Common Prayer, and its use was required by an Act of Uniformity. This Prayer Book was strongly criticized by Catholics and Protestants alike, and in 1552 it was revised in a more Protestant direction. The Book of Common Prayer was the greatest religious achievement of the English Reformation, and it stamped Cranmer as a great liturgical genius. Cranmer also prepared a creedal statement: the Forty-two Articles.

Edward died in 1553 and was succeeded by his Catholic half sister, Mary. Under Mary, the Edwardian reforms were cast aside, and in 1554 Parliament voted to restore papal authority over the Church of England. The Protestant leaders were severely persecuted, and some, like Cranmer, were sent to the stake. These persecutions and Mary's marriage to Philip II of Spain made her very unpopular with her subjects.

When Elizabeth I ascended the throne in 1558, she reinstituted the Reformation, but more for political reasons than religious. In 1559 Parliament passed a new Act of Supremacy which made Elizabeth the Supreme Governor of the Church. The second Prayer Book of 1552 was revised and the use of the revised edition was required in all the churches. The Forty-two Articles were also revised, and as the Thirty-nine Articles they became the Anglican statement of faith.

### The Spread of the Reformation in Europe

Lutheran ideas spread into the Scandinavian countries, where Lutheran state churches were established. The Reformation leaders were Hans Tausen in Denmark, Jørgen Erikssøn in Norway, Olaf and Lars Petersson and Laurentius Andreae in Sweden, and Mikael Agricola in Finland.

In France, Luther's influence was superseded by that of Calvin. The French Calvinists, or Huguenots, grew in numbers and influence, in spite of persecution. They became intimately involved in French politics, and their fortunes constantly shifted. Toleration was achieved when Henry IV, a former Protestant, issued the Edict of Nantes in 1598.

In the Low Countries Lutheranism soon gave way to Anabaptism, but eventually Calvinism became the dominant form of Protestantism. The fortunes of the Reformation were bound up in the political struggle for independence from Spain. Calvinism was identified with resistance to Spanish rule, and it became the religion of the majority in the northern provinces which broke from

Spain, the modern Netherlands. In the south, modern Belgium, Catholicism was revived by the Counter Reformation.

Calvinism became the state religion in the German Palatinate when its elector, Frederick III, embraced it. Under the leadership of John Knox, the Scottish Church was reformed and organized into a Calvinist state church. In Poland, Hungary, and Bohemia, both Lutheranism and Calvinism scored striking successes. Anabaptist and antitrinitarian ideas also found adherents in these lands. That the Reformation was not ultimately triumphant in eastern Europe was due to the vigorous work of the forces of the Counter Reformation and the weak political organization in these countries. Reformation ideas found scattered adherents in Italy and Spain; but in neither country was there a strong evangelical movement.

### Catholic Renewal and Reform

The Roman Catholic Church had been awakened by the Reformation to the necessity of a reform and renewal of its life. Yet the political interests of the Popes prevented them from doing anything concrete about the situation. In the 1540's two important events occurred which mark the beginning of that Catholic revival commonly called the Counter Reformation. These were the papal authorization in 1540 of the Society of Jesus, which was founded by Ignatius Loyola, and the convening of the Council of Trent in 1545. The Jesuits formed the loyal army of the Counter Reformation, and Trent established the doctrinal basis of Roman Catholicism down to the present. The Tridentine decrees constitute a vigorous rejection of the distinctive Protestant beliefs. This Catholic revival spread throughout Europe and regained many lands previously lost to the Reformation.

Basically a religious movement, the Reformation occupies a place of the greatest importance in Western history. The struggle over the ideas which it generated changed the entire complexion of Europe for centuries. Along with the spirit of the Renaissance, it marked the death of the Middle Ages and the birth of the modern world.

**REVELATION** [rĕv-ə-lā'shən], in Christian theology, God's disclosure of Himself, as distinct from any merely rational or natural knowledge of God. In the Bible, God reveals Himself by His acts in history (Deut. 11:2–7), His Word to the prophets (Amos 3:8) and supremely in His Son (Luke 10:22).

St. Thomas Aquinas holds that even without revelation we could know through rational proof that God exists, but that revelation is needed to know that God is three in one or that He became incarnate in Jesus Christ. Calvin's view is rather that without revelation any natural knowledge we may have of God, even as our Creator, becomes erroneous. For both Aquinas and Calvin revelation was essentially a number of propositions contained in Scripture (and, for the former, also in the tradition of the Church).

This propositional view of revelation was still current when the 18th-century Deists attempted to construct a religion without revelation on various grounds. According to Matthew Tindal (1655–1733), revelation implied unfairness on the part of God. According to John Toland (1670–1722), revelation in any case had to be checked by reason. Bishop Butler's reply in his *Analogy* (1736) was that the religion of reason had difficulties analogous to those of a religion of revelation, and William Paley (1743–1805) contended that even with revelation we did not have too much light.

Faced with criticism of the historical accuracy of the Bible, a 19th-century apologist like A. B. Bruce brought out the distinction between revelation and the record of revelation. The Bible, he maintained, is the record of revelation, not revelation itself, and therefore need not necessarily be entirely free from error.

In the 20th century most theologians, apart from those in the Roman Catholic Church, have maintained that revelation does not take the form of propositions, since the supreme revelation is Christ Himself, a person. Karl Barth, the Swiss theologian, contends that revelation comes only in Christ.

**REVIVALS,** historically, periods of religious resurgence such as the Puritan Awakening in 17th-century England, the Wesleyan Revival there in the 18th century, and the Great Awakenings of 1734 and 1800 in America. These revivals were usually launched by some powerful preacher, such as John Wesley or Jonathan Edwards. The term is also applied to a series of special services, generally marked by emotionalism, individualism, and pietism, emphasizing a sudden personal conversion rather than a gradual Christian growth or an awakening of social responsibility. Revivals of this type have been carried on by such outstanding evangelists as Charles G. Finney, Dwight L. Moody, "Gipsy" Smith, Billy Sunday, and Billy Graham. The week of preaching missions held annually in many local churches of the South is also popularly called a revival.

**ROMAN CURIA** [kūr'ē-ə] (Lat., "court"), the papal court, in Rome. As the spiritual ruler of many millions, the Pope, like any ruler of large numbers, must have assistance. The development of the Roman Curia was the work of centuries, a long process of evolution. The Congregations, now so important, are of comparatively modern origin. The energetic and able Sixtus V (reigned 1585–90) established them as a permanent section of the Roman Curia in 1588.

The Roman Curia today consists first of all of the College of Cardinals. Then come the Sacred Congregations, over each of which a cardinal presides. These are the Congregations of the Holy Office, the Consistory, the Eastern Church, the Sacraments, the Council, the Religious, Propagation of the Faith, Rites, Ceremonies, Extraordinary Ecclesiastical Affairs, Seminaries and Universities, and the Basilica or Fabric of St. Peter's.

Then there are three judicial organizations or tribunals: the Penitentiary, the Signatura, and the Rota. The Penitentiary takes care of the internal forum, that is, matters of the soul. The Signatura is a sort of supreme court. There can be no appeal from its verdicts. The Rota takes care of most ordinary judicial actions. It is not usually a court of first instance. It is to the Rota that many marriage cases are appealed.

Then come the Roman Offices. These are the Chancery, Datary, Apostolic Camera, Secretariat of State, Secretariat of Briefs, and Secretariat of Latin Letters.

Although not all papal commissions are strictly speaking a part of the Roman Curia, they are closely connected with the government of the Catholic Church and with the Curia. Some important papal commissions are the Biblical, the Interpretation of the Code of Canon Law, the Revision of the Vulgate, Sacred Archeology, and the Protection of Historical and Artistic Monuments of the Holy See.

**ROMAN RITE,** the prayers and ceremonials used for religious functions in the city of Rome and (with a few exceptions) in all Roman Catholic churches of Western Europe, including Poland, as well as in all the countries colonized from Western Europe. The Roman rite evolved in the Latin language during the 4th, 5th, and 6th centuries. By the 12th century, at latest, it had superseded such divergent rites as the Gallican and Spanish (Mozarabic). Complete uniformity was achieved after the Council of Trent, when new and revised editions of the liturgical books were published: Breviary (1568), Missal (1570), Pontifical (1596), Ceremonial of Bishops (1600), and Ritual (1614). The Roman rite is noted for its antiquity, dignity, and beauty, and for the comparative brevity of its ceremonies.

**ROSARY,** form of prayer, common among Roman Catholics, consisting of 15 decades, each accompanied by meditation on one of the events connected with the redemption. A decade consists of the Lord's Prayer, 10 repetitions of the Hail Mary, and the Gloria Patri. Usually only five decades are recited at one time, and the prayers are counted on a string of beads, also called a rosary. The custom of counting prayers on beads or on a string with knots was common in the Eastern Church from the earliest times. In the Western Church by the 11th century prayer beads, called paternosters, were used to count repetitions of the Lord's Prayer, which in Latin begins with the words *Pater Noster*. The use of beads for counting Hail Mary's started in the 12th century, and meditation on the mysteries, now considered essential to the devotion, became common in the 15th. The Popes have frequently commended the devotion to the faithful. The Feast of the Holy Rosary is celebrated annually on Oct. 7.

**SACRAMENTALS,** in the Roman Catholic Church, certain religious rites and objects, distinct from the essential matter and form of the sacraments, but connected with the administration of the sacraments or otherwise intended for pious use. Peter Lombard (d.1160) first used the word "sacramentals" to designate ceremonies preparatory to baptism. Thereafter, the word was extended to include ceremonies and objects which the church officially designates for spiritual effects. Among the sacramentals are the dedication of churches, blessed ashes, palms, candles, bells, water, rosaries, statues, medals, and many other things. Catholic theologians teach that, because of the intercession of the church, the sincere user of such sacramentals receives forgiveness of venial sins and other spiritual benefits.

**SACRAMENTS** [săk'rə-mənts], rites and ceremonies distinctive of the Christian religion, and observed with special solemnity. They consist of a visible sign or symbol—whether a material substance such as water, oil, bread and wine, or a ceremonial gesture such as joining or laying on of hands—and an invisible spiritual grace imparted with and in the sign. A ritual form of words accompanies the outward sign, stating the intention and significance of the grace bestowed. Sacraments differ from other external symbols and actions in that they do not only signify a gift of grace promised by God but also actually convey it.

The forms of Christian sacraments were derived from Judaism and given express institution by Christ. But it is debated whether Judaism had sacraments in the Christian sense. Ancient Gentile religions had sacraments, but none of them was borrowed by Christianity. The early Church had no defined number of sacraments, but medieval theologians limited them to seven: baptism, confirmation, Eucharist, penance, matrimony, unction, and holy orders. Most Protestants admit only two: baptism and Eucharist (generally called the Lord's Supper). But the Lutherans also account penance, and many Anglicans account all seven as sacraments, as do Roman Catholic and Eastern Orthodox Christians. Baptism, confirmation, and holy orders may be conferred only once.

**SAINTS,** certain distinguished Christians who after their death are officially honored by public commemoration and veneration in the worship of the Church. Usually the date set apart for special commemoration is the anniversary of the saint's death. Saints may also be adopted as patrons for individuals, groups, or institutions, as when a saint's name is selected for one's own Christian name given in baptism, or for the name of a religious society, school, hospital, or edifice. To win recognition as a saint a person must have displayed during his or her lifetime as a Christian a distinctive quality of holiness and purity of life and manners and one or more of the religious and moral virtues in a heroic degree.

In New Testament times all Christians were called saints by reason of being the holy people of God and participating in Christ's gifts of holiness in the sacraments. But beginning in the 2d century a tendency developed to reserve the term to individual heroes and leaders of the Church—first the martyrs, later the distinguished bishops, teachers, ascetics, and missionaries. The title was often an outgrowth of unorganized popular veneration. But beginning in the 4th century the bishops began to control the process of formal admittance of saints to the Church's calendar of observances, a procedure known as canonization.

In the Roman Catholic Church the Papacy alone, since 1634, has the right to authorize the veneration of new saints. In other churches (chiefly Eastern Orthodox, Lutheran, and Anglican), formal commemoration of saints in public worship is subject to approval by bishops or by supreme governing councils and synods.

**SCHOLASTICISM** [skə-lăs'tə-sĭz-əm], primarily, philosophy and theology taught in the medieval schools (*scholae*); secondarily, modern philosophy and theology that is similar to medieval philosophy and theology. Scholasticism holds the following positions. (1) Even though philosophy is the work of reason alone, it must be guided by Christian revelation. (2) Philosophy and theology, harmoniously related, should transmit the Judaeo-Christian tradition as well as the culture of the ancient classical world. (3) Philosophy and theology as sciences can be organized and taught as academic subjects.

Within this general framework, there is considerable diversity. Thus sharply conflicting positions were taken by medieval philosophers in the debate over universal ideas. St. Thomas' theory of knowledge is Aristotelian, and St. Bonaventure's is Platonic. Most of the surviving medieval scholastic works are either commentaries upon texts (for example, upon the logical writings of Aristotle or the *Sentences* of Peter Lombard) or *Summae*—summaries or syntheses of philosophy and Christian theology. The principal medieval scholastics were St. Anselm of Canterbury, William of Auvergne, Alexander of Hales, Albertus Magnus, Abelard, St. Thomas Aquinas, St. Bonaventure, Duns Scotus, and William of Occam. Waning with the decline of medieval universities, scholasticism was revived in Spain during the Renaissance by Francisco de Suárez, Francisco de Vitoria, Dominic Soto, and Cajetan. In the 20th century scholasticism prevails chiefly in Catholic universities. Its leading figures are Jacques Maritain and Etienne Gilson.

**SERMON ON THE MOUNT,** public discourse of Jesus, recorded in Matthew 5–7, containing His most characteristic teaching about the way of life which must mark His disciples. A shorter version is given in Luke 6:20–49. Matthew says that Jesus "went up into a mountain" to deliver this teaching. A parallel is probably intended between the "Mount of the Beatitudes," where Jesus promulgated the law of the kingdom of Heaven, and Mount Sinai, where Moses' law was promulgated. Luke's version says that Jesus spoke on "a level place." The location has been identified with a level piece of ground on the ridge running parallel to the west shore of the Sea of Galilee between Tell Hum (Capernaum) and Tabgha (Bethsaida). One goes up to this place from the lake but looks down on it when coming from the west (as Luke probably did when he came from Caesarea to visit the scenes of Jesus' Galilean ministry).

Both versions begin with the Beatitudes and end with the parable of the two foundations. Matthew's version is perhaps amplified by the insertion of related sayings of Jesus spoken on other occasions.

Jesus restates the Mosaic law by emphasizing that the springs of action lie in the thought life and insists that the law of love to one's neighbor knows no limits. Those who practice undiscriminating love are true children of God, for He is undiscriminating in His love. The golden rule sums up this aspect of Jesus' teaching. He restates the principles of religious practice—charity, prayer, and self-denial—by showing that it is their inner motive that counts, not their outer display. In this context we find Matthew's version of the Lord's Prayer. Finally, Jesus emphasizes the necessity of a clear-cut decision for the kingdom of God, and warns His hearers that His way provides the only secure foundation for life.

**SHRINES, CATHOLIC.** Places of Catholic pilgrimage are as old as the church, beginning with the Holy Places in Palestine and the tombs of the martyrs in 1st-century Rome. At the present day, shrines are of different types, but all have in common the idea of some sacred image, remains, or historic event which attracts pilgrims, who pray at the shrine and are often specially favored with spiritual or temporal blessings.

Most Catholic shrines are dedicated to the Blessed Virgin or the saints and are frequently associated with some revelation or apparition which occasioned their erection as places of pilgrimage. Every major country in the world has its variety of shrines. In France there are Lourdes (Blessed Virgin) and Montmartre (Sacred Heart of Jesus); in Spain, Santiago de Compostela (St. James); in Portugal, Our Lady of Fatima; in Italy, numerous shrines, especially to Mary and the martyrs; in England, at Canterbury and Walsingham; in Wales, at Holywell; in Scotland, at Iona; in Germany, at Cologne; in Mexico, at Guadalupe; in Canada, Ste. Anne de Beaupré. In the United States the National Shrine of the Immaculate Conception in Washington, D.C., is the most famous.

Depending on traditions and church legislation, shrines are normally connected with some church or oratory and directed by a select group of clerics or religious. Special indulgences and other spiritual privileges are often granted for visiting the shrine and making the prescribed prayers or acts of devotion.

**STATIONS OF THE CROSS,** among Roman Catholics, a religious devotion in which one pauses at 14 wooden crosses placed at intervals around the wall of the church (or sometimes outside) and prays or meditates on the Passion of Christ. Undoubtedly the devotion was originally that of pilgrims to Jerusalem following the Via Dolorosa, Jesus' route from Pilate's house to Calvary. Subsequently this devotion was popularized and transferred to local churches by the Franciscans in the later Middle Ages. Ordinarily the crosses are accompanied by painted or bas-relief images depicting certain events in Christ's journey to Calvary.

The 14 stations are (1) The condemnation of Christ, (2) His bearing the Cross, (3) His first fall, (4) His meeting with Mary, (5) His being assisted by Simon of Cyrene, (6) Veronica's wiping the blood from His face, (7) His second fall, (8) His meeting with the women of Jerusalem, (9) His third fall, (10) The stripping off of His garments, (11) The nailing to the Cross, (12) His death, (13) His removal from the cross, (14) His entombment.

**TRANSUBSTANTIATION** [trăn-səb-stăn-shē-ā'shən], literally the passage of one substance into another substance, and in Christian theology used technically only of the Eucharist. Coined by theologians about 1150 to explain the constant teaching of the Church, it attained official acceptance at the fourth Lateran Council (1215). In 1551 the Council of Trent defined it as "the marvelous and singular conversion of the whole substance of the bread into the body of Christ, and of the substance of the wine into the blood, with only the appearances of the bread and wine remaining unchanged." The Catholic understanding of the words of Christ, "This is my body . . . this is my blood" (Matt. 26:26–28), has always been literal, to the exclusion of all metaphor or merely symbolic presence or representation.

**TRINITY** [trĭn'ə-tē], **THE HOLY,** Christian doctrine that in the one substance of the Godhead there are three persons equal in status, Father, Son, and Holy Spirit. In the New Testament the three persons of the Godhead are grouped together in the baptismal injunction of Matthew 28:19 and the Pauline benediction of II Corinthians 13:14. But the doctrine of the Trinity did not form part of the apostles' preaching, as this is reported in the New Testament. In its final form it is a product of many factors. Some of these are Biblical, for instance the Johannine and Pauline doctrine of the pre-existence of Christ (John 3:16, 17; 8:58; Col. 1:15–17), the fact that prayer was offered to Christ (Acts 7:59), the experience of being filled with the Holy Spirit at Pentecost (Acts 2:1–4) and afterward as a divine gift (Acts 8:17; 10:44–47), and the identification of Jesus with the divine Logos operative in creation as well as in redemption (John 1:1–3).

On the other hand, behind other strands in the development of the doctrine are considerations at least partly philosophical. Behind Tertullian's vehement assertion that God the Father did not suffer on the Cross lies the philosophical conviction that unless there is an element in God which remains unaffected by the world, He would not be God. Conversely, Augustine's conviction that the unity of Father, Son, and Holy Spirit is much greater than the

unity, for example, of three good men links with his view that each of the three persons of the Godhead does not merely partake in goodness but is goodness. Otherwise goodness would be greater than God. And this in turn implies a Platonic view of universals and predication.

The reformers retained the view that the doctrine of the Trinity describes the essence of the Godhead, but later Protestant theologians have argued this point. F. D. E. Schleiermacher (1768–1834) tends toward the view that the Trinity does not describe God as He is in Himself but rather three distinct ways in which He is revealed to us. Karl Barth rejects Schleiermacher's position mainly on the ground that revelation does reveal God as He is in Himself.

**VATICAN** [văt'ə-kən], **THE,** official residence of the Pope at Rome. Whether or not Constantine either built or restored a palace for the Pope when he built the Basilican Church of St. Peter's, it is certain that from early times the Pope had a residence adjoining the basilica.

Pope Symmachus (reigned 498–514) certainly either built or restored a residence next to St. Peter's. The medieval Popes, Blessed Eugene III (1145–53), Alexander III (1159–81), Innocent III (1198–1216), and Nicholas III (1277–80), added considerably to the old residence to make it into a large palace. When the Popes returned from Avignon in the late 14th century, they found the Lateran palace, formerly the principal papal residence, in a ruined condition and began to use the Vatican for this purpose.

The Vatican began its period of artistic glory with the 14th century. Pope after Pope brought artist after artist to augment and embellish the great complexus of palaces. Nicholas V (1447–55) built a belvedere, the Blessed Sacrament Chapel, and an oratory adorned with frescoes by Fra Angelico. Sixtus IV (1471–84) built the library and began the famous Sistine Chapel. Alexander VI (1492–1503) is responsible for the Borgia Apartments, beautifully decorated by the paintings of Pinturicchio. Julius II (1503–13) completed the Sistine Chapel and set Michelangelo to work on his mighty paintings. Under Leo X (1513–21) Raphael worked to beautify the loggia of St. Damasus. Paul III (1534–49) built the Pauline Chapel and the Scala Regia. Sixtus V (1585–90) built the hall of the Vatican Library and the wings of the courtyard of St. Damasus. It was this energetic old Pope who moved the obelisk of Caligula from the sacristy of St. Peter's to its present position in the center of the piazza. And down through the centuries Popes continued to add to and adorn the Vatican. Pius XI (1922–39) and Pius XII (1939–58) did much in modern times to restore and augment the buildings of the Vatican.

Today the Vatican contains over 1,000 rooms, halls, and chapels. The Pope's apartment is in the main palace overlooking the piazza. Many bureaus of the papal government have their offices in the Vatican.

The Vatican contains a railroad station, a radio station, a garage, and a post office. The Vatican Museum reflects the arts and crafts of centuries. The Vatican Apostolic Library is a vast storehouse of historical material.

**VIRTUES, CARDINAL** (from Lat. *cardo*, "hinge"; *virtus*, "strength"), the virtues of prudence, temperance, fortitude, and justice. St. Ambrose (c. 339–97) called these "cardinal" virtues to indicate that they were the *cardines* ("hinges") upon which all other natural moral virtues depend. The earliest reference to the importance of these virtues is found in the writings of Plato (429–347 B.C.). Roman writers, such as Cicero (106–43 B.C.), followed Plato, and in medieval Latin literature Plato's view was commonly accepted

In traditional Christian thought a virtue is defined as a habit of doing right. Prudence is regarded as the most important natural virtue, because as a quality of the intellect it enables a man to make judicious choices, pointing out the norms of temperance, the bounds of fortitude, and the means and the measure of justice. But prudence is not to be identified with intelligence. A man who sees what should be done but does not do it is not a prudent man.

The other virtues are said to be qualities of man's will. Justice inclines a man to give to others what he owes them. Temperance restrains the natural appetites and their immoderate craving for pleasure. Fortitude steels man's natural impulse to flee from danger and causes him to follow a mean between rashness and cowardice.

**VIRTUES, THEOLOGICAL,** faith, hope, and charity—the three spiritual gifts listed by St. Paul as the sources of Christian life and holiness (I Cor. 13). Christian writers distinguish them from the cardinal virtues, which can be naturally acquired, whereas faith, hope, and charity can be obtained only through divine grace. Moreover the cardinal virtues are primarily concerned with man's duties to himself and to his neighbor, whereas the theological virtues relate man directly to God.

Faith is defined by the author of the Epistle to the Hebrews (11:1) as "the substance of things hoped for, the evidence of things not seen." By means of this virtue, the Christian is inclined to believe what is revealed by God, even when the truth revealed, being supernatural, is beyond his human comprehension. Faith is also said to bring about a loving reliance upon God and upon His promise of salvation through Christ. The infused virtue of hope is described as a power enabling man to trust that God will grant him eternal life and all the means necessary to it. Want of hope is called despair. Named the greatest of the theological virtues by St. Paul (I Cor. 13:13), charity is said to reside in the soul, enabling it to love God above all things and one's neighbor for the sake of God

# Holidays

**ADVENT,** ecclesiastical season of preparation for Christ's coming, which precedes Christmas and begins the Christian liturgical year. Its observance can be traced back to the 6th century. In the West, it starts on the Sunday nearest St. Andrew's Day (Nov. 30) and includes four Sundays, while in the East it begins on Nov. 14 (Old Style) and is a 40-day season analogous to Lent. It is a preparation for Christmas and also for Christ's second coming in judgment. As such it is a penitential season, for which the liturgical color is purple, and during which marriages are not solemnized.

**ALL SAINTS' DAY,** feast celebrated Nov. 1, commemorating all Christian saints, especially those not remembered in the church calendar. Originally only martyrs were so honored, but gradually other saints were included. A feast of the highest rank, its liturgical color is white.

**ALL SOULS' DAY,** the commemoration, on Nov. 2, of the souls of all the faithful departed. Prayers are said for their continual growth in God's service, thus supplementing the celebration of All Saints' Day. The Mass of the day is a special Requiem, containing the famous "Dies Irae."

**ASCENSION DAY,** the fortieth day after Easter, upon which is commemorated Christ's Ascension, or return to Heaven after His post-resurrection appearances (Acts 1:3–11). It celebrates especially Christ's human nature being raised into the eternal realm. The feast was known to Chrysostom and well-established by Augustine's time. Traditionally, the Ascension occurred from Mt. Olivet.

**ASH WEDNESDAY,** day of solemn penitence and fasting which marks the beginning of Lent. It occurs 40 days before Easter (excluding Sundays). The name derives from the rite of burning the palms of the preceding Palm Sunday, blessing the ashes, and imposing them upon the penitent's forehead with the words, "Remember, O man, that dust thou art and unto dust shall thou return." Ashes are the ancient symbol of deep penitence and mourning.

**ASSUMPTION OF THE BLESSED VIRGIN MARY,** the Catholic belief that "the Immaculate Mother of God, Mary ever virgin, when the course of her earthly life was finished, was taken up (assumed) body and soul into heavenly glory." This definition of Pope Pius XII (1950), which crystallizes what the Church has always held whether implicitly or explicitly, likewise indicates the Scriptural basis and theological reasons of the doctrine: Since God in choosing Mary to be the Mother of Christ had preserved her from original sin (Immaculate Conception) and had kept her a virgin even in her motherhood, it was fitting that He grant her the final victory over death by freeing her body from all corruption and bringing it together with her soul to the glory of heaven. Testimony to the universal belief in this doctrine can be traced to early Christian times. The feast, on Aug. 15, certainly antedates the decree of the Byzantine Emperor Maurice (582–602) that it be celebrated throughout his empire.

**CANDLEMAS** [kăn'dəl-məs], feast commemorating the Presentation of Christ in the Temple and the Purification of the Blessed Virgin Mary, kept on Feb. 2, 40 days after Christmas. In the Western rite, candles, symbols of Christ the True Light, are blessed, distributed, and lit while the *Nunc Dimittis* (Luke 2:29–32) is sung.

**CHRISTMAS,** feast celebrating the birth of Christ, now generally observed on December 25. The actual date of Jesus' birth is unknown, and Christians did not have a Nativity feast until the 4th century. At first, January 6, the Epiphany, was observed as the feast of Jesus' Baptism, with a secondary emphasis on His birth. The Armenian church still keeps Christmas on that day. The earliest certain mention of December 25 as Christ's birthday occurs in the Philocalian calendar (354), and that date seems to have become general throughout the West by the 5th century.

December 25 was already a major festival in the pagan Roman world, the *Dies Natalis Solis Invicti*, or "Birthday of the Unconquered Sun," falling within the week-long celebration of the Saturnalia, a feast honoring the renewal of the sun at the winter solstice. Pagan celebrations on December 25 had included feasting, dancing, lighting bonfires, decorating homes with greens, and giving gifts. So when this became a Christian festival, the customs continued, but with a Christian meaning imparted to them.

Throughout the Middle Ages, Christmas was a richly varied religious holiday. However, during the Commonwealth, the English Puritans, repelled by both the pagan practices and the religious ceremonies, forbade any religious or secular celebration of Christmas. The English celebration returned with the restoration of the Stuarts, but Christmas observances were still outlawed in Puritan New England for many years; and not until the 19th century did Christmas become a legal holiday in America.

Christmas customs vary widely around the world, but the retelling of the Christmas story (Luke 1-2:20; Matt. 1:18–2:12) forms an important part of the celebration everywhere. Church services begin on Christmas Eve and continue through the great midnight Masses of the Catholic churches to the day itself. In many European countries, especially France and Italy, the center of the celebration, both in church and home, is the crèche or crib, a model of the manger scene. St. Francis of Assisi introduced this into Italy in the 13th century, in an effort to bring the real meaning of Christmas to the people. In Austria and Belgium nativity plays are an important feature of Christmas. Christmas carols arose in the 13th century and are a part of the Christmas celebration in every country. Singers go

## CHRISTMAS AROUND THE WORLD

Christmas customs vary around the world but a festive spirit pervades the celebration of the feast everywhere.

*Roger Schall—Birnback*

The lamb, often mentioned in Christian Scriptures, is made part of the Christmas celebration in Les Baux, France.

*John Lanois—Black Star*

A group of Tokyo Santas carrying advertising placards amuse some passing children.

*Hans Truoel—Pix*

Christmas services in Amras, Austria.

A blindfolded boy tries to break the piñata, a clay pot covered with colored paper and filled with sweets and gifts, in a traditional Mexican Christmas ritual.

*Marilu Pease—Monkmeyer*

Swiss children have fun parading through city streets wearing oversized miters to drive away the "evil demons."

*Black Star*

*Jordan Tourism Information Service*

The day before Christmas the Roman Catholic Patriarch enters the Church of the Nativity in Bethlehem to begin the holiday ceremonies.

*Columbia University*

Students at Columbia University in New York celebrating Christmas in a simple candlelight service.

*Lon Landauer—Black Star*

from house to house, and are welcomed with food and gifts, especially in England and Scandinavia.

The exchange of gifts symbolizes God's gift of His Son to men, gifts the Wise Men brought to the Christ Child, and the bond of Christian love in the family and with friends. Santa Claus, a secularized version of St. Nicholas, the patron saint of children, is known also as Father Christmas or Kris Kringle. St. Nicholas' feast, December 6, is the day of gift-giving in the Low Countries, where December 25 is a quiet, purely religious festival.

**CORPUS CHRISTI, FEAST OF,** feast celebrating Christ's Real Presence in the Eucharist, kept on the Thursday following Trinity Sunday, when the consecrated Host is displayed and carried in procession. Its institution was due to St. Juliana of Liége (1192–1258), and the offices of the day were composed by St. Thomas Aquinas.

**EASTER,** the feast of the Resurrection of Christ, the greatest and most ancient of the Christian festivals. Easter is celebrated on the first Sunday after the full moon following the vernal equinox. Thus, with our modern calendar, Easter may fall between March 21 and April 25.

The earliest Christians seem to have celebrated the Resurrection every Sunday; but gradually the annual feast, preceded by Lent and Holy Week, and followed by Paschaltide, developed. The origin of the name "Easter" is uncertain: Bede connects it with the Anglo-Saxon spring goddess Eostre; but it may have come from the German *ost* ("east"), the direction from which the sun rises. Christians celebrate the feast by attending church, often rising early to greet the day, in commemoration of those who went early to the tomb "as it began to dawn toward the first day of the week" (Matt. 28:1). The services are elaborate and joyous, the churches decorated with flowers and candles, with white, the color of purity and joy, predominating. Alleluia ("Praise Yah"), the expression of joy and thankfulness, resounds. Sometime during the Easter season, Roman Catholics must make confession and receive communion.

Many of the customs associated with Easter are derived from various spring fertility rites of the pagan religions which Christianity supplanted. Eggs were a primitive symbol of fertility; but Christians saw in them a symbol of the tomb from which Christ rose, and continued the practice of coloring, giving, and eating them on Easter. The Easter rabbit, legendary producer of Easter eggs, was also a symbol of fertility and new life. The practice of wearing some new article may derive from the white garments of those newly baptized on Easter in the early church.

**EMBER DAYS,** three days of fasting and prayer in the Western Church occurring four times yearly. They are the Wednesday, Friday, and Saturday after the first Sunday in Lent, after Whitsunday, after Holy Cross Day (Sept. 14), and after St. Lucy's Day (Dec. 13). The name perhaps comes from the Latin *quattuor tempora*, "four seasons." Originally they were days of prayer for crops; now, in the Roman Catholic and Anglican churches they are days of prayer for the ordination of the clergy.

**EPIPHANY** [ĭ-pĭf′ə-nē] (Gr. *epiphaneia*), "manifestation" of Christ to the Gentiles, represented by the wise men who visited Him as an infant (Matt. 2:1–12). Their star-guided journey was early interpreted as the fulfillment of Isaiah 60:3, "the Gentiles shall come to thy light, and kings to the brightness of thy rising," whence also the wise men (actually astrologers) were taken to be kings. Its celebration as a Christian festival on Jan. 6 (Twelfth-night), which also traditionally commemorates Christ's baptism, is of greater antiquity in the Church than the observance of Christmas on Dec. 25.

**FEASTS, ECCLESIASTICAL,** days set aside for the public worship of God, sometimes with special reference to the saints, angels, Our Lady, or to an event in the life of Our Lord. The Jews observe the Sabbath as a divinely appointed day of rest. Other feasts such as the Passover and Tabernacles commemorate significant events in Jewish history. The Day of Atonement is an important Jewish penitential feast.

In the Christian Church Sunday has been observed since Apostolic times in commemoration of Christ's resurrection. In 321 Constantine declared Sunday a general holiday. Martyrs were commemorated in the early centuries, and by the 5th century the number of feasts was very large. Some days, such as Pentecost and Ascension, are movable feasts because their celebration depends on the date of Easter, which is determined by the lunar cycle. Other feasts, such as Christmas and saints' days, have permanent dates for their celebration. Originally they were sometimes scheduled to counteract the effects of pagan festivals. A new classification of feasts according to their importance became effective in the Roman Catholic Church Jan. 1, 1961. A new calendar is also being prepared by the Protestant Episcopal Church.

**GOOD FRIDAY,** the Friday preceding Easter, which marks the anniversary of Christ's crucifixion. In the Roman Catholic and some other churches it is a day of strictest fasting, penitence, and mourning. The liturgical color is black, churches are stripped of candles and ornaments, and music is generally omitted. In the Roman rite, lessons and prayers are followed by ceremonial veneration of the cross and the Mass of the Presanctified, in which a previously consecrated Host is used. A three-hour service, from noon to 3 P.M. (commemorating Christ's last three hours on the cross), is held in many churches.

**HOLY WEEK,** the week from Palm Sunday to Easter. During its days Christians commemorate the Passion of Christ. The climax of the week is on Maundy Thursday,

day of institution of the Eucharist and of Christ's betrayal, and Good Friday, day of the Crucifixion. Holy Saturday rites anticipate the joy of Easter. The Roman Catholic Church has designated services for the most significant days. Protestant churches have prayers and readings of scriptures, with Good Friday afternoon in many denominations a time for special devotions.

**LADY DAY,** Feast of the Annunciation, Mar. 25. It commemorates the visit of the angel Gabriel to the Virgin Mary to tell her that she would bear the Messiah (Luke 1:26–38). Formerly "Lady Day" applied to any feast of the Virgin.

**LENT,** 40-day season of fasting and penitence in preparation for Easter. The period of fasting in the early Church was generally only a few days. Gradually it was extended and the 40-day fast, imitating Christ's temptation in the wilderness, became standard. Sundays are not included in computing the days.

Originally the fast was very severe, permitting only one meal a day and forbidding the eating of meat and all things that come from flesh, including milk, cheese, and eggs. It has gradually become less severe, but festivities are curtailed and extra time is devoted to prayer.

**LITURGICAL YEAR,** ecclesiastical calendar in which the great events in the Christian church's history are annually remembered and celebrated in the liturgy. Most of the year is devoted to a roughly chronological observance of the events of Christ's life, and the remainder to His teachings. The liturgical year begins in November with Advent, the preparation for Christmas. Then Epiphany emphasizes Christ's manifestation to the world. This is followed by Pre-Lent and Lent, penitential seasons, and Easter. Ascensiontide marks the end of Christ's earthly life, Whitsunday (Pentecost) the coming of the Spirit, and the following Sundays (after Pentecost or after Trinity) are devoted to Christ's teachings. Throughout the year, saints and specific events are commemorated on certain days.

**MAUNDY** [môn′dē] **THURSDAY,** (from Lat. *mandatum,* "command," in John 13:34), the Thursday in Holy Week. Primarily a festival of the institution of the Lord's Supper, or Eucharist (Mark 14:17–25), it is a solemn remembrance. The Eucharist is celebrated, often in the evening, as at the first Lord's Supper. Other traditional features of the observance are the reconciliation of penitents (long since obsolete), the blessing of holy oils for use during the year, and the ceremonial washing of feet (John 13:3–15).

**PALM SUNDAY,** the Sunday before Easter, observed in Christian churches as the day on which Christ made his triumphal entry into Jerusalem as some of the multitude "cut down branches from the trees, and strewed them in the way" (Matthew 21:1–11). The custom of carrying palms or olive branches at Jerusalem in observance of the day has been reported from the 4th century. In the Middle Ages in Europe a special rite similar to the Mass evolved in the blessing of the palms. The Roman Catholic Church greatly simplified this service in 1955. The Orthodox Church also observes the day, and some Protestant sects have retained modified forms of the ceremonies.

**RED LETTER DAY,** an important feast or saint's day which is printed on ecclesiastical calendars in red ink, as opposed to the lesser "black letter days." In the Anglican communion only those feasts provided with liturgical prayers in the Prayer Book are red letter days.

**SHROVE** [shrōv] **TUESDAY,** the day before Ash Wednesday. The name comes from the "shriving" (confession and absolution) of the faithful on this day. Pancakes, utilizing foods formerly forbidden in Lent, are traditionally eaten.

**TRINITY SUNDAY,** in the Christian ecclesiastical calendar, the Sunday after Whitsunday. Since the 10th century it has been kept as a feast in honor of God the Father, Son, and Holy Ghost. It marks the beginning of a long season of teaching and growth after the observance of the events of Christ's life in the liturgical year.

**TWELFTH NIGHT,** January 5, the 12th night after Christmas, counting Christmas. It is the eve of Epiphany, the Christian feast celebrating the arrival of the Wise Men. Twelfth Night is the end of the Christmas holiday. It is a time of great celebration in England, where it is perhaps the most convivial night of the year. Large masquerade parties similar to the Mardi gras celebrations in Catholic countries are held, and employers give dinners, called beanfeasts, for their workers. In the folklore of southern Germany, Twelfth Night is the time when Berchta, a witch who is often invoked to frighten children who misbehave, is supposed to be abroad.

**VIGIL** [vĭj'əl] (Lat. *vigilia,* "night watch"), among Christians, a day of prayer, and sometimes of fasting, prior to the celebration of a great feast. In the ancient Church, vigils were long nocturnal prayer services ending with the Eucharistic sacrifice. From the 8th century it became customary to "anticipate" the vigil service, and from about the 14th century the day preceding the feast was devoted to preparation. Vigils are kept for 16 feast days in the Church of England, for 14 in the Byzantine Rite, and for 7 in the Roman Rite.

**WHITSUNDAY,** Christian feast occurring at Pentecost, the fiftieth day after Easter, celebrating the descent of the Holy Ghost upon the apostles (Acts 2). Whitsunday is sometimes called the birthday of the Church, as the apostles were then empowered to preach the Gospel of Christ. The term "Whitsunday" refers to the white garments of those baptized on this day. The liturgical color for Whitsunday is red.

## Literature

**APOCRYPHA** [ə-pŏk′rə-fə], Greek word meaning "hidden" or "secret," used by early Christians to designate books not contained in the canonical Old and New Testaments. The term first occurs toward the end of the 2d century in reference to the "secret and spurious writings" of the Gnostics—one Gnostic book bears the title *Apocryphon of John*. The word may have been applied to such apocalypses as II Esdras because of their emphasis on secrecy. In the 4th century it was used of Old Testament apocrypha and of the Book of Revelation (not then regarded as canonical). Jerome set the style for the West; for him apocrypha were semiscriptural writings outside the canon.

### Old Testament Apocrypha

The title Old Testament Apocrypha is usually given to the 12 books, or parts of books, included in the English Bible, but not regarded as Scripture by Protestants: I and II Esdras; Tobit; Judith; "the rest of" Esther; Wisdom of Solomon; Wisdom of Jesus son of Sirach (Ecclesiasticus); Baruch (with Epistle of Jeremiah); additions to Daniel; the Prayer of Manasses; and I and II Maccabees. The Council of Trent (1546) rejected I and II Esdras and the Prayer of Manasses, but treated the other books as Scripture.

In the early Church, many of these books—along with others—were regarded as authoritative. Thus, the New Testament Epistle of Jude makes use of the Assumption of Moses and explicitly quotes I Enoch, while the Epistle of Barnabas (early 2d century) gives quotations from I Enoch, II Baruch, and II Esdras. In Palestinian and Alexandrian Judaism of the 1st century A.D. the list of approved books was similarly quite fluid. It was shortened, probably in a move against apocalyptic literature, at the Council of Jamnia (c.90 A.D.), though some of the apocrypha continued to be read by Jews (among others, Sirach, Judith, and Tobit).

Some Protestant scholars have held that the apocrypha belonged to a Greco-Jewish canon used at Alexandria; but the evidence for this view is slight, the only apocryphal books clearly Greek in origin being the Wisdom of Solomon, II Maccabees, and parts of Esther. The Old Testament apocryphal books were read everywhere before the process of canonization resulted in the drawing of more rigid lines. The Greek Bible read by early Christians (the Septuagint) included not only the books mentioned above but also III and IV Maccabees, 14 "odes" from the Old and New Testaments (as well as the *Gloria in Excelsis*), and the 18 Psalms of Solomon (1st century B.C.). Actually it is hard to differentiate between the "apocrypha" and the "pseudepigrapha" (books ascribed to someone not the real author) in regard to form, content, and date, and there are pseudepigrapha in the canon (for example, the book of Daniel).

The value of the books of the Old Testament apocrypha, or of any group of them, can be considered either theologically or historically. Theologically, they are authoritative for members of those groups which, in various ways, have accepted them. Historically, they are significant since they illuminate the life and thought of Judaism in the century or so before the fall of Jerusalem, and in most instances show what was regarded as worthy of translation into Greek, and provide evidence for at least part of the Jewish background of the life and thought of early Christianity. (Some of these books, for example, Tobit, were found in the Dead Sea Scrolls.) In this sense they provide a bridge between the Old and New Testament. The significance of the bridge, of course, depends on the view taken of the relation between Judaism and Christianity.

### New Testament Apocrypha

The title New Testament Apocrypha is really a misnomer, since the Old Testament Apocrypha are recognized by some churches, whereas these books have been recognized by none since at least as early as the 4th century. Among them are two completely different classes of books: (1) the writings of some of the Apostolic Fathers, regarded by some early Christians as belonging to the New Testament canon, but later excluded; and (2) various gospels, acts, epistles, preachings, "teachings," and revelations never included in the canon by orthodox Christians. The latter group is what is usually referred to when this term is used.

Most of the apocryphal gospels were lost, except for fragments in early church writers; but papyri from Egypt have yielded fragments of the Gospel of Peter, a second Gospel of Thomas, and some gospels not otherwise known. These gospels seem to be based on some or all of the canonical four, although it has been claimed that "Thomas" uses independent and genuine sources. Among the oldest of the apocryphal gospels (perhaps early 2d century) are the Gospel according to the Hebrews and the Gospel according to the Egyptians, both of which seem to come from Jewish Christians or semi-Gnostics in Egypt.

Among the Apocryphal acts, the most important are those (also 2d century) which describe the careers of Paul, Peter, and John. All are marked by a love of romance: Paul converses with a lion he has baptized; Peter is a second Christ on his way to crucifixion; John instructs docile bedbugs to leave him alone. At the same time, they contain a strong note of asceticism; and the apostles encounter difficulties when they try to persuade wives to live apart from husbands. In later times these works, and others, were regarded as heretical, but their theology is probably merely immature.

From the 2d century we possess an apocryphal correspondence between Paul and the Corinthians which explains what heresies the latter should avoid. These letters were first published in 1958 in Greek, from a papyrus of the early 3d century. Fragments of a few other apocryphal letters survive. As for "preachings" and "teachings," several ascribed to Peter and Paul survive in fragments. They are the orthodox equivalent of the secret revelations which Gnostics liked to ascribe to the apostle John especially, and reflect the common outlook of Christianity in the 2d century.

Revelations particularly flourished in great numbers. Apart from Christian revelations ascribed to Old Testament figures, and the Revelation of John in the New

Testament itself, there were also revelations of Peter and Paul, and of other apostles. Some of these contain lurid pictures of the fate of the wicked; others, descriptions of the heavenly world, about which the New Testament is quite reticent. In general these apocryphal writings seem to have been intended to supplement the New Testament documents, by modifying the teachings of Jesus, by amplifying the teaching of the apostles, and by introducing a novelistic element, which presumably would gain the attention of rather secular-minded readers. They are valuable witnesses to the life of the Church in the 2d century and after; but they contribute nothing to our understanding of the apostolic age.

**BIBLE** [bĭ'bəl], **THE,** the collection of books which the Christian Church acknowledges as sacred. The word "Bible" is derived from Latin *biblia*, which in turn is derived from Greek *biblia*, a plural form meaning "books." The books of the Bible are thus "the books" in a special and supreme sense. The first Christian occurrence of the phrase "the books" with this meaning comes in a 2d-century document called the Second Epistle of Clement ("the books and the apostles declare . . . that the Church . . . has existed from the beginning"). A pre-Christian use of the phrase is found in Daniel 9:2 ("I Daniel understood by the books"), where it refers to the volume of Old Testament prophetic writings.

Another common designation of these books is "The Scriptures." This phrase is frequently used in the New Testament to denote the Old Testament documents in whole or in part. It simply means "the writings"—the writings which take precedence over all other writings because they are "given by inspiration of God" (II Tim. 3:16). In one place in the New Testament a collection of Christian documents is included in these "writings"— II Peter 3:16 includes "all" the epistles of Paul along with "the other scriptures," by which probably the Gospels as well as the Old Testament books are meant.

The Old and New Testaments are recognized in the Koran (the sacred book of the Muslims) as earlier divine revelations. The Old Testament without the New constitutes the Jewish Bible. The first five books of the Old Testament constitute the Bible of the Samaritans, who survive to this day as a religious community a few hundred strong.

### Contents and Authority

Christians regard the Old and New Testaments together as making up the Bible, but they are not in entire agreement about the contents of the volume. The Ethiopic Bible includes the books of Enoch and Jubilees. Some branches of the Syriac Church do not include II Peter, II and III John, Jude, and Revelation in the New Testament. The main Christian bodies, however, are in agreement on the contents of the New Testament; it is with regard to the Old Testament that they differ. The Roman Catholic and Eastern Orthodox churches include in the Old Testament 12 or 14 books over and above those which make up the Hebrew Bible. These additional books are commonly called the "Apocryphal or Deuterocanonical

books." The Lutheran and Anglican communions agree that these books may be read "for example of life and instruction of manners," but consider that they cannot be appealed to for the establishment of doctrine. Other Protestant churches do not regard them as Biblical in any sense.

In the Roman Catholic and Eastern Orthodox churches, and in some other ancient communions, the living tradition of the Church stands alongside the written record of Scripture as the final authority in religion. In the Churches of the Reformation, on the other hand, the Bible alone is the ultimate court of appeal. Thus the Church of England declares that "Holy Scripture containeth all things necessary to salvation," while the *Westminster Confession of Faith*, venerated by Presbyterians throughout the world, describes the 66 books of the Old and New Testaments as "the rule of faith and life." The use of the Bible in this way, of course, must not be mechanical, but presupposes a proper use of Biblical criticism and exegesis, based on sound hermeneutics. Central to the Christian use of the Bible is the fact that the divine revelation which it records culminates in Christ, and is to be understood in relation to Him.

When we call the two divisions of the Bible the Old and the New Testaments, we employ the word "testament," not in its current sense of "last will and testament," but as a synonym of "covenant." The Old Testament contains the literature associated with the "old covenant"—that is, the covenant which God established with Israel in the days of Moses (Exod. 24:3–8). Six centuries after Moses, another prophet declared that that covenant would one day be replaced by a new and more effective one (Jer. 31:31–34). In Christian belief this new covenant was inaugurated by Christ (I Cor. 11:25), and the New Testament is so called because it contains the foundation documents of the new covenant, the title deeds of the Christian Church.

### The Old Testament

In the form in which the Old Testament is most familiar to us, it consists of four divisions: (1) the Pentateuch, or five books of the law (Genesis to Deuteronomy); (2) the historical books (Joshua to Esther); (3) books of poetry and wisdom (Job to Song of Solomon); and (4) the prophetic books, comprising the Major Prophets (Isaiah to Daniel) and Minor Prophets (Hosea to Malachi). The Minor Prophets are so called not because they are less important but because their books are shorter. Lamentations, which is a poetical book, is appended to Jeremiah, one of the Major Prophets, instead of appearing with the other poetical books.

This order of Old Testament books goes back, in essentials, to the Latin Bible, and even farther back to the Greek version called the Septuagint. In the Hebrew Bible, however, the books appear in a different order, and in three divisions. The first division consists of the Pentateuch (Genesis to Deuteronomy). The second division, called the "Prophets," contains the "Former Prophets" (Joshua, Judges, Samuel, and Kings) and the "Latter Prophets" (Isaiah, Jeremiah, Ezekiel, and the "Book of the Twelve Prophets"—that is, the Minor Prophets, reckoned together as one book). The third division, called the "Writings," contains the rest of the Old Testament books, in the order: Psalms, Proverbs, Job; Song of Solomon, Ruth, Lamentations, Ecclesiastes, Esther; Daniel, Ezra-Nehemiah, Chronicles. Traditionally the books of the Hebrew Bible are reckoned as yielding a total of 24 (mainly by counting the Minor Prophets as one book, and by counting as one each of the books which in the Christian versions are divided into "First" and "Second"); but the 24 books of the Hebrew reckoning correspond exactly to the 39 books of the Protestant Old Testament.

The origin of the threefold division of the books of the Hebrew Bible cannot be certainly determined. It is commonly supposed that it reflects three stages in which these books were recognized as "canonical"; but in the absence of direct evidence, this cannot be positively affirmed.

The Old Testament took shape over a period of a thousand years, from the drafting of Israel's earliest law code before the nation settled in the land of Canaan in the 13th century B.C., to the period following the propagation of Greek culture over all Western Asia as a result of the conquests of Alexander the Great in the late 4th century B.C. The history which the Old Testament records covers an even greater expanse of time, going back a long way before the beginnings of Israel's nationhood. But it is not related in the form of what we call secular history; from first to last it is presented as the chronicle of God's dealings with His people. Yet so true to real life is this chronicle, which is practically coextensive with the history of civilization in the ancient Near East, that it has received repeated illumination and confirmation from the archeological research of recent times, to a point where it stands revealed as accurate and reliable beyond the expectations of scholars of an earlier generation.

### The New Testament

The New Testament falls naturally into four divisions. First come the four Gospels, in which the ministry of Jesus, culminating in His death and resurrection, is narrated from four different points of view. Basic to all four Gospels is the primitive oral preaching about Jesus and arrangement of His teaching for communication to converts. The second division consists of the Acts of the Apostles, originally written as the sequel to the Gospel of Luke, which tells the story of the advance of Christianity in the first 30 years following the death and resurrection of Christ, principally along the road from Jerusalem to Rome. In this book the leading figure is the Apostle Paul. He also dominates the third division of the New Testament, the Epistles, for 13 out of the 21 Epistles bear his name. It is important to bear in mind that most of Paul's Epistles were written before the earliest Gospel (the Gospel of Mark). The fourth division of the New Testament comprises one book, the Revelation of John. This book belongs (like the Old Testament book of Daniel) to the literary category called Apocalyptic, and proclaims in symbolical terms the triumph of Christ at a time when His cause seemed doomed to annihilation under the persecuting power of the Roman Empire.

The New Testament documents were written within the span of one century. But they were not gathered together in the form in which we know them immediately after they were written. Around 100 A.D. we have evidence that the four Gospels began to circulate as a collection, instead of pursuing a local and independent existence. About the same time, too, Paul's letters appear to have been collected from the various centers where they had been preserved and began to circulate as a corpus throughout the Christian world. Later it was appreciated that the Acts of the Apostles formed an admirable link binding the Gospel collection to the Pauline collection; and other surviving writings of Apostles, or of men associated with the Apostles, were included in the growing list of authoritative books of the new covenant. The main outlines of the New Testament as we know it were established before 200 A.D., though it is not until 367 A.D. that we first find a list enumerating precisely the 27 books which are now recognized as making up the New Testament.

| The Books of the Old Testament King James Version | The Books of the Old Testament New Catholic Edition |
|---|---|
| Genesis | Genesis |
| Exodus | Exodus |
| Leviticus | Leviticus |
| Numbers | Numbers |
| Deuteronomy | Deuteronomy |
| Joshua | Josue |
| Judges | Judges |
| Ruth | Ruth |
| I. Samuel | 1 Kings |
| II. Samuel | 2 Kings |
| I. Kings | 3 Kings |
| II. Kings | 4 Kings |
| I. Chronicles | 1 Paralipomenon |
| II. Chronicles | 2 Paralipomenon |
| Ezra | 1 Esdras |
| Nehemiah | 2 Esdras, alias Nehemias |
|  | Tobias |
|  | Judith |
| Esther | Esther (and Supplements) |
| Job | Job |
| Psalms | Psalms |
| Proverbs | Proverbs |
| Ecclesiastes | Ecclesiastes |
| Song of Solomon | Canticle of Canticles |
|  | Wisdom |
|  | Sirach |
| Isaiah | Isaias |
| Jeremiah | Jeremias |
| Lamentations | Lamentations |
|  | Baruch |
| Ezekiel | Ezechiel |
| Daniel | Daniel |
| Hosea | Osee |
| Joel | Joel |
| Amos | Amos |
| Obadiah | Abdias |
| Jonah | Jonas |
| Micah | Micheas |
| Nahum | Nahum |
| Habakkuk | Habacuc |
| Zephaniah | Sophonias |
| Haggai | Aggeus |
| Zechariah | Zacharias |
| Malachi | Malachias |
|  | 1 Machabees |
|  | 2 Machabees |

| The Books of the New Testament King James Version | The Books of the New Testament New Catholic Edition |
|---|---|
| Matthew | St. Matthew |
| Mark | St. Mark |
| Luke | St. Luke |
| John | St. John |
| Acts | Acts |
| Romans | Romans |
| I. Corinthians | 1 Corinthians |
| II. Corinthians | 2 Corinthians |
| Galatians | Galatians |
| Ephesians | Ephesians |
| Philippians | Philippians |
| Colossians | Colossians |
| I. Thessalonians | 1 Thessalonians |
| II. Thessalonians | 2 Thessalonians |
| I. Timothy | 1 Timothy |
| II. Timothy | 2 Timothy |
| Titus | Titus |
| Philemon | Philemon |
| Hebrews | Hebrews |
| James | St. James |
| I. Peter | 1 St. Peter |
| II. Peter | 2 St. Peter |
| I. John | 1 St. John |
| II. John | 2 St. John |
| III. John | 3 St. John |
| Jude | St. Jude |
| Revelation | The Apocalypse |

The Christian Church inherited the Old Testament books as its sacred Scriptures, and was not long in placing the Gospels and the Apostolic writings alongside the law and the prophets for use in worship and preaching. It was natural that, as Christianity spread among people whose native language was not Greek (in which all the New Testament books were originally written), the New Testament, as well as the Old, should be translated into other languages for the benefit of new converts.

### Early Bible Translation

Even before the rise of Christianity a beginning had been made with the work of Bible translation. In the 3d century B.C. the Old Testament began to be translated from Hebrew and Aramaic into Greek, primarily for the benefit of the large Jewish community in Alexandria, Egypt, whose language was Greek. This Greek translation of the Old Testament is called the Septuagint (from *septuaginta*, the Latin word for "seventy," because of a legend that it was the work of 70 learned Jews). When once the Old Testament had been translated into Greek, it could be read all over the eastern Mediterranean lands, and it performed a useful missionary service in introducing Gentiles to the revelation of Israel's God. When Paul and other Christian preachers began to carry the Gospel to the Gentile lands, they based their preaching on the Septuagint, before the first New Testament document was penned. And to this day the Septuagint remains the "authorized version" of the Old Testament for Greek-speaking Christians.

By 200 A.D. there were Latin and Syriac translations of the New Testament, and one in Coptic (the vernacular of Egypt) within the following century. From Syriac it was further translated into Armenian and Georgian. For English-speaking Christians, the Latin versions of the Bible are of chief importance, as these versions stand on the line of transmission along which they have received their Bible.

The earlier translations of the Bible into Latin were unofficial and inadequate, but about 382 Pope Damasus commissioned his secretary, Jerome, to revise the existing Latin translations so that one trustworthy version might be adopted throughout Latin-speaking Christendom. No better man could have been chosen for this task. Jerome revised the Latin New Testament, but instead of merely revising the Latin Old Testament, he decided to produce a completely new translation and to base it on the Hebrew original. Earlier Latin versions of the Old Testament had been translated from the Septuagint. Jerome completed his work of translation about 405. Like all new translations of the Bible, it met with considerable initial resistance, but its intrinsic merit triumphed at last. It is generally known as the "Vulgate" (that is, the common) translation, and is still the official version in the Roman Catholic Church.

### The English Bible

The English people were pagans when first they settled along the east coast of Britain but a start was made with their evangelization in 597. It was necessary to teach them the contents of the Bible after they became Christian, and this was first done in poetry and song. Then, between the 8th and the 11th centuries many parts of the Bible were translated from the Latin Vulgate into Old English; and some of these translations still survive.

A number of translations of parts of the Bible into Mid-

One of the 773 existing leaves of the Codex Alexandrinus, a Greek 5th-century manuscript of the Bible.

*British Museum*

dle English have come down to us from the 13th and 14th centuries, but the principal Middle English versions are those associated with the name and work of John Wycliffe (c.1330–84). There were two "Wycliffite" translations of the Latin Bible into English—one extremely literal, and the other, the work of a disciple of Wycliffe named John Purvey, much more idiomatic. In spite of official disapproval and restriction, Purvey's version continued to enjoy considerable popularity among literate English people well into the 16th century.

The revival of learning and the invention of printing in the 15th century, together with the Reformation in the 16th century, provided fresh stimuli for Bible translation. William Tyndale's translation of the New Testament from the Greek original was first printed in 1525. He also translated considerable portions of the Old Testament from Hebrew. The work which he began was eagerly prosecuted by his colleagues and successors; and successive versions of the English Bible appeared one after another —Coverdale's Bible (1535), Matthew's Bible (1537), Taverner's Bible (1539), the Great Bible, which in 1539 and the following years was placed by royal decree in every parish church in England, the Geneva Bible (1560), the Bishops' Bible (1568), and the King James Version (1611). All these were basically revisions and completions of Tyndale's work, and the same may be said of later revisions— the Revised Version, the American Standard Version, and the Revised Standard Version. On the other hand, the New English Bible is a completely new translation.

The first English Bible for Roman Catholics after the Reformation was produced by exiles in the north of France between 1582 and 1610; it is known as the Douay Bible and was subjected to thorough revision in the 18th century. Roman Catholics in Great Britain and Ireland acquired a second official version to stand alongside the Douay Bible in the translation of Ronald A. Knox. This is a most readable version. Like the Douay Bible, its basis is the Latin Vulgate. The Douay New Testament was revised in America by the Episcopal Committee of the Confraternity of Christian Doctrine; this revision, a very real improvement, was published in 1941. Instead of revising the Douay Old Testament, the Confraternity decided to produce a completely new translation on the basis of the Hebrew original. A Catholic edition of the Revised Standard Version was published in 1966, and later in the same year appeared The Jerusalem Bible, a magnificent product of Catholic scholarship.

It is almost impossible to enumerate the private versions of the Bible which have appeared in the English-speaking world during the 80 years between the appearance of the Revised New Testament in 1881 and of the New Testament section of the New English Bible in 1961. Most of these have been versions in modern speech. Among the most successful may be mentioned *A New Translation of the Bible*, by James Moffatt, and *The Complete Bible: An American Translation*—The Old Testament translated by J. M. Powis Smith, and a group of scholars; the Apocrypha and the New Testament

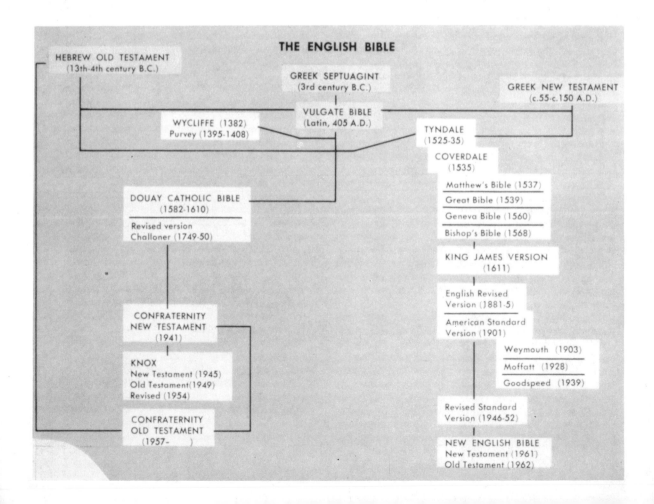

**THE ENGLISH BIBLE**

HEBREW OLD TESTAMENT
(13th-4th century B.C.)

GREEK SEPTUAGINT
(3rd century B.C.)

GREEK NEW TESTAMENT
(c.55-c.150 A.D.)

VULGATE BIBLE
(Latin, 405 A.D.)

WYCLIFFE (1382)
Purvey (1395-1408)

TYNDALE
(1525-35)

COVERDALE
(1535)

Matthew's Bible (1537)

Great Bible (1539)

Geneva Bible (1560)

Bishop's Bible (1568)

DOUAY CATHOLIC BIBLE
(1582-1610)

Revised version
Challoner (1749-50)

KING JAMES VERSION
(1611)

English Revised
Version (1881-5)

American Standard
Version (1901)

Weymouth (1903)

Moffatt (1928)

Goodspeed (1939)

CONFRATERNITY
NEW TESTAMENT
(1941)

KNOX
New Testament (1945)
Old Testament(1949)
Revised (1954)

CONFRATERNITY
OLD TESTAMENT
(1957-    )

Revised Standard
Version (1946-52)

NEW ENGLISH BIBLE
New Testament (1961)
Old Testament (1962)

translated by Edgar J. Goodspeed. Many more versions of the New Testament alone have appeared; of these may be mentioned *The New Testament in Modern Speech*, by R. F. Weymouth (1903), an accurate translation such as might be expected from a classical scholar and headmaster, and *The New Testament in Modern English*, by J. B. Phillips (1958), a free and vigorous rendering originally undertaken for members of a youth club.

### The Bible in Civilization

The Bible has played a notable part in the course of world civilization, and continues to do so, either directly, where its message is publicly accepted, or indirectly, in unsuspected ways, even where its message is formally repudiated. One external indication of its civilizing influence is the fact that many languages have been reduced to writing for the first time in order that the Bible might be translated and published in them.

We may properly speak of the message of the Bible, in spite of the manifold diversities inevitably presented by such a collection of writings from various times, places, and authors. The ethical emphasis of the Old Testament laws, the aspirations of psalmists, the examples of history, the lessons of the prophets, have all a self-consistent message which, for the Christian, finds its living embodiment in Jesus Christ, as His works and words are recorded in the New Testament. Here God confronts man with His grace and truth; here man, made in God's image, is taught the way to God, so that in obedient response to Him, man may find his highest good. The Bible exercises its undying appeal because it deals with the deepest concerns in human life, those concerns which do not change with the passing of the centuries. Far from laying the dead hand of the past on man, the Bible liberates his mind and encourages him to think and act as one who finds perfect freedom in the knowledge and service of God, and who loves grace and truth without reservation for the sake of the God of grace and truth.

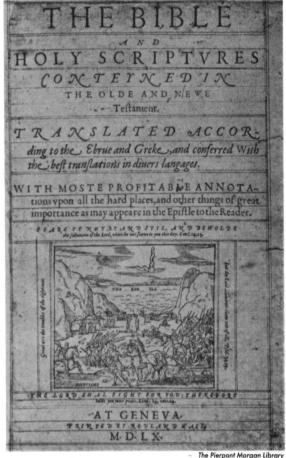

*The Pierpont Morgan Library*

The Geneva Bible, first published in 1560, was popular with early American settlers.

### RARE EDITIONS OF BIBLES

Title page from the first printing of the King James Authorized Version of the Bible.

*New York Public Library—Rare Book Collection*

The Gutenberg Bible, printed in Mainz, Germany (1452–56).

*Yale University*

King James I, by Daniel Mytens. King James ordered a new translation of the Bible, which was finished in 1611 and is still widely used.

*National Portrait Gallery*

**BIBLICAL CRITICISM.** Since the Bible is a collection of documents which has come down to us from antiquity— the latest parts from about 100 A.D. and the earliest parts over 1,000 years before that—its study demands the application of certain techniques which are used in the examination of other ancient literature. Since even the oldest surviving manuscripts of the Biblical books are copies, several times removed, of the original documents (the "autographs"), and since we have always to reckon with copyists' errors when we are dealing with copies of original documents, textual or lower criticism must be employed in order to establish as precisely as possible the original wording. When that has been done, higher criticism is then employed in order to determine as far as possible the way in which the individual documents were composed, together with the questions of their date and authorship. Even then the task of criticism is not finished; sometimes it is necessary to go back to the time before the material was written down and try to discover what it was like when it was handed down from one generation to another by word of mouth. One aspect of this branch of criticism is known as "form criticism"; this examines the pattern and structure of the material in its oral stage on the very reasonable hypothesis that the pattern and structure survive even when the material has been reduced to writing.

It is most important to recognize that there is nothing in all this inconsistent with the character of divine revelation which the Bible has for believers. The aim of Biblical criticism is to find out as much as possible about the way in which the various parts of the Bible took shape and the way in which they have been preserved to our day. Biblical criticism in no way involves "criticizing" the Bible in the popular sense of the term.

A certain amount of critical interest in the Biblical records may be traced in the earlier centuries A.D., among Jewish, Christian, and pagan scholars. Jerome, for example, about 400 A.D. recognized that the lawbook discovered in the Jerusalem temple in the reign of King Josiah (II Kings 22:8) was the book of Deuteronomy; a fresh recognition of this fact 1,400 years later was a crucial moment in the development of the critical study of the Old Testament. But the modern age of Biblical criticism may be considered to have begun in the Reformation age (16th century). Literary criticism of certain parts of the Bible (especially the Pentateuch, the first five books) was pursued in the 17th and 18th centuries, and by the beginning of the 19th century conclusions were reached about the literary structure of the Pentateuch which continue to be widely held today. What the critical approach to the Pentateuch did for Old Testament study, the critical approach to the Gospels did for New Testament study. An epoch in Gospel criticism was the demonstration in 1835, by Carl Lachmann, that Mark's Gospel is basic to the other two Synoptic Gospels (Matthew and Luke).

In the 19th century it was increasingly appreciated that literary analysis alone could not solve all the critical problems raised by the study of the Biblical documents. It was important that the documents themselves, together with such earlier sources as could be discerned behind them, should be placed in their proper historical context. Unfor-tunately critical scholars in the 19th century did not have adequate data at their disposal for this task, especially where the earlier Old Testament writings were concerned. They therefore drew upon analogies from other fields in religious history, and constructed hypotheses on the basis of current trends in the philosophy of history, particularly those associated with the name of Hegel. This tendency may be seen in the critical studies in the New Testament and the Early Church produced by F. C. Baur and other scholars of the University of Tübingen, Germany, and also in the Old Testament studies of Julius Wellhausen, one of the most influential figures in the history of Biblical criticism. Their insistence on the importance of placing the documents in their historical context was sound, even if their methodology was defective. The increase of historical knowledge since their time, especially in the archeological rediscovery of the Old Testament background, has changed the critical situation.

It remains true that one of the most important services that Biblical criticism can render is to place the various parts of the Bible in their original "life-setting." It is only when we read the records against their contemporary background that we understand them properly; it is only then that we are really in a position to reapply to our own day the message they conveyed to their day.

The civilization of the ancient Near East for the period with which the Bible deals has now been reconstructed for us on the basis of archeological research and interpretation. When we look at the Biblical history against this background, we cannot fail to be impressed with the way in which each successive stage of the Biblical history fits the appropriate part of the background. For example, the Pentateuch, whose criticism is of central importance for all Old Testament study, is traditionally associated with two names—Moses and Ezra. Ezra is presented to us in the tradition not as author but as editor, and it is certain that to his time (about 400 B.C.), and probably to his activity, we must ascribe the promulgation of the Pentateuchal law as the constitution of the Jewish state after the return from the Babylonian captivity. But when we examine the Pentateuch in detail, in the light of the archeological record, we can trace in it elements going back not only to the time of Moses, Israel's first and greatest legislator (about 1250 B.C.), but earlier still. Much of the contents of the patriarchal narratives in the book of Genesis can be shown to reflect the cultural and social life of the Middle Bronze Age (about 1900–1580 B.C.), and must have taken shape in that period, in an oral, though not in a written, form.

Similarly, New Testament criticism has uncovered, beneath all the diversity of viewpoint represented in the written records, the primitive consistency of the apostles' oral witness to Christ.

**GOSPELS, THE,** the first four books of the New Testament. They give an account of the work and teaching of Jesus, and witness to the faith of the early Church in Jesus as Christ and Son of God. This is most obvious in John, the fourth Gospel, which differs from the other three, not so much in theological interest, but in style and historical framework. Thus John lacks parables, but has long, interwoven discourses on such themes as light and love. Teaching about the Kingdom of God is almost entirely replaced by teaching about eternal life. Most attention is given to Jesus' activity in Judaea, especially at the time of Jewish festivals, and little space is given to His Galilean ministry. Jesus' cleansing of the Temple comes in John at the beginning, while in the others at the end of the narrative. John makes it almost impossible for the Last Supper to have been a Passover, which it is in Mark.

Matthew, Mark, and Luke, commonly called the Synoptic ("seen with the same eye") Gospels, are much closer, though not identical, in historical outline, and have long passages word for word the same. In matter common to all three, Matthew and Luke never agree together against Mark in the order of events, and seldom agree in wording. These facts are best explained if Mark was used by both Matthew and Luke. These two contain more teaching than Mark, much of it in similar or identical wording, and this may have come from the same oral and written sources. In addition, each Gospel has material of its own, which gives it a special coloring. The four Gospels show the variety of tradition in the early period of the Church's mission; but they recognizably deal with the same central, historical person.

**KING JAMES VERSION,** English translation of the Bible published in 1611 under the sponsorship of King James I of England, commonly called the Authorized Version. It was undertaken in accordance with a resolution passed at the Hampton Court Conference of 1604, called by James to provide for a new version without partisan notes, which should be the only version used in services of the Church of England. The task was entrusted to 54 scholars. Formally it was a revision of the Bishops' Bible (1568) but in fact all existing English versions were laid under contribution, together with many foreign versions, and above all (of course) the Hebrew, Aramaic, and Greek texts. One of the translators, Miles Smith, subsequently Bishop of Gloucester, contributed a lengthy introduction, "The Translators to the Reader," containing a detailed statement of the principles on which the translators worked. The widespread acceptance of the version after 350 years attests the excellence of their workmanship.

**NEW ENGLISH BIBLE, THE,** completely new translation of the Bible from the original languages (not a revision of existing versions) produced by panels of scholars and literary experts responsible to a joint committee representing the principal non-Roman churches of Great Britain and Ireland, the British and Foreign Bible Society, the National Bible Society of Scotland, and the Oxford and Cambridge university presses. The New Testament was published on Mar. 14, 1961, and more than 1,000,000 copies were sold in the next few days. The rest of the work involves the translation of the Old Testament and the Apocrypha.

**NEW TESTAMENT,** the second part of the Christian Bible, consisting of 27 books: the four Gospels, the Acts of the Apostles, 21 Epistles, and the Revelation of St. John or the Apocalypse. These 27 books are the definitive documents of Christianity, containing the principal record of Jesus of Nazareth and of the apostolic preaching of Him as Christ, Son of God, and Redeemer of Mankind.

The earliest Christians accepted the Old Testament, the Jewish Scriptures, as the revelation of God. There were no distinctly Christian Scriptures until later, but in Jesus Christians saw the fulfillment of the Old Testament and a new covenant between God and His people, fulfilling (or even superseding) the old covenant made with Moses. The Christian books, written later, were collected and in due course distinguished as the Scriptures of the new covenant, or New Testament.

Except for some of the Epistles of St. Paul, the books of the New Testament cannot be dated precisely; but nearly all were written between 50 and 100 A.D. Many of them were quoted as authoritative from c.100. We find lists from later in the 2d century defining the books of the New Testament canon. Most of the 27 were generally included, but there was disagreement about a few. This disagreement continued as late as the 4th century in the West, and much longer in the East. The criteria applied to a disputed book were belief in its apostolic authorship, its intrinsic merit, and its acceptance in the chief Christian centers.

The Christian claims for Jesus as Son of God made man, who was crucified and raised from the dead, are closely related to historic events. The historical reliability of the records is therefore a matter of great concern and has been questioned and searchingly examined in the last two centuries. To many Christians who have accepted the traditional estimate of the divine inspiration and infallible truth of the entire Bible, this inquiry has seemed shocking and dangerous. But of the results of Biblical scholarship in general we may say (1) that treating the books of the New Testament as human and fallible has not proved incompatible with the belief that they enshrine the word and act of God, and (2) that, although many details of the narratives are questioned, there is no doubt of the historicity of Jesus and His death nor of the apostolic belief in His Resurrection and saving power. The ultimate beliefs themselves lie beyond historical proof and remain a matter for personal decision.

St. Paul's Epistles give us early and authentic testimony to the Christian faith and preaching. The first three Gospels clearly preserve a reliable impression of Jesus, His teaching, and His impact. Scholars do not agree, however, as to how much of the central Gospel (that Jesus is the Son of God and Redeemer) goes back to Jesus Himself. How far were the traditions of His teaching colored by the beliefs of those who handed them down? Answers range from conservative to radical. But it should be noted that many scholars combine the most radical historical criticism of the Gospels with a profound faith in Jesus as Redeemer.

The New Testament books were written in Greek; they vary in literary quality and in their manner of presenting the Christian teaching.

**PARABLES** [păr'ə-bəlz] **OF JESUS.** Jesus' most characteristic method of teaching was by parables: as regards His instruction of the general public, "without a parable spake he not unto them" (Mark 4:34). His parables are confined to the three Synoptic Gospels; the similitudes of the Good Shepherd (John 10:1–16) and the True Vine (John 15:1–6) are not parables in the ordinary sense.

The parables are regularly incidents from the world of nature, or from daily life, from which may be drawn some important lesson regarding the principles of the kingdom of God, a man's duty to God or his neighbor, or God's dealings with men and women. These incidents are usually related for the sake of one particular feature, in which the point of comparison lies. The lesson is obscured if we try to find a spiritual analogy for every detail of the story. For example, the parable of the Good Samaritan (Luke 10:30–37) is told in order to explain the meaning of the word "neighbor" in the commandment "Thou shalt love thy neighbor as thyself." The true neighborly relation is established between someone who is in need and someone who is able and willing to supply that need. There is no need to spiritualize the priest, the Levite, the inn, and the innkeeper in the story; the one lesson is expressed in Jesus' concluding words: "Go, and do thou likewise."

Similarly the parable of the Prodigal Son (Luke 15:11–32) is told to illustrate the welcome which God gives to the repentant sinner. The parable of the Unjust Steward (Luke 16:1–8) illustrates the wisdom of making preparation in this life for the life to come. The parable of the Unjust Judge (Luke 18:1–8) does not teach that God is like an unrighteous judge who is slow to see justice done to his petitioners, but that His children should persevere in prayer and not give up. If even an unrighteous judge paid heed at last to the plea of a persistent widow simply for the sake of peace, all the more may God be expected to hear the prayers of His people.

Of those parables which illustrate the working of the kingdom of God, some illustrate its unseen but invincible operation in the world. When the grain is sown, the farmer can do no more; he cannot see the process of germination, but when at last a good crop springs from seed that has been sown on good ground, the hour for decisive action has struck: "straightway he putteth forth the sickle, because the harvest is come" (Mark 4:29).

Other parables emphasize that the kingdom of God is the one thing above all others which men should seek and prize; it is the treasure hidden in the field, it is the pearl of great price, for which a man may well give up everything that he has (Matt. 13:44–46). There are others which set forth its final manifestation, at the coming of the Son of Man; such are the parables of the Ten Virgins, the Talents, and the Sheep and the Goats (Matt. 25). "With many such parables spake he the word unto them, as they were able to hear it" (Mark 4:33).

**REVISED STANDARD VERSION,** the most recent and thorough-going revision of the King James Version, Revised Version, and American Standard Version of the Bible. It was produced by a committee of 32 American scholars appointed in 1937 by the International Council of Religious Education. The New Testament appeared in 1946, the complete Bible in 1952, and the Apocrypha in 1957.

**REVISED VERSION,** a revision of the King James Version (q.v.) of the Bible, undertaken by a resolution of the Anglican Convocation of Canterbury in 1870. Two companies of revisers were established, one to work on the Old Testament and one on the New. Biblical scholars of churches other than the Church of England were co-opted. Two parallel companies of American scholars were formed to co-operate with the British revisers. The result of their labor was the American Standard Version. The Revised Version of the New Testament appeared in 1881, the complete Bible in 1885, the Apocrypha in 1895. This version is unsurpassed for grammatical and verbal accuracy.

**SYNOPTIC** [sĭ-nŏp'tĭk] **GOSPELS,** the gospels of Matthew, Mark, and Luke, so called because they share much common material and phrasing. These similarities enable the texts to be studied conveniently in parallel columns.

**VULGATE** [vŭl'gāt], Latin translation of the Bible, regarded as authoritative in the Roman Catholic Church. It was based on the work of St. Jerome (c.342–420), who certainly translated the Old Testament and the Gospels himself, but apparently did not revise earlier Latin versions of the rest of the New Testament. Beginning his translation of the Old Testament in 382 at the request of Pope Damasus (c.304–84), he gradually reached the conclusion that it had to be based only on the Hebrew text. St. Augustine (354–430) and others criticized him for neglecting the Septuagint, but ultimately his view prevailed, along with his work.

"The Procession" (1957), by Elbert Weinberg. The man leading carries a Torah, or scroll of the law. Behind him walk three men, one carrying a prayer book and another a holy seven-branched candelabrum, or Menorah.

Frank J. Darmstaedter—Jewish Museum

# 2 · JUDAISM

**JUDAISM** [jōō′də-ĭz-əm], religion of the Jews. Jewish religious faith and practice are based on the doctrinal and legal content of the Old Testament, as interpreted in the literature of Pharisaic-Rabbinic Judaism, and as developed by legalists and mystics, philosophers and pietists through the ages. In the absence of a supreme ecclesiastical authority recognized by all Jews, at least since the destruction of the Temple and Jewish state in 70 A.D., Judaism, with a few notable exceptions, has not engaged in the formulation and imposition of dogmas. It is thus best approached as a climate of beliefs and opinions which at no time in its long history represents a monolithic structure but rather contains a variety of manifestations: Pharisees, Sadducees, Essenes, in New Testament times; Rabbinites and Karaites, Rationalists and Anti-Rationalists, in the Middle Ages; Orthodox, Conservative, Reform Judaism, at the present time.

**Faith.** Common to all manifestations of Judaism, however, is commitment to the covenant between God and Israel in the Bible, which, in its doctrinal and legal implications, is Judaism's reason for being and the inspiration of its doctrinal content and religious observance. Common, too, to all forms of Judaism is the awareness of the existence of God, of the world, and of man, as well as of the relationships obtaining between them. If Judaism can be said to have a "confession of faith," it is to be found in Deuteronomy 6:4 ("Hear, O Israel: The Lord our God,

the Lord is One"), proclaimed by the Jew every morning and night, thus emphasizing Judaism's stress on the unity of God. God may be experienced on various levels, approached by diverse routes, but all experiences and routes point to the One God, of Whom no physical representation is permitted. God is "our Father and our King." The question of His attributes occupies all Jewish thinkers. Some deny altogether man's ability to fathom God's attributes, and recognize only God's "attributes of action," the ways in which He relates to the world of man. It is generally recognized, however, that God, in His dealings with men, manifests two "qualities": the "quality of justice" and the "quality of mercy." The maintenance of the world requires a combination of both.

God is related to the world through creation. The Bible speaks of a six-day creation, but Judaism does not insist on a literal interpretation of Genesis. The Jewish prayer book speaks of God "Who, in His goodness, daily renews the work of creation." Creation is thus an ongoing process. The fact that God created the world means that the world is "very good" (Gen. 1:31). Judaism therefore discountenances the more extreme forms of asceticism, and insists, instead, on man's duty to live *in* the world which God created "to be inhabited" (Isa. 45:18).

Man, himself a part of that creation, owes both his body and his soul to the work of God, and must, therefore, care for the welfare of each. He is endowed with both

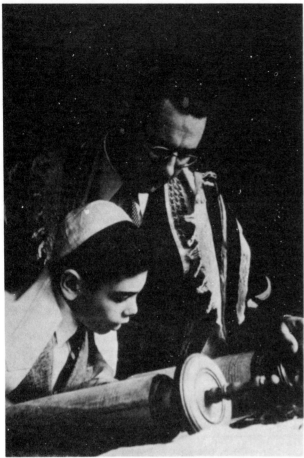

Cornell Capa—Magnum

Reading the Torah, or scroll of the law, man and boy wear prayer shawls and skull caps, in accordance with Jewish law.

Frank J. Darmstaedter—The Jewish Museum, New York

Brass Hanukkah candelabrum, or Menorah, made in Poland c.1760.

a "good inclination" and an "evil inclination," and also with freedom of choice. Sin, which is rebellion against God, is not inherited. The soul as it comes from God is pure. Though sin is universal, man, through repentance, may obtain divine forgiveness. The Pharisees taught the doctrine of the resurrection of the dead, which was denied by the Sadducees, but which became an essential ingredient of Rabbinic Judaism. However, the medieval philosophers laid greater stress on the implied immortality of the soul, while modern Reform Judaism denies the doctrine of a physical resurrection altogether.

God is related to man through revelation. God reveals Himself to man because of His love. Out of this revelation, two major commandments are born: "And thou shalt love the Lord thy God with all thine heart, and with all thy soul, and with all thy might" (Deut. 6:5), and "Thou shalt love thy neighbour as thyself" (Lev. 19:18). These commandments, in turn, give rise to further commandments—until all areas of life are drawn into the orbit of religion and covered by legislation affecting man's relation to God, and man's relation to his fellow man.

Man's relation to the world is envisaged in terms of redemption. God's creation is, so far, only potentially "very

good." It will be so in actuality when men "shall not hurt nor destroy in all my holy mountain: for the earth shall be full of the knowledge of the Lord, as the waters cover the sea" (Isa. 11:9). That is the time of Messianic fulfillment. The Hebrew prophets described it by using the metaphor of the ideal king, the Messiah. The advent of the Messiah requires the co-operation of God and man. Depending upon the political conditions of the time, the emphasis was placed either on the former or on the latter. Thus, in the 2d century A.D., after the failure of the last Jewish rebellion against Rome, the stress was on God's miraculous intervention; in the 19th century it was on man's efforts.

**The Halakhah.** While Judaism is poor in dogma, allowing considerable leeway to individual predilections (the detailed descriptions of the Messianic Age and of the hereafter, for instance, being matters of folklore rather than of dogmatics), it is rich in literature formulating the *Halakhah* (Heb., "the way"), the Jewish style of living. Here, what the Jew does in his home and at his place of work far outweighs in importance even what he does in the synagogue. From the moment he rises in the morning until he goes to sleep, from his eighth day until his burial, his life is replete with the symbols and demands of his religion. Even after answering the call of nature, the Orthodox Jew recites a benediction, thanking God for the wondrous manner in which the human organism works. Every meal is surrounded by a framework of prayers. And what the Jew eats is governed by elaborate dietary laws, which, contrary to a widespread view, were not ordained for reasons of health but in order to inculcate "holiness,"

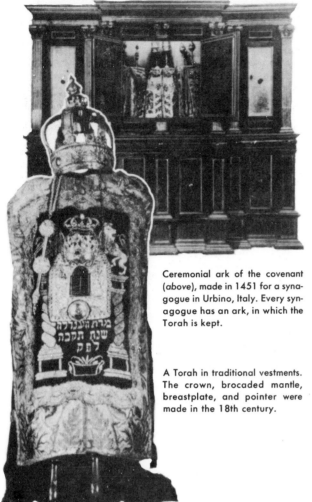

Ceremonial ark of the covenant (*above*), made in 1451 for a synagogue in Urbino, Italy. Every synagogue has an ark, in which the Torah is kept.

A Torah in traditional vestments. The crown, brocaded mantle, breastplate, and pointer were made in the 18th century.

*Frank J. Darmstaedter—The Jewish Museum, New York*

God decides the fate of nations and individuals. The latter, described in the Bible almost exclusively in terms of the Levitical ritual, has been transformed into a day which the Jew spends wholly in the synagogue, in prayer and in confession of sins. Fasting is still a means of observing the day, but the obtaining of divine forgiveness is made dependent upon the sincerity of man's repentance and upon his having pacified his wronged fellow man prior to the beginning of the Day of Atonement.

In addition to the Day of Atonement, there are a number of other fast days in the Jewish year—in connection with various sad historic memories. Chief among them is the Ninth Day of Av, commemorating the destruction of both the first and the second Jerusalem Temples as well as other catastrophic events in Jewish history.

There are also two minor festivals in the Jewish calendar: Purim, a carnival occasion, based on the Biblical Book of Esther, and Hanukkah ("Feast of Dedication"), celebrated in memory of the rededication of the Temple after the Maccabean victory in 165 B.C.

**Prayer and Study.** But the most important occasion in the calendar is the Sabbath, celebrated on Saturday, beginning with sunset on Friday. The two motivations given in the Bible, Creation (Exod. 20:11) and the Exodus from Egypt (Deut. 5:15), are incorporated in the liturgy of the day and in the meaning given to the Sabbath in Judaism. Its main observance lies in the abstention from "all manner of work," and a considerable part of Jewish legal literature is devoted to the definition of "work." Notwithstanding, by means of legal fictions, on the one hand, and of convivial domestic rituals, on the other, the Jewish Sabbath is far from being a day of gloom associated with its probable Babylonian antecedent. Instead, Jews celebrate it as a "day of light and of joy for Israel." Moreover, the rest enjoined for that day is not the mere cessation of work, but, on the positive side, the process of spiritual regeneration through prayer and study.

Study, in fact, is regarded by Judaism as a form of worship. The study of God's teaching ranks as the most important commandment. Those engaged in it may even curtail their prayers, while, according to rabbinic teaching, "the ignorant man cannot be truly pious." Every Jewish worship service, on weekdays as well as on Sabbath, contains selections from Biblical and post-Biblical literature for study purposes.

Biblical religion was centered in the Jerusalem Temple and its hereditary priesthood, but post-Biblical Judaism has been able to survive without animal sacrifice and a hereditary priesthood. Cognizance is still taken of descent from the latter in cases where family tradition has been preserved, but no priest is required for the conduct of later Jewish worship services. The rabbi (Heb., "teacher") is, technically, a layman, and Judaism is, basically, a layman's religion. This goes back, on the one hand, to the Pharisees' contesting of the priestly monopoly, and, on the other, to the evolution of the synagogue (with its non-sacrificial service) when the Jerusalem Temple was still in existence. Prayer and charitable acts were regarded as adequate substitutes for the sacrifices after the Jerusalem Temple was destroyed.

**Membership** in the community of Judaism is achieved through birth, for the covenant at Sinai was made "also

self-discipline for the sake of a higher ideal. Little parchment scrolls containing basic Biblical verses are affixed to all doorposts. Prayer shawl and phylacteries are worn for daily morning prayers. There are two other times of daily prayer on weekdays and three on the Sabbath. Thunder, lightning, and rainbow are greeted with praises to God, as are the first blooms in spring.

**Festivals.** Characteristic of Judaism is its festival calendar. Based on Biblical festivals, the sacred seasons of Judaism have been invested with historical and religious associations—often to the neglect of their original agricultural connotations. Thus Pesah (Passover), originally a farmer's spring festival, commemorates the Exodus from Egypt and celebrates the ideal of freedom. Shavuoth (Pentecost), originally the "Feast of First Fruits," is observed as the Festival of Revelation, the season of the giving of the Ten Commandments. Sukkoth (Tabernacles), originally a harvest and vintage festival, is celebrated in commemoration of God's providential care for Israel throughout their desert wanderings.

Two other Biblical festivals have been taken over, and adapted, by Judaism: the Day of Memorial and the Day of Atonement. The former, having no particular characteristics in the Biblical list of festivals, becomes the New Year, celebrated in solemn joy as the "birthday of the world" as well as the "day of judgment" on which with him that is not here with us this day" (Deut. 29:14, 15). Circumcision of the male child on the eighth day is a commandment. But it does not "make" the native Jewish child into a Jew, any more than does the observance of the 13th birthday (*bar mitzvah*). All of these rites are undergone by him who is already a Jew through the mere fact of birth. Judaism, however, is also open to converts. They can join the covenant community after a period of study and a searching examination, and, by traditional Jewish law, after undergoing circumcision and ritual immersion.

## Denominations

**HASIDISM** [hăs'ə-dĭz-əm], religious movement in Judaism founded by Israel Baal Shem Tov in eastern Europe in the 18th century. In its teachings Hasidism stresses joy in the worship of God and the mystical idea that the world of the senses is a veil concealing the essence of reality, which is the divine spark of holiness in everything. It thus exalts religious melody and dance. Hasidic communities were founded throughout eastern Europe in the 18th century and are now functioning in the United States and Israel. They have produced a rich literature of Biblical commentary, philosophical speculation, and tales about Hasidic teachers, which have been translated into most modern languages.

**JUDAISM, CONSERVATIVE,** that modern interpretation of Judaism which tries to combine adherence to the traditional forms of the faith with concessions to modern conditions of life. The position crystallized when Zacharias Frankel left the 1845 conference of Reform Rabbis after the latter declared against the absolute necessity of Hebrew in the worship service. In the United States, Solomon Schechter laid the foundations of the Conservative movement, which now includes the Jewish Theological Seminary of America, the Rabbinical Assembly, and The United Synagogue of America. Conservative Judaism lays a strong emphasis on Jewish peoplehood, but has generally avoided defining its religious position. Although it stands midway between Reform and Orthodox Judaism, its radical, "Reconstructionist," wing opposes supernaturalism.

**JUDAISM, ORTHODOX,** that formulation of Judaism which arose in the early 19th century in opposition to nascent Reform Judaism. It considers as binding divine revelation the totality of traditional Jewish law, rejects the findings of the higher criticism of the Bible, and upholds, as against Reform rejections of these beliefs, the doctrines of the personal Messiah, the resurrection of the dead, and the ultimate restoration of the sacrificial service in the Jerusalem Temple. The Orthodox Jewish worship service is conducted entirely in Hebrew, men and women sit in separate parts of the building, there is no instrumental music, head coverings and prayer shawls are worn by the men, and the service is usually of considerable length, since respect for the entirety of the accumulated tradition precludes any conscious process of selection. Samson Raphael Hirsch is responsible for that statement of the

Orthodox position which enables its adherents to combine strict observance of the Law with full participation in the cultural and civic life of the environment. Orthodox Judaism in the United States has several competing organizations, divided on the issue of whether Hirsch's position is to be maintained or whether secular learning is a hindrance to true piety.

**JUDAISM, REFORM,** that form of Judaism which arose in the 19th century in response to the changing conditions of emancipated Jewish life in Germany. Beginning with mere aesthetic reforms of the worship service, it soon led to a complete reappraisal by men like Abraham Geiger and Samuel Holdheim of the whole nature of Judaism. This was now conceived of in evolutionary terms, the traditional view of a once-for-all revelation at Sinai giving way to the doctrine of "progressive revelation." Only such traditional ceremonies were to be maintained as were meaningful to the modern Jew. The outward forms of religion are always changing, and the "spirit of the times" is also God's revelation. Transplanted to the United States, Reform Judaism found its greatest organizer in Isaac Mayer Wise, who established the Union of American Hebrew Congregations, the Hebrew Union College, and the Central Conference of American Rabbis. A period of radical departure from traditional usage was followed by a greater appreciation of the emotional aspects of the Jewish heritage.

## Personalities

**AARON** [âr′ən], in the Biblical account, elder brother of Moses, and progenitor of Israel's priests. The name is Egyptian and there is no reason to doubt that Aaron was a historical figure, the ancestor of a priestly family serving in the Israelite sanctuary of Bethel, where God was worshipped as riding on a bull. Later Old Testament writers regarded this worship with disapproval and considered it a sin (Exod. 32). Aaron himself may never have been in Bethel, living rather in the south of Palestine, where tradition recorded his tomb on Mount Hor in Edom (Num. 20:22–29). In the growth of Israelite tradition Aaron was linked with Moses and Miriam as their brother, and after the exile of 586 B.C., when Bethel ceased to be an accepted sanctuary, Aaron's descendants were the sole legitimate priests of Jerusalem.

**ABRAHAM** [ā′brə-hăm], traditional progenitor of the Hebrews, a historical figure from antiquity who migrated with his family from Mesopotamia to Palestine (Gen. 11:31). No exact date for his life can be fixed, though the story of Abraham's battle against a confederacy of kingdoms in Genesis 14 contains the names of historical kings. None, however, can be certainly identified. Abraham lived a seminomadic life, with flocks and herds, settling for brief periods when pasture was good, then moving elsewhere. He received a revelation from God (Gen. 15:1ff.), who became known as "the Shield of Abraham," in which he was promised numerous descendants and permanent possession of the land where he pastured his flocks. Abraham lived in the south of Palestine, near Hebron, where the later Calebite clan remembered him. With the permanent settlement of Israelite tribes after the conquest of Canaan, the traditions were enlarged with stories of Beersheba, Shechem, and Bethel, and the divine promise was extended to include all the land of Canaan. Other tribal ancestors were then related to Abraham to present a picture of the family of the Patriarchs. Abraham thus came to be regarded as the father of all Israelites. David's kingdom was thought to be the divine fulfillment of the original promise to Abraham, and the Shield of Abraham was identified with Yahweh, the God of Israel. With the breakup of the kingdom, a renewed fulfillment of the promise was looked for in the future.

**AKIBA BEN JOSEPH** [ä-kē′vä bĕn jō′zəf] (c.45–c.135), father of rabbinic Judaism, compiler of the Oral Law. An illiterate shepherd, Akiba in middle age devoted himself to study, becoming the foremost scholar and teacher of his day. He regarded Bar Kokhba as the "Messiah," and with nine other prominent teachers ("the ten martyrs") was executed for teaching the Law in defiance of an edict of the Emperor Hadrian. The circumstances of his martyrdom, however, are clouded by legend.

**ELIJAH** [ĭ-lī′jə], one of the great prophets of the Old Testament, who exercised his stormy ministry in Israel during the reigns of Ahab and Ahaziah (869–849 B.C.). He is known from the record of his activity in the books of Kings (I Kings 17–19, 21; II Kings 1–2). A gaunt figure of forbidding appearance and fierce conviction, he fought for the distinctiveness of the Mosaic faith when it was threatened by the cults of Canaan (I Kings 18:17–40; II Kings 1:1–17) and for social justice when it was threatened by royal tyranny (I Kings 21). Standing in the tradition which runs from Moses to Amos, he earned the title "Troubler of Israel" (I Kings 18:17) and knew the burden of his prophetic commission (I Kings 19:4–8). His reputation became legendary in Jewish tradition. He was expected to return before the coming of the Kingdom of God (Mal. 4:5).

**EZRA** [ĕz′rə], priest and scribe who obtained a decree from King Artaxerxes I (458 B.C.) to introduce Biblical law as the constitution of the re-established Jewish commonwealth in Palestine. As expounder of the law, he was the first of the scribes, a precursor of rabbinic Judaism. Modern scholarship, beginning with Spinoza, sees his hand in the editing of the Pentateuch.

**HILLEL** [hĭl′ĕl], founder of a rabbinic school, called after him, Beth Hillel, and generally revered as the spiritual leader of Jewry during the period of 30 B.C. to 10 A.D. Born in Babylonia, he went to Palestine at the age of 40 with the intention of perfecting himself in the science of Biblical exposition. Love of man was considered by Hillel as the core of the entire Jewish teaching. He once said "Do not unto your fellowman what you would not have him do unto you; this is the whole Law; the rest is commentary." He was the grandfather of Gamaliel, the teacher of St. Paul.

**ISRAEL BAAL SHEM TOB** [bäl shĕm′tōv] (Heb., "Israel, the Master of the Divine Name") (c.1700–c.1760), founder of Hasidism, a pietistic movement among the depressed Jews of Eastern Europe in the 18th century. Beginning about 1740 he taught the principles of Hasidism to many disciples. His sayings were collected by his disciples and published after his death.

**MAIMONIDES** [mī-mŏn′ə-dēz], **MOSES** (1135–1204), Jewish philosopher, Talmudic jurist, and physician. Born in Córdoba, Spain, he sojourned in Morocco and Palestine before settling in Cairo, where he earned his living by practicing medicine in the court of Saladin. His *Guide of the Perplexed* was the most important Jewish attempt to

Portrait of Moses Maimonides, from an 18th-century Italian locket.

to the place of his own earlier sojourn in Sinai. There he instituted a rule of law, administered by elders, with the Ten Commandments (Exod. 20:2–17) as its core. Here and in the region of Kadesh, south of Palestine, Moses, serving as prophet and priest, taught the people to interpret their deliverance from Egypt as a gift from Yahweh, and established a covenant between Israel and Yahweh. In this covenant Israel was to be Yahweh's people and was required to worship Yahweh alone.

The personality of Moses left an indelible impression on all subsequent generations of Hebrews. Tradition records that his character was marked by great humility (Num. 12:3), but that he was subject to outbursts of fierce anger (Exod. 32:19). Perhaps his greatest quality as a leader was his unselfish identification of his own interest with that of his people (Num. 14:11–19).

The later union of 12 tribes in Palestine was the outgrowth of the religious movement instituted by Moses, whom all the tribes considered as the mediator of Yahweh's revelation to them (Num. 12:7, 8). Few men have exerted a more enduring influence on history.

Renaissance conception of Moses, Biblical Hebrew leader, by Michelangelo, in the Church of St. Peter in Chains, Rome.

establish a *rapprochement* between Scriptural religion and Aristotelian philosophy, the latter being known to Maimonides through the writings of al-Farabi and Avicenna. One of the most characteristic of Maimonides' principles is that Aristotelian philosophy is fully reliable only in its account of the present state of the physical world. In accordance with this principle, he argues that in so far as Aristotelian philosophy touches upon the origin of the world it should not be followed. Thus Maimonides justifies his belief in the religious doctrine of creation *ex nihilo* ("from nothing"). Maimonides' position on this and other points influenced Thomas Aquinas. Besides his philosophic writings, Maimonides produced one of the most important codes of Talmudic law. He was also a noted physician and wrote a number of medical treatises in Arabic.

**MOSES** [mō'zĭs], historical founder of Israel. The name is Egyptian, and according to the Old Testament account, Moses was born in Egypt among a group of Hebrew slaves who were used for forced labor on national building. Owing to a fortuitous circumstance, he was adopted as a child by Pharaoh's daughter and brought up in Pharaoh's household (Exod. 2:1–10). After killing an Egyptian for smiting a Hebrew, Moses fled to the Sinai Peninsula, where he lived with a Midianite nomad tribe in the desert, married the daughter of its priest, and received a revelation from Yahweh, the god of the area, who identified himself as the God of the Hebrew patriarchs. Yahweh commanded Moses to return to Egypt to deliver his people, and after a conflict with Pharaoh, Moses eventually led the Hebrews out of Egypt and across the Sea of Reeds

**PATRIARCHS, THE,** in the Old Testament, the ancestors of the race, such as Noah, and more particularly of the nation of Israel—Abraham, Isaac, and Jacob. These men were Aramaean seminomads who had migrated from Mesopotamia in the first half of the 2d millennium B.C. and lived in the east and south of Palestine, where traditions of their lives (Gen. 12–50) were kept by the later tribes of Israel who settled there. The Biblical presentation shows Abraham as the father of Isaac, and Jacob as Isaac's son; but originally their lives were separate and their settlements were in different localities. They worshiped God under the form of patron deities who were believed to accompany them on their journeys and were known by the name of the chief of the clan by whom they were worshiped: Shield of Abraham, Fear of Isaac, and Mighty One of Jacob.

With the formation of the 12-tribe confederacy of Israel about 1200 B.C., all the tribes were claimed as descended from Jacob through 12 sons, and Yahweh, the God of Israel, was identified with the gods of the patriarchs. The patriarchs were presented as one family, with Abraham as its head, to whom was promised possession of the land of Palestine.

**PHARISEES** [făr'ə-sēz], the most important religious division of the Jews in the period preceding the rise of Christianity, developing into rabbinic Judaism in the Christian era. Its origins and name are obscure and have been variously interpreted. The name is related to the Hebrew root *PRSH* ("to separate"), but whether it originally meant self-separation or forcible separation by others is uncertain. The group as an identifiable party was active in the reign (134–104 B.C.) of John Hyrcanus, but its origins are much earlier. There was a connection between Pharisees and the Hasidim of the early Hasmonean period, and also with the "Wise of Israel," a group of lay teachers at the beginning of the 2d century B.C.

Pharisees represented a progressive challenge to the priestly authorities over the right of lay teachers to interpret Scriptures. Eventually confirmed in their right, they developed a notable body of teachings, the Oral Law, composed of interpretations of Scripture and nonscriptural traditions believed to have been revealed along with the Bible. Their goal was the building of a community of faith and observance out of the entire Jewish nation in conformity with their doctrines and practices.

Far from being a reactionary element, they sought new expressions for Judaism and were responsible for the survival of Judaism after the end of the Jewish state. The New Testament represents them not only as opponents of Jesus but as hypocrites. It has been shown that while there may have been such in the group, on the whole they were pious and learned men, motivated by sincere religious belief and aims.

**PROPHETS** [prŏf'ĭts], **THE,** second major division of the Hebrew Bible (the first being Law, the third and last,

Writings). The great prophets of the Old Testament were the heart and soul of ancient Israel, and through their insight into the nature and purpose of God mankind has been given a revelation of permanent validity. Prophecy was practiced in many religious traditions of the ancient Near East, as the Old Testament itself bears witness (I Kings 18:19; II Kings 10:19). But its greatest representatives in Israel so far surpass the traditional institution that they must be regarded as constituting a distinctive and unique religious phenomenon.

The golden age of Hebrew prophecy lasted almost exactly two centuries—from 750 to 540 B.C.—and included men of the stature of Amos, Hosea, Isaiah, Micah, Jeremiah, Ezekiel, and the anonymous prophet "Second Isaiah," author of Isaiah 40–55. These prophets, however, were not simply isolated individuals. They stood in a succession and were heirs to a prophetic tradition which can be traced through outstanding personalities such as Micaiah (I Kings 22), Elijah (I Kings 17–19), Nathan (II Sam. 12), and Samuel (I Sam. 15:22) to the early years of the monarchy and ultimately to the archetypal prophetic figure of Moses (Deut. 34:10). Thus it was the original Mosaic faith of Israel and not a new religion which became incandescent in the experience and conviction of the succession of prophets and which fully emerges into the light of history with Amos. The nearest access we can gain to their personal experience is afforded by the accounts of their individual calls to act as God's spokesmen to his people (Amos 7:14, 15; Isa. 6; Jer. 1:4–10; Ezek. 1:4–3:15; compare Exod. 3–4) and such confessions of divine constraint as Jeremiah 6:11 and 20:9.

The prophet's ministry was essentially to his contemporaries in Israel in particular political and social situations, where it was given to him to discern and fearlessly to proclaim the will and purpose of God. The prophetic books, composed largely of short spoken pronouncements faithfully preserved and perhaps recorded by the master's disciples, still bear unambiguous witness to the revolutionary insight with which these messengers, heralds, watchmen, and servants of God confronted His people. For them, obedience consisted not in ritual observance but in righteousness, that is, response to the divine order and divine purpose for history and society (Mic. 6:6–8).

The prophets were also concerned with the future, not, however, because they were interested in prediction (as the very word "prophecy" has come to suggest), but because they were aware that God was working out His purpose in ongoing history and because they believed that it was by the final consummation of that purpose (the Day of the Lord and the Kingdom of God) that Israel's response at all times must be judged.

**RASHI** [rä'shē], (initials of his full title and name *Rabbi Shelomo* (Solomon) ben *Isaac* (1040–1105), most popular Jewish Bible and Talmud commentator. Born in Troyes, France, he was by profession a wine grower and dealer and served the Jewish community in an honorary capacity. He is famous for the simplicity of his style. The influence of his Bible commentary is evident in Luther's German translation of the Bible.

**SOLOMON** [sŏl'ə-mən], son of David and Bathsheba and successor of David as King of united Israel and Judah (reigned c.970–930 B.C.). Through the influence of Bathsheba, David on his deathbed was persuaded to designate Solomon instead of the older Adonijah as the next King. After David's death Solomon strengthened his position by ordering the execution of Adonijah and Adonijah's supporter Joab. In like manner Abiathar was deposed from the priesthood (I Kings 1–2).

Solomon's reign was marked by splendor and brilliance. The King was himself a gifted and charming man, noted for his wit and wisdom. He organized his kingdom efficiently, dividing it into 12 districts. He married a number of foreign princesses to improve his nation's relations with its neighbors (I Kings 3:1; 7:8; 11:1–3). He conducted extensive building operations, the most important achievement in this area being the famous Temple at Jerusalem, erected with the help of Hiram, King of Tyre (I Kings 5–8; II Chron. 2–6). The national defense was provided for by the fortification of cities (I Kings 9:15–19) and the development of chariotry (I Kings 10:26; II Chron. 9:25). On the economic side Solomon sponsored maritime trade with Red Sea ports (I Kings 9:27,28; II Chron. 9:21–24) and overland caravan trade with Arabia (I Kings 10:15). He established a copper-smelting plant at the Red Sea port of Ezion-geber, as shown by archaeology. Finally he established a lucrative business as a middleman in the sale and transport of horses and chariots among nearby countries (I Kings 10:28, 29). A corresponding literary development saw the beginning of some of the more important parts of the Old Testament, such as the Books of Samuel, the early sources in the Pentateuch, and Psalms and Proverbs.

But there was also a darker side to Solomon's reign, as may be seen in I Kings 11. The luxurious harem and the easy familiarity with foreigners and foreign religions conduced to a moral and religious laxity contrary to the ancestral traditions of the people. Moreover, Solomon did not have his father's military skill, and surrounding satellite states began to rebel and secede with impunity. Internally the King was compelled to resort to heavy taxes and forced labor to support his vast enterprises (I Kings 5:13; 11:28; 12:4). Jeroboam, an overseer of labor gangs from the tribe of Ephraim, plotting revolution, fled to Egypt to bide his time. Upon the death of Solomon the northern tribes (Israel) rebelled, recalling Jeroboam to be their King, while Rehoboam, Solomon's son, retained only Judah as his kingdom (I Kings 12:1–20).

*Alinari—Art Reference Bureau*

"Judgment of Solomon" (Uffizi Gallery, Florence), attributed to the Renaissance painter Giorgione. The King of Israel and Judah determines the true mother of a disputed child (I Kings 3:16–28).

## Terms

**ADONOI** [ăd-ə-noi'] **or ADONAI** [ăd-ō-nā'ī], an appellation for God (lit., "My Lord") used in the Hebrew Scriptures, for example, in Gen. 18:27. In early times, Adonoi was used as a substitute for the unpronounceable name of God, YHWH. Because of this substitution the name YHWH (also transliterated as Javeh or Yahweh) was translated "Lord" in the Septuagint, a Greek version of the Hebrew Bible from the 2d century B.C., and in the earliest English translations. Later, since Adonoi was always read for YHWH, when the vowel points were put in the Masoretic text YHWH was pointed with the vowels of Adonoi, and this was the cause of the erroneous reading of YHWH as Jehovah. In later Jewish usage, the substitute Adonoi itself became sanctified, and pious Jews avoid the pronunciation of it except when reading from the Torah scroll or in the liturgy. At other times, they substitute the term Hashem ("the Name") for Adonoi.

**ASHKENAZIM** [ăsh-kĕ-năz'ĭm], Hebrew designation for the Jews of medieval Franco-Germany and their descendants, in contradistinction to Sephardim (of Spain). The term is based upon a fanciful identification of Ashkenaz (Gen. 10:3) with Germany. The rise of Ashkenazi Jewry is traceable largely to the Muslim-Christian cleavage which resulted in the destruction of Babylonian Jewry's hegemony over its coreligionists in Christian Europe. European Jewry then came under the influence of Palestine and carried over many of its traditions. It is this which ultimately accounts for Ashkenazi-Sephardi differences in pronunciation of Hebrew, and in liturgy, ritual, and law, especially pertaining to matrimony and diet.

Church-imposed segregation stimulated the rise of highly organized, self-governing Ashkenazi communities with their own Judeo-German dialect, Yiddish. Since they had little intellectual contact with the outside world, their cultural patterns were distinguished by an almost exclusive concentration upon Talmudic studies, a limited Biblical exegesis, and an overwhelmingly religious poetry.

In the 12th century Ashkenazim constituted only 6.7% of Jewry, but they reached numerical parity with Sephardim about 1700, and now account for about 86% of all Jews, the largest concentration being in the United States. In Israel, Ashkenazim and Sephardim are more or less evenly balanced and the differences between them are being effaced.

**BAR MITZVAH** (Heb., literally "son of a Commandment") denotes the coming of age of a Jewish youth. Once he becomes *bar mitzvah*, the boy's parents are no longer responsible for his fulfillment of the Biblical injunctions and the Halakhah. As a Jewish adult, he himself assumes the obligations and receives the privileges of the religious community. A Jewish boy becomes *bar mitzvah* automatically on his 13th birthday. The event is usually celebrated in the synagogue by "calling up" of the boy to read a portion of the Law or the Prophets.

**BIBLICAL LAW.** The content of Revelation is, in Hebrew, *torah*, commonly translated—since the Septuagint—as "law," but actually meaning "instruction," of which "law" is only a part. But law does represent an important aspect of Biblical religion. The Hebrew commonwealth is pictured as a theocracy—God functioning as the Author of its constitution. Separation of church and state being unknown, Biblical law is both cultic and civil, and its observance is understood as Israel's obligation under the Covenant, as well as man's supreme joy (Ps. 119). Rabbinic Judaism finds in Biblical law a total of 613 commandments, of which 248 are positive, 365 negative; but there is no unanimity in Rabbinic sources about the identification of this number with specific Biblical provisions.

Various types of legislation are reckoned with, for instance, "ordinance," "commandment," "judgment," "testimony," and "charge." Their exact differentiation is now doubtful, although "judgment" (*mishpat*) definitely refers to civil law. Most of the latter is found in Exodus (21–23), and Deuteronomy (21–25); much of the cultic law in Leviticus. But Leviticus (19), with its mixture of moral, cultic, and civil provisions, shows that modern distinctions were far from the mind of the Biblical writers. Cases of civil law seem to have been tried by "the elders in the gate," while the priesthood of the Jerusalem Temple functioned as the supreme legal authority (Deut. 17:8–13; Mal. 2:7). Whatever the actual application of Biblical law may have been prior to the Babylonian Exile, the reconstituted commonwealth of returned exiles, in the 5th century B.C., explicitly adopted the "law of Moses" as its constitution (Neh. 8–10).

Critical scholarship claims to know of various "strata," in chronological sequence, of Biblical legislation, and adduces parallels from other ancient law codes. These findings may differ from traditional notions in the assignings of dates to the various legal documents; but it is still recognized that law codes were accepted by the people in "covenantal assemblies," as their part of the Covenant obligations. On the other hand, the question of dating is extremely complicated in view of the more recent assumption, particularly by Scandinavian scholars, that, in ancient civilizations, a long oral tradition precedes written law.

**CABALA or KABBALA** [kăb'ə-lə] (Heb., "Tradition"), the mystical religious tradition in Judaism. It was believed to have been handed down from the beginning of time, first orally, then in writing. Some of the problems discussed were the way an infinite God created a finite world; the existence of evil; and the religious and moral duty of man.

Originally studied by only a few, Cabala became a mass movement among Jews in the 16th century, and was influential also among Christians. It is one of the central elements in Hasidism. The classic of Cabala, the *Book of Splendor* (Zohar), came to light through Moses de Leon in the 14th century.

**CANTOR** [kăn'tər], precentor, literally a singer. Specifically, the title connotes an official in charge of music in a cathedral, college chapel, monastery, or synagogue. In Lutheran Germany, as in Bach's case in Leipzig, he was director of music at the church and its adjoining school. In the Catholic rite the term refers to singers who perform solo portions of the chant. Called hazzan in the Jewish synagogue, he is a solo singer who chants the service.

**CIRCUMCISION** [sûr-kəm-sĭzh'ən], ritual cutting of the foreskin of a boy or the labia of a girl. It is part of the initiation rites of various peoples. Among Australian aborigines and many African tribes a man who has not undergone this rite is considered a boy by the group, and he cannot participate in tribal affairs. The operation is less frequently performed on girls, but where it is customary it has the same significance as that for the male—the bestowal of adult social status. There are various theories regarding the meaning of the rite, but there is no evidence of when or why it originated.

In the New World only the Aztecs practiced circumcision. It was in vogue in Egypt before 3000 B.C. Circumcision of boys is considered an obligation by Muslims. In modern medical practice circumcision is frequently performed as a hygienic measure.

**The Jewish Rite.** In Genesis (17:10–14) God commands Abraham to circumcise all males on the eighth day after birth as a "sign of the Covenant." Thus among Jews this rite assumed a religious character and applied only to males. The Covenant of Abraham came to distinguish Jews from non-Jews. Male proselytes to Judaism still undergo circumcision. It assumes symbolic significance in Jeremiah (4:4), "Circumcise yourselves to the Lord, and take away the foreskin of your heart." Christian thought, in full awareness of Jesus' actual circumcision, stresses the symbolic meaning and regards baptism as the proper substitute. Rabbinic thought, stressing the actual observance, also saw ethical implications: "Just as some creations in nature do not attain perfection until modified by man, so man's natural inclinations need channelling by man's ethical will." Originally carried out with a flint, Jewish circumcision is now performed with surgical instruments. Circumcision ceremony among Jews is a joyous occasion, a name-giving ceremony followed by a festive meal.

**COVENANT** [kŭv'ə-nənt], **ARK OF THE,** wooden chest (described in Exod. 25:10–22) in the Tabernacle of Moses, and later, in the Temple of Solomon. It was made of acacia wood, approximately 3 ft. 9 in. long, 2 ft. 3 in. wide, and 2 ft. 3 in. deep. The wood was overlaid with gold, and the lid was of pure gold. The lid was termed "the mercy seat"; Yahweh was understood to dwell between the two golden cherubim on top of it. Hence, the ark was enshrined in the innermost sanctuary, the Holy of Holies. The ark originally contained the two tablets of stone on which were written the Ten Commandments, and other cultic objects were also placed in it for a time (Heb. 9:4). It was carried at the front of the Israelite host in the wilderness; and after some vicissitudes in Canaan (including

capture by the Philistines) it was enshrined at Jerusalem during David's reign, before being placed in Solomon's Temple. Its later disappearance is a mystery, though it was probably stolen by Nebuchadnezzar's troops, who destroyed the Temple in 587 B.C.

**COVENANT, BOOK OF THE,** originally the legislation of Exodus (20:22–23:33), which, with the Ten Commandments (Exod. 20:2–17), listed Israel's obligations to Yahweh under the terms of the divine covenant. Many of its enactments are similar to sections of the Code of Hammurabi. How much of this legislation really dates from the time of Moses is impossible to say, but it undoubtedly had its beginnings then. It is, in fact, a commentary on the Ten Commandments, which in their earliest, abbreviated form were almost certainly Mosaic. Later the term was applied to the whole "Law of Moses."

**ELOHIM** [ĕl-ō-hēm', ĕ-lō'hĭm], one of the names of God used in the Hebrew Bible. Though used with singular verbs and adjectives, its ending is plural. This is probably because the plural ending designates majesty. The origin of the word is uncertain. Scholars believe that the term "Elohim" designates deity in general, in contrast to the more specific name Yahweh. In Rabbinic literature, the term Elohim is interpreted as referring to the attribute of justice of God. "Elohim" is also used to designate idols and the gods of the nations. When used in this way, it takes plural verbs and adjectives.

**ESSENES** [ĕs'ēnz], a group of Jewish ascetics who flourished from about 200 B.C. to 100 A.D. The name has been variously derived from Hebrew, Aramaic, and Syriac words covering a wide range of meanings. As described by such ancient authors as Josephus (in the *Antiquities* and *Wars*), and Philo (in the *Apology for the Jews*), they lived for the most part among, but separated from, the larger community, observing their own interpretation of the laws of ritual purity with great vigor.

"They shunned pleasures as a vice and regarded temperance and the control of the passions as a special virtue. Disdaining marriage, they adopted other men's children" (Josephus). They lived a communal existence, in which all possessions were owned jointly, and elected officers to attend to the interests of the community. The communal meal was an important function in the life of the group. They were devoted to charity and to study. Entrance into the group was preceded by a strict period of probation; infringement of its rules resulted in expulsion. The doctrine of the soul's immortality was strongly affirmed.

Since the discovery of the Dead Sea Scrolls at Qumran in 1947, there has been renewed interest in the Essenes. A number of scholars have identified the community of Qumran with them, and have used the writings of that group to explain long-standing mysteries concerning the Essenes. The occurrence of the name Hasidin (*see*

HASIDIM) in one document revived the identification of the Essenes with the Assideans of the Maccabean period.

**EXILE, THE,** also called the Babylonian Captivity, the period following Nebuchadnezzar's conquest of Judah in the 6th century B.C., during which the leaders of the Jewish community were exiled in Babylon. The first deportation occurred after the devastation of Judaean towns in 597 (II Kings 24) and the second deportation after the destruction of the Temple and city of Jerusalem in 587 (II Kings 25). The return of the exiles began fitfully after Cyrus the Persian conquered Babylon in 539 and issued his edict of religious toleration (Ezra 6:3–5). He appointed Sheshbazzar to restore the sacred vessels to Jerusalem and lay the foundations of the Second Temple (Ezra 1:7–11; 5:14–16). A larger number of Jews returned home with Zerubbabel, a Davidic prince appointed Governor of Judah, some time before 522, and in conditions of great difficulty (Hag. 1:1–11) the new Temple was completed in the spring of 515 (Ezra 6:13–18). The Jews in Babylon during the "Captivity," so far from being prisoners, lived in their own communities (Ezek. 3:15; 33:30–33) and were free to develop such distinctive religious observances as the Sabbath and Circumcision. Many families settled and prospered in their new surroundings (Jer. 29:5–13) and never returned to Palestine. Although Jewish religious life was maintained amid the ruins of Jerusalem throughout this period (Jer. 41:5), the Exile was the most decisive turning point in Old Testament history. It brought to an end Israel's existence as an independent state, and with it the institution of the Davidic monarchy. It inaugurated the priestly and scribal community of postexilic Judaism.

**HALAKHAH** [hä-lä'KHä] (from Heb. *halakhi*, "to go"), that part of the Jewish oral law dealing with legal matters in contrast to Aggadah or Haggadah, the nonlegal elements. Halakhah can also mean a specific law or regulation. It covers all phases of private and communal life, dealing with ritual, civil, and family law.

**HASIDIM** [hä-sē'dĭm] (Heb., "men of steadfast love," plural of *hasid*), name applied to three distinct Jewish groups: (1) Strict observers in the time of Judas Maccabeus who joined in the revolt against the Seleucids (167–162 B.C.); (2) mystics in the Rhineland at the end of the 12th century; and (3) members of a mystical pietist movement called Hasidism (q.v.) that began in the 18th century.

**HEBREWS,** synonym for "Jews," specifically the designation of the descendants of the patriarch Abraham, who settled in different parts of Canaan. Some scholars maintain that the origin of the word "Hebrew" specifies the people whose ancestors had dwelt in the land beyond the river Euphrates, or "on the other side of the flood."

The term "Hebrews" is used in the Pentateuch as the name for Israelites in contrast to Egyptians, Philistines, and other peoples. Also, in their early history up to the conquest of Palestine, the Israelites were known to the Babylonians and Persians by the name "Hebrews."

**HIGH PRIEST.** The Pentateuch speaks of the tribe of Levi as being chosen for the service of the Lord. Within the tribe of Levi, it is the family and descendants of Aaron, Moses' brother, who are charged with the major priestly functions, and the presiding officer of the priesthood, of whom Aaron himself is the prototype, is the High Priest. This is undoubtedly anachronistic, representing the final stage of a long development. But in the days of the Second Temple, the High Priest, under the Persian administration, does indeed figure as the religious and civil head of the Jews. Only certain families were eligible to furnish candidates for this office, which was governed by strict rules of Levitical purity. During the Roman administration the office could be bought, and it fell largely into disrepute. It ceased altogether with the destruction of the Temple in 70 A.D.

**JEHOVAH** [jĭ-hō'və], modern form of the Hebrew sacred name of God, probably originally "Yahweh." From c.300 B.C. the Jews, from motives of piety, uttered the name of God very rarely and eventually not at all, but substituted the title "Adonai," meaning "Lord," the vowels of which were written under the consonants of "Yahweh." In the Middle Ages and later, the vowels of one word with the consonants of the other were misread as Jehovah.

**JEWISH CALENDAR.** The Jewish religious year has twelve lunar months: Nisan (March-April), Iyyar, Sivan, Tammuz, Av, Elul, Tishri, Heshvan, Kislev, Tevet, Shevat, and Adar; a second Adar is intercalated every 2 or 3 years, the common year having only 354 days. Years are reckoned from the traditional date of Creation, which is, in Christian terms, 3761 B.C. The most important Jewish feasts are Tabernacles, Passover, and Pentecost, beginning on 15 Tishri, 15 Nisan, and 6 Sivan respectively. New Year is 1 Tishri, and the Day of Atonement is 10 Tishri.

**KOSHER** [kō'shər] **FOODS AND JEWISH COOKERY.** One of the oldest and most international types of cookery is the Jewish. Individual dishes vary according to national origin; yet a certain basic unity exists in that traditionally

Jewish cookery has been greatly influenced by the dietary laws of the Old Testament and the Talmud. Scholastic interpretation of the dietary laws has been a source of controversy for thousands of years. A common misconception today is that the laws are merely health measures and, as such, out of date. Although these laws include strict commands for "cleanliness" and "purity," the terms are used in a ritual sense and their main purpose is *holiness*. Their primary objective is to hallow the act of eating by teaching reverence for life. All food that is prepared and served in keeping with the dietary laws is called *kosher*, meaning "fit for use" or "proper."

**Dietary Laws.** Among the many dietary laws are those decreeing that when an animal is killed it must be slaughtered under rabbinical supervision in the most humane way possible; that the blood must not be eaten, for blood is the symbol of life; and that meat and milk must not be served or eaten at the same meal ("Thou shalt not seethe a kid in his mother's milk"; Deut. 14:21). Foods permitted under the dietary laws are:

(1) All fruits and vegetables.

(2) All animals which are cloven-hoofed and chew their cud such as cattle, sheep, and goats. Only the forequarters of these are eaten; special preparation of the hindquarters, required by the Law, involves complicated removal of veins and tissues, thus making this meat prohibitive in cost.

(3) Those fish having both fins and scales, and their roe.

(4) Most domesticated fowl, including chicken, turkey, goose, duck, and squab. (Scavengers and birds of prey are prohibited.)

Meat must also be processed so that the blood is purged. This is known as *kashering*. The meat is first dressed. It is then soaked in cold water for a half-hour, salted for one hour, and washed again under cold running water. Since broiling is an effective means of removing blood, broiled meats which have been first salted need not be *kashered*. Eggs having blood spots may not be eaten.

These and the many other dietary laws have resulted in the establishment of a Jewish cuisine. The Jewish cook who keeps a kosher home must use imagination and ingenuity to comply with these somewhat limiting dietary edicts. For instance, a kosher cook must not use milk or milk products (dairy) in preparing or serving a meat (*flaishig*) meal. Conversely, she must not include meat or meat products in a dairy (*milchig*) meal. Thus milk for the coffee, whipped cream with dessert, or butter for the bread are prohibited at a meat meal. Nor may ice cream be served. Such substitutes as a pure vegetable milkless margarine and ices, however, are permissible.

In the kosher home two completely separate sets of pots, pans, silverware, and dishes are required—one set for meat, the other for dairy. The two sets must not come into contact with each other in any way. Some authorities approve the use of the same glassware, however, for both cold meat and dairy meals.

Food that is neither milk nor meat is called *pareve* (neutral) and may be eaten at any meal. Fruits, vegetables, fish, and eggs fall within this category.

Kosher wine (wine made under the rabbinical supervision) is used for sacramental purposes and in modern as well as traditional dishes.

"Kosher for Passover" means "fit or proper for Passover." Certain foods, if certified for Passover use by rabbinical authority, are permitted. These may include matzo or matzah (a thin waferlike "bread" made without leavening agent), matzo flour, Passover noodles, candy, cake, beverages, canned and processed foods, milk, butter, jams, cheese, jelly, relishes, dried fruits, salad oils, vegetable gelatin and shortenings, vinegar, and wines, which have been specially prepared for the holiday. Certain foods such as fresh fruits and vegetables need not be certified by rabbinical authority. The use of peas or beans, however, is altogether prohibited. Frozen fruits and vegetables are permitted if they have not been precooked or processed. Natural coffee, sugar, tea, salt, and pepper are allowed if they are in unopened packages or containers at the advent of Passover.

Foods forbidden during Passover include leavened bread, cakes, biscuits, and crackers; cereals; coffee substitutes derived from cereals; and all liquids containing ingredients or flavors made from grain alcohol.

**MATZAH, MATZO, or MATZOH** [*mät′sə*], unleavened bread eaten in connection with the observance of Passover (Exod. 12:8). The order of service for the table liturgy explains that it is eaten to recall the haste with which the Israelites left Egypt (Exod. 12:39).

**LEVITES** [*lē′vīts*], in the Old Testament, members of the Israelite tribe of Levi, who were priests' assistants. In early Biblical literature priests and Levites are not differentiated. In Exodus 28 the Levites Aaron and his sons are chosen for the priesthood, with the remaining Levites aiding them, short of approaching the most holy things. In Deuteronomy, priests and Levites are synonymous; and Deuteronomy 12:18 recommends to the people's mercy "the Levite that is within thy gates," referring to Levites expelled from the "high places" which had been abolished. But Ezekiel points out the inferiority of Levites to priests, and in II Chronicles 5:12; 8:14 Levites are singers and doorkeepers in the temple.

**MESSIAH** [*mə-sī′ə*] (Heb. *māshīaḥ;* Gr. *Christos;* Eng. *Christ*), term which originally meant "anointed," to indicate divine appointment for some special task. Thus, in the Old Testament, "messiah" is used of priests, kings, and even of the Persian King Cyrus. Eventually, however, the word came to be used for *one* Anointed One whom God was yet to appoint. It would be his duty to overcome the enemies of God's chosen people and establish Israel as the great and central nation of the world, with Jerusalem as his capital.

There was no universal agreement as to who Messiah would be. Some expected an angel, others a man. Some thought he would come miraculously from the skies, others that he would be a physical descendant of David. At times (as recorded in the Dead Sea Scrolls) *two* Messiahs were expected, each with separate tasks in the restoration of a glorified Kingdom of Israel.

Some of Jesus' followers thought of him as Messiah in the popular, politico-military sense. Although this was not his role, the Church continued to apply the title to Jesus, interpreting it, however, in terms of the Suffering Servant of Isaiah 53.

Present-day Jews still differ widely about the Messiah. Some think of a personal Messiah coming in the future, others of an impersonal Messianic Age that is yet to dawn.

days were all of a taboo character. The Biblical interest in the well-being of man and the worship of God is unique.

In the Christian Church the Old Testament demand for a day of rest and worship was gradually transferred to the first day of the week in memory of the Resurrection of Christ. But the New Testament never calls this day the Sabbath. Indeed, both days were observed, separately, in Apostolic times.

**PHYLACTERY** [fĭ-lăk′tər-ē], square leather box containing Scripture passages dealing with God's unity, man's love for God, retribution, and the Exodus from Egypt, written on little parchment scrolls. One phylactery is worn on the forehead and one on the left arm by Jews during morning prayer on weekdays. In Talmudic times they were worn throughout the day. The practice is based on the Pharisaic interpretation of Deuteronomy 6:8; 11:18 and Exodus 13:9,16.

**RABBI** [răb′ ĭ] (Heb., "my master"), title of the ordained Jewish spiritual leader. Originating in Palestine in the 1st century A.D., the title carried with it authorization to render decisions in civil and ritual law. In addition, the rabbi was a teacher, though no ordination was required for either the teaching or the preaching function. Rabbinic Judaism being a layman's religion, the rabbi was not a priest, and until comparatively modern times the rabbinate was not a profession. Holders of that title earned their livelihood through a trade, often as physicians. The title was conferred by master to disciple. In modern times individual ordination has become rare, Jewish congregations preferring to get rabbis from recognized rabbinical seminaries. In modern times, too, the function of the (now professional) rabbi has changed. The legal aspect has receded into the background, and the modern rabbi is primarily a preacher, teacher, pastor, and administrator.

**SABBATH** [săb′əth], the seventh day. The observance of the seventh day as holy was considered by the Israelites to date from the creation (Gen. 2:3), and it was re-enacted in the Ten Commandments (Exod. 20:8–11). In the tabernacle and temple ritual, the Sabbath was marked by an extra sacrifice and by the presentation of the shewbread. In later times the Sabbath became the chief day of worship in the synagogue ritual. The principal feature of the day, which in the Jewish calendar extends from Friday evening to Saturday evening, has always been the prohibition of work of any kind. Detailed regulations, defining what is and what is not permissible, have been worked out by the rabbis over many centuries.

The observance of specially holy days was frequent in the ancient world, and the name "Sabbath" probably derives from the Akkadian word *shabattu*. But the ancient

**SABBATICAL** [sə-băt′ĭ-kəl] **YEAR,** every seventh year, considered holy by the Hebrews, for whom the number seven had a peculiar sanctity. In that year, the land was to lie fallow, neither sowing nor reaping being permitted (Lev. 25:1–7). The year also served to release Hebrew slaves from bondage and Hebrew debtors from their debts (Deut. 15:1–15). These were well-intentioned economic measures, to restore the earlier status quo. There is occasional historical evidence of the observance of sabbatical years between the time of the 5th-century-B.C. Jewish leader Nehemiah and the 1st-century-A.D. historian Josephus. In modern academic usage the term refers to a paid leave of absence for research or travel granted every seventh year to professors.

**SADDUCEES** [săj′ŏŏ-sēz], one of the religious divisions of the Jews in the period preceding the rise of Christianity. The name may be derived from a certain Zadok who, in one source, is said to be its founder, or from the phrase "sons of Zadok," referring to the family that controlled the high priesthood after the return from the Babylonian exile (538–438 B.C.). Both the Jewish historian Josephus (c.37–100 A.D.) and the rabbinic sources report the Sadducees' opposition to the Pharisees on the basis of their rejection of the latter's insistence that the oral tradition was of equal validity with Scripture. In addition the Sadducees held a highly transcendent view of God, emphasized the freedom of the human will, and denied retribution and resurrection. Josephus reports that they were "boorish in their behavior" with one another and rude with others. They seem to have been made up of priestly and aristocratic families. After the fall of Jerusalem, in 70 A.D., they lost all influence and apparently ceased to exist as a cohesive group.

**SANHEDRIN** [săn′hē-drĭn], the high council of the Jews, with 71 members recruited from the high-priestly families (the current high priest being president), the scribes, and other lay elders. Its religious influence extended to Jewish communities everywhere, and in Roman times it was the administrative council for Judaea, and was the supreme court. The Sanhedrin, abolished with the destruction of Jerusalem in 70 A.D., was later revived by the Jewish community in Palestine but ceased to function by the end of the 4th century A.D.

**SCRIBES** [*skrībz*] (literally, "those who know the art of writing"), the line of teachers begun by Ezra (5th or 4th century B.C.), who taught the Law to the Jewish people. First reading the Hebrew text, they translated it into the Aramaic vernacular and commented upon it. Builders of the oral tradition after the Babylonian Exile (586–538 B.C.), they raised Jewish knowledge to a higher level. They also transmitted, and occasionally revised, the Biblical text. As an organized group they functioned for some 200 years, until the time of Alexander the Great.

**SEPHARDIM** [*sĭ-fär'dĭm*], Hebrew designation for the Jews of the Iberian Peninsula before the expulsions of 1492 and 1497, and later for these exiles and their descendants, in contradistinction to Ashkenazim (Jews from Germany). The term is based upon similarity of sound between "Sepharad" (Obad. 20) and "Hesperia" (Spain).

The Sephardim were incorporated into the Islamic world and their intellectual life was influenced by the famous Babylonian Jewish schools (3d–11th century). From these they received their distinctive Hebrew pronunciation, their main liturgical forms, and their ritual and legal traditions. Since they were less isolated than the Ashkenazim, they generally enjoyed a greater social prestige and a cultural superiority. Their Talmudic texts were regarded as being more reliable, and their method of study was more systematic. Sephardi Biblical and linguistic studies were highly developed, and a rich, variegated secular literature was produced in Hebrew, influenced by Arabic language and style. For many centuries the Sephardim maintained their own Spanish-Jewish dialect, called Ladino, and the Sephardi pronunciation has become standard in modern spoken Hebrew.

Up to the 13th century Sephardi influence was preponderant. But during the 14th and 15th centuries the Ashkenazim, because of their rapid growth, became predominant, and the gap between the two Jewries widened. Despite the cultural, legal, and ritual differences between the two, however, they have generally coexisted peacefully. Although in Israel the Sephardim have achieved numerical parity with the Ashkenazim, they constitute no more than 14% of world Jewry.

**SHOFAR** [*shō'fär*], ancient horn or trumpet, used in the synagogue by the priests. The instrument is made from an actual ram's horn and has a cup-shaped mouthpiece at the small end. The two tones produced are of a strident quality. After thousands of years the shofar is still in use today during certain religious holiday seasons, particularly the New Year.

**SYNAGOGUE** [*sĭn'ə-gŏg*] (Heb. *kneset*, "assembly"), Greek designation of an ancient Jewish institution: the gathering of the community to worship and receive instruction. Its origins are obscure and traditionally are traced to the days of Moses. Historically it can be traced to the Babylonian Exile, for it existed side by side with the

Touro Synagogue in Newport, R.I., was dedicated in 1763.
(THE JEWISH MUSEUM)

Temple in Jerusalem after the return from the Exile (end of the 6th and beginning of the 5th century B.C.), as a nonpriestly institution. With the destruction of the Temple in 70 A.D. the mode of worship developed in the synagogue became the usual practice for Judaism.

The particular contribution to the history of worship made by the synagogue was that it provided, as the Jewish scholar Ismar Elbogen (1874–1943) said, for "regular gatherings for worship at places that required no other consecration than the presence of those united for that purpose." Nonetheless it is evident that the synagogue received some of the structure of its worship from forms used in the Temple. The recitation of Deuteronomy 6:4–9, beginning with the words "Hear, O Israel, the Lord our God, the Lord is one," which remained central to the service, apparently goes back to the early period of Temple

Hebrew University of Jerusalem synagogue (1957), by Emanuel Rau.
(THE JEWISH MUSEUM)

worship. This, together with other Biblical passages and the introductory and concluding prayers, formed the earliest structure of synagogal worship.

As this developed, daily gatherings, analogous to the sacrificial hours of the Temple, were instituted, giving rise to the three regular daily services. In addition, the public reading of Scriptural selections on the Sabbath and market days (Monday and Thursday) became increasingly important. After the destruction of the Temple (70 A.D.) the synagogue became the central institution in the life of the Jewish community. The liturgy continued to develop and grow, reflecting the experiences and moods of the people. The teaching aspect of the synagogue was emphasized through the regular reading and interpretation of Scripture.

The contemporary synagogue in all of its forms continues to reflect the ancient structure of worship and teaching. Because of the nature of its worship service, its physical structure is basically quite simple. Requisite are the *aron ha-kodesh*, the Holy Ark, a cabinet containing the handwritten scroll of the Pentateuch, and the *bimah*, the platform and desk from which the Scripture is read. In the traditional synagogue, the reader of the service stands before and facing the Ark. The order of service for weekdays and Sabbaths is found in the siddur (Heb., "order"), and for festivals and holy days, in the mahzor (Heb., "cycle").

**TABERNACLE** [tăb'ər-năk-əl], portable shrine used by the Israelites prior to their conquest of Canaan. It or some temporary structure also served for a time after the conquest, until superseded by the Jerusalem Temple during Solomon's reign. The structure and furniture of the tabernacle are described in Exodus 25–27. The structure measured 30 by 10 cubits and consisted of two compartments, the holy place and the Holy of Holies, which were separated by a curtain. It faced west and was surrounded by a court. The most important piece of furniture was the Ark of the Covenant, housed in the Holy of Holies. Other items were the altar of incense, golden lampstand, table of shewbread, and in the outer court the altar of burnt offering and the laver.

Although the description may be idealized and from a later period, the existence of some sort of portable shrine to house the Ark of the Covenant in preconquest times is very likely. Indeed, there are early Canaanite and other parallels. It is also probable that the Temple was modeled on it.

**TALMUDISTS,** primarily the Jewish rabbis quoted in the Talmud, who lived from about 200 B.C. to 500 A.D. in Palestine and Babylonia. But the term "Talmudist" is also applied to students of the Talmud, and since the Talmud has been the core of the curriculum of Jewish schools for the past 15 centuries, the number of such Talmudists is legion.

**TEMPLE, JEWISH,** center of Jewish worship, in ancient Jerusalem. The first Jewish Temple, superseding earlier temporary structures (tabernacles), was erected in Jerusalem in the middle of the 10th century B.C. It was instigated by Solomon, and the work was largely done under Phoenician supervision (I Kings 5; 6). Throughout Solomon's reign it served as the central sanctuary for the whole Israelite nation, but after his death, when the kingdom had split in two, it was used only by the southern Kingdom of Judah. Though once or twice plundered and damaged, it stood until 587 B.C., when the Babylonian armies under Nebuchadnezzar burned down Jerusalem and the Temple with it (II Kings 25:8–16).

After half a century of exile, when the Jews returned, one of their first concerns was to rebuild the Temple, presumably on the pattern of that of Solomon. This second Temple, however, was far less glorious. Zerubbabel, the Jewish governor, was behind the work, and it was completed in 515 B.C. (Ezra 1–6). This temple, too, had its vicissitudes, but it never suffered destruction. It was desecrated by Antiochus IV Epiphanes in 168 B.C., but was triumphantly rededicated under Judas Maccabeus four years later. Pompey the Great forced his way into it in 63 B.C. but he took no plunder. Herod the Great (37–4 B.C.) decided to rebuild it, but without interrupting the services of worship. He began the magnificent work of renovation and embellishment in 19 B.C. (John 2:20), and the main part of the new building was finished by 9 B.C. All the courts, however, were not completed until between 62 and 64 A.D. This Temple stood until 70 A.D., when the Roman troops under Titus destroyed it by fire at the end of the Jewish War. The temple area is now occupied by the sacred Arab enclosure, Haram esh-Sherif, with the two 7th-century-A.D. mosques of Aqsa and of Caliph Umar built by Caliph Abd al-Malik, the latter mosque called the Dome of the Rock and consecrated as a rival sanctuary to the holy places of Mecca and Medina. Part of the Haram wall is the Wailing Wall, relic of the Temple of Solomon and among the holiest and most revered of Judaic sites.

**Description.** Cedar wood was the chief material in the first two Temples, though gold and silver were also lavishly used. Herod used huge blocks of white stone. In all three Temples, but particularly in Herod's, there was a complex of buildings and courts, so that the Temple area was sometimes used as a fortress. Jesus and His contemporaries found the courts and colonnades suitable sites for teaching the crowds who frequented the Temple area. One court served for commercial purposes, and Jesus took exception to this, and once or twice ejected the salesmen (John 2:13–16; Mark 11:15–18). But the Temple proper was reserved for the priesthood alone, and only the high priest ever entered the inner sanctuary. The shrine itself consisted of an outer and inner sanctuary, the latter containing the Ark of the Covenant until that most sacred object disappeared. Afterward the innermost chamber remained empty. Another important feature of the several Temples was the entrance porch, which was originally flanked by two great pillars. The entire structure was rectangular, facing east and west.

**YAHWEH or JAHVEH** [yä'wĕ], the most common name for God in the Hebrew Bible. It appears 6,823 times. It is the proper name for the God of Israel, in contrast to the more general name for the Deity, "Elohim." From earliest times in the synagogue, the name was not pronounced, the word "Adonoi" being used instead. Since the word was pointed with the vowels of its substitute Adonoi when the vowel points were finally put into the Hebrew text, "YHWH" was mistakenly read as "Jehovah." The now more common pronunciation Yahweh is based on inconclusive evidence from ancient sources.

The meaning of "Yahweh" is also not certain. The most convincing scholarly opinion is that it is derived from a Hebrew root meaning *to be*, and thus "Yahweh" would mean either "He Who Always Is" or "He Who Brings Everything into Being." In rabbinical literature "Yahweh" is interpreted as referring to God's attribute of Mercy. Because the name Yahweh has four letters in Hebrew, it is frequently referred to as the Tetragrammaton (Gr., "four-lettered").

**ZION, MOUNT,** Biblical name used as a synonym for Jerusalem, or else for one part of it: originally for the City of David (II Sam. 5:7; I Kings 8:1), and then for the hill on which Solomon's temple was built (Isa. 2:3; 8:18). Beginning in the Middle Ages a popular tradition located Zion on the southwestern hill, where a church existed over the supposed spot of Jesus' last supper. Archeological work has shown this tradition to be wrong, for the city of David existed on Ophel (the southeastern hill).

## *Holidays*

**ATONEMENT, DAY OF** (Heb. *Yom Kippur, Yom Ha-Kippurim*), the most solemn day in the Jewish calendar, occurring on the 10th of Tishri (the 7th month). The Biblical account (Lev. 23:26–32) is taken by some scholars to represent a late stage in a long development. However, in the period of the Second Commonwealth (beginning with Ezra, 5th century B.C.), its character was firmly established as a day of fasting and prayer. The ceremonies performed in the Temple by the High Priest are described in minute detail in rabbinic sources. In addition to the usual offerings, two goats were set aside. One was offered on the altar; the other, the scapegoat, was sent out into the wilderness. According to these traditions, it was on this day that the High Priest entered into the Holy of Holies to confess for himself and the whole people. After the destruction of the Temple (70 A.D.) the observance of the day centered in the synagogue. Its priestly aspect vanished and its character as a period of personal repentance was enlarged. The liturgy of the day is extremely elaborate. The 24-hour fast begins at sundown with the recitation of *Kol Nidre* (All Vows), a formula asking for release from obligations of man to God which he cannot fulfill. This is sung to a touching medieval melody. Some parts of the service recount the ancient rites, but in general, the meditations and prayers are devoted to introspection, self-examination, confession, contrition, and resolution. The day ends with the sounding of the Shofar (the ram's horn).

**HANUKKAH** [hä′nōō-kə], Jewish Feast of Dedication, observed for eight days from the 25th of Kislev (November-December). Instituted in commemoration of the rededication of the Jerusalem Temple in 164 B.C., it is celebrated by kindling lights, adding one for each evening and reciting benedictions over them.

**PASSOVER** (Heb. *Pesah*), a major festival in the Jewish calendar, lasting eight days. One of the three Biblical pilgrimage festivals (Deut. 16:16), Passover, according to critical views, was originally observed by the sacrifice of a lamb on the night of the 14th of Nisan (March–April) and was later connected with the Feast of Unleavened Bread beginning on the 15th of Nisan to form one festival (Lev. 23:4–8). During the existence of the Temple the individual sacrifices were offered there, but the flesh was consumed elsewhere in Jerusalem. After the destruction of the Temple (70 A.D.) the sacrificial cult came to an end and the family table liturgy was enlarged.

The central theme of the observance was the "Going out from Egypt" (Exod. 12:43–51), and from this developed a ritual narrative recited at the family table. This recitation (Haggadah), emphasizing the mighty acts of God, elaborates upon the Biblical story of the Exodus and explains the significance of the Passover offering, the unleavened bread (matzah), and the bitter herbs eaten during the meal. The eating of leaven is proscribed during the festival.

**PENTECOST** [pĕn′tə-kôst] (Gr. *pentekoste*, "fiftieth day"), a major festival in the Jewish calendar observed on the 6th and 7th of Sivan (May-June). Originally a pilgrimage festival in connection with the offering of the first fruits, it followed Passover by seven weeks and was celebrated on the 50th day, hence its Hebrew name (*Shavuot*, "weeks") and its Greek appellation. Following the destruction of the Temple in 70 A.D., the harvest aspect of the festival diminished and emphasis was placed on the Revelation at Sinai, which according to tradition occurred on this day.

**PURIM** [pōōr′ĭm], a minor Jewish festival, observed on the 14th of Adar (February-March) in commemoration of the deliverance of the Jews from the plot of Haman as recounted in the Book of Esther. The distinctive features of the day are the reading of the Book of Esther, the exchanging of gifts, and a children's masquerade. Critical scholarship has cast doubt upon the historicity of the events, but the major emphasis upon religious freedom has given the day an enduring importance.

**ROSH HA-SHANAH** [rŏsh hə-shä′nə], the New Year Festival of the Jewish calendar, falling on the 1st and 2d of Tishri (September–October). It introduces the Days of Awe, culminating in the Day of Atonement. Mentioned briefly in the Bible as the Day of Memorial (Lev. 23:23–25), it developed into a major holy day. The distinctive feature of the worship is the sounding of the shofar (ram's horn), and its main themes are summarized in the prayers recited in connection with this act: the proclamation of the Kingdom of God, of God's providence and His revelation and redemption. The order of worship is intended to arouse the individual to introspection in preparation for the Day of Atonement.

**TABERNACLES, FEAST OF** (Heb. *Sukkot*), the most joyous festival in the Jewish religious calendar, observed in the autumn for nine days (eight in Israel and among Reform Jews). Its origins go back to the agricultural festivals commemorating the harvest (Exod. 23:16; 34:22; Lev. 23:34,39; Deut. 16:13,16). It is also connected with the Exodus from Egypt and the wilderness wanderings (Lev. 23:43). During the festival, meals are eaten in a booth (tabernacle) erected out of doors, and, as part of the worship service, palm branches are waved during the recitation of certain psalms. The eighth day is called *Shemini Atzereth* (Eighth Day of Assembly); and the ninth, *Simhath Torah* (Rejoicing of the Teaching).

## *Literature*

**AGGADAH or HAGGADAH** [hə-gä′də], that part of the Jewish Oral Law which does not deal with legal matters, or *halakhah*. It includes homiletical interpretations of Biblical verses, stories, parables, moral sayings, proverbs, and biographies of Biblical and Talmudic personalities. The word is probably derived from a Hebrew verb meaning to tell or to relate.

**DEAD SEA SCROLLS,** popular designation for the collection of Hebrew and Aramaic manuscripts discovered at the northwest end of the Dead Sea between 1947 and 1956. In Apr., 1948, cables from Jerusalem reported the discovery of sheepskin manuscripts dating from some 2,000 years ago. Found by Bedouins (1947) in a cave south of Jericho, half of the scrolls had been acquired by the Syrian Metropolitan Athanasius Samuel and half by Professor E. L. Sukenik of the Hebrew University. All seven of the scrolls are now in the Shrine of the Book, part of the Israel Museum in Jerusalem, which was opened in 1965. The cave in which they were found was excavated by the French Dominican archeologist, Father Roland de Vaux, in 1949, and hundreds of additional fragments were discovered. By 1956 most of the inscribed material from Cave I was published. These scrolls evidently belonged to a particular Jewish sect of the period.

In 1949 De Vaux began excavating the ruins of Qumran, nearly a mile south of Cave I. There he found community buildings which had served as a kind of monastery. Farther south, he later excavated ancient workshops and the remains of gardens belonging to the same Jewish sect whose scrolls had been discovered in Cave I. This was soon identified with the third most important of the early Jewish sects, the Essenes, who are described by Josephus and Philo, and who are said by Pliny the Elder to have had their settlement in this precise region, where they had flourished for two centuries.

Since 1948 hundreds of caves in this area have been examined, and a dozen of them have yielded scrolls and fragments. Most important are Caves IV (1952) and XI (1956); the former had preserved fragments of some 400 scrolls, while the latter contained some relatively complete manuscripts. There are probably many still undiscovered caches of manuscripts in the Qumran area. (The manuscript remains from Murabbaat and En-gedi nearly all date from the time of the Second Jewish Revolt, c.132–135 A.D., and have nothing to do with the earlier Essenes.)

The Qumran manuscripts may all be dated paleographically between c.225 B.C. and the third quarter of the 1st century A.D., but most of them were copied during the 1st century B.C. This is confirmed by coins, pottery, and radiocarbon datings, as well as by linguistic and historical analysis of the contents of the scrolls. Qumran itself seems to have been occupied by the Essenes between c.100 B.C. and the early years of Herod the Great (reigned 37–4 B.C.), and again, more briefly, until the destruction of the community by the Romans c.69 A.D. The scrolls are

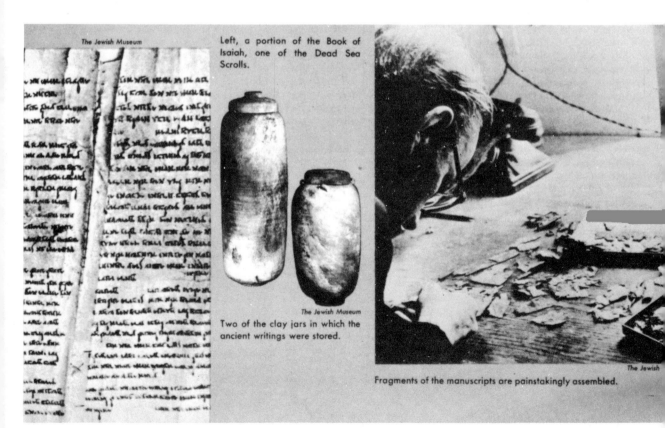

The Jewish Museum

Left, a portion of the Book of Isaiah, one of the Dead Sea Scrolls.

The Jewish Museum

Two of the clay jars in which the ancient writings were stored.

Fragments of the manuscripts are painstakingly assembled.

The Jewish

largely copies of Old Testament books and are on the average a good millennium older than the earliest Hebrew Biblical manuscripts previously known. They are only slightly later than the Greek translation (Septuagint) and are of inestimable value for the historical and textual reconstruction of the Hebrew Bible.

Besides Hebrew Biblical writings, there are remains of pre-Essene Intertestamental books (Tobit, Jubilees, Enoch), as well as of Essene sectarian books. Among the latter are the Scroll of Discipline, the so-called Damascus Covenant, the Thanksgiving Hymns, the War, commentaries on Biblical books, which interpret the text prophetically, and translations of the latter into Aramaic. The Essene literature is of the greatest importance for the light it sheds on the New Testament and the beginnings of Christianity.

**GEMARA,** part of the Talmud (q.v.), a commentary on and supplement to the other part, the Mishnah.

**HAGIOGRAPHA** [hăg-ē-ŏg′rə-fə] (Gr. *hagios*, "holy"; *grapha*, "writings"; Heb. *ketuvim*, "writings"), third part of the Hebrew Scriptures, comprising Psalms, Proverbs, Job, the Five Rolls (Song of Songs, Ruth, Lamentations, Ecclesiastes, Esther), Daniel, Ezra, Nehemiah, and I and II Chronicles. This is the order followed in the synagogue; but in the Alexandrian canon (the Septuagint) these books are in a different order. The existence of such a collection is attested in the 2d century B.C. in the prologue to *Ecclesiasticus*, but the final fixing of its content took place around 90 A.D.

**HASMONEAN** [hăz-mə-nē′ən] **DYNASTY** (167–29 B.C.), Jewish dynasty founded by the Maccabees. They were descendants of Mattathias, the priest who led the revolt against the Seleucid King, Antiochus IV Ephiphanes (176–163 B.C.). The victory over the Syrians, achieved by Judas Maccabeus and his brothers Jonathan and Simon, resulted in independent status within the Seleucid empire. The family took the high priestly office (152 B.C.).

**HEBREW LITERATURE,** the literature in the Hebrew language, together with literature pertaining to the Jewish religion written in other languages.

**Old Testament and Apocrypha.** The Old Testament contains writings from more than 3,000 years ago to the 2d century B.C. Some of the books excluded from the Biblical canon and some works in Biblical style of later origin (up to c.100 A.D.) were preserved (mostly in Greek translation) in the Apocrypha and in the Pseudepigrapha.

**Hellenism.** The spread of Greek civilization generated contacts between Judaism and Hellenism, especially in Ptolemaic Egypt. In the 3d century B.C. the Pentateuch was translated into Greek. The Greek version of the Bible, known as the Septuagint, of which this translation of the Pentateuch was the first part, was intended both for Greek-speaking Jews and for intelligent heathen. The Apocryphal Wisdom of Solomon (2d century B.C.) fused

Judaic with Greek ideas. Philo Judaeus, also known as Philo of Alexandria (c.30 B.C.–c.40 A.D.), advocated a synthesis between Hebrew and Greek wisdom. Flavius Josephus (38–c.100 A.D.), of Jerusalem and Rome, described the Judaeo-Roman war of 66–73 A.D. (*The Jewish War*) and wrote a history of his people (*Jewish Antiquities*) and a treatise in defense of Judaism (*Against Apion*), all in Greek.

**The Dead Sea Sect.** Since 1947 we have possessed some of the writings of the Essenes (fl.2d century B.C.–1st century A.D.). The Scroll of Discipline records the rules by which they lived; the Thanksgiving Hymns, their devotional life; and the War of the Sons of Light with the Sons of Darkness, their Messianic beliefs.

**Rabbinism and Biblical Scholarship.** After the destruction in 70 A.D. of the Second Temple and with the rise of new centers of Judaism (for example, in Babylonia), more and more emphasis was placed on exegesis of the Bible, interpretation of the Law (as originally given in the Torah, or Pentateuch), and study of the classical traditions. The basic record of these investigations is contained in the Palestinian and Babylonian versions of the Talmud, which were completed in the 4th and 5th centuries, respectively. Nonlegal, theological, historical, and legendary materials are contained in numerous Midrashim, homiletic works of the same period. The post-Talmudic Geonim, heads of academies in Babylonia, wrote *Responsa*, or scholarly answers to legal inquiries. In the Gaonic period (589–1038), too, a uniform Biblical text (the Masorah) was established.

Rabbinism was attacked by the Karaites, a Jewish sect founded in the 8th century which advocated a return to the Bible; Karaite scholars wrote their own works on Hebrew grammar and Biblical exegesis. However, rabbinic activity continued both in the East and in Europe. *The Epistle* of Gaon Sherira (d.1000) of Pumbeditha, Babylonia, offers a concise history of Talmudic tradition. Nathan ben Jehiel (fl.11th century), of Rome, compiled the *Arukh*, a Talmudic lexicon. Solomon ben Isaac, known as Rashi (1040–1105), of Troyes, wrote extensive commentaries to the Bible and the Babylonian Talmud and initiated the school of the Tosaphists, who wrote glosses on the Talmud. Other commentators on the Bible were the rationalist Abraham ibn Ezra (Spain, 1092–1167) and the mystic Moses Nahmanides (Spain, c.1195–c.1270). Moses Maimonides (Spain and Egypt, 1135–1204), the greatest of medieval Jewish scholars, wrote in Arabic a commentary to the Mishnah, which is a part of the Talmud, and a Hebrew code of the entire Law (*Mishneh Torah*). Joseph Karo (Palestine, 1488–1575) composed the Shulhan Arukh, the definitive code of Jewish law. Talmudic studies flourished in eastern Europe during the period from the 16th through the 18th century; they culminated in the works of Elijah of Vilna (1720–97).

**Philosophy, Ethics, and Poetry.** Most medieval Jewish philosophers aimed at a systematic presentation of Judaism—a rational demonstration of the concept of God—and at a reconciliation, however conditioned, of reason and revelation; they discussed issues such as creation, free will, evil, reward and punishment, prophecy, immortality. Saadia Gaon (Babylonia, 892–942) wrote *Doctrines and Beliefs*; Maimonides wrote the *Guide for the Perplexed*, a

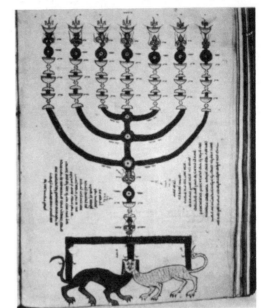

The *Mishneh Torah* (1180) of Moses Maimonides is one of the great Jewish theological works of the Middle Ages. At left is a page from the original manuscript, in Maimonides' handwriting, with his corrections and suggestions to the copyist. Above is a page from a 13th-century German copy, with a diagram explaining the symbolic details of the seven-branched Menorah.

work used by the Scholastics. In his *Kuzari*, Judah ha-Levi (Spain, 1085–c.1140) represented a nonrationalist approach to faith. The Talmudist and astronomer Levi ben Gershon (France, 1288–1344) was an Aristotelian. Opponents of Aristotelianism were Hasdai Crescas (Spain, 1340–1410) and Joseph Albo (Spain, 1380–1444); the former's *The Light of the Lord* influenced Spinoza. Writers on ethics stressed "the duties of the heart" (Bahya ibn Pakuda, Spain, c.1040–c.1110) and simple, mystic devoutness (*The Book of the Pious*, Germany, c.1200). Poets, using contemporary art forms, composed liturgical pieces (*Piyyut*): they wrote on the love for God and on Israel's past history and current exile, her sufferings, and her hope for the Messianic redemption. The chief poets were the Spaniards Solomon ibn Gabirol (Avicebrón, 1021–58), Judah ha-Levi (1085–c.1140), and Moses ibn Ezra (c.1070–c.1140).

**Mysticism and Hasidism.** Rooted in early mystical and Gnostic teachings of the first centuries A.D., Jewish mysticism (cabala) matured in medieval Spain. The Zohar (Book of Splendor), 13th century, expounded the mysteries of creation and divine revelation, and the communion of the soul with God. Isaac Luria (1534–72) headed a school of mystics in Palestine; his teachings provided the doctrinal background of the Hasidic movement, founded in eastern Europe by Israel Baal Shem Tob (1700–60).

**Enlightenment and After.** From the 18th century on, Western thought entered Jewish literature. Moses Mendelssohn (Germany, 1729–86) combined Judaism with Europeanism (*Jerusalem*, 1783; trans., 1838), translated the Bible into German, and initiated the Haskalah (Enlightenment) movement. A secular Yiddish literature arose

in eastern Europe. Leopold Zunz (1794–1886) applied modern historiographic methods to Hebrew literature. Heinrich Graetz (1817–91) and Simon Dubnow (1860–1941) wrote large-scale histories of the Jewish people. Modern poetry is represented by Hayyim (Chaim) Nahman Bialik (1873–1934), the modern essay by Ahad Haam (1856–1927). Contemporary religious thinkers are the orthodox mystic Abraham Isaac Kook (1864–1935); the philosophers Martin Buber, author of *I and Thou* (1923; trans., 1937), and Franz Rosenzweig (1886–1929), author of *The Star of Redemption* (1921); and Mordecai Kaplan, author of *Judaism as a Civilization* (1934). Important contemporary scholars are G. G. Scholem, author of *Major Trends in Jewish Mysticism* (1941), and S. W. Baron, author of *A Social and Religious History of the Jews* (2d ed., 9 vols., 1952–60).

**MASORETIC or MASSORETIC TEXT** [măs-ə-rĕt′ĭk], Hebrew text of the Old Testament in the form representing the tradition preserved by Jewish scholars (Masoretes, "transmitters") both in Palestine and Babylonia during the first Christian millennium. The consonantal text was fixed no later than 100 A.D., while the vowel points were added, beginning with the 5th century, on the basis of older oral traditions concerning the correct reading and pronunciation of the words. The Masoretic text is divided into three sections, Torah, Prophets, Hagiographa. The books are arranged differently in the Septuagint, the Alexandrian Greek text, which furnished the order of arrangement in the Christian Old Testament.

**MIDRASH** [mĭd'răsh] (from Heb. *derash*, "to search"), a Jewish interpretation of Scripture beyond the literal meaning (*Peshat*), created by the Talmudic rabbis. There are two types: Midrash Halakhah, dealing with the legal books; and Midrash Aggadah, concerned with narrative and hortatory sections. Midrashim were complied into separate collections for specific books of the Bible and are also found throughout Talmudic literature.

**MISHNAH** [mĭsh'nə] (from Heb. *shanah*, "to repeat"), compendium of Jewish Oral Law compiled by Rabbi Judah ha-Nasi in the beginning of the 3d century A.D. in Palestine. It ranks second only to the Bible as an authoritative source of teaching for Judaism, and served as the basis of the Gemara, which, together with the Mishnah, forms the Talmud. The Mishnah is divided into six *sedarim* ("orders"): (1) Seeds (*Zeraim*), dealing with agricultural activities and ritual problems; (2) Festivals (*Moed*), treating the laws connected with the Sabbath and festivals; (3) Women (*Nashim*), dealing with the legal aspects of marriage, divorce, and the relations between the sexes; (4) Damages (*Nezikim*), concerned with civil and criminal law; (5) Holy Things (*Kodashim*), containing the laws of sacrifice and the ritual of the Temple; and (6) Purities (*Tohoroth*), presenting the regulations governing ritual impurity. The Mishnah is written in a Hebrew dialect known as Mishnaic Hebrew.

**OLD TESTAMENT,** the Hebrew Bible, first of the two sections into which the Christian Bible is divided, witnessing to the Old Covenant, or Testament, between God and Israel. In the English versions it comprises 39 books arranged in four parts: the Pentateuch (Genesis—Deuteronomy), the historical books (Joshua—Esther), the poetical books (Job—Song of Solomon), and the Prophets (Isaiah—Malachi). This is roughly similar to the order of the Greek versions of the Old Testament.

In the Hebrew Bible there is a threefold division into the Law, or Torah, containing the Pentateuch; the Prophets, containing also most of the historical books; and the Writings, containing the remainder. The total number of books in the Hebrew reckoning is 24, counting the 12 minor Prophets as one book, Ezra and Nehemiah as one, and the historical books which are separated into two in the English Bible as one each: Samuel, Kings, and Chronicles. The Hebrew order reflects that in which the collections grew up and were regarded as authoritative for Jewish faith. The Pentateuch was of first importance, and by c.444 B.C. was accepted by the Jewish community substantially in its present form; the final edition of the prophetic books was made at the latest by 200 B.C.; and by the Council of Jamnia (90 A.D.) the Hebrew Old Testament contained all those books which it now has. Certain books appearing in Greek translations of the Old Testament, but no longer appearing in the Hebrew, were rejected by the Jewish Council as of sec-

ondary authority, but were retained in the Christian Church to form the Apocrypha.

The original language of the Old Testament was Hebrew, with the exception of a few passages (Ezra 4:8—6:18; 7:12—26; Jer. 10:11; Dan. 2.4—7:28) which were in Aramaic. The text was originally written with only a partial representation of the vowels, but Jewish scribes, the Masoretes, evolved a system of points, which were later added, together with marginal notes, to produce the Masoretic Text. The standard edition was the work of the family of Ben Asher and appeared in the 10th century A.D.

The Old Testament bears witness to the life and faith of the people of Israel and was written down during the years from c.1000 B.C. to c.164 B.C. Older traditions of the origins of Israel were related orally before being finally fixed in writing.

**PENTATEUCH** [pĕn'tə-tūk] (Gr. *penta*, "five"; *teuchos*, "book"), first five books of the Bible: Genesis, Exodus, Leviticus, Numbers, and Deuteronomy. They contain the major collections of ancient Israelite laws and are frequently called the Law, or Torah. They contain the old covenant law of Moses, with expansions adapting it to new situations as these arose in Israel.

**PRAYER BOOK OF THE JEWS,** the individual and communal prayers from the ancient Temple service. With additional liturgy accrued through the centuries, the prayers have been collected and formalized in the *siddur*, or *tephillah*, for daily prayers, and the *mahzor* for festivals. While the general structure and main text of daily, Sab-

*The Jewish Museum*
A page of the Soncino Bible (1492).

bath, festival, and holy day services are similar, minor variations reflect geographical and historical differences between various Jewish communities.

**SEPTUAGINT** [sĕp'tū-ə-jĭnt], the Greek translation of the Hebrew Scriptures begun in the first half of the 3d century B.C. and concluded well into the 2d century B.C. The Letter of Aristeas tells the legend of its separate translation by 72 Jewish elders in 72 days, all translations agreeing with one another. It is not a unified translation but a collection from many hands. Some books have been rendered quite freely; others, word for word. In some cases it appears that the translators may have been working from a somewhat different Hebrew text than the one that has come down to us from Palestine. Created for the Jewish community of Alexandria in Egypt, this translation was the means of conveying to the Greek world knowledge of Hebrew thought and religion. The order of the books is that found in the usual English translations, though it contains material accounted noncanonical in the Jewish and Protestant traditions but included in the Roman Catholic canon.

**TALMUD** [tăl'mŏŏd, tăl'mŭd] (Heb., "teaching"), compilation of the Jewish oral law. It contains the Mishnah, which is the legal codification of the oral law, with the Gemara, which is the amplification of, and commentary on, the Mishnah. The Mishnah, which is divided into 63 tractates, is written in Hebrew, while the Gemara is written mainly in Aramaic.

There are two Talmuds: the Babylonian and the Palestinian. The Babylonian Talmud is a record of the discussions of the Babylonian rabbis and the Palestinian Talmud is the work of the Palestinian teachers. The discussions recorded in the Talmuds cover material created over the course of 700 years. The Palestinian Talmud was redacted in 400 A.D., and the Babylonian about 500 A.D. The Talmud not only records the decisions of the rabbis, but their discussions as well. The Babylonian is estimated to contain about 2,500,000 words, the Palestinian about a third that number. The Babylonian Talmud is the authoritative source book of Judaism, while the Palestinian Talmud holds a subordinate position.

The Talmud comprises both *halakhah*, or legal elements, and *aggadah*, or nonlegal elements. Next to the Bible, it is the most important work in Judaism. It formed the central subject of the curriculum of Jewish schools for 15 centuries, and has been the subject of thousands of books of commentary and elucidation. It is the source of Jewish law and ritual as well as the basis of Jewish theology and religious ideas. It has been translated into several modern languages, the latest being the English translation known as the Soncino translation.

**TARGUM** [tär'gŭm] (from Akkadian *targumanu*, "interpreter"), Aramaic translation of the Hebrew Scriptures. From the earliest times of the Second Temple (c.400 B.C.) it was customary to add an Aramaic translation during the public reading of Scripture, since Aramaic was the spoken language of the masses. The best-known Targum is that of Onkelos to the Pentateuch. It is usually printed together with the standard Hebrew text. There are also Targums of lesser importance to the Pentateuch, as well as to the other books of the Hebrew Bible.

**TEN COMMANDMENTS,** known also as the Decalogue, ancient Jewish code. It is the core of the religious and moral teachings revealed by God on Mount Sinai and the basis of God's covenant with Israel. Though modern scholarship has suggested some alternatives, Jewish and Christian tradition finds the authoritative version of the Ten Commandments in Exodus 20:2-17 and Deuteronomy 5:6-21. After God is shown to be the deliverer from Egyptian bondage, there follow religious commandments concerning worship of false gods, misuse of God's name, and the sanctity of the Sabbath. Then came moral commandments concerning parents and prohibition of murder, adultery, theft, perjury, and covetousness. The wording of the Exodus and Deuteronomy versions is at variance, but the contents are essentially the same. However, the sanctity of the Sabbath is motivated in Exodus by the consideration of God's creation; in Deuteronomy, by God's liberation of Israel from bondage. There are variations in the numbering of the Ten Commandments, but their contents have become the foundation of both Jewish and Christian religious teaching.

**TORAH** [tôr'ə] (Heb., "teaching"), word used in Jewish thought with a wide variety of references. In its narrowest construction it refers to the Pentateuch, and in the phrase "Sefer Torah" (Book of Teaching) it indicates the scroll used for the public reading of Scripture in the Synagogue. More broadly construed, "Torah" means the entire range of Jewish teaching, including the Scriptures and the whole oral tradition (the Midrash, Mishnah, and Talmud). The translation of this word as "law" fails to do justice to its more inclusive meaning, for in Judaism it is the term for religion in its broadest and most encompassing sense.

Ananda, a favorite disciple, attending the *Pari-Nirvana* of the Buddha. *Pari-Nirvana* is the death and final entry into *Nirvana* of a perfect being. This 12th-century rock cut is in Polonnaruwa, Ceylon.

# 3 · BUDDHISM

**BUDDHISM** [boo'dĭz-əm, bood'ĭz-əm], comprehensive name given to the doctrine believed to be that of the historical Buddha, Siddhartha Gautama, to the philosophy and religion that evolved from it, and to the related sects, dead and extant.

Buddhism originated in India, and the Buddhist world, which has included the whole of Asia east of Iran, is divisible philosophically into two main parts: the Southern and Northern schools of Buddhism. The former preserves its sacred literature in the dead Indian language, Pali, while the latter has its scriptures in Sanskrit, Chinese, Japanese, and Tibetan. "Southern" and "Northern" refer to the location of the communities in relation to the Himalayas. Thus, Southern Buddhism obtains in Ceylon, Burma, Siam (Thailand), and Cambodia; while Northern Buddhism is, or was, associated with Nepal, Kashmir, Tibet, China, Annam, Mongolia, Korea, and Japan. In India Buddhism lost its identity 1,000 years ago.

Unlike most other sages of 6th-century-B.C. India, who were of the Brahman (priest) caste of Aryan society, Siddhartha belonged to the warrior caste. His clan name was Gotama in Pali, Gautama in Sanskrit. Brahmanism, the authoritative teaching of the Brahmans, claimed for itself a monopoly in religion, and therefore condemned the Buddha's doctrine as unorthodox, or evedic, that is, not derived from the traditional source of Hindu thought contained in the ancient Vedas (the Aryan sacred lore dating from 1500 to 1000 B.C.). After the four Vedas and their appendages, the Brahmanas, came the Upanishads— books containing philosophical systems by which the mystical Realization of Liberation from mundane life could be attained by means of Knowledge. Primitive Buddhism was, in early Indian speculative thought, representative of this Upanishadic period; it claimed that by Knowledge plus Compassion one might realize Liberation, which Buddhists call *Nirvana* (in Sanskrit), *Nibbana* (in Pali).

**Buddhist Canon.** Doubt exists as to what amount of the Buddhism contained in even the oldest of the Buddhists' canonical writings was actually the teaching of the historical Buddha, Gautama. The Theravada, the only surviving sect of the Southern School, claims that its Pali Canon contains the original doctrines in words actually spoken by Gautama. However, its books were not committed to writing until the 1st century B.C., which was 500 years after the Buddha began to teach, following his Enlightenment. Since his death, therefore, these words had been passed down orally through some 15 generations of teachers and pupils in collections of recitations called *suttas* (Pali) or *sutras* (Sanskrit). Not only must the words themselves be considered, but also shifts in their interpretation throughout the centuries.

Meetings of Buddhists, called "Buddhist Councils," were convened early in North India to discuss these questions. The First Council was held in 483 B.C., a few months after the death of Gautama, by his leaderless disciples. The Second Council (383 B.C.) considered the rules of discipline and procedure in the *Sangha* (Buddhist order of monks and nuns), against the growing rigidity of which a number, calling themselves *Mahasanghikas* (members of the Greater Sangha), protested. A Third Council (c. 250 B.C.) deliberated as to which of the then current recitations should be regarded as canonical and worthy of preservation. This is the most historic of all Buddhist Councils, because at it the decisions of a minority dictated the contents of the Pali Canon. A schism resulted, and the dissatisfied majority seceded, calling its doctrine the *Maha*

("Great") *Yana* ("Vehicle"), while that of the minority they termed *Hina* ("Lesser") *Yana*. The Hinayana coincides with the Southern School, the Mahayana with the Northern. Thereafter, both parties held councils independently, until in 1956 the Theravadins arranged a convention in Burma, called by them "The Sixth Council," which was also attended by some Mahayani Buddhists of Japan and Tibet.

### Doctrine of the Historical Buddha

Gautama posited Three Characteristics that condition life and all that lives, including human beings. These are:

(1) Impersonality, unsubstantiality (Pali *anatta*; Sanskrit *anatman*);

(2) Impermanence, change (Pali *anicca*; Sanskrit *anitya*);

(3) Imperfection, sorrow (Pali *dukkha*; Sanskrit *dukkha*).

"Just this have I taught and do I teach," declared the Buddha, "sorrow, and the ending of sorrow." Sorrow, then, is the basis of the Buddhist philosophy; and it is this which has sometimes brought an exaggerated charge of pessimism against Buddhism. The Indian—Hindu and Jain, as well as Buddhist—finds life essentially unsatisfactory and imperfect; and sorrow and pain, mental and physical, he recognizes as characteristic of mundane life. Hinayana Buddhism, like other Indian religions, aimed primarily at Release from this world of sorrow, at Liberation or *Nibbana*. Hence the self-perfected Buddhist (*Arahat*) was regarded by many as the skillful escapist. There was nothing derogatory about this appellation, however, since the *Arahat* had to renounce family life, social position, all possessions, and every luxury in order to succeed. Quite differently, Mahayana Buddhism claimed that this objective world is in reality *Nirvana*, and aimed at the subjective Realization of this Truth. To both the Hinayani and Mahayani, the Buddha's Doctrine (Sanskrit *Dharma*; Pali *Dhamma*) is merely a means to the end, to be discarded when that end is reached.

The Buddha's stock definition of *dukkha*, or suffering, is made as a statement of truth. It is the first of the Four Noble Truths, which are:

(1) That life is subject to sorrow;

(2) That this sorrow is caused by ignorance, which results in desire-attachment;

(3) That this sorrow can be eliminated by the elimination of desire-attachment;

(4) That the way to eliminate desire-attachment is to follow the Eightfold Path.

**Noble Eightfold Path.** In effect this is the Middle Way of life between extremes of excessive austerity and sensuality. Both are equally deplored as hindrances to spiritual progress. This way of moderation and detachment is the Buddhist's criterion, and the Buddhist philosophy of life is sometimes referred to as "The Middle Way."

The sections of the Noble Eightfold Path are:

(1) Right Views: seeing life as it is, in accord with its fundamental Three Characteristics, and appreciating the Four Truths;

(2) Right Mindedness: being motivated by friendly thoughts, without prejudice, toward one's fellow human beings and toward all other forms of sentient life;

(3) Right Speech: speaking kindly and truthfully, and narrating incidents accurately;

(4) Right Action: acting skillfully and sympathetically, while avoiding vain or violent effort;

(5) Right Livelihood: practicing a means of living that does not cause oneself or others to infringe lawful morality;

(6) Right Endeavor: self-perfection by avoiding and rejecting ignoble qualities, while acquiring and fostering noble qualities;

(7) Right Mindfulness: the cultivation and practice of self-awareness and compassion, resulting in self-reliance and equanimity;

(8) Right Concentration: contemplation culminating in intellectual intuition, wisdom.

The Eightfold Path is divisible under three main headings: Morality (items 3, 4, 5: right speech, action, livelihood); Mental Culture (items 6, 7, 8: right endeavor, mindfulness, concentration); and Wisdom (items 1, 2: right views, mindedness). Some of the later Buddhist sects originated from an emphasis on one or another of these three divisions of the Noble Eightfold Path.

Thus, the Buddha concerned himself primarily with the causes of sorrow in order to arrive at its elimination. "That being present, this becomes; from the arising of that, this arises," he declared. "That being absent, this does not become; from the cessation of that, this ceases." The Theory of Dependent Origination, or Causal Formula, is one of 12 mutually conditioning links, and served as a corollary to the Four Truths. Truths 2 and 3 state, respectively, that sorrow is caused by ignorance resulting in desire-attachment, and that this sorrow can be eliminated by the cessation of desire-attachment. Therefore, starting from Ignorance, the formula is:

Ignorance conditions one's characteristic actions;
Character and actions condition consciousness;
Consciousness conditions mind and body;
Mind and body condition the senses;
The senses condition sense impression;
Impression conditions sensation;
Sensation conditions craving;
Craving conditions attachment;
Attachment conditions becoming;
Becoming conditions again-becoming (rebirth);
Birth conditions old age, death.

A Chinese painting (9th–10th century) in the British Museum portrays the Buddha bidding farewell to his servant and his horse before taking up the life of a hermit.

*Art Reference Bureau*

Or alternatively expressed: Old age and death depend on birth, birth on living, living on attachment, attachment on craving, craving on sensation, sensation on impression, impression on the senses, the senses on mind and body, mind and body on consciousness, consciousness on one's characteristics and actions, and these depend on ignorance. This is also known as the Wheel of Becoming, which can be summed up in this way: Ignorance causes desire-attachment, which causes activity, which causes reincarnation.

**Law of Karma.** The mechanics of this, and of all processes, are governed by the Law of Karma (Pali *Kamma*), or the principle which states that everything which happens is the result of a previous cause, and will itself cause a further result, and so on and on. All Indians accept this law of action and reaction, by which principle they explain moral retribution, which demands for its functioning a continuity of lifetimes, either here or on other planes of existence. This means that death is necessarily followed by another life, since the results of one's actions (measurable by the amount of volition that gives rise to them) are not annulled by death, but will find their appropriate expression independent of time. This process goes on and on until obviated by the attainment of *Nirvana.* Hence one is born to the parents, and into the environment, that one deserves. And since rebirth is caused by desire-attachment, the Buddhist must abstain from desires and attachments. Because the factor motivating reincarnation is volition, karmic reaction is the opposite of fatalism: man is, ultimately, "the master of his fate."

**Attainment of Nirvana.** *Nirvana* is a supernormal condition. Didactic Buddhism defines the normal healthy human being as (a) possessing six senses—the five physical ones plus mind (thinking) and (b) as composed of five parts (Pali *khandhas;* Sanskrit *skandhas*)—form, sensation, perception, mental tendencies and conditions, and consciousness. All these are subject to transience (*anicca*), for man exists in a state of flux; not only is his physical body continually changing, but also his mind—his opinions, enthusiasms, ambitions, likes, and dislikes.

Mind-consciousness is indicated as the vehicle of that mysterious identity that is carried on after death, through reincarnation, during the series of lives that continues until *Nirvana* is attained. Buddhists look for the explanation in *anatta* (impersonality). The word *anatta* is a negative one, from *an* ("not," or "no") and *atta* ("self"). But how exactly the Buddha applied this to the individual human being became a source of controversy among his later followers, and discussion over it persists among Western scholars today. The majority of Hinayani Buddhists, including the orthodox Theravadins of South Asia, define *anatta* literally, thus denying that any changeless, enduring personal entity exists. The minority of Hinayana Buddhists, together with Mahayani Buddhists and many distinguished Western Buddhologists, affirm that *anatta*, while meaning no separate self, implies no self permanently separated from the Higher Self—that Self which the Realized man perceives as the Whole, the cosmic Self, the "Buddha-essence" that pervades the universe. This view equates the essential in Buddhism with the essential in Hinduism, since this universal Buddha-nature is none other than Brahman; both are names for the unnamable Absolute. Orthodox Hinayana denies that a Higher Self

*Art Reference Bureau*

"The Dream of Maya" (9th–10th century) is a Chinese painting in the British Museum. While the future Buddha awaited his coming to earth, his mother, Mahamaya, dreamed that a white elephant, symbol of the miraculous birth of a great teacher, entered her side. According to tradition, the Buddha was born from her right side.

exists; Mahayana replies that the Hinayani interpretation of *anatta* is a too literal exoteric one, which knows nothing of the esoteric Self. And so Mahayana denies that Gautama denied that a Higher Self exists, and posits the non-duality of the phenomenal and noumenal.

The imperfect self that suffers reincarnation, when it becomes the perfected Self that knows the bliss of *Nirvana*, is reduced by Buddhist metaphysics to a condition of being which only those who have attained the Goal can appreciate. *Nirvana*, the Buddha taught, can be won here and now, in one's present lifetime. When it is, when the Truth is Realized, the body, of course, has to complete its natural span of years, although it is no longer subject to karmic reaction. At death the body of one who is Enlightened, who has Realized *Nirvana*, disintegrates, and there is no further reincarnation or again-becoming: one has Become. This state of cessation is called *Pari-Nirvana*, or Utter Nirvana, when the identity is lost in the Whole, the One, the Absolute.

The etymology of *nirvana* gives *nir-va* the meaning "to blow"; in old texts references are found to the simile of the wind blowing out the flame. While it can be said that *Nirvana* is the result of the annihilation of ignorance and sorrow, Buddhists emphatically deny that *Pari-Nirvana* is annihilation. Mahayanists term it *Tathata*, or Suchness, and claim that it cannot even be named "the One," since it is not distinct from anything. Hinayanists equate it with Cessation, holding that "the cessation of becoming is *Nibbana*." When urged to say more than this, the Buddha replied: "No measure measures him who has reached the Goal: by what measure is the immeasurable measured? No words describe the indescribable!"

### Buddhist Meditation

One-third of the Eightfold Path is devoted to Meditation, the exercise of which plays the most important part in the actual practice of Buddhism. It serves to improve and perfect the character and to stimulate intuition and wisdom. Buddhist mental culture, or *yoga*, commences with simple breathing exercises; by control of the breath one learns to calm and ultimately to control the physical body. With the body under control, the more difficult and important task of controlling the mind follows. With one's thoughts controlled and purified, the character can be perfected; then wisdom and intuition mature, until finally the mystical Realization is won. It is the individual who has to change and not the "outside" world. The wisdom that enables one to accomplish this is not to be confused with factual knowledge, such as that acquired by conventional education; rational thinking, intellectual reasoning, can be an obstacle to attainment, which is, essentially, a process of passing beyond the mind.

The Buddha insisted that knowledge must be tempered with kindness and understanding; neither Knowledge nor Compassion alone ensures Perfection. In the Southern School of Buddhism the science of Meditation is divisible into three principal groups of exercises:

(1) Contemplation of the Four Sublime States of Mind: Benevolence, Compassion, Sympathy, and Equanimity.

(2) Practice of the Four Applications of Mindfulness. These are more comprehensive, involving exercises in concentration upon one's body, one's sensations, one's states of mind, and one's mental conceptions.

(3) Absorption in the Material and Immaterial Spheres (*Jhanas*). These are the most important of all, and involve the contemplation of a series of four material and four immaterial spheres. Meditation on the objects of form results in successive withdrawals from objective stimuli until the mind and senses become tranquilized. Meditation on formless objects involves the contemplation of infinite space, unlimited consciousness, emptiness, and neither perception nor nonperception.

The exercises in meditation practiced by monks of the Northern School include many of the aforementioned, and are generally more varied and less systematized; they also include contemplation of the characteristics of the Compassionate Buddha, and of principles of Buddhist doctrine. In Lamaism and in some of the Mahayani sects of China and Japan, elaborate systems of meditation were devised, the lessons of which were applied to such things as wrestling, archery, flower arrangement, and painting. Meditation is the most significant occupation of the monks of the Buddhist Order.

### The Buddhist Order

The newly Enlightened Buddha soon attracted a number of devotees, who, like himself, were wandering mendicants who had renounced family life. Several of his earliest disciples were Brahmans "well versed in the Vedas," though the Compassionate One made no distinctions among those seeking him as their *guru* or teacher. For most of the year they moved from place to place, meditating and sleeping in caves or under trees, while begging a daily meal from merit-seeking villagers. During

Frances Mortimer—Rapho-Guillumette

"Penitent Buddha" (2d–4th century) is an Indian work in the Central Museum, Lahore, Pakistan. The Buddha lived an ascetic life for a short time, but finally decided that Enlightenment could not be achieved through the mortification of the flesh.

the rainy seasons, when travel became impossible, temporary shelters were provided by householders. Before many decades—while Gautama was still living, it appears —these shelters developed into sizable buildings, organized monasteries housing the brotherhood (*Sangha*).

The primitive *Patimokkha* (rule for Buddhist monks) contains the heart of the Buddha's teachings:

> "Abstain from all evil; acquire merit; purify your thoughts.
> "Patience is the greatest penance; *Nibbana* is the Goal.
> "No ascetic, no recluse is he who injures, who vexes another!
> "Hurt none by word or deed: live so bounden, and restrained, moderate in eating, in resting and sleeping; devoted to contemplation."

This, the Pali scriptures teach, is the message of all Buddhas. From it were evolved the *Patimokkha* rules, 145 in number, for the monks (Pali *bhikkhus*; Sanskrit *bhikshus*) of the *Sangha*. To this nucleus each sect added more regulations, many quite petty. The *Vinaya Pitaka* of the Theravadins contains a total of 227 rules, all attributed to the Buddha, though it seems unlikely that more than the first few were promulgated by Gautama himself, whose *Dhamma* stressed detachment, free-thinking, and the avoidance of all fetters.

Of these *Vinaya* rules the first four are of fundamental import, the breaking of any one of which results in expulsion from the Order. These stipulate that no *bhikkhu* should indulge in sexual intercourse, take anything not given him, deprive a human being of life, or boast of possessing supernormal powers.

A simple system of initiation into the Buddha *Sangha* was employed and later elaborated into two regular ceremonies of ordination: a preliminary (*Pabbajja*), and a higher (*Upasampada*). Each novice monk (*Samanera*) is given eight requisites which are his sole possessions: three saffron-dyed robes, a girdle, a needle, a razor, a water strainer, and a food bowl. Today donors add to these a pair of sandals and an umbrella.

Some years after the establishment of the Buddhist *Bhikkhu Sangha* women were admitted for ordination as *bhikkhunis*, or nuns. They lived apart from the monks; a Hinayani canonical legend relates that Gautama was reluctant to include women in the *Sangha*, and prophesied that their presence in it would shorten the life of his *Dhamma's* dispensation in the world by half. Buddhist nunneries flourished better in the countries of the more tolerant Mahayana, though today few *bhikkhunis* remain anywhere. The vows taken by monks and nuns are not binding for life, and they remain free to quit the Order and revert to lay life. Buddhist householders observe the Five Precepts, by which they undertake to abstain from killing, stealing, adultery, lying, and intoxication.

The comparatively sheltered life in the monastery served its proper purpose of providing the ideal environment for the practice of meditation, the cultivation of intuition, and the perfection of wisdom, though the supreme Realization may be attained anywhere, at any time. Gautama, at his death, appointed no successor as leader; the *Sangha* remained without a Patriarch, though subsequently some sects elected chiefs. The Order necessarily depended upon lay society for its maintenance, from its initial recruitment to its members' two daily meals. And although wealthy donors and princes sometimes granted land and revenue to individual monasteries, the *Sangha's* livelihood, and therefore its attitude, remained ultimately dependent upon public opinion and favor.

In India the Buddhist Order underwent four successive stages of development: the Ascetic Stage, when contemplative recluses strove for immediate Realization; the Monastic Stage, when unregimented monks aimed at personal perfection, or, at least, propitious rebirth; the Sectarian Stage, when rigid rules and orthodoxy diverted the monks' attention to pedantic competition; the Popular Stage, when the monks sought to make their *Dharma* available and attractive to the pious householder—the era of a universal religion.

### Mahayana: Buddhism as a Universal Religion

Mahayana Buddhism accepts as fundamental the teachings of the historical Buddha recorded in the Pali Canon, but asserts broadly that the Hinayana contains the comparative truth and gives the literal interpretation of those teachings, whereas the absolute Truth, together with the means of its Realization, is more comprehensively set forth in the Great Vehicle.

Historically Mahayana dates from the Second Council of the 4th century B.C. in India. The Buddha's doctrine

(*Dhamma*) is followed in the Pali Canon by the *Abhidhamma* (After-Dhamma), which constitutes a cold psychoanalysis of the *Dhamma*. As a reaction to this lifeless dissection there evolved the warm-hearted "New Wisdom School" of Indian Mahayana. In Buddhist literature the borderline between Hinayana and Mahayana is reached with the Early *Prajnaparamita* (Perfection of Wisdom), *sutras*, some of which date from the 1st century A.D. They introduce new metaphysical ideas and novel doctrines about previous Buddhas and *Bodhisattvas* (Buddhas-to-be), on whom the householder, unable to enter the *Sangha*, could pin his faith. Mahayana in outlook, these *sutras* are, however, attributed to the *Sabbatthavadins* (Pali *Sarvastivadins*), the most important of the Hinayani sects of Northwest India, whose scriptures were written in Sanskrit. They introduce the doctrine that the world of experience (*samsara*) is comparatively unreal because all is void (*shunya*) of permanent self-substance. Such was the metaphysical basis of the "New Wisdom" of the Great Vehicle.

**Nagarjuna.** "The Father of Mahayana" was the teacher Nagarjuna, a Brahman born at Berar, India, in the 2d century A.D., who formulated the nondual doctrine of *Shunyata*, or emptiness, which proclaims the Oneness of the phenomenal and noumenal. A corollary of this teaching was the doctrine of Three Bodies (*tri-kaya*): the Dharma-body of the Buddha as the Absolute; the noumenal, or Enjoyment-body, of the Bodhisattvas of the Pure Land or Paradise; and the phenomenal body of the historical Gautama. His followers were called *Madhyamikavadins*, followers of "The Middle Way," between the unreality of *samsara* and the Supreme Reality of *Nirvana*. Their literature is known as the Larger, or later, *Prajnaparamita* (the words of which *sutras* were attributed to the Buddha to enhance their prestige). To Mahayanists, Nag-

While the Buddha sat meditating under a bodhi tree, he was tempted by Mara, an evil spirit, to renounce his quest for Enlightenment. A Tibetan temple banner shows him pointing to the earth to bear witness that he has not succumbed to temptation.

*American Museum of Natural History*

A 10th-century Japanese Buddha, carved in wood, is seated in the traditional position of meditation.

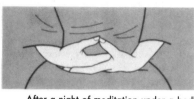 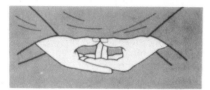

After a night of meditation under a bodhi tree, the Buddha attained the supreme mystical experience of *Nirvana*. The way of deliverance from the world was revealed to him. According to tradition, he sat in the position shown at left, with crossed legs and hands in his lap. This arrangement of the hands (two variations shown above) is associated with contemplation and concentration.

arjuna remains "The Second Founder of Buddhism," who reasserted the Middle Way and revealed the true interpretation of Gautama's *Dharma* (Doctrine). His greatest known work is the Sanskrit *Mula-Madhyamika Karikas*, in which he demonstrated that no individual thing (*dharma*) can be positively asserted, since only the Whole is real—which doctrine of relativity has been misunderstood as nihilism. Nagarjuna composed several works, and to him were subsequently attributed (in the usual Oriental style) books written by other, later teachers.

**Mahayana Sects.** Each of the sects derived its support and inspiration from one or more *sutras* or groups of writings. The *Prajnaparamita* group of the Madhyamikas became so copious that abridged *sutras* were composed, the most famous of which were the *Hrdaya* (Heart) and *Vajrachhedika* (Diamond-cutter) *sutras*, good translations of which appear in some Western anthologies.

It was the Mahayana Buddhism of Faith in, and Devotion to, Amitabha Buddha of Infinite Light, the personification of Compassion, that brought Buddhism completely out of the monastery. Popular in India, it became more famous in the Far East with the Pure Land Sects, where Amida (Japanese for Sanskrit *Amitabha*) Buddha became the foremost object of worship. The Four Stages to *Nibbana* of the Hinayani aspirant—Stream-attainer, Once-returner, Never-returner, *Arahat*, or Perfected one—are now replaced by the Mahayani Six Stages to spiritual perfection—charity, morality, resignation, vigor, meditation, wisdom (*prajna*)—called the Six *Paramitas* or Perfections. They reflect the idealism of the *Bodhisattva* (Pali *Bodhisatta*), whose Compassion demanded that he renounce *Pari-Nirvana* in order to help humanity. These "Buddhas of Compassion" became objects of adoration.

**Yogacara School.** In 5th-century India the *Yogacara* school of Mahayana Buddhist idealism, teaching that the entire objective world, composed of Buddha-essence, is a manifestation of the eternal Buddha-mind, followed Nagarjuna's *Shunyavada*, when the Brahman brothers Asanga and Vasubandhu, of Peshawar, founded their *Vijnanavada* school. In *Yogacara* or *Vijnanavada*, the consciousness (*vijnana*) becomes the one undeniable factor of personal continuity in a world of cosmical illusion (*maya*). Whereas Nagarjuna had explored and elaborated the early *Prajnaparamita* works, the brothers took their inspiration from *sutras* the principal of which were (a) The

*Reunion with the Absolute* (*Abhisamaya-alankara*) by Maitreyanatha, their distinguished teacher, whose particular doctrine was one of pure subjective idealism; and (b) the *Lankavatara sutra*. A systematization of the latter called *The Awakening of Faith in the Mahayana* posits that nothing exists independently of *Tathata* (Thusness, that is, the Absolute). This is a step beyond the *Shunyata* of *Madhyamikavada*, which identified *Tathata* with *Dharmakaya*, "the One," which is not distinct from anything; for it expresses *shunya*, nothing, positively as *Alayavijnana* (in Sanskrit), that which contains the "Suchness" of things.

By the 7th or 8th century the Buddhist religion was on its way out of the land of its origin, passing northward into Tibet and Mongolia. The school of Indian Buddhism characteristic of this last period is the *Tantra*, which by the 10th century was flourishing throughout Northern India, where it subdivided into four sects: Mantrayana, Kalacakrayana, Sahajayana, and Vajrayana.

**Decline in India.** The apparent decline of Buddhism in India was due to various factors. For several centuries great Buddhist universities had existed in India, particularly in the northwest, the most famous of which was Nalanda University (founded, c.2d century A.D.); to them students came from as far away as Java and Japan. But in the 8th century the first waves of fanatical Muslim invaders from Arabia reached Northwest India. These were followed by a Muslim occupation of all North India, when every monastic building and religious organization foreign to Islam was systematically destroyed, including Nalanda, which succumbed early in the 9th century. By 1150 A.D. the Buddha *Sangha* was extinct in India.

There is no evidence that Buddhists were actually persecuted by Hinduism, which had borrowed much from the metaphysics of Nagarjuna and Vasubandhu. But Indian Buddhism had become submerged in the devotional Saivite *Tantra*, and in the intellectual Advaita Vedanta of Gaudapada and the remarkable religious reformer Sankaracarya (788–828 A.D.). Gaudapada admitted his indebtedness to *Madhyamikavada* and *Yogacara*, while Sankara was called a "secret Buddhist." But while Buddhism lost its identity in the country of its origin, later schools of Mahayana continued to develop beyond India.

### Buddhism Beyond India

Although Indian Buddhism is now dead, Buddhism in one form or another still constitutes one of the great world religions. Asoka, proclaimed Emperor of India in 269 B.C., adopted Hinayana Buddhism as a sort of state religion, received ambassadors from Syria and Greek Egypt, and patronized Buddhist missions to Iraq, Palestine, Egypt, and Macedonia. Mahinda, a Prince of the same

Mauryan Dynasty, personally introduced Theravada in 246 B.C. into Lanka (Ceylon), on which island the Pali Canon was first put into writing, during the 1st century B.C.

Meanwhile, the Sanskrit Buddhism of Northern India had spread northwest into Bactria, and questions put by its Grecian King Menander to the Sarvastivadin missionary Nagasena are recorded in *Milindapanha* (preserved in Pali). Although Bactria and Northwest India were subsequently invaded by Kushanas, one of the earliest Scythian Kings, Kanishka, embraced Mahayana Buddhism about 80 A.D.

**China.** A more important event for Buddhism was the introduction of Mahayana in about 65 A.D. into China, where it was patronized by some Emperors, persecuted by others, yet continued to fructify into a number of sects. Some famous Chinese pilgrims visited their Holy Land of India, in particular Fa-hsien (4th century), and I-tsing and Hsüan-tsang (7th century), who visited Nalanda. Their accounts remain valuable records.

The *Madhyamikavada* of Nagarjuna formed the basis of several sects in the Far East, and Mahayana Buddhism soon spread beyond China to Annam (3d century), and to Mongolia, Korea, and Burma (4th century). Around 400 A.D. the devotional White Lotus Sect (forerunner of the Pure Land School) was founded in China by Hui-yüan. From the *Vijnanavada* school of the 4th and 5th centuries there developed other *tsung* (sects) in China. The mystical *dhyana* (contemplative) side of *Yogacara* was introduced by Bodhidharma from South India, who founded in 520 A.D. the Ch'an Tsung. During the second half of the 6th century Chih-i started the T'ien-T'ai Tsung. From Korea, Buddhism was taken to Japan, around 550 A.D.

In the 5th century the Magadhese monk Buddhaghosa visited Ceylon, where he composed the *Visuddhimagga* and other commentaries on the Pali canonical books. At the same time, Mahayana was being introduced into Cam-

bodia and Siam, and thence, in the 6th century, into Sumatra and Java. Around 640 A.D. the Tantric Buddhism of Bengal was taken to Tibet by the Indian saint Padmasambhava, the virtual founder of Lamaism. In Burma during the 8th century Mahayana gave way to the orthodox Hinayana of the Theravada sect.

**Japan.** In Japan Buddhism found favor with the Imperial family. One of the earliest Japanese *shu* (sects) was the Hosso (Yogacarin), brought from China by Dosen in 736 A.D., which subsequently became the Kegon Shu. Although it remained one of the smallest communities, its influence upon the future Buddhism of Japan was considerable. In 805 A.D. the T'ien-T'ai Tsung of China became the Japanese Tendai Shu, and in 806 the Chen-yen Tsung was established as the True Word, or Shingon Shu. The Japanese founders of the Tendai and Shingon sects were Saicho (Dengyo Daishi) and Kukai (Kobo Daishi), respectively, who succeeded in blending Mahayana Buddhism with indigenous Shinto (Shin-Tao), a fusion similar to that which had already taken place in China, and which was to persist in Japan for a thousand years.

But the first of the distinctively Japanese Amida sects did not come into being until the beginning of the 12th century, when the Yudzu Nembutsu was founded by Ryonin. Faith in Amida Bodhisattva was believed to suffice for rebirth in the Paradise, or Pure Land, where the attainment of *Nirvana* is ensured. Toward the mid-12th century Honen Shonin brought the White Lotus Sect from China, to be known in Japan as the Pure Land, or Jodo Shu. From it developed the Jodo Shin Shu founded by Shinran Shonin (1173–1262), a disciple of Honen. The Japanese scripture of the native Jodo Shin sect is the *Kyogyoshinshu Monrui* by Shinran, which offers salvation by the mere repetition of the holy name *Amida*. Shinran, a married man, advocated marriage for priests—(a revolution in the monastic ethics of Buddhism). To these three Jodo Shu the addition of the minor Ji Shu completes the Four Pure Land Sects of Japanese Buddhism, the devotees of which still revered the saint Nagarjuna as their First Patriarch. Esoterically, Amida is the Higher Self, and rebirth into his Pure Land is synonymous with Realization. As an object of devotion in China and Japan, Amida Buddha is closely followed by the Bodhisattva Avalokitesvara, the male manifestation of the Supreme Reality which became metamorphosed in China into the goddess Kwan Yin (Japanese *Kwannon*), "The Regarder of the Pleas of the Universe." In Tibet and Mongolia, Avalokitesvara, known also as Padmapani, the Embodiment of Compassion, ranks as the primary object of devotion.

In 1191 A.D. the first Zen sect was founded in Japan by Yeisai (Japanese *Zen-na*; Chinese *Ch'an*, Sanskrit *Dhyana*; Pali *Jhana*; in all four languages the word means "contemplation"). In China the Ch'an Tsung had divided into Northern and Southern sections, and the three Zen sects of Japan stem from the latter. They are Rinzai Zenshu (12th century), Soto Zenshu (13th century), Obaku Zenshu (17th century). The last of the important indigenous Japanese sects was the popular Nichiren Shu, founded by the reformer Nichiren in 1253 A.D., when the metaphysics of Mahayana reached its fullest maturity. In Siam Mahayana

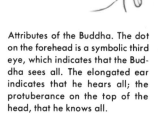

Amida, the Buddha of Boundless Light, whose cult emphasized faith rather than works. This 11th-century statue of gilded wood is in Kyoto, Japan.

Attributes of the Buddha. The dot on the forehead is a symbolic third eye, which indicates that the Buddha sees all. The elongated ear indicates that he hears all; the protuberance on the top of the head, that he knows all.

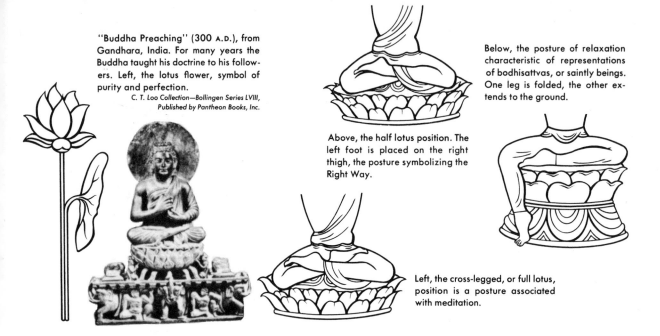

"Buddha Preaching" (300 A.D.), from Gandhara, India. For many years the Buddha taught his doctrine to his followers. Left, the lotus flower, symbol of purity and perfection.

C. T. Loo Collection—Bollingen Series LVIII, Published by Pantheon Books, Inc.

Above, the half lotus position. The left foot is placed on the right thigh, the posture symbolizing the Right Way.

Below, the posture of relaxation characteristic of representations of bodhisattvas, or saintly beings. One leg is folded, the other extends to the ground.

Left, the cross-legged, or full lotus, position is a posture associated with meditation.

was superseded by the Theravada during the 14th century.

**Europe.** In the 20th century Buddhist societies or groups of Buddhologists sprang up in almost every European country. In London The Buddhist Society was formed in 1924; in Paris Les Amis du Bouddhisme was founded in 1928; in Germany several groups came into being, and Europe's first native Buddhist temple was built in Berlin. In the United States numerous Buddhist societies exist; some Japanese communities, especially in California and Hawaii, run sectarian "churches"; while in New York a Buddhist Academy operates an information bureau.

There are some resemblances between the maxims and precepts of the Compassionate Buddha and Jesus of Nazareth, although more striking similarities are apparent between Indian Buddhism and the ancient Taoism of Laotzu, and the philosophy of the Greek Stoics. Theories of borrowing have been offered. Early Christianity may well have been influenced by the Essenes of Palestine, who perhaps had contacts with Buddhism, and in later centuries Lamaist ritual may have adopted practices of Nestorian Christian missionaries.

Some reckless estimates have been offered as to the number of Buddhists in the world; but no registration exists in Buddhist countries. Millions of Chinese have referred to themselves as both Buddhist and either Taoist or Confucian. Even these comprehensive labels are dying out in Communist central and eastern Asia, where Buddhism has obviously declined. This decrease of millions of Buddhists in China and Mongolia has not been compensated for statistically by the several thousand Indian *Harijans* (Hindu "Untouchables") who, during the 1950's, declared themselves "Neo-Buddhists," for little else than social reasons. Nepal, however, the historical Buddha's native land, remains officially Buddhist.

### Authorities: Literature of Buddhism

Much valuable research into Buddhism is found in the works of Western Buddhologists between 1844 and 1914 —a period beginning with the French Orientalist Burnouf

and ending with the beginning of World War I. But since the end of the 19th century, archeological discoveries in Turkestan, West Pakistan, and Northwest India have added little to our knowledge of Buddhist history. The greatest authority with regard to Hinayana Buddhism remains the Pali Canon, which is divided into three copious sections (*pitakas*): the Vinaya, which includes the monastic rules; the Sutta, consisting of four *Nikayas*; and the Abhidhamma. A vast expository literature came into existence during the first six to ten centuries following the closing of the Canon. Much of the Sanskrit literature of Indian Mahayana Buddhism has been lost, and many books remain only in their Chinese and Tibetan translations.

## Denominations

**HINAYANA** (Skr., "Lesser Vehicle"), Southern School of Buddhism emphasizing salvation by objective attainment. Prevailing in Burma, Cambodia, Ceylon, Laos, and Thailand, its only surviving sect is Theravada ("Way of the Elders"). Hinayana scriptures, the Pali Canon, preserve fundamental teachings of the historical Buddha.

**JODO SHIN SHU or JODOSHINSHU,** Japanese Mahayana Buddhist sect founded in 1224 by Shinran Shonin, a disciple of Honen, founder of the Pure Land sect. Shinran taught that salvation is attained by mere repetition of the name "Amida," the Infinite (Buddha). In effect, death and *Nirvana* then become synonymous, resulting unconditionally from the grace of the Bodhisattva, who, out of compassion for the welfare of humanity, renounced supreme enlightenment. Thus Shinran interpreted Buddhism entirely emotionally. He married and advocated marriage of Buddhist priests (who are not recognized members of the *Sangha*, the order of Buddhist monks) and popularized lay worship. Shin, the largest single Japanese sect, is an active missionary organization with headquarters at the famous Honganji Temple in Kyoto.

**KEGON SHU,** oldest Japanese Buddhist sect. Founded in China and based on the Yogacara school of Indian Buddhist idealism, it was introduced into Japan in 736 A.D. by Dosen, and headquarters were established at the Todaiji Temple. It was only a small sect, but its influence was considerable because the Mahayani doctrine of *jijimuge* (monism) offered universal realization of Buddhahood.

**LAMAISM** [lä'mȧ-ĭz'm], Western name for the religion of Tibet, which is also practiced in Mongolia and other neighboring territories. It comes from the Tibetan word *La-ma*, meaning "Superior One," a title reserved for abbots of monasteries and teachers of junior monks. The religion is a mixture of Buddhism and Bon, an indigenous primitive animism, or nature worship, whose shamanist leaders wear black hats.

Buddhism was first introduced into Tibet from India in the 5th century A.D., but it was the patronage of the 7th-century Tibetan King Srongtsen Gampo that really established it. In the 8th century Padmasambhava, an Indian saint who was given the title of Guru Rimpoche ("Precious Teacher"), founded the first Tibetan Buddhist brotherhood of monks. This still exists as the unreformed sect of Nyimba or Nyingmapa ("Ancient Ones" or "Old Style"). Its members are distinguished by their red hats, and their practices include much of the indigenous primitive Bon.

In the 11th century Atisha, another Indian Buddhist, finding Lamaism degenerate, purged the monastic order of its grosser elements, and, with his Tibetan pupil Bromton, founded the Kadampa sect. This provided a new stimulus to Buddhist monasticism and inspired a number of reform movements, chief of which was the later Sakyapa ("Tawny Earth") sect, which, over the years, was favored by the Chinese authorities who dominated Tibet politically. And in the 13th century, the chief Lama of the Sakya monastery became virtually the temporal ruler of the country.

Toward the end of the 14th century the great reformer Tsong-k'a-pa, from China, reorganized the Kadampa sect and built the famous Gan-Dan monastery near Lhasa, the capital city. There he established the headquarters of his Gelugpa ("Virtuous Order") sect, whose members are identified by their yellow hats. Their practices retain little of Bon origin compared with those of the unreformed "Red Hats."

Much of the temple ritual of Lamaism is very elaborate. Their principal religious ceremony closely resembles High Mass, and may have been copied from early Nestorian Christian missionaries. The historical Buddha and other Buddhas are depicted as purely transcendental and are worshiped as such. Invocative formulas are repeated numerous times each day, orally, and also on fluttering flags and inside hand-manipulated "prayer-wheels."

The succession of the Grand Lamas depends upon their reincarnation in human form within 18 months after death, and the infant Lama, selected by an elaborate ceremony, undergoes a rigorous training until he reaches maturity. The Lamaist hierarchy, in addition to the ruling Dalai and Panch'en Lamas, consists of ordinary lamas (abbots of monasteries and religious teachers), monks, and novices, all of whom take vows of celibacy and live in monasteries. No other country in the world contains such a large percentage of monastic celibates as Tibet, and since the formation of the first Lamaist brotherhood in the 8th century, the population has dwindled to perhaps one-tenth of what it was formerly.

Although the Lamaist hierarchy had exercised temporal power from the 13th century on, their dominance of all the religious, social, and political life of Tibet dates only from the 17th century. Thereafter the dual Grand Lamas of the Gelugpa sect, the Dalai Lama and the Panch'en, or Tashi, Lama, controlled the country's destinies, though their power was absolute only in those districts of central and western Tibet and parts of Mongolia where the Gelugpa sect predominates. Their rule, however, was interrupted by the Chinese Communist invasion of Tibet in 1950 and the flight of the Dalai Lama to India in 1959.

**MAHAYANA** [mä-hä-yä'nə] (Skr., "great vehicle"), Northern school of Buddhism, which emphasizes salvation by subjective realization, and whose voluminous scriptures preserve the esoteric Buddhism. It prevails in Japan, Korea, Nepal, Tibet, Mongolia, and parts of China.

**SHINGON** [shĭn'gōn], Japanese sect of Mahayana Buddhism. In 719–20 A.D. the sect was brought from India to China, where it was called Chen-yen Tsung, or Ni Chiao Tsung, Secret Teaching Sect of the tantric, or esoteric, school of Buddhism. Chen-yen was introduced into Japan c.800 A.D. as Shingon Shu, or the True Word Sect, by the Japanese mystic Kukai (Kobo Daishi) of Mount Koya, who harmonized it with the indigenous Shinto religion. Shingon doctrines include (1) The Ten Stages, from beastly man to the Great Illuminator, a belief in the Buddhanature of Supreme Reality, of which the historical Gautama Buddha was a manifestation; (2) The Two Elements, the passive, or mental, and the active, or material, reflecting Wisdom and Compassion; and (3) The Three Secrets, that everything possesses body, thought, and speech.

**TENDAI,** Mahayana Buddhist sect founded by Chih-i (531–97 A.D.) at T'ien-T'ai Mountain in China and based on doctrines brought from India about 400 A.D. It was introduced into Japan about 800 A.D. by Saicho (Dengyo Daishi), who built the Tendai monastery on Mount Hiei, which became a center of Buddhist learning. Tendai advocates extreme tolerance of "The Middle Way," recognizes all Buddhist sects, and is itself a miniature Buddhism. Very popular in Japan is its fundamental teaching that not only everyone, but also everything, attains Buddhahood, and that Buddha is Supreme Reality, manifested as the historical Gautama Buddha, who gave his doctrines in five grades to suit varying intelligences. The Tendai ideal is to live in harmony with Reality by vowing (to oneself) imitation of Buddha. Like Shingon, Tendai harmonized with the indigenous Japanese religion, Shinto.

**VAJRAYANA** [wə-jrŭ'yə-nə] (Skr. *vajra*, "thunderbolt," "diamond"; *yana*, "vehicle"), a sect of the tantric school of Mahayana Buddhism. Vajrayana is sometimes called *Mantrayana*, the vehicle of attainment of nirvana by the recitation of mantras, or invocatory formulas from the tantras. The tantras are textbooks which instruct the worshiper in the esoteric use of spells, diagrams, gestures, and ritual dances.

Practices of sympathetic magic and sexual mysticism, by which supernormal powers are acquired, originated in North Indian nature worship. By the 7th century A.D. codifications of the religions had developed rites and formulas and had become popular among both Shaivite Hindus and Buddhists, who distinguished "right-handed" and "left-handed" paths associated with male and female elements, respectively. The former represents compassion, the latter wisdom, the twin characteristics essential to enlightenment. While the right-handed path reflects the profound philosophy of *shunyata* (void), the left-handed path stresses union with the primordial Adi-Buddha, symbolized by sexual imagery. Some Western critics, finding it inconceivable that the sexual act could portray a reverent purpose, condemned Vajrayana. But for the tantrist, the sex-yogic ritual is above considerations of morality and immorality.

In the 8th century Vajrayana spread to Tibet, where it became an essential part of Lamaism, and to Japan, where the right-handed path is followed by members of the Shingon sect of Buddhism. The body of tantric literature is enormous, the Sanskrit Guhyasamaja-Tantra being perhaps the earliest scripture. Most of the tantric literature survives only in Tibetan translations of the original Sanskrit, but there are some Chinese translations.

**ZEN** (Jap., from Chin. *Ch'an*, from Skr. *dhyana*, "meditation that leads to insight"), Japanese name for the "meditation sect" of Mahayana Buddhism. The uniqueness of Zen among the various Buddhist sects lies in the stress it places on meditation as the means to enlightenment. Legend traces the beginnings of Zen back to Gautama Buddha himself. One day when a crowd had gathered to hear the Buddha deliver a sermon, he merely held up a flower and

said nothing. All his disciples were baffled except Mahakasyapa, who smiled, showing that he had understood the meaning of this gesture. Thus did the Buddha convey the essence of his spiritual insight in nonverbal exchange: that is, he transmitted the "enlightened" state directly from his own mind to the mind of his disciple.

In order to attain enlightenment, or Buddhahood, according to Zen, a person must plumb the depths of his own "self." When he comes to know his own consciousness fully, he will find it to be identical with the spiritual reality which is coterminous with all that is. Even a single flower will reflect the mystery and wonder of the entire universe. If a person cannot perceive reality in the most commonplace objects and activities, he will not find it anywhere.

According to tradition, the Indian monk Bodhidharma carried Zen to China in 520 A.D. But some scholars contend that Zen sprang up of its own accord from the confluence of Indian Buddhism with Chinese Taoism. In any case, Chinese Zen (*Ch'an*) proceeded by patriarchal succession to the Sixth Patriarch, Hui-neng (637–713), and thereafter branched into five separate schools. Of these, the most prominent are the Rinzai and Soto schools, which migrated to Japan in the 12th century and still survive there today. Soto emphasizes the attainment of enlightenment (*satori*) through seated meditation without conscious striving for any goal. Rinzai, on the other hand, employs the technique of *koan* study, wherein the student focuses his meditation on *koans*, or problems, which the Zen master gives him, and confronts the master regularly until he arrives at acceptable solutions.

# Personalities

**ASANGA** [ä-sän'gə] (c.315–90), Indian Buddhist monk and philosopher. Born in Peshawar and converted to Mahayana Buddhism, he founded the Idealistic, or Yogacara, School of the Great Vehicle, which deeply influenced Sino-Japanese Buddhism. He was the author of the earliest text of this school and in it he elaborated the main theme of consciousness as the source of man's sense of reality.

**ASHOKA** [ə-shō'kə] **or ASOKA** [ə-sō'kə] (d.232 B.C.), third and greatest Emperor (reigned c.272–232 B.C.) of the Mauryan Dynasty of India, son of Bindusara, and grandson of Chandragupta. Ashoka was proclaimed Emperor after four years of fratricidal war following his father's death. Upon securing the throne, he proceeded to conquer the Kalingas (modern Orissa), but the horror of war so repulsed him that he turned to Buddhism. This fact was not only a turning point in Ashoka's career, but also proved to be of great consequence in the history of South Asia. After the Kalinga campaign, Ashoka abandoned military conquest in favor of *Dharma*, the law of piety. Through his efforts, Buddhism spread to Ceylon, Burma, and Thailand. His missionaries were sent as far west as Syria, Egypt, and Greece. Ashoka ordered officials throughout his vast realms to inscribe Buddhist teachings on rocks and pillars to instruct the people. Some of these rock edicts, such as the one at Sarnath, remain. Aside from maintaining law and order, Ashoka's government was also known to have provided for medical aid to his people and to have built hostels along the main roads for travelers. Ashoka also patronized religious architecture; legend attributes 8,400 Buddhist temples to his inspiration. Before his death, Ashoka's empire included all of northern India and Afghanistan, from Herat in the west to Assam in the east and from the Himalayas in the north to Madras in the south.

**ASHVAGHOSA** [äsh-və-gō'sə] (fl.100 A.D.), Indian writer in Sanskrit. Little is known about his life; even his exact name and the extent of his writings are uncertain. A Tibetan version of his famous epic *Buddhacharita* (Life of Buddha, trans. as *The Light of Asia* in 1879 by Sir Edwin Arnold) mentions his birth in Saketa (India). A contemporary of the Indian ruler Kanishka, he was converted to Buddhism and worked in northern India as preacher, poet, and musician. His works include the epic *Saudarananda* (Nanda the Fair), trans. 1928; *Vajra-Suchi* (Diamond Needle), a work criticizing the caste system; and *Mahayana-Shraddhotpada* (Awakening of Faith in Mahayana), an influential study of Buddhist beliefs.

**BUDDHA** [boo'də, bood'ə], title given to one spiritually Awakened or Enlightened, it means "awake." As a personal name, "Buddha" refers to Siddhartha Gautama, the name of the historical Buddha. It distinguishes him

from previous legendary Buddhas, of whom, at first seven, and later 24, were posited by Buddhist tradition. "Buddha" thus refers to any of these fabulous teachers of prehistoric eras, while "the Buddha" is the historical personage born in mid-6th century B.C. in Lumbini in the Himalayan kingdom of Nepal, then called Sakya.

The following brief biographical details of the historical Buddha are necessarily those which his later followers believed about him, since the earliest written records date from the 1st century B.C., about 500 years after his Enlightenment. His father, Suddhodana, was the Raja, or chief, of Sakya, a ruler elected from the warrior or kshatriya class of early Aryan society. His mother, Mahamaya, died seven days after giving birth to Siddhartha. The boy grew into a strikingly handsome young man who was anatomically perfect, possessed a wonderful intelligence, and excelled at sports. He married his cousin, Yasodhara, and they had one son, Rahula.

At the age of 29 he renounced a luxurious family life and became a wandering mendicant. His quest for Enlightenment lasted six years, during which he studied the philosophical systems expounded by the Brahman, or priestly, teachers and endured extreme bodily austerities in the

The Shaka Trinity (623 A.D.), in Nara, Japan. The Buddha is seated on a lotus throne, symbol of the world. The cross-legged position indicates meditation and the hands assume the gestures of reassurance and charity. He is flanked by two bodhisattvas, beings who have renounced *Nirvana* in order to help mankind.

*Bollingen Series LVIII, Published by Pantheon Books, Inc.*

company of ascetics. He rejected such practices as the means to Enlightenment and ultimately attained the supreme mystical experience of Nirvana while meditating under a bodhi, or pipal tree at Gaya, in what is now the Indian state of Bihar. This occurred c.528 B.C.

The Buddha Gautama, endowed with knowledge and compassion, proceeded to assist his fellow men toward liberation, and the remaining 45 years of his life were devoted to teaching his doctrine, or dharma. After establishing the monastic order, the Sangha, he died at the age of 80 at Kusinagara c.483 B.C. His corpse was cremated and eight urns of ashes were divided among devotees seeking the holy relics, over which mounds, called *stupas*, were erected.

The Buddha's personality remains largely legendary. For decades after his death his bodily form was considered too sacred to reproduce in sculpture or painting and he was represented by such symbols as the footprints, the vacant preaching throne, the wheel, and the pipal tree. Later statues of the Buddha, found in temples and shrines of Buddhist monasteries, vary in type and exhibit the physical characteristics of their countries of origin. The Buddha became well-known in northern India as "The Sakyan Sage," and he referred to himself impersonally as "Tathagata," that is, one who has attained Truth. Buddha images are venerated, not worshiped; the Buddha is not a god. A Buddhist messiah is named in Buddhist scripture; he is Buddha Maitreya, the Buddha of Benevolence-to-come. Hindu mythology includes Buddha as the 9th avatar or incarnation of Vishnu.

**FA-HSIEN** [fä'shē-ĕn'] **or FA-HIEN,** (c.340 A.D.–?), Chinese Buddhist monk and writer. Born in Shanshi Province, he entered a Buddhist monastery while still a child. After his ordination, he lived as a monk until 399, when he left China and traveled to India. Arriving there in 402, he visited the traditional holy places, spent three years in Pataliputra learning Sanskrit, went to Ceylon for two years, and returned to Nanking by way of Java c.413. Greatly interested in *Vinaya*, or Discipline, he brought back the rules of two sects: the Mahasanghika, which he translated, and the Sarvastivadin. His *Record of Buddhist Countries*, written in 415, became a favorite classic of the Far Eastern Buddhist communities.

**KUAN-YIN** [kwän'yĭn'], also known as Kuan-shih-yin, the most popular Buddhist deity in China. A goddess, she was derived from the Indian male divinity Bodhisattva Avalokitesvara. In the 7th century the Chinese transformed him into the female Kuan-yin, which means "the seer of the sound of suffering." It is written that when she was about to enter into her Buddhahood, Kuan-yin turned back to listen to the cry of suffering which arose from the earth and vowed to postpone her deification until the level of existence of her own sublime elevation had been achieved by all other living creatures. She is regarded as the chief deity of Chinese Amidism, the Buddhist sect which claims that the only road to salvation and of escaping the torments of Hell is to be reborn in the marvelous Sukhavati (Paradise), or what the Chinese call Hsi-t'ien (Western Heaven). As a substitute for Gautama, who preaches the arduous life of abstention and contemplation, Amidism praises Amida, the Buddha of Boundless Light who is the ruler of Sukhavati. In order to achieve Buddhahood one must invoke the name of Amida and must worship and follow the precepts of Kuan-yin by devoting one's whole life to benevolence toward all men. In the mind of the Chinese, Kuan-yin thus became known as the compassionate Goddess of Mercy, who is the giver of male descendants and the guardian of children and womanhood.

**NAGARJUNA** [nä-gär'jŏŏ-nə] (fl.2d century A.D.), Buddhist philosopher and founder of the Mahayanist school of the Middle Way (*Madhyamika*), was born in Berar, Central India. A legendary personality, Nagarjuna is credited with the authorship of many texts, probably composed between the 1st and 9th centuries A.D. He certainly wrote the basic strophes of Madhyamika philosophy (*Mula-Madhyamika Karikas*) in 27 chapters, in which he analyzed many philosophical subjects to show that nothing exists per se, everything being caused and cause; behind every reality, there is only one reality, the Emptiness (*Shunyata*). Nagarjuna's followers, the Madhyamikavadins, regard him as the true interpreter of the Buddha's doctrine.

## Terms

**BOROBUDUR** [*bō-rō-boō-doŏr'*], the largest and most impressive Buddhist monument in Java, Indonesia It is a massive pyramid of seven stone terraces rising from a hill on the plains north of Jogjakarta. The sides of the four rectangular lower terraces are covered with elaborate bas-relief sculpture depicting scenes from Mahayana Buddhist texts. The three circular upper terraces are flanked with bell-shaped stupas (ceremonial mounds) enclosing statues of Buddha. A huge central stupa surmounts the whole. The monument stands 150 ft. high and contains 400 statues of Buddha. Its construction is believed to have been started in 772 A.D. during the reign of Pancapana, the first Buddhist ruler of the Sailendra Dynasty of the ancient Javanese kingdom of Mataram.

**BUDDH GAYA,** historic and religious site of eastern India, in the state of Bihar, 7 mi. south of Gaya. The town is the holiest place of pilgrimage for Buddhists, who believe that Gautama Buddha attained enlightment here under the pipal (*Ficus religiosa*) tree. The Buddhist temple, built in the 11th century, is richly decorated with images in its niches, and is enclosed by an old railing surrounded by votive stupas (mounds).

**DAIBUTSU** [*dī-boō-tsoō*], Japanese word meaning "great Buddha," generally refers to two famous statues of Buddha, one at Nara and the other at Kamakura. The one at Nara, the first capital of Japan, is 53 ft. high and was completed in 179 A.D. It is housed in a hall which is part of the Todaiji (Great Eastern Temple). The one at Kamakura, which is usually known as Kamakura Daibutsu, cast in the 13th century, is 43 ft. high. It was originally enshrined, but a tidal wave carried the enclosure away in 1495, and ever since it has been exposed to the elements. Both Daibutsus are in a sitting pose. The outdoor Daibutsu is the better known of the two because pictures of it have been widely circulated throughout the world. As a tourist attraction, it has become almost as much of a symbol of Japan as Mount Fuji and cherry blossoms.

*Waagenaar—Pix*

A bas-relief panel from the many that decorate the monuments. The panels illustrate scenes from the life of Buddha.

One of the seven terraces of Borobudur.

*Marc Riboud—Magnum*

The bronze Buddha, or the Daibutsu, of Kamakura, Japan.

*Share—Annan*

**DALAI LAMA** [dä-lī' lä'mə], title of the religious and political ruler of Tibet. *Lama*, a Tibetan word meaning "superior," technically refers only to a man considered to be an emanation in human form of some metaphysical aspect of the absolute Buddha, although it is used out of courtesy to address learned monks in high monastic positions. *Dalai*, a Mongolian word meaning "ocean" and implying "wisdom as vast as the ocean," was first bestowed as a title on the head lama of the Gelugpa, or Yellow Hat sect, in 1578 by the Mongol Altan Khan. The title Dalai Lama is not commonly used by the Tibetans themselves, who refer to their religious ruler as the *Yidbzhin nor-bu*, the "Wish-granting Jewel."

In 1642, the Fifth Dalai Lama (1617–82), through Mongol military support from Gushri Khan, became the first of the Dalai Lamas to rule Tibet. The century following his rise to power was marked by severe political upheavals. By the middle of the 18th century, however, the structure of the theocratic government, consisting of religious and secular officials pyramiding in rank and authority up to a council of four senior ministers directly under the Dalai Lama, had become firmly established. It remained virtually unchanged until the Communist Chinese occupation of Tibet in 1951.

The Tibetans regard the Dalai Lama as an emanation of the bodhisattva Spyan-ras-gzigs (Sanskrit: *Avalorkiteshvara*), who is derived from the Amitabha Buddha. (The Panch'en Lama is regarded as the emanation of the Amitabha Buddha himself.) When a Dalai Lama died, a senior lama was appointed as regent to administer the government *pro tem*. A search, relying on the interpretation of omens, prophecies, and signs was then conducted to locate the rebirth of the Dalai Lama. Once a likely candidate was found, the child was subjected to various tests by senior lamas to determine whether he was the true rebirth of the previous Dalai Lama. One of the tests was the identification of personal possessions of the deceased Dalai Lama which had been placed alongside identical ordinary objects. Once the lamas were satisfied that the boy was the true rebirth, he was enthroned in the Potala, the Dalai Lama's palace in Lhasa. He was given extensive religious education and had to pass the same monastic examinations in Buddhist metaphysics given to ordinary monks. When he attained his majority at 18 years of age, he assumed the administrative duties of the Tibetan government and the regent retired from office.

**Past Dalai Lamas.** The Fourth Dalai Lama (1589–1617) was the only one of the rebirths who was not Tibetan. He was born as the great-grandson of Atlan Khan. His selection was a decisive factor in the conversion of the Mongols to the Yellow Hat sect. The Fifth Dalai Lama was discovered in an influential Red Hat family, which then shifted its religious and political allegiance to the Yellow Hat sect.

The Tibetan written language was reserved for religious purposes and *belles-lettres* did not develop as a literary genre in Tibetan literature. Ironically, one of the few examples of nonreligious poetry is the 62 poems, many romantic in content, attributed to the Sixth Dalai Lama (1683–1706).

The Ninth to the Twelfth Dalai Lamas all died young.

The Thirteenth Dalai Lama (1876–1933) lived to be a remarkable religious and political figure. Following the invasion of central Tibet in 1910 by imperial forces from China, he fled into exile in India, where he formed lasting friendships with British officials. After the 1911 Chinese revolution and the fall of the Manchu Dynasty, the Thirteenth Dalai Lama returned to Tibet and effected Tibetan independence from China in 1913. During the rest of his reign, he tried to introduce British-inspired reforms to update civil and military organizations in Tibet. Most of these reforms were abandoned because of opposition from monastic groups, which in effect controlled Tibetan political and religious life.

**The Present Dalai Lama.** The Fourteenth Dalai Lama was born on June 6, 1935, to a peasant Tibetan family living in Ch'ing-hai province of China. After official recognition, he was enthroned in the Potala in Lhasa in 1940. Tibet remained neutral during World War II and refused to allow the Allies to transport military supplies to China via Tibet. After the war, the Communists rose to power in China and in Oct., 1950, the armies of the Chinese People's Republic invaded the eastern frontier of Tibet. Although only 15 years old at the time, the Dalai Lama was given the responsibility of the Tibetan government. His appeal to the United Nations in Nov., 1950, went unanswered, and Tibet was forced to sign an agreement with Red China in May, 1951.

Contrary to several of the 17 articles of the 1951 agreement, the Communist Chinese began to implement reforms and to make alterations in the structure of the centuries-old Tibetan government. Revolt against the Chinese began in eastern Tibet and spread in area and intensity until its culmination in Lhasa on Mar. 10, 1959, when the Dalai Lama fled into exile in India followed by loyal officials and tens of thousands of Tibetan refugees. The Dalai Lama now resides with members of his government in exile in Dharamsala in northwest India. Since the 1959 revolt, he has written his autobiography, which marks the first time that a Dalai Lama has caused his life story to be written in English for readers around the world.

**NARA** [nä-rä], city of southern Honshu, Japan, capital of Nara Prefecture, equidistant about 20 mi. from Osaka to the west and Kyoto to the north. Nara's religious and historic importance, its deer park covering 1,250 acres, museums and art treasures, shrines, and temples make it one of the nation's foremost tourist centers. Industries are confined largely to producing souvenir handicraft objects including Nara dolls, writing brushes, inks, fans, and lacquerware.

Nara was the earliest Japanese stronghold of Buddhism, introduced from China in the early 7th century. In 710 it became the first permanent capital of the country, but the seat was removed to Kyoto in 784. Nearby are the remains of the Horyuji temple, the oldest Buddhist temple in Japan and possibly the oldest wooden building in the world. After the establishment of the capital in Nara many other fine temples and buildings were constructed. These include the famous Todaiji with its Daibutsu-den, or Hall of Great Buddha, containing a bronze Buddha, completed in 752, that stands 53 ft. high. In the Nara National Museum are sculpture treasures from the Nara period of art in the 7th and 8th centuries. Pop., 134,577.

**NIRVANA** [*nĭr-vä′nə, nər-văn′ə*] (Skr., "blowing out"), the ideal end of the Buddhist spiritual life, essentially an escape from repeated reincarnations. The historical Buddha defined *Nirvana* (Pali *Nibbana*) as bliss. The holy man, or Arahat, who is supposed to attain *Nirvana* by overwhelming the negative elements of existence by good acts of body, word, and mind, is defined as one who has lived the life, done the task, and laid down the burden of past acts. As a negative conception, *Nirvana* is suggested by the mystical terms "Unchangeable," "Calm," "Other-Shore," and "Arrest."

**PALI** [*pä′lē*], member of the Indic branch of the Indo-Iranian subgroup of the Indo-European language family. Pali is the principal language of the earliest Buddhist scriptures. It was a spoken language in northern India before the middle of the 1st millennium B.C. and continued to be used as a literary medium into the Christian era. The center of the region where Pali was spoken was probably the northeastern Indian kingdom of Kosala, which flourished in the 7th century B.C. in the Himalayan foothills. Our principal sources of knowledge of Pali are the Buddhist canonical works, commentaries and ancillary works, and inscriptions. The canon itself is not very extensive; outside the canon, Pali literature is varied and quite extensive.

**PANCH'EN LAMA** [*pän′chən lä′mə*] **or TASHI LAMA** [*tä′shē lä′mə*], titles of the second highest lama in the Gelugpa (Yellow Hat) sect in Tibet. The title Tashi Lama is derived from the name of the Panch'en Lama's monastery, called Tashilhumpo and located near Shigatse in west-central Tibet. The Panch'en Lama was traditionally regarded as more withdrawn from the mundane world of political affairs than the Dalai Lama because he was an emanation in human form of Amitabha, the Buddha of Meditation (called Ö-pä-mĕ in Tibetan).

After 1728, the Panch'en Lama was head of a local government at Tashilhumpo, which administered a few districts in west-central Tibet. This government was subject to the ultimate authority of the Dalai Lama's central government in Lhasa, however. On one occasion, the Fourth Panch'en Lama (1781–1854) served as administrator of the Tibetan government for about eight months while a regent was being selected during the minority of the Eleventh Dalai Lama (1838-56).

The first Panch'en Lama to be recognized as such was Lō-säng Chö-ke Gyĕ-tsĕn (1567–1662), a religious teacher of the Fifth Dalai Lama (1617–82). After the Fifth Dalai Lama achieved political control of Tibet in 1642, an apocryphal text was "discovered." This revealed that his teacher was an emanation of the Amitabha Buddha, and he installed his teacher at Tashilhumpo as the first of the Panch'en Lamas. It is to be noted that the Dalai Lama was an emanation of Avalokiteshvara, the *spiritual son* of the Amitabha Buddha. Consequently, it was appropriate that the Fifth Dalai Lama "discovered" that his teacher, or *spiritual father*, was an emanation of the Amitabha Buddha.

As in the case of the Dalai and other lamas, the successive rebirths of the Panch'en Lama were discovered by the interpretation of omens and prophecies and confirmed by mystic tests. Over the centuries, the Dalai Lama and the Panch'en Lama administered the vows of monkhood to each other depending upon which was the senior lama at the time.

Relations between the Dalai Lamas and Panch'en Lamas were traditionally cordial until the time of the Thirteenth Dalai Lama (1876–1933) and the Ninth Panch'en Lama (1883–1937). Following a dispute with the Lhasa government over a tax-arrears, the Ninth Panch'en Lama fled into exile in China in 1923 and never returned to Tibet. He died in 1937 in the province of Ch'ing-hai, where the present, or Tenth, Panch'en Lama was born in 1938. Because of the dispute with the Lhasa authorities, followers of the previous Panch'en Lama would not allow the young candidate to go to Lhasa for the customary examinations. The candidate fell into the hands of the Communist Chinese when they occupied Ch'ing-hai province in 1949.

In accordance with the 1951 agreement signed between Tibet and Red China, the Tenth Panch'en Lama was escorted to Tibet in 1952 and installed in the Tashilhumpo monastery. The Chinese maintained that the Panch'en Lama was second to the Dalai Lama in the political as well as the religious hierarchy in Tibet, and appointed the Panch'en vice chairman of various new "committees."

When the Dalai Lama fled to India after the Mar. 10, 1959, revolt in Lhasa, the Panch'en Lama was elevated to the position of acting chairman in his place. Finally in early 1965, the Panch'en Lama was removed from office for being a "reactionary" and since then his whereabouts remain unknown.

**POTALA** [*pō′tä-lä*] traditional palace seat of the Dalai Lama in Tibet, on a rocky hill rising above the western suburb of the Tibetan capital of Lhasa. The Potala grew from a fortress built by the Tibetan King Srongtsen Gampo when he removed his capital from Yarlung to Lhasa in the 7th century. It was expanded to its present form in the time of the fifth Dalai Lama (1617–82). The Potala has 13 stories with a massive façade towering over 400 ft. high. Official functions and public audiences customarily took place in the uppermost story in order to observe the rule that no one must look down upon the Dalai Lama. In 1959 when the Chinese Communists seized Tibet, they installed the Panch'en Lama in the Potala.

**TANTRAS** [tăn'trəz] (Skr. *tantra,* "fundamental doctrine"), textbooks of ritual worship of certain Buddhist sects. There is also a tantric tradition in Hinduism, the parallel Hindu texts often being called Agamas. Tantrism is very old in India. In some ways it inherits the tradition of the Brahmanas, in which the worshiper, by proper performance of ritual and by repetition of magical formulas (*mantras*), compels the gods to grant him divine powers and lead him to the highest bliss.

The most commonly cited beliefs of tantrism are that man is the microcosm (embodying all the material and spiritual elements of the universe and having the potential for experiencing divine bliss) and that the seeming dualities of the universe (human-divine and male-female) are unreal. Reality is unity, experienced by the worshiper, who realizes his divinity by discipline, and by performing ritual sexual intercourse. The psychology of the tantric sects has been examined often. In ritual worship, all taboos are lifted. The worshiper eats forbidden meat and fish, drinks wine, and indulges in sexual intercourse, though not promiscuously. Some observers feel that these rites are a glutting of bodily desires in order that they may be controlled better.

**TRIPITAKA** [trĭ-pĭt'ə-kə] (Skr. *Tripitaka;* Pali *Tipitaka,* "Three Baskets"), the three divisions of sacred and classical writings which make up the Buddhist canon. The Tripitaka includes the Vinayapitaka, "the Basket of Disciplines"; the Suttapitaka, "the Basket of Discourses"; and the Abhidhammapitaka, "the Basket of Metaphysics." The compilers of the Tibetan and Chinese canons added the sections known as Prajnaparamita, "the Perfection of Wisdom"; Avatamsaka, "the Buddha's Wreath"; and Tantra, "the Esoteric Teaching."

*T. S. Satyon—Black Star*

Young Tibetan lamas studying ancient Buddhist scriptures.

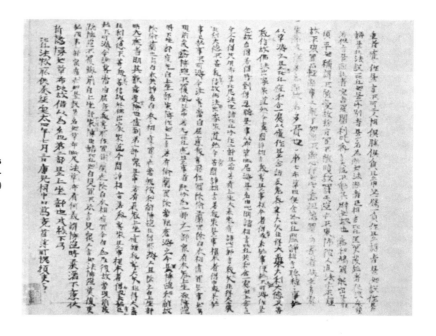

Chieh-yuan, a Buddhist scripture. It was written in 448 A.D. and is one of the oldest manuscripts extant in China. (EASTFOTO)

The Dome of the Rock (completed 691 A.D.) in Jerusalem is the oldest extant example of Islamic architecture. One of the holiest places of Islam, the shrine shelters the rock from which the Prophet reputedly entered heaven.

# 4 · ISLAM

**ISLAM** [ĭs'ləm, ĭs-läm'], which means "submitting oneself to God," is the name Mohammed gave to the faith of which he was the prophet. It is the second most widespread religion. A follower is called a Muslim (also spelled Moslem). Modern Muslims commonly object to the use of the terms "Mohammedan" and "Mohammedanism" lest Christians suppose that Muslims worship Mohammed.

Mohammed first preached in the 7th century in the towns of western Arabia, and in his lifetime most converts to the faith were Arabs. But Islam has long ceased to be identifiable with Arabs. In most areas there are no exact censuses, but approximate figures for the mid-20th century are as follows, by major groups: in Arab lands (Arabia, the Fertile Crescent, Egypt, Sudan and North Africa), 68,-000,000; in the rest of Africa, 31,000,000; in Turkey and eastern Europe, 25,000,000; in the Soviet Union, 21,000,-000; in Iran and Afghanistan, 27,000,000; in Pakistan, 66,000,000; in India, 40,000,000; in Indonesia and Southeast Asia, 76,000,000; and in China, 10,000,000. There are important Muslim groups in several other countries. For instance, about a quarter of the population of Surinam, the former Dutch Guiana, in South America is Muslim. There are congregations of immigrants and converts in most countries; such congregations exist in the major cities of the United States. In all, a sixth or a seventh of mankind now adheres in some degree to Islam.

**Origins and Relation to Other Religions.** Mohammed taught that God had created the world and mankind in it; that men's duty is to obey God's will; that He has made His will known through the messages of prophets whom He has sent to all peoples (among the prophets were Moses, Jesus, and Mohammed himself); and that at the end of history God will judge all human beings, condemning the disobedient to Hell, but rewarding the obedient in Paradise. God's will, as Mohammed presented it, was that

men should worship Him alone, associating no other being with Him; that they should act justly and generously with each other; and that if possible they should join and defend, under Mohammed's leadership, the community of the faithful, in which God's way for men was to be established.

Mohammed believed that he was preaching the same faith as the founders of Judaism and Christianity had preached in earlier times. Most of the Arabians were pagans in Mohammed's time, as was his own tribe at Mecca. But Judaism, Christianity, and related religions were to be found in Arabia, and it was undoubtedly their influence which gave him his first impulse as a religious seeker. In expounding the faith, he intended to hold to what he believed to be true in the Judaeo-Christian tradition. His later adherents also looked to the older religions for historical information. Hence many points in Islam correspond closely to points in Judaism and Christianity. But Mohammed believed that, though they had originally been divinely inspired, these faiths had been corrupted by their adherents. Where he was convinced that the truth was other than what they taught, he did not hesitate to differ with them. He even made use of some old Arabian elements in secondary matters. Mohammed's vision was vitally independent, and in the end he created an essentially new religion. Muslims hold that it supersedes the older faiths, which are therefore no longer valid. They believe that he is the final Prophet, and his religion the final religion for all mankind.

**Development of Islam as a Religion.** Mohammed's community, first established in the Arabian farming town of Medina, soon won, by zealous preaching and by diplomacy backed by occasional force, the allegiance of most of Arabia. The united Arabians thereupon conquered half the Roman Empire and all the Persian Empire, establishing themselves as rulers from Spain to Afghanistan, under the caliphs. Instead of adopting the faith and ways of the conquered peoples and then losing their own identity, as has more often been the case with such empires, the Muslims maintained the integrity of their faith and their community. Gradually many of the subject people adopted Islam, for the most part by voluntary conversion. A new society was formed, based on the Muslim faith but built upon the varied cultural experiences of all the peoples who were converted to Islam. The civilization of this society (justly called the Islamic civilization because of the central role Islam played in it) has undergone many phases of great creativity, in philosophy, in science, in the arts, and in political and social life; it has also passed through phases of decadence and disruption. In the later Middle Ages, however, the Islamic was the most widespread society on earth, dominating human life from the Niger Basin to Siberia and from the Danube River to Java.

In the context of this flourishing new Islamic society, Mohammed's religion developed, as other religions have, from its first elements, as the immediate followers of Mohammed had known them, into a varied and sophisticated expression of spiritual needs and experiences of wide sections of mankind. The more pious among the Muslims sought to understand what their acceptance of Mohammed's mission meant in detail as to what they should believe and how they should live. They looked for answers above all in the Koran, the record of the explicit messages which Mohammed believed had been given him by God. When they could not find sufficient guidance there, they tried to discover what Mohammed himself had said or done in various situations; for the example he gave, called Sunna, would be approved by God. Reports of Mohammed's Sunna, called hadith (derived from eyewitnesses in some cases, in others based on conjecture), were gathered in collections. Some of these collections were sifted with special care to make sure that their reports went directly back to eyewitnesses; two, those made by al-Bukhari (810–70) and by Muslim (d.875), have been considered especially dependable. Together with the Koran, the six most revered collections of hadith form a canon of what may be called Muslim scripture.

On the basis of the Koran and of Mohammed's Sunna, the Muslims worked out a full system of rules governing all aspects of the life of the Muslim community. All possible actions were listed as either required, or approved but not required, or forbidden, or disapproved but not forbidden, or simply permitted according to personal need or wish. Not only individual but social needs were covered. Some actions were required of the Muslim community as a whole; for instance, the maintenance of public order; but if some Muslims were performing them satisfactorily, the others were released from those duties. Other actions were required of every responsible man or woman. This system as a whole is called the Sharia. The Sharia has almost never been integrally enforced in any Islamic society, but in most Islamic lands large parts of it have been the law of the land, at least until quite modern times. All of it has formed an ideal norm for Muslims everywhere.

There have always been several forms of the Sharia,

which are not to be confused with sects, though each is accepted by a different group of Muslims. These vary only in matters of detail. Four of these, the Sunnite schools (Hanafi, Shafii, Maliki, and Hanbali), are recognized by most of their adherents as equally valid. Adherents of certain other forms of the Sharia, chiefly Shiite Muslims, hold their own forms to be the only correct ones.

**Principal Duties of Muslims.** Each Muslim must believe in the exclusive sovereignty of God (who is called in Arabic, Allah) and that Mohammed is the final prophet. To make the formal declaration, "There is no god but God, and Mohammed is God's messenger," suffices to enroll one legally as a Muslim. One must also believe in the truth of the sayings of all the other prophets, in the reality of the coming Last Judgment and of Paradise and Hell, and in the existence of certain supernatural beings, notably angels, Satan, and the jinn. Muslims possess in the Koran and the hadith very graphic accounts of the Last Judgment, when, later Muslims came to believe, Mohammed will successfully intercede for his adherents; of hell-fire, which is to burn eternally, but from which most Muslims expect to be saved sooner or later; of Paradise, where the blessed will enjoy supernatural fruits and wines and maidens, but where the supreme delight will be the vision of God Himself.

There are no ordained priests in Islam. Each Muslim man and woman must perform worship on his own account, as laid down in the Sharia. On five occasions each day, each believer should perform certain acts of worship called the salat, consisting of prostrations in a fixed manner and of Arabic formulas of praise to God, largely taken from the Koran. Before performing worship, he must wash himself ceremonially. In his prostrations he must face toward Mecca, which for the majority of Muslims is more or less toward the west. Worship may be performed in any clean spot. If several perform it together, they should normally choose one of their number as leader, called an imam, the rest performing it behind him, keeping time with his actions. At midday each Friday, Muslims should gather for special worship. The service is much like that

In sight of an ancient pyramid, Egyptian Muslims kneel toward Mecca to say their prayers, a duty performed five times daily.

*Birnback Publishing Service*

John G. Ross—Photo Researchers

sques are silhouetted against the Cairo sky. From the slim mina-
s, criers, called muezzins, summon the faithful to prayer.

of every day but with a sermon added by the imam or another leader. But otherwise Friday is not a specially holy
day.

Muslims commonly set aside special places called
mosques, which are usually buildings, for performing
worship, especially the Friday worship, and for other
religious purposes, such as the study of the Koran. Muslim
governments appoint imams to the more important
mosques, as well as other officers such as muezzins, who
summon the faithful to worship at the appointed times
by a musical chant. The mosques are often adorned very
beautifully, but not with animal or human figures, for
Muslims distrust any such figures lest they become objects of adoration in place of God. Many pious Muslims
have carried the same atitude over into all art; this has
not prevented a high development of painting at all
periods and in many Islamic lands, though sculpture has
been little cultivated. The art of decoration with plant
forms and geometrical intricacies has flourished, leading
to the arabesque.

In addition to performing the daily worship, a Muslim
is required to fast during daylight hours in the month of
Ramadan, to give a fixed proportion of his property (if he
is well-to-do) for the relief of the poor and the advancement of the faith (this legal alms, or zakat, is paid to a
Muslim government under favorable conditions or else is
given away privately), and to make a pilgrimage to Mecca
(called the hajj, sometimes hadj) at least once in his life,
if he can afford it, at the time of the yearly ceremonies
there. The public declaration of faith, the daily worship,
the fast of Ramadan, the zakat, and the pilgrimage to
Mecca are sometimes grouped as the "five pillars of Islam,"
as pre-eminent Muslim rites. But certain other ritual
matters are almost equally important. At the end of Ramadan and at the time of the yearly pilgrimage ceremonies
in Mecca, Muslims everywhere celebrate holidays called
id, or Bairam. There is also an annual celebration of Mohammed's birthday. All Muslims, both girls and boys, are
normally circumcised, at an age which varies from land to
land. Muslims do not take wine, pork, or any meat not
slaughtered according to prescribed forms.

Beyond such ritual matters, the Sharia covers personal
etiquette and public obligations, contracts and inheritance, marriage and divorce, civil status, crime and its punishment, and all other legal questions; all are considered,
strictly speaking, as integral to religion as is ritual. Many
governments, even if not Muslim, have applied parts of

the Sharia, especially those governing personal status, to
their Muslim subjects as "Islamic law." The criminal law
is on the whole mild, especially by medieval standards.
Women are subordinate to men, but have important personal and financial rights. Slavery is permitted but discouraged.

In the cities of most Islamic lands, custom long demanded severe segregation of upper-class women from
men, a practice strange to the earliest Muslims. Unless
they were members of the family, men were not permitted
in the inner part of a home (called the harem, or haram),
which was the women's domain. While on the streets
women went veiled (in some lands very heavily veiled)
from men's view. Such segregation of women has been
done away with among many Muslims in the 20th century,
and in most lands the Sharia law has been modified in
favor of women's rights.

Men and women who are learned in the Sharia are
called ulema (also ulama). They are expected to act as authorities, wherever they are, in guiding individual believers in living according to God's will. Those who merely
give opinions on what should be done in stated cases are
called muftis; those appointed by a government to decide
actual cases brought before them at law are called qadis.
The qadi of a town was a major figure in the Middle Ages,
usually having charge also of the many pious foundations
for charitable purposes, which formed the economic backbone of Muslim life.

**Islam and Non-Muslims.** It is an essential duty of the
Muslim community to see that justice and a godly order
prevail in the world. In the Middle Ages this was generally interpreted to mean that Muslims, committed to
carrying out God's laws, should alone rule. Under prescribed circumstances, fighting in a war to defend the
area already governed by Islam or to extend it was regarded as a major obligation of those Muslims who were
able to do so. Those who died in such a battle were regarded as martyrs assured of Paradise. Such a war was
called a jihad, or "holy war." Since its purpose was to

Heart of the Haram, Mecca's mosque, is the Kaaba, in which is set
the Black Stone, believed to have been given to Abraham by God.

Alpha Photo Associates

assure the prevalence of godly order on earth, a jihad was very often proclaimed by reformers against nominal Muslims, who were ruling unjustly. Modern Muslims generally regard a jihad as legitimate only for defensive purposes.

The aim of a jihad was not normally conversion, contrary to what many Westerners have supposed. Mohammed did not tolerate those who did not acknowledge God the Creator. Those Arabians who were heathen, he insisted, must become Muslims. But he allowed Jews and Christians to carry on their own religions in Muslim territory, provided they accepted Muslim rule. (Some of the Arabians who helped establish the Caliphate continued to be Christian; and many present-day Arabs are Christians.) This tolerance was extended by later Muslims to any religion that could claim to be monotheistic and to possess revealed scriptures. Non-Muslims under Islamic rule were expected to live under their own laws, coming under Muslim law only when general public policy was involved. (In recent times many Islamic states have given Muslims and non-Muslims an essentially equal standing under a common secular law.) Conversion to Islam, as to Christianity, has sometimes been forced, but more often it has taken place for the sake of gaining social advantages in a society ruled by Muslims, or of taking part in the superior culture that Islam has often carried with it, or simply in response to the devoted missionary zeal of Muslim preachers. On the other hand, conversion from Islam to another faith was punished by death.

**Major Interpretations of the Faith.** Like other developed religions, Islam required a theology to provide intellectual discipline against distortion by overzealous partisans of one or another approach to it and as a defense against critics and doubters. The most successful early school of theology was that of the Mutazilites. These aroused opposition by their too logical consistency in denying positions which, though no clear part of the earliest Islam, had come to be favored by most of the pious. The pious asserted on the one hand that God is so utterly exalted that He is not to be judged by human moral standards, but on the contrary must be granted to have eternally predestined men's acts, both good and evil—a position which to the Mutazilites seemed to deny divine justice and human freedom. The pious asserted on the other hand that God is so close to the believer that the Koran which the believer recites is His very speech, eternally divine. To the Mutazilites, this contention seemed to set up an eternal Koran to be adored alongside God. Many early Muslims, dissatisfied with the Mutazilite logic on such points, distrusted any attempt at intellectual formulation other than the use of God's own words in the Koran. But later theological thought, led by al-Ashari, made room for the favorite dogmas of the pious, and was accepted as a normal part of religious training. It introduced into Islam many of the methods of Greek philosophical thought, as had earlier been the case with Christianity. Predestination, or kismet, was admitted, but modified by subtle distinctions to save human freedom; the uncreated and eternal character of the Koran was admitted, again with subtle modifications. The immediate and inscrutable sovereignty of God over all events was reconciled with the fact of a predictable natural order by means of an atomistic metaphysics.

A religion requires not only a theology but a sense of history. Disputes over how Islam was to fulfill its historic mission on earth began early. In the second generation after Mohammed, a group of purist Muslims, the Kharijites, demanded that Muslim rulers be deposed unless they were absolutely upright, and separated themselves from Muslims who accepted less perfect rulers.

A more popular tendency was to expect high standards to be set by the descendants of Mohammed. For many Muslims, a personal devotion to Mohammed and his family has been an essential part of Islam. Increasingly, Mohammed, respected as divinely chosen to show men how to live, came to be regarded as perfect and sinless; to insult him became the grossest of offenses. He was, moreover, represented in his family. Any descendant of Mohammed (called a sayyid) was to be respected and given special privileges. The ancestor of these sayyids in the male line, Ali, Mohammed's cousin and husband of his daughter Fatima, was revered as a great hero; while very orthodox Muslims insisted that the first three caliphs stood higher in rank than he, many believed he was the best man after the Prophet. Ali's son Husayn, Mohammed's grandson, had been killed at Karbala in Iraq in an abortive rebellion against the Umayyad Dynasty of caliphs, descendants of men who had at first opposed Mohammed. The Umayyads have been condemned as corrupters of Islam, and the deaths of Husayn and his brother Hasan were thought of as martyrdoms, and in India and other lands their deaths were commemorated in sorrowful ceremonies. It was hoped that as times grew worse and Islam became still more corrupt, another leader like Mohammed, bearing his name and known as the Mahdi (the Rightly Guided One), would arise to purify Islam and lead it to final triumph in the world. Most Muslims have expected this would be one of Mohammed's descendants.

Some Muslims have stressed devotion to Mohammed's family to the point of insisting that only Ali and his descendants could be the rightful leaders of Islam after Mohammed's death. They have denied that others were true Muslims and have established a number of sects, together known as Shiite Islam, in contrast to Sunnite Islam. These Shiites have special holidays in addition to the ordinary Muslim ones, notably the day of Ghadir Khumm, when they believe Mohammed formally required his followers to accept Ali. The Imamis, the largest sect of Shiite Islam, commemorate the death of Husayn in the month of Muharram with tearful reading of elegies and sometimes with plays and processions culminating in bloody self-lacerations. Most Shiite sects traditionally curse the first three caliphs as usurpers, thus bringing down the wrath of other Muslims; but they hold it lawful to conceal their Shiite faith if necessary. The Shiites have their own systems of Sharia, based on the Koran and Sunna. At most, a tenth of all Muslims are now Shiites.

Although the outer life of a Muslim is governed by the Sharia, the inner life of Islam, especially Sunnite but also Shiite, came to be largely dominated by a spiritual movement called Sufism. This was rather slow in developing,

United Press International

In Meknès, Morocco, guests at a Muslim wedding celebration gather to drink mint tea and listen to music.

in a world-wide, sophisticated community. But it has found converts also in such lands as the United States, notably among the Negro population. Genuine historical Islam is to be distinguished, however, from a self-styled "Islam" under local Black Nationalist leadership, which is not recognized by the original Muslims but has, like historical Islam, had some popularity in the United States.

but after the 10th or 11th century it was almost universally accepted except among certain purist groups. Individual Muslims who cultivated mystical experiences came to be looked on as saints especially close to God. Their disciples formed great brotherhoods to follow their spiritual teachings, each with its own centers for worship and study of mystical theories. In some lands almost every Muslim was affiliated in one way or another with some such brotherhood. Reverence for Sufi saints, especially at their tombs, was sometimes made the excuse for the survival of pre-Islamic shrines and rituals; wandering devotees called dervishes, claiming to be Sufis, often practiced the jugglery, magic, and charlatanry so common in all medieval societies. By the 20th century organized Sufism was falling into disrepute among educated Muslims, though the Sufi spiritual tradition continues strong.

In the 19th and 20th centuries Muslims, like all other modern peoples, have been confronted with radical changes in the conditions of social and intellectual life, which have been reflected in the religious as in other spheres. Many Muslims have tried to purify the faith, not only of the excesses and superstitions that had come to be associated with Sufism, but of many of the prejudices and petty regulations that had been associated with the Sharia and that hampered adjustment to modern times. Among the Arabs, one of the most intellectually important of these movements was called the Salafiya. Indian Islam has been stimulated by the most profound of modern Muslim thinkers, Iqbal (1873–1938), whose Muslim vision helped produce Pakistan. Attempts to reinterpret Islam for modern times have ranged widely. Zealous revivalist movements often seek to seize power and impose a purified but strict rule of Sharia, inspired by the puritan reforms of Wahhabism in Arabia. At the other extreme, individual Muslims have seen Islam as a purely spiritual ideal, set forth in the Koran alone, which should not intervene directly in law or politics. In practice, the Muslim religion has become increasingly separated from government in Islamic states.

Meanwhile, Islam has continued to spread. Well-organized missionary societies have appeared, but it still spreads mostly through incidental personal contacts. Its most marked growth has been in Africa, where it offers, in exchange for the limited horizons of tribalism, membership

## Denominations

**DRUSES or DRUZES** [drōōz'sĕs] (Arab. *Duruz*), a Syrian people, mostly landholders and peasants, mainly located in the Lebanon, Anti-Lebanon, and Hauran mountains They have their own religion, developed in the 11th century from the Ismaili branch of Islam and based on the adoration of the Egyptian Caliph al-Hakim, who is regarded as a manifestation of God. They expect al-Hakim to return a conqueror and fill the earth with righteousness. Meanwhile the more pious of the Druses (who alone are initiated into the secrets of the faith) try to purify their souls, which are held to be reincarnated generation after generation, by disciplined and truthful living, so as to be worthy of him. The Druses have often ruled the parts of Syria in which they live. They are as famous for their brigandage and feuds as for their chivalry and hospitality.

**IMAMIS** [ĭ-mä'mĭs], the largest sect of Shiite Islam. The Imamis recognize a series of 12 imams, or legitimate successors of Mohammed, starting with Ali and his two sons Hasan and Husayn (Mohammed's grandsons by his daughter Fatima); and continuing among Husayn's descendants to the hidden imam, Muhammad al-Muntazar, who disappeared in 873 and is expected to return at the end of history to rule the world justly, as Mahdi. They have accepted the Jaafari form of the Muslim law, named after their sixth imam; and are led by independent religious authorities, mujtahids, recognized as learned and pious representatives of the hidden imam. The mujtahids, who are loosely organized, live and teach at Najaf in Iraq, where Ali is buried, and at other cities sanctified by members of Mohammed's family. For Shiites, pilgrimage to these places is almost as important as pilgrimage to Mecca. Imamis, the greatest body of Shiites in the 20th century, form the majority of the population in Iran, in both Iranian and Soviet Azerbaidzhan, and southern Iraq, and important minorities in eastern Arabia, northern Syria, northern India, and the Indian Deccan.

**KHARIJITES** [kä'rĭ-jīts] **or KHAWARIJ** (Arab., "the seceders"), adherents of several Muslim sects who insisted that the ruler of Islam must be of pure character and elected by the faithful. The Kharijites in the two centuries after Mohammed (c.570–632), declaring all other Muslims renegade for accepting sinful rulers, rose repeatedly and bloodily against the caliphs. One Kharijite sect, the Ibadis, remains in the 20th century in North Africa, Oman, and East Africa. They are noted for their independent spirit, puritan morals, and widespread commercial activity.

**SHIITE** [shē'ĭt] **ISLAM,** originally a political movement loyal to the house of Mohammed. It took the form of the party (Arab *shia*) of Mohammed and his son-in-law, Ali, the fourth Caliph. Shiite Islam early developed into a group of Muslim sects. Each has borne allegiance to its own divinely sanctioned leaders, called imams, and has maintained a bitter and often bloody opposition to the larger Sunnite branch of Islam.

Among these sects, the Zaydis have remained closest to the primitive Shiite impulses and have established a state in Yemen. Others sought a deeper meaning in their allegiance, ascribing a cosmic role to the imams. The Alawites of Syria represent a large group of early sects, now mostly extinct, which often rejected much that is central to orthodox Islam. Most modern Shiites stem from two main branches. The Ismailis worked out an elaborate esoteric interpretation of the Koran and established the Fatimid caliphate in North Africa and Egypt. They divided into several groups and survive in many lands in this century. From them sprang the Druses. The Imamis, who were also inclined to read the Koran symbolically, never raised their imams to power, but have come to be far the most numerous Shiites. Various minor Shiite movements, such as the Ahl-e Haqq, have an Imami background. In the 20th century Shiites form at most one-tenth of all Muslims.

**SUFISM** [sōō'fĭz-əm]. A phase of Muslim spiritual life, Sufism is centered on mystical religious experience. Early in the development of Islam, individual Muslims, partly inspired by Christian monks, adopted lives of ascetic piety. (Celibacy was frowned on, however.) They rejected worldly comforts in favor of giving what they could in charity and spending much time in conscious remembrance of God. They acknowledged their faults and the terrible justness with which they would be punished in Hell. Hasan of Basra (d.728), for instance, was noted for almost continually weeping at the prospect. Gradually such ascetics came to lay stress on adoration and love for God. Thus Rabia (d.801) found her heart so full of love for God that she hardly had time to fear Hell. She was willing to renounce even Paradise, contented with God alone.

**The Mystical Aspects of Sufism.** This movement led to full-blown mysticism, the seeking of experiences of unity with the divine. Outstanding mystics taught their disciples to examine themselves morally and spiritually and to renounce the world. They led their more devoted followers along paths of ever more subtle and intense mystical experience. These teachers and their disciples were called Sufis, from the rude garb of wool (Arab. *suf*) that they wore.

Devotees meditated on the Koran or on the names of God and repeated pious exercises, called *dhikr* or *zikr*. These induced extreme states of concentration partly through the control of breathing and posture. An individual progressing in the mystical way was expected to pass through numerous attitudes of the soul. These ranged from simple belief to total acceptance of God's will, and the individual moved from one stage to the next as he was found ready for it by his spiritual guide (called sheikh or *shaykh*, or *pir*). It was only by divine grace, however, that the seeker could achieve the much prized holy states of consciousness, ranging from certainty of faith, through the ecstasy of love, to utter absorption in the divine being.

**Theology of Sufism.** To explain their experiences, the Sufis developed elaborate systems of thought about men, the universe, and God. To a large extent they were founded upon Neoplatonic and Gnostic theories of late classical Greek times. Many mystics saw the creation of the universe as an outgoing impulse of the Absolute One, God. In the human organic synthesis, creation reached its greatest complexity, remotest from the original simplicity of the One. Yet at the same time creation achieved a consciousness capable of returning to God in love. God, they said, was a hidden treasure, and He created the universe that men might find Him. The devoted worshiper of God was, therefore, the very goal of creation. Mohammed, Islam's Prophet, was regarded as the prototype of such saints, and it was held that in every generation the chief of the saints, or *Qutb*, maintained the creation by fulfilling its goal in his consciousness of God. Some Sufi theories have been called pantheistic, because in this way they saw the whole universe as an extension or reflection of the being of God.

**Historical Development of Sufism.** After some centuries Sufism was generally accepted among Muslims as embodying the more intimate side of Islam. The schools of Sufi thought developed into organized brotherhoods or orders, to which ordinary laymen, both men and women, commonly attached themselves for spiritual guidance and blessing, even if they did not devote full time to the mystical search. Craft guilds were often affiliated with one or another Sufi order, taking the order's founder as its patron saint. The brotherhoods received great endowments. Special buildings, constructed especially at the tombs of noted saints, housed the Sufis and their religious exercises. Numerous individual devotees wandered as dervishes (holy mendicants) from one Sufi residence to another throughout the lands of Islam. In these ways Muslim social life was strengthened locally and was knit together internationally.

Popular devotion, however, was often excessive. Sometimes honor was paid to saints, dead and even living, such as had once been paid to local gods. Miracles were looked for and were forthcoming. In later centuries many kinds of magic and superstition came to be associated with the dervishes and the Sufi brotherhoods. In the 20th century Sufism has lost favor among educated Muslims.

**SUNNITE** [sŭn'ĭt] **ISLAM,** also known as Sunni Islam, the prevailing form of Islam. Sunnite Islam, unlike Shiite and

Kharijite Islam, recognizes the religious authority of all the first generation companions of Mohammed. At least nine-tenths of all Muslims are Sunnites.

**WAHHABISM** [wä-hä'bĭz-əm], a Muslim reform movement founded in Arabia by Muhammad ibn Abd al-Wahhab (d.1792). Following the strictest of the Sunni Muslim schools, he rejected much of the law and custom of medieval Islam as not genuinely stemming from Mohammed, but applied rigorously the law that he accepted. He condemned adoration of Muslim saints and their tombs and regarded most Muslims as infidels on this account. He won the support of a local chieftain, Muhammad ibn Saud, who built a state in central Arabia on the basis of the reformer's teachings.

The Wahhabis then tried to enforce those teachings in neighboring lands. During the first decade of the 19th century they captured Mecca and Medina and shocked the Muslim world by destroying sacred tombs. Ottoman Turkish authority was soon restored, but the movement lingered on in central Arabia. Meanwhile its militant puritanism stimulated the formation of several similar groups in various Muslim countries early in the 19th century. These groups often fought against Western encroachments. Subsequently the Wahhabis' rejection of medieval superstition attracted Muslim intellectuals and influenced their efforts at reforms. In the 20th century the movement's power was revived by a descendant of Muhammad ibn Saud, Abd al-Aziz ibn Saud, who founded the state of Saudi Arabia and made Wahhabism its official creed. Mecca was again conquered, but since then the Wahhabis have remained on better terms with other Muslims.

**ZAYDIS or ZAIDIS** [zā'dĭs], a sect of Shiite Islam. The Zaydis hold that any descendant of Ali and Mohammed's daughter, Fatima, may be a legitimate imam, or ruler of the Muslims, provided he is both expert in the law and effective in claiming his rights by the sword. They are named after Zayd, the fourth of the imams whom they recognize. They have their own form of Muslim law, but differ little from ordinary Sunnite Muslims. They have established several states and are now the ruling majority in Yemen.

## *Personalities*

**ASHARI, AL-** [*ăl*ăsh-ă-rē'] (c.873–935), Arab Muslim theologian of Basra and Baghdad. In his earlier life al-Ashari (Arab. Abu al-Hasan Ali al-Ashari) was a Mutazilite, rationalist theologian, but was converted to a more traditional view about 913. Thereafter, he defended a doctrine of Islam based on an almost literal interpretation of the Koran and the Islamic Traditions, and emphasized God's omnipotence. This doctrine was developed and systematized in later centuries by the Asharite school, which became prevalent in medieval Sunnite Islam.

**FATIMA** [*fä'tĭ-mə, făt'ĭ-mə*] (c.605–632), daughter of the Prophet Mohammed and Khadija. For later Shiite Muslims (members of one of the major branches of Islam) she embodied all that was noblest in woman, although little is known of her actual life. She was born in Mecca, went to Medina with Mohammed, and there married his cousin Ali about 623. Her sons Hasan and Husayn were, after Ali, the first of the imams (supernatural leaders) acknowledged by the Shiites and are ancestors of the sayyids and sharifs of today. The Shiite Dynasty of Fatimids in Egypt took its name from her.

**HARUN AL-RASHID or HAROUN AL-RASCHID** [*hä-rōōn' äl-rä-shēd'*] (763?–809), the fifth Caliph of the Abbasid Dynasty. The dynasty reached the height of its power under Harun, who later achieved legendary fame in the *Arabian Nights*. Harun's career was decisively influenced by two developments which occurred in his youth. In 782, during a victorious campaign against the Byzantine Empire, Harun so impressed his father, the Caliph al-Mahdi, that the latter nominated him as the second in the line of succession, according him also the honorific title al-Rashid, meaning the "Straightforward." The second development was the appointment of Yahya ibn Khalid, a prominent member of the Iranian family of the Barmecides, as Harun's tutor. As a result of this association, the Barmecides controlled the affairs of state from the accession of Harun in 786 until his brutal liquidation of them in 803. The social and economic prosperity of Harun's reign was mainly achieved by the administrative talents of these Iranian viziers.

The general prosperity was also enhanced by the relative security of the empire both internally and externally. Harun's armies successfully coped with a number of rebellions, and the security of the empire was strengthened by new fortresses erected along the Byzantine frontier and by raids launched against Christian territory. The Caliph's military campaigns in 789–99 forced the Byzantine Empress Irene to pay tribute to the Muslim ruler. When Emperor Nicephorus rejected that treaty, Harun reimposed even more humiliating terms on the Byzantine Empire by means of victorious campaigns between 802 and 806.

Although the anti-Byzantine wars did not result in any permanent territorial gains, they contributed greatly to Harun's international prestige. His court was visited by foreign diplomats; according to Western sources even Charlemagne exchanged embassies with his great Muslim contemporary. Apart from economic, political, and military splendor, the reign of al-Rashid was famous for scientific and artistic activity in which the Caliph showed great interest.

With all its splendor, the reign of Harun al-Rashid had an adverse effect on the development of the Abbasid Caliphate. By allowing a Governor in Africa to establish a hereditary dynasty, Harun legalized a secessionist tendency among provincial governors, which led ultimately to the disintegration of the empire. The brutal suppression of the Barmecides alienated the Iranian aristocracy, the support of which had been so essential to the rise of the Abbasid Caliphate. His incompetent handling of an oppressive Governor in Khurasan (eastern Iran), and above all his division of the empire between his two sons, al-Amin and al-Mamun, cast further doubt on his abilities as a statesman. It was mainly because of Harun's political errors that, soon after his death, the Caliphate was plunged into bloody civil war.

**IQBAL** [*ĭk-bäl'*], **SIR MUHAMMAD** (1873–1938), Indian Muslim poet and philosopher. He was educated in Lahore, Cambridge, and Munich. As a poet he reflects the hopes and aspirations of Indian Muslims, of whom he was the most distinguished literary representative. He firmly believed that Islam was flexible and dynamic enough to be adapted to modern conditions. In 1930 he advocated a separate Muslim state in India; it has been said that if Jinnah was the founder of Pakistan, Iqbal conceived of the idea and through his poetry prepared the ground for it. His poems, both in Persian and in Urdu, have been translated and are being read all over the Muslim world. *Poems from Iqbal* (1955) presents a selection of his poems in English translation by V. G. Kiernan.

**MOHAMMED** [*mō-hăm'ĭd*] **or MUHAMMAD** [*mōō-hăm'məd*] (c.570–632), Arab religious and political leader, founder of the religion of Islam and of the Arab (Islamic) empire or caliphate.

**Call to Be a Prophet.** Born after his father's death, Mohammed grew up as an orphan in Mecca. His grandfather, who acted as guardian, had been head of the clan of Hashim and prominent in Meccan affairs; but the influence of the clan was declining as that of other clans increased. Mecca was a town of merchants. Built around a sanctuary, the city's taboo against blood feuds enabled men to trade there freely. By 600 the great Meccan merchants had obtained control of the lucrative trade up the west coast of Arabia. Mecca was prosperous, but its outlook had become materialistic and self-centered. The rich cared nothing for those without money or influence. By his marriage to a rich widow, Khadija, about 595, Mohammed had enough capital to play a small part in the trade of the town. About 610 he felt that he was called to be a prophet. He began to receive messages which he believed were from God and which God was commanding him to proclaim to his fellow citizens. The messages or revelations summoned them to worship God (Arab. *Allah*, literally, "the god"), to be generous with their wealth and to believe that they would appear before God on the Last Day. On that day they would have eternal reward or punishment assigned to them for their deeds in this world.

**Followers and Opponents in Mecca.** Some Meccans believed Mohammed's messages and joined him in special forms of worship at the Kaaba (a holy shrine in Mecca) and elsewhere. These included many younger men. After a time, however, the richest merchants became afraid of Mohammed, perhaps because they realized he might become the strongest man in Mecca. They criticized him and said his messages were false; and they made life difficult for the members of their clans who adhered to Mohammed's movement. From about 615 to 618 all the other clans of Mecca joined in boycotting Mohammed's clan of Hashim, but the boycott seems to have failed. Eventually the new chief of the clan of Hashim, Mohammed's uncle, Abu Lahab, who had common commercial interests with some of the rival clans, decided that Mohammed had forfeited the protection of the clan by some of his doctrines. This made it impossible for Mohammed to go on as he had been doing in Mecca, and when an opportunity came to move to the oasis of Yathrib (later called Medina), 250 mi. north, he eagerly took it.

**Migration to Medina.** Negotiations with the people of Medina began in 620. By July, 622, most of the Arab clans of Medina had accepted Mohammed's religion and pledged themselves to defend him as they would their own kinsmen. Their readiness to do this was largely due to the fact that there had been fighting with much bloodshed between two tribes or groups of clans in Medina, and Mohammed, with the prestige of his prophethood, was a suitable person to act as arbiter in disputes. Over 70 of Mohammed's Meccan followers traveled in small parties to Medina. Last was Mohammed himself with Abu Bakr, his chief lieutenant. They arrived in Medina on Sept. 24, 622. This migration is called the Hegira or Hijra.

**Vindication Against His Opponents.** Nearly all the people of Medina except the Jews accepted Mohammed as prophet, but he had no special political powers, ranking only as the chief of the "clan" of emigrants along with eight other clan chiefs. How he originally expected his followers to gain their livelihood at Medina is not clear. In Mar., 623, they began to go out on raiding expeditions (*razzias*), according to the normal Arab custom. Their aim was to capture rich caravans going from Mecca to Syria. Not till Jan., 624, did they have any success. Then on Mar. 15, 624, at Badr a raiding party of 315 men met a force of 900 which had come from Mecca to protect a caravan. The Meccans were defeated, over a dozen of the leading men and some 50 others killed, and a similar number taken prisoner. Mohammed and his followers regarded this as God's vindication of His prophet.

**The Meccans Subdued and Reconciled.** The loss of life and lowering of prestige stung the Meccans to vigorous counteraction. An expedition of 3,000 men sent to the oasis of Medina in Mar., 625, inflicted serious casualties

on the Muslims (the adherents of Mohammed's religion) in a battle at the hill of Uhud; but the Meccans were unable to follow up their advantage. Urged by the desperate need to restore their prestige, they formed a confederacy and marched on Medina with 10,000 men in Apr., 627. Mohammed had dug a trench to protect the parts of the oasis open to cavalry attack. After a fortnight the confederacy broke up, and the Meccans had to retire ignominiously with nothing accomplished. Mohammed, however, was now working not for their defeat but for their reconciliation. In 628 he made a treaty calling off his attacks on Meccan caravans, and showed he was ready to be friendly. When the treaty was broken, he collected 10,000 men in Jan., 630, and advanced on Mecca, which submitted to him on generous terms. Those Meccans who became Muslims were able to share fully in the administration of Mohammed's growing state.

**The Unification of Arabia.** Immediately after the submission of Mecca, Mohammed led his force, together with most of the Meccans, against a threatening concentration of nomads and defeated them at Hunayn. This made him the strongest ruler in Arabia. Deputations began to come to Medina from most of the Arab tribes seeking alliance with him. He insisted on acceptance of Islam, the name given to Mohammed's faith, and payment of a kind of tithe. In many cases one faction in a tribe approached him to gain his support against a rival faction. By 632 most of the Arab tribes, except those in the north under Byzantine influence, had some kind of treaty with Mohammed, though sometimes a minority had made the treaty.

**Mohammed's State.** The state Mohammed founded at Medina was conceived as a federation of clans or tribes; but it implied the acceptance of Mohammed as prophet and in this way was based on religion and not kinship. A document has been preserved known as the Constitution of Medina. This conception of a federation was developed when other Arab tribes wanted to become allies of Mohammed. Jewish and Christian communities were added to the Islamic state as "protected groups" (*dhimmis*), in much the same way as strong nomadic tribes protected weaker ones. This organization, simple as it was, proved capable of becoming the framework for the phenomenal expansion which began under Umar I, the second caliph or ruler of Islam.

**The Koran and the New Religion.** The messages or revelations which Mohammed had begun to receive about 610 continued at frequent intervals until his death, and were later collected to form the book known as the Koran. At first they dealt with mainly spiritual matters such as the signs in nature of God's power and how God vindicated his prophets and those who believed in them. Mohammed was spoken of as the latest in a series of prophets which had included Old and New Testament figures such as Abraham, Moses, David, Job, John the Baptist, and Jesus, though the death of Jesus on the Cross was denied. Later passages insisted on God's unity and described the pleasures of Paradise and the terrors of Hell. Those messages revealed at Medina had instructions for many aspects of the daily life of the community and interpretations of some of the main historical events such as the battles of Badr and Uhud. The main religious duties of Muslims came to be regarded as (1) public witness that "there is no god but God, and Mohammed is his prophet," (2) formal prayers or worship five times a day, (3) the payment of alms or tithes, (4) the fast by day throughout the month of Ramadan, (5) the pilgrimage to Mecca at least once in a man's life. Sometimes participation in the "holy war" or military expeditions was added.

**The Achievement.** When Mohammed died on June 8, 632, he left a prosperous state and a growing religion, although the extent of his achievement was not yet apparent. His personality is somewhat hidden in the mist of legend, but he is known to have been tenderhearted toward children and animals. Although the times made his success possible, it would not have been achieved without his qualities of character—the vision to see what was wrong in his world and what could be made of it, the statesmanship to frame practical policies, and the administrative skill and tact to carry them out.

**SALADIN** [săl'ə-dĭn], Arabic name Salah al-Din, "honor of the faith" (1138–93), the founder of the Ayyubid Dynasty in Egypt, and famous as a victorious leader of Muslim armies against the Crusaders. A member of a Kurdish family in Iraq, Saladin first rose to prominence during the conquest of Egypt (1164–69) by the forces of his Syrian overlord, Nur al-Din. After assuming command of the army in Egypt, he abolished the Egyptian dynasty of the Fatimids and, following the death of Nur al-Din in 1174, established his virtual independence of Syria. Saladin proceeded with an economic and military build-up of Egypt which was to enable him to launch an effective assault against the Crusaders.

Between 1174 and 1186, by asserting his authority over many important regions in Syria and Iraq, Saladin achieved a consolidation of the Muslim front. His advantageous political, military, and economic position was further enhanced by the popularity of the Muslim Holy War (jihad) against the Crusaders, an idea to which he frequently appealed. After a provocation by the Crusaders, Saladin crushed their army at Hattin in 1187. He then overran Palestine and on Oct. 2, 1187, received the surrender of Jerusalem. His subsequent conquests were brought to a stop by a new expedition of European land and naval forces, best known as the Third Crusade. But the effort of the European counteroffensive petered out around Acre, where the heroic Muslim garrison, bravely assisted from the outside by Saladin, resisted the attacks of the Crusaders (1189–91).

In spite of the ultimate fall of that coastal fortress, Saladin succeeded in turning this temporary setback into his final success. The prolonged siege operations had a demoralizing effect on the Crusader forces, most of which returned home after seizing Acre. The strength of the remaining contingent of the Crusaders, bravely commanded by Richard the Lion-Hearted, King of England, was not sufficient to defeat Saladin. After several military engagements a deadlock was reached, which led ultimately to the conclusion of an armistice agreement in 1192. Its provi-

sions clearly demonstrated the success of Saladin. Except for a limited coastal strip in Syria to be retained by the Crusaders, the rest of the formerly contested territory, including Jerusalem, remained in the hands of Saladin. Thus, by this great achievement, Saladin established the forces of Islam in a strategically powerful position against the Crusaders. Shortly after that triumph, Saladin's brilliant career was brought to an end by his death in Damascus. His political heritage was safeguarded by his brothers and their immediate descendants, who perpetuated the regime of the Ayyubids in Egypt and Syria.

**UMAR** [oo'mär] **I,** also Omar, Arabian name Umar ibn al-Khattab (reigned 634–44), second Caliph, or ruler, of the Islamic state, who organized its transformation into an empire. At Mecca he at first opposed the Prophet Mohammed, but about 615 he became a Muslim. At Medina he was second to Abu Bakr as adviser to Mohammed, his position being confirmed by Mohammed's marriage to his daughter Hafsa in 625. In 632 his energetic advocacy prevailed on the Muslims of Medina to accept Abu Bakr as Mohammed's Caliph, or successor. On Abu Bakr's death in 634 he succeeded to the title. The quelling of the Arab revolts under Abu Bakr had opened the way for the long-foreseen expansion of Islam into Iraq and Syria. The Persian Empire was shattered in 637, and Muslim forces defeated the Byzantines in Syria in 636 and in Egypt in 641. Umar organized the occupation of these vast territories. This decade of unparalleled expansion was closed by his murder in 644.

## Terms

**ABBASID** [ăb'əsĭd, ə-băs'ĭd], dynasty of caliphs ruling Islam from 750 to 1258. The name was derived from al-Abbas, the uncle of Mohammed.

**Rise to Power.** The Abbasids were originally one of several factions struggling for power during the Umayyad caliphate (661–750). Their position was strengthened when they assumed leadership of the extreme anti-Umayyad sect of the Hashimiyya. In 716 Abu Hashim, the sect's leader and claimant to the caliphate, bequeathed his authority to Mohammed ibn Ali, the head of the Abbasids. By utilizing the sect and its propaganda organization, the Abbasids intensified their efforts against the Umayyads. Their task was facilitated by uprisings against the Umayyads by the Shiites and Kharijites, Islamic sectarians, as well as by internal feuds between leading Arab tribes. Directing their operations from the turbulent Mesopotamian city of Kufa, Abbasid leaders concentrated their clandestine propaganda on Persian Khurasan.

In 745 Ibrahim, the son of Mohammed ibn Ali, sent Abu Muslim, a Persian freedman, to Khurasan to direct the Abbasid movement there. Under his leadership the movement spread among the Persian Muslims, the Yemenite Arabs of Khurasan, and even among the Zoroastrians and Buddhist squires who had been converted by Abbasid missionaries. In 747 Abu Muslim led these groups in revolt against their rulers. Defeating one Umayyad army after another, his armies advanced westward. In 749 they captured Kufa, where the jubilant Abbasid supporters acclaimed Abu'l-Abbas, a brother and successor of Ibrahim, as the new caliph of the Muslim Empire. Their triumph was complete with the defeat of the last Umayyad caliph, Marwan II, in the Battle of the Great Zab (750). The Abbasids thereafter consolidated their position by brutally executing their former revolutionary supporters, including Abu Muslim and the Hashimiyya, as well as survivors of the Umayyad regime.

**Character of the Abbasid Caliphate.** Contrary to the assertions of 19th-century scholars, the success of the Abbasids cannot be regarded as a victory of the Persians over the Arabs. Although Persians played their part in the victory, the Abbasid movement was Arab in origin. It was directed by the Arabs from the Arab city of Kufa, and it resulted in the supremacy of an Arab family over the Muslim Empire. Furthermore, Arabic continued to be the sole official language, Arabian land remained fiscally privileged, and some of the high offices were at first reserved to the Arab aristocracy. Nevertheless, the establishment of the Abbasids was followed by changes in the character of the ruling regime. They shifted the capital of the caliphate from Syria to the new city of Baghdad in Iraq. The result was both a geopolitical and social reorientation in the Muslim Empire. The highly evolved bureaucratic administration of the state as well as court etiquette were molded by Persian influences. Non-Arabs could rise to the high office of vizier, even controlling the affairs of state as in the case of the Barmecide family. Furthermore, non-Muslims came to exercise considerable power in the economic life.

To maintain their supremacy over this quickly developing, cosmopolitan empire, the Abbasids adopted a new basis for their authority. Whereas Arabism, or rule by the Arabs, was the guiding political principle of the Umayyads,

Under the Abbasid caliphs Arabic civilization attained its golden age. Abbasid society enjoyed high cultural, scientific, and economic standards.

*The Bettmann Archive*

Above, the scientist and philosopher Avicenna lectures to students. Science was advanced with such instruments as the astrolabe. Below, a caravan returns from China.

*Photographie Giraudon*

*New York Public Library*

the Abbasids resorted to the idea of Islamism, since Islam could serve as a bond uniting the various ethnic components of the vast empire. In pursuit of this religious policy, they insisted on the co-operation of Muslim theologians, and persecuted Muslim heretics.

**History of the Abbasid Caliphate.** The Abbasid caliphate evolved brilliantly and swiftly. A series of powerful rulers, including al-Mansur (r.754–75), al-Mahdi (r.775–85), Harun al-Rashid (r.786–809), and al-Mamun (r.813–33), generally succeeded in preserving the empire, which extended from North Africa to Central Asia. An efficient administrative organization permitted Abbasid society to attain a high standard of scientific, cultural, artistic, and economic development. Even during its flowering, however, forces were at work which led to the gradual decline of the caliphate. The need to defend the empire as well as to cope with internal revolts compelled the caliphs, beginning with al-Mutasim (r.833–42), to establish regiments of trained slaves, known as mamelukes. After a time the soldier-slaves grew so powerful that the caliphs surrendered their political authority to their military commanders. Moreover, petty dynasties arose in various provinces of the empire, acknowledging the nominal suzerainty of the Abbasids, but weakening the empire with their jealousies and struggles. Egypt and Syria were lost to the Tulunid dynasty (r.864–905) and the Ikhshidid dynasty (r.935–69). The effective political authority of the Abbasids was gradually restricted to Iraq. A succession of internal revolts was even more decisive in reducing Abbasid power. Although some of these were staged by socially underprivileged elements, as in the case of the Zanj revolt in Mesopotamia (868–83), most of them had the character of religious movements. The most extreme and persistent was that of the Shiite Ismaili group, which aimed at the replacement of the Abbasid caliphs by the descendants of Ali and Fatima (the cousin and daughter of the Prophet, respectively). This group succeeded in 909 in establishing the rival caliphate of the Fatimid (q.v.).

By the middle of the 10th century the Abbasids were politically impotent. Their humiliation became complete when Iraq was invaded in 945 by Daylamite troops of the Persian Buwayhids. The religious as well as the political prestige of the Abbasids suffered, since their new masters professed the Shiite creed. The emergence in 1055 of the orthodox regime of the Seljuk (q.v.) sultans restored some of the prestige of the Abbasid caliphate, though none of its political power. Caliph al-Nasir (r.1180–1225) managed to re-establish the caliphate's power over a small state centered around Baghdad. However, in 1258 the Mongols abolished the Abbasid caliphate entirely, and though a shadow Abbasid caliphate was established in Cairo in 1261 by Baybars I to serve the interests of Mameluke (q.v.) sultans, this too was abolished in 1517 by the Ottomans.

**AGA KHAN** [ä′gə kän′], title of the religious leader of the Ismaili Shiite Muslims. The Aga Khan is the imam (spiritual and temporal leader) of 20 million Ismaili Muslims, who live mainly in the subcontinent of India, Central Asia, the Middle East, and East Africa. The best-known Aga Khan of modern times was Aga Khan III, Sir Sultan Muhammad Shah (1877–1957), who became the imam in 1885, when he was eight years old. Born in India and educated in England at Eton and Cambridge, Aga Khan III exercised considerable influence among upper-class Indian Muslims. He was one of the principal leaders who established the All-India Muslim League in Dec., 1906. He led the Indian delegation to the League of Nations in 1932 and 1934–37, and was elected president of the League Assembly in 1937. Aga Khan III was also renowned as an international sportsman. His income was reputed to be several million

dollars a year. Though his followers annually contributed to this amount, much of his wealth was derived from shrewd investments. After his death on July 11, 1957, he was succeeded by his grandson, Karim Al Hussaini Shah (1937–    ), Aga Khan IV, who graduated from Harvard University in 1959.

As Ismaili Muslims live scattered in Africa and Asia, belong to different cultures, and speak different languages, it is the institution of the imam that binds them together. Most of the money that they contribute to the imam is returned to their communities to finance social welfare projects. Wherever considerable numbers of Ismaili Muslims live, there is a Supreme Ismaili Council, whose members, besides being responsible for the welfare and education of the community, also function as justices of the peace in cases where only members of the Ismaili community are involved. The Aga Khan presides over the entire organization of the Ismaili community.

**ALIGARH MOVEMENT,** the drive to teach the Muslim population of preindependence India modern ideas of political and social life. One of its aims was to convince the Muslims that the acquisition of Western knowledge was not necessarily incompatible with ancient religious traditions. The movement centered around Aligarh Muslim University, founded by Sir Sayyid Ahmad Khan in 1875. Muslims were urged to take part in public life but to withhold support from the growing Hindu nationalist movement. The Muslims believed that a rapprochement with the British provided the best solution to their problems. The ultimate effect of the Aligarh movement was the founding of the All-India Muslim League, and the eventual establishment of Pakistan as a separate Muslim state in Aug., 1947.

**ALLAH** [ăl′ə], Muslim name for God. In the Koran, the holy book of Islam, the name is used for the creator of the world, God of Abraham, of Moses, of Jesus, and of Mohammed. God is presented as unconditioned lord of all things, good and evil. He is merciful to human beings, guiding aright those who submit to Him and rewarding them for their good deeds; but if men rebel, He leads them into wrong ways and punishes them.

For orthodox Islam, God is utterly transcendent. He is not to be compared to any of His creatures; no image may be made of Him. His omnipotence is asserted to such an extent that human free will is almost denied—over the protests, however, of many Muslims, especially the Mutazilites. There can be no mediator between God and men. God tells men what He expects of them through prophets, His spokesmen; but the prophets, however excellent, are merely men. God demands above all the recognition of His own oneness; the greatest sin is worship of any other being, real or imaginary, alongside Him. The Christian doctrine of the Trinity is rejected as making a mere man, Jesus, divine. The Muslim finds this inconsistent with God's absolute unity.

God is at the same time very close to men, "nearer to a man than his jugular vein." Each can approach God directly in personal prayer and especially in reciting the Koran, which is the very speech of God. Moreover, in Sufism, a mystic movement within Islam, Muslims have developed ways for the individual to enter a mystical relationship of ecstatic love with a God who is sometimes conceived almost pantheistically.

**ALL-INDIA MUSLIM LEAGUE,** Muslim organization dedicated to independence for India and later to a separate Muslim state on the subcontinent. Toward the middle of the 19th century, apprehension developed among the Indian Muslims concerning their future as a minority in a predominantly Hindu nation. In order to press their demands, Muslim leaders, led by Aga Khan III, established the All-India Muslim League on Dec. 30, 1906, at Dacca. By 1909 the league had persuaded the British government to grant separate representation to Muslims in various legislatures.

Following World War I, the influence of the Muslim League decreased. Muslims co-operated with the All-India National Congress and participated in the Khilafat movement which was launched against the British in support of the Muslim caliph in Turkey. However, when it became clear that British policy was to concede political power to Indians by progressive stages, differences arose between Hindu and Muslim leaders as to how this power should be shared. Under the leadership of Muhammad Ali Jinnah, the league was reorganized during the provincial elections of 1936–37. Jinnah's claim that the league was the sole spokesman of the Muslims was contradicted by the election results. Nevertheless, his popularity increased when the Hindu-controlled governments in the provinces refused to work with the Muslim League representatives. In Mar., 1940, the Muslim League voted in favor of a separate independent state for Muslims. The All-India Muslim League was divided into the Indian Muslim League and the Pakistan Muslim League after the partition of India in Aug., 1947.

**ARABIC LITERATURE** properly denotes creative and deliberate writing in Arabic from about 550 A.D. onward.

Classical Arabic is the language of pre-Islamic poetry, the Koran, and a vast body of literature dating from about the 7th century A.D. As a result of early Islamic conquests, Classical Arabic was spread from Spain in the west to Chinese Turkestan in the east. It replaced many languages spoken in conquered areas, and was also used for literary purposes by people who spoke other languages.

**Poetry.** This is the oldest and most continuous form in Arabic literature. The most typical genre preserved is the *qasida*, a stylized ode of varying length, uniform rhyme, and complicated meter, extolling the merits of desert life and abounding in descriptions of nature; usually it vaunts the poet's tribe, his steed, and his (often tragically separated) beloved. The best known early collection is the *Muallaqat* (sometimes called *Golden Odes*); they number seven, but there is not universal agreement on more than five, the collection having been made perhaps two centuries after its original composition.

The authenticity of such poetry has often been questioned, most sharply by Taha Husain (1889–    ). After its eclipse in the "Mohammedan" period, poetry revived under the Umayyads and the Abbasids; at this time it was often used as source material for philological research in the ultimate interests of Koranic exegesis. The *qasida* has never entirely died out, but it was subordinated, over the centuries, to other purposes, and other genres developed from it.

In the earlier post-"Mohammedan" period individual poets are numerous, and there are at least three famous collections: the *Kitab al-Aghani* (Book of Songs), compiled in many volumes by Abu'l-Faraj al-Isfahani about 950; and two smaller compilations, both called *Hamasa* (Valor), put together respectively by Abu Tammam (d. about 850) and Buhturi (d.897). Two poets meriting special mention are the enigmatic and tragic al-Maarri (d.1057) and the Moorish mystic Ibn al-Arabi (d.1240). Acknowledged as the greatest of Arabic poets is al-Mutanabbi (d.965).

**Koran.** Strictly speaking, the *Koran* (q.v.) should not be termed "literature," since for all Muslims it is, in different degrees of literalness, the very word of God, revealed to Mohammed during some 20 years prior to his death in 632; but its importance within Arabic literature is capital. About the length of the Christian New Testament, it is divided into two types of units, the chapter (*sura*) and the verse (*aya*). These are both of greatly varying length, but it is the latter that represents the unit of revelation, the chapter arrangement having largely followed the standardization of the text that culminated in the version of 646. There is much contrast of content and style throughout the *Koran*. This has given rise to an immense body of commentary and analysis, theological and historical, grammatical and devotional, and some of these studies later gained independence of Koranic sanction.

**Tradition and the Law.** The Tradition (*hadith*) records words and deeds ascribed to Mohammed himself. Even after repeated purging of fabrications, a vast residue survives. Of six canonical collections, those of al-Bukhari (d.870) and Muslim (d.874) take precedence. From the Tradition grew jurisprudence (*fiqh*); there are four recognized schools of Islamic law, all sustaining a great body of literature. The most influential have perhaps been those of Malik (d.795) and al-Shafü (d.820).

**History, Biography, and Travel.** Historical writing, often monumental in scope, is a major glory of Arabic literature. Its origins too may be in the Tradition. Important annalists are Tabari (838–923), Masudi (d.956), and Ibn al-Athir (d.1234); Ibn Khaldun (d.1406) achieved additional renown as a pioneer historical theorist. Ibn al-Tiqtaqa wrote a popular work, *al-Fakhri*, about 1300. From the 9th century onward, biography flourished steadily; particularly common were classified biographies, covering the adherents of a town, a profession, or a legal school, to name only a few significant categories. Somewhat related to both history and biography were travel narratives, of which two fine examples are those of the Spaniard Ibn Jubayr (1145–1217) and the Moor Ibn Battuta (1304–77).

**Philosophy, Theology, and Mysticism.** Much medieval Arabic literature served to transmit Greek thought (often otherwise lost) to the West; but it also offered original contributions of its own, not only in philosophy, but also in theology and mysticism. The pioneer philosopher was al-Farabi (Alfarabius, d.950), whose work awaits proper study; he was overshadowed only by Ibn Sina (Avicenna, d.1037), who was also a scientist and a physician. A third major figure is Ibn Rushd (Averroës, d.1198). Two great theologians are the orthodox master al-Ashari (d.935) and the brilliant and unique al-Ghazzali (Algazel, d.1111); the latter was one of the sublimest mystical prose writers.

**BARMECIDE** [bär'mə-sīd] **or BARMAKID,** Iranian family of government officials that dominated the political life of the Abbasid caliphate during the second half of the 8th century. The family rose to prominence with **KAHLID IBN BARMAK** (d.781 or 782), who became the vizier, or chief administrator, for the Abbasids and governor of several provinces. His son, **YAHYA** (d.805), was appointed tutor of the crown prince, and when the latter became caliph as Harun al-Rashid in 786, Yahya was created vizier in charge of the caliphate. Yahya's sons **AL-FADL** and **JAAFAR** also acted as viziers and held responsible positions in Baghdad and in the provinces. After accepting the political preponderance of the Barmecides for 17 years, Harun al-Rashid decided to eliminate this powerful family whose influence had been perpetuated by nepotism and tremendous wealth. Therefore, in spite of their many positive achievements in the political, economic, and cultural fields, the family was brutally liquidated in 803; Jaafar was executed, the rest of the family imprisoned, and their wealth confiscated.

In one of the tales of the *Arabian Nights*, a Barmecide invites a beggar to an elaborate dinner, then pretends to enjoy it though in fact there is no food on the sumptuous plates served to him and the hungry man. The term "Barmecide feast" therefore refers to illusory magnificence.

**CALIPHATE** [kǎl'ĭ-fāt], Islamic form of government by a caliph, the essential purposes of which are to establish the Law of God among Muslims and to extend the realm of Islam in the world. Apart from these features the caliphate has varied widely both in its historical reality and the way it has been viewed by Muslim thinkers. It can therefore best be understood by surveying its history in practice and theory.

**The Four "Upright" Caliphs (632–61 A.D.).** The earliest period of the caliphate vitally affected the later development of that institution. However, two major accounts of this history have been current in the two main groups of the Muslim world, the Sunnite Muslims and the Shiite Muslims, and have led to different conclusions about the original caliphate as intended by the first Muslims.

The Sunnite version is accepted by the great majority of Muslims today, and is regarded by most critical historians as correct in its main historical features. According to this tradition, the Prophet Mohammed received a divine code of law and morals, which was revealed in the Koran, and he also gave further guidance to the Muslim community through his example and sayings. He made it clear that the state is an essential organ of Islamic action in the world, but left it to his companions to devise the state's political organization after his death and to appoint his successor as head of this state. On his death in 632, a small group in Medina elected Abu Bakr (reigned 632–34), the Prophet's closest companion, as the first Caliph (Arab. *Khalifa,* successor) of Islam. The second Caliph, Umar I (reigned 634–44), was designated Caliph by Abu Bakr before his death and was accepted without question by the Muslims and their leaders. It was under Umar's vigorous direction that the Arabs carried out most of the first great expansion of the Islamic state outside Arabia. He was the first Caliph to add the title "commander of the believers" (*amir al-muminin*) to that of Caliph. A panel of six, appointed by Umar, elected Uthman from among themselves as the third Caliph.

It was Uthman's caliphate (644–56) that raised the first serious problem about the functioning and rules of succession of the new institution. Owing to his partisan appointments to government positions this Caliph became the target of attack by a group of insurgents, who assassinated him at his residence in Medina. The fourth Caliph, Ali (reigned 656–61), Mohammed's first cousin and the husband of his daughter Fatima, was elected by the elders but failed to seize and punish the murderers of Uthman. Consequently he soon became involved in a civil war with the avengers of Uthman, led by Muawiya, one of the Umayyad family and Uthman's kinsman. Muawiya was the Governor of Syria; Ali's base of operations was Iraq. After an indecisive battle at Siffin in northern Syria (657) the two parties agreed to arbitrate their dispute. But in the course of arbitration Ali was outwitted and found himself reduced to a mere candidate for the caliphate on an equal footing with Muawiya. For his blunders Ali was deserted by a group of his followers, the Kharijites. One of these assassinated him, thus leaving the field clear for Muawiya.

From the events of these four reigns Sunnite Muslims generally have drawn certain conclusions about the caliphate. They regard the first four Caliphs as upright Muslims and companions of the Prophet, and the 30 years of their reigns as a golden age for Islam. The period therefore establishes certain standards for the ideal caliphate for the Sunnites: (a) The Islamic state initiated by Mohammed should have a single caliph, as an accepted head of the Islamic community and source of all governmental authority. (b) The main duties of the caliph are to secure obedience to the divine law by means of governmental action and personal example, and to bring more people to the blessings of Islam by appropriate means, peaceful or warlike. (c) The caliph should be an Arab of the Prophet's tribe, the Quraysh, and should be fully qualified to rule effectively. (d) He may be appointed by designation or election. The appointment must be sanctioned by a council of elders representing the Islamic community; it is never automatically valid by inheritance or by divine grace. In sum, the Sunnite caliphate is a human office with a divine purpose, the promotion of Islam.

The Shiite view of the early caliphate differs widely both in its account of events and in the theory based on it. The Shiite movement in fact probably began as a political party supporting Ali. But during the first three centuries of Islam the Shiites developed the doctrine that Mohammed had expressly designated Ali not only as his political successor (*khalifa*) but also as a spiritual leader (*imam*). To enable Ali to guide the Muslims in the understanding and practice of the Law, Mohammed revealed to him secrets of divine knowledge. Ali was chosen for this high position because of his unique virtue and his close relationship to Mohammed. However, the Shiites maintain that after the Prophet's death the rightful claims of Ali were pushed aside by the first three Sunnite "caliphs" and their supporters. Then when Ali was finally accepted, he was cheated of his office by Muawiya and his followers, being induced by a trick that played upon his piety to accept a truce at the point of victory; and in the arbitration his delegate was duped by Muawiya's delegate. At the time of his death, therefore, Ali was still the true Caliph, or rather Imam, of Islam, and Muawiya was a usurper.

According to the Shiites, then, of the first four actual rulers Ali alone legitimately held the imamate, the position belonging to him by right of designation by Mohammed.

A third view of the early caliphate was held by the Kharijites. These believed that the first four caliphs were properly elected, and remained caliphs so long as they maintained a high standard of conduct. Hence they supported Ali at the beginning, but regarded him as automatically deposed the moment he accepted arbitration with his wrongful challenger. Family and tribe were irrelevant as qualifications for the caliphate, whereas morality and piety were all-important to the Kharijites.

**The Umayyads of Damascus (661–750).** After the death of Ali, Muawiya, who was generally recognized as Caliph, proceeded to restore stability to the Islamic empire. Backed by the Arab aristocracy, he ensured the succession by designating his own son as heir apparent. He thus introduced the hereditary principle in fact, though not in form since allegiance by the elders was still considered necessary. Thus the Umayyad dynasty, which ruled the empire from Damascus and enlarged it to include North Africa, Spain, Turkestan, and Sind, was established. The principle of dynastic succession to the caliphate was followed by all later caliphs, though it was later criticized for being un-Islamic.

Serious revolts of Kharijites and Shiites threatened the Umayyads. When Ali's son Husayn, in leading a revolt, was killed by a Umayyad commander in Iraq (680), Shiite feelings in favor of Ali's descendants were immensely strengthened by the tragedy. In time the Umay-yads were overthrown by a combination of Shiite and Sunnite forces. The latter were led by the Abbasids, descendants of the Prophet's uncle Abbas. They revolted on behalf of "the Prophet's family"—a deliberately ambiguous phrase covering both the descendants of Ali and themselves—organizing a rebellion in northern Iran, which enabled them to overthrow the Umayyads and succeed them in the caliphate.

**The Early Abbasids (750–945).** Like their predecessors, the Abbasids suppressed Shiite pretenders. The Kharijites were no longer a menace. At first tranquillity was restored, and the Abbasids succeeded better than the Umayyads in appearing as champions of Islamic civilization rather than as Arabs imposing Arab domination. Their new capital of Baghdad soon became the large metropolis of a prosperous empire, achieving fabulous luxury under Harun al-Rashid (786–809). Science and literature flourished. In the 9th century, however, a serious decline set in, both at Baghdad where the caliphs were no longer able to control their unruly guards, and in the eastern provinces where the Abbasid governors founded dynasties paying sometimes homage and tribute, sometimes only homage, to their lawful sovereign. Independent states arose in Spain and North Africa. By the mid-10th century the Abbasids had lost most of their power, which they never regained.

**Shiite Dynasties.** While the Abbasid power was collapsing, many Muslims nourished Messianic hopes of an Islamic revival through some descendant of Ali. Secret Shiite movements took on new life. One in particular, the Ismailite sect, was able to emerge openly in Tunisia soon after 900, proclaiming a "Fatimid" Imam, descended from Ali and Fatima. Fatimid forces conquered North Africa from Algeria to Egypt, as well as Sicily and Syria, and the Fatimid dynasty reigned from their new capital of Cairo for two centuries (969–1171). They threatened the Sunnite caliphs of Baghdad both by military power and by spreading propaganda in all Muslim countries. Their missionaries described the Fatimid imams as infallible and sinless, who received illumination in unbroken apostolic succession from their ancestor Ali, and even ultimately from the prophets and patriarchs of the Old Testament. Armed with spiritual and secular authority, they had come to introduce a reign of Islamic justice on earth. For educated initiates, Ismailite theorists explained the imams' illumination in terms of Hellenistic psychology, according to which the Active Intellect manifests itself particularly in the purest souls.

Meanwhile another Shiite movement was widespread in Iran and Iraq, the "Twelvers" (Imamis). Their doctrines on the nature and mission of the imams resembled those of the Ismailis, but they believed that the line of imams appearing on earth had ceased after the first twelve—Ali and his descendants. These twelve had held spiritual authority, while being wrongly deprived of secular power, during the first 250 years of Islam. The later imams were concealed, and would not reappear until the last days; thus the Fatimid claims were not accepted by the Twelvers. For over a century (945–1055) a Persian dynasty of this persuasion, the Buwayhids or Buyids, actually ruled in Baghdad and held the Sunnite caliph in subjection and humiliation.

**The Later Abbasids (945-1285).** Throughout the period of Shiite predominance the Abbasid caliphs were allowed to survive, and eventually they enjoyed a revival of prestige though not of power. The Sunnite majority continued to regard Shiite doctrines as extravagant, and before long a Sunnite military and political recovery occurred, starting at the western and eastern extremes of Islam. In Muslim Spain, which had never come under Abbasid rule, a strong Umayyad king at Córdoba, Abd al-Rahman III (912-61), assumed the title of caliph (929), primarily to counter the Fatimid caliphate in North Africa; his descendants held it until their dynasty ended (1031). In Iran, Persian and Turkish monarchs championed the Abbasid caliphs against Shiite heresies, and a Turkish Seljuk sultan took Baghdad from the Buwayhids (1055). From then on the Abbasids were free of Shiite control, but either remained under the "protection" of the Seljuks or governed only a small state around Baghdad. What authority they retained in the Muslim world was due to an enduring Sunnite conviction that they alone, as caliphs, could delegate power to all other Muslim rulers. The last Caliph of the dynasty at Baghdad was put to death by order of Hulagu when the Mongols sacked the city in 1258.

It was during this period that Sunnite theories of the caliphate were fully developed, perhaps in reaction to Shiite doctrines. The classical statement is that of al-Mawardi (974-1058), a Baghdad jurist. According to him the caliphate is in essence a contract between the caliph and the Islamic community, the terms of which are set by the divine Law of Islam. Its purpose is the welfare of Muslims in both this life and the next. He describes the military and administrative functions of the caliph. (Judicial functions are left to the Muslim judges or *qadis*. Legislation was performed once for all by the Prophet of God.) A caliph may delegate some powers to other men (as he was forced to do in al-Mawardi's time), but should not become a mere head of state. He describes the moral, intellectual, physical, and tribal qualifications for holding the office, and the conditions for a valid designation or election of a new caliph. He holds that a caliph who fails seriously in his duties or loses an essential qualification breaks his contract and is liable to deposition. In that case another caliph must be elected immediately, for the caliphate is a necessary institution of Islamic society.

The great religious thinker al-Ghazzali (1058-1111) accepted al-Mawardi's theory in general, but a more resigned tone is noticeable when he speaks of the practical inadvisability of deposing caliphs because of the civil disturbance which would ensue. Such a strain of quietism appears constantly in medieval Islamic political thought, partly because there were no constitutional organs of peaceful change.

**The Mameluke Period (1250-1517).** The Mameluke sultans of Egypt and Syria established as Caliph in Cairo (1261) a man who was supposed to be an uncle of the last Abbasid of Baghdad. His descendants were installed there regularly until the Ottoman conquest of Egypt in 1517, when the last one was deposed. But the Cairo caliphs had no power and were not often recognized beyond the Mameluke kingdom. The title of "caliph" began to be adopted as an honorific title by both Arab and non-Arab monarchs.

The fact that the Abbasid caliphs were now powerless, and had never competed with the religious scholars (*ulema*) as learned authorities on the Law, raised the question more acutely than ever for Sunnite theorists whether caliphs had any function in Islam. Ibn Jamaa (1241-1333) held that their essential function was only to give legitimacy to sultans and to preserve the formal unity of Islam. Thus he could carry quietism to an extreme, by admitting any qualified caliph as adequate even if installed by force and without power. Ibn Taymiya (1263-1328) was more realistic, discounting the significance of the caliph and emphasizing instead the importance of Muslims working with their sultans to make Islam a living force. Ibn Khaldun (1332-1406) thought the ideal Islamic community should have a caliph, but he did not recognize such a caliph as existing in his time nor did he discuss means of restoring one.

**The Ottomans (c.1300-1924).** The Ottoman sultans assumed the title "caliph" from an early date, but attached little significance to it until their empire was declining. Sultans after 1774, reacting to the encroachment of Christian powers on the Near East, claimed that as caliphs they had a right to the "spiritual" allegiance of Muslims beyond the Ottoman boundaries. When the Ottoman empire collapsed after the First World War, the Sultan was deposed by the Turkish nationalists, but a Caliph was allowed to remain until 1924, when the caliphate too was abolished.

**Modern Views on the Caliphate.** For a few years after 1924 there was serious discussion in Egypt about the nature and prospects of the caliphate. Ali Abd al-Raziq argued in 1925 that the original caliphate was a spiritual headship only, a view which aroused strong protest among Egyptian Muslims. Rashid Rida (1865-1935) proposed the revival of a universal caliphate, and this was discussed at Islamic congresses in 1926 held in Mecca and Cairo, but no practical steps were taken. Since that time interest has languished. Modern Muslims have been preoccupied with problems of national independence and economic development. But the question has remained theoretically open.

**FATIMID** [*fǎt′ǐ-mǐd*] (909-1171), Caliphate which at the peak of its strength extended from North Africa to Iraq. It was established by an extreme Muslim sect of the Ismailis, themselves a sect of Shiite Islam. The latter regarded their Fatimid leaders as true descendants of the fourth Caliph, Ali, and his wife, Fatima (Mohammed's daughter). They believed the Fatimids were destined to replace the orthodox Abbasid Caliphate. Thus, apart from efficient military and administrative organization, the Fatimid Caliphate rested on strong religious foundations. As heads of the Ismaili sect, the Fatimid Caliphs held the position of infallible pontiffs endowed with supernatural attributes by divine ordination. Furthermore, an elaborate religious organization not only secured the inner cohesion of their regime but promoted the Fatimid cause by means of external missionary activities which culminated in a temporary proclamation of Fatimid sovereignty in Baghdad (1058–59).

After a period of consolidation in North Africa (909–69), the Fatimids captured Egypt, transferring their capital to the newly founded city of Cairo (969). The Fatimid Caliphate enjoyed a long period of cultural and economic development, particularly under the Caliphs al-Muiz (reigned 952–75) and al-Aziz (reigned 975–96). But in the second half of the 11th century the dynasty began to decline. It survived with difficulty a grave economic and social crisis under Caliph al-Mustansir (reigned 1036–94). Internally, the prestige of the Caliphs suffered from the emergence of military usurpers and from a major split in the Ismaili sect. Externally, the emancipation of North African provinces and the invasions of the Seljuk Turks and of the Crusaders reduced Fatimid possessions to Egyptian territory. In 1171 Saladin suppressed the Fatimid Caliphate and restored Egypt to her former Abbasid allegiance.

**HADJ or HAJJ,** the pilgrimage to Mecca which every Muslim is obliged to make at least once in his life if he can afford it. Anyone who has performed it is highly honored as a hadji.

**HAREM** [hâr′əm] (Arab. *harim*, "forbidden"), term designating the separate living quarters of women in Muslim households, where strict separation and seclusion were enforced. It also means the collective women of the harem. In India the harem was called *zenana* or *purdah*. Except for close relatives, no male visitors were allowed and women were veiled to all men, except husband, son, and father.

Although the practice of secluding women was known in many ancient cultures, it was chiefly Islam that perpetuated this practice into the present. The Koran sanctions concubinage and polygamy, allowing four wives. In later centuries, the most elaborate harems were those of the sultans of the Ottoman empire. The imperial harem was a highly structured community consisting of wives, concubines, slaves, servants, and children, often ruled by the sultan's mother, with security enforced by eunuchs. While social intercourse was free within the harem, its women ventured outside only in veil and with attendants. Although prestige and privileges accrued to women of the harem (Turkish women had many legal rights, including possession of property), the rigid isolation and lack of education and employment frequently led to boredom and vacuity in harem life. Plots involved with succession to the throne were hatched in the imperial harem, often leading to espionage, infanticide, and assassinations.

The imperial seraglio of Constantinople was broken up in 1909 and in 1926 Turkey legally abolished polygamy. In the last 30 or 40 years, modern influences have rendered the harem obsolete in the more progressive Muslim communities, where women have slowly begun to seek education and enter public life. Nevertheless,

Muslim women of the less developed areas still wear veils and live in seclusion.

**HEGIRA** [hĭ-jī′rə] **or HIJRA** [hĭj′rə], the migration (less accurately, flight) of the Prophet Mohammed and his followers from Mecca to Medina. Mecca was not friendly to the religious doctrines of Mohammed when he first declared them, whereas in Medina, an oasis about 200 mi. from Mecca, the people accepted him as their religious leader. He therefore migrated to Medina in 622 A.D. The Muslim era, still used by Muslims for dating events, began on the first day of the Arab year in which the Hegira took place, namely July 16, 622. The Hegira probably occurred on Sept. 20, 622.

**ISLAMIC LAW,** or Sharia, the attempt to define the will of Allah for Muslim society in terms of a person's rights and obligations. The main elements of divine revelation are found in the Koran, to the Muslim the very word of Allah himself, and in the Sunna, the divinely inspired rules of conduct enunciated by the Prophet Mohammed.

It was not until about 900 A.D. that the task of fashioning

Women walk down a corridor toward the tomb of Mohammed in a shrine in Medina, Saudi Arabia, where the Prophet died in 632 A.D.
United Press International

a comprehensive legal system from this limited material was completed. Scholar-jurists known as *mujtahids* interpreted, expanded, and systematized the precepts of the Koran and the Sunna, using particularly the method of *qiyas*, or reasoning by analogy. Differences of opinion resulted in the formation of different schools of law.

Among the Sunnites (or Sunnis), the majority group in Islam, four such schools survive today: the Hanafi school, which predominates in the Middle East and the Indian subcontinent; the Maliki school of North and West Africa; the Shafii school of East Africa, Aden Colony and the Hadhramaut, and Southeast Asia; and the Hanbali school, which is confined to Saudi Arabia. Where the schools agree, as they do on all basic matters, the principle of *ijma*, or consensus, proclaims such rules to be an established and certain expression of Allah's will; where the schools disagree the *ijma* ratifies the different rules as all equally probable definitions of Allah's will.

Fundamentally different considerations apply to the minority movement of the Shiites (or Shia) in its various branches, the Ithna Asharis in Iran, the Ismailis in the Indian subcontinent and East Africa, and the Zaydis in Yemen. As opposed to Sunnites, Shiites in theory reject human reason, in the form of *qiyas* or *ijma*, relying instead upon the word of their divinely inspired imam, or religious leader, who is thus the infallible mouthpiece of the law.

By the end of the 10th century the law had been crystallized in the texts that were regarded as authoritative expositions of the Sharia in the different schools. The theory of *taqlid*, or "imitation," took firm root: future generations of jurists were bound to follow the established doctrine, and for more than 10 centuries the medieval texts held a paramount and exclusive authority. Thus, as social and economic circumstances changed, a rift developed between the terms of the rigid and immutable Sharia and practical needs. Parts of the Sharia were perforce abandoned. Jurisdiction in the fields of contract and crime was exercised by non-Sharia courts, for the Sharia law of contract rested upon an impractical prohibition of any form of interest on capital (*riba*) or any element of risk or uncertainty in commercial dealings, while the criminal law was suited only to the needs of a tribal society.

**Family Law.** By the end of the 19th century the jurisdiction of the courts of the *qadis*, the judges of Sharia law, was confined in the great majority of Muslim countries to family law. The general nature of this law may be illustrated by a brief reference to the two major topics of marriage and divorce.

Marriage, according to Sharia law, is a simple contract requiring no formalities beyond the presence of two witnesses. In return for the general obedience of his wife, the husband is obliged to pay her a dower and to provide for her maintenance. In intention, marriage is a lifelong union; only the Ithna Asharis recognize temporary marriage (muta), where the period specified may range from one day to 99 years. Minor children may be contracted in compulsory marriage by their guardians, and though the Hanafis allow an adult woman to contract herself in marriage the other schools require her guardian to conclude the contract on her behalf. Polygamy is allowed subject to two main restrictions: a Muslim may not have more than four wives concurrently, nor may he be married at the

same time to two women closely related to each other. There is no exception to the rule that a Muslim woman may marry only a Muslim; a Muslim male may marry either a Muslim or a Kitabiyya, a woman professing a religion which has a kitab, or revealed scripture.

Divorce may be effected in three principal ways. Firstly, the husband has an unrestricted power to repudiate (*talaq*) his wife at will. No intervention by the court is necessary and questions of motive are irrelevant. Secondly, divorce by mutual consent is recognized. Thirdly, the court may dissolve a marriage on certain specified grounds, restricted to sexual impotence in Hanafi law, but including cruelty and desertion in the other schools. Adultery per se is not a ground for judicial dissolution; but the penalty for adultery, a criminal offense, is death by stoning.

But even in matters of family law, which have always been regarded as an integral part of the religion of Islam, opposition to the traditional doctrine materialized under the impact of Western civilization. In Turkey in the 1920's the Sharia law was wholly abandoned in favor of a family law based on the Swiss Civil Code. By the early 1960's no other Muslim country, however, had followed this extreme step. Since 1913, when Egypt first restricted child marriage by a regulation providing that no marriage would be recognized by the courts unless the parties had reached the minimum ages of 18 and 16 for males and females respectively, far-reaching reforms have been achieved in the Sharia law. Moving cautiously at first by indirect methods, the reformers now openly deny the doctrine of *taqlid* and claim the right to reinterpret the original sources, the Koran and Sunna, in the light of modern conditions. Two outstanding examples of reforms so achieved are contained in the Tunisian Law of Personal Status of 1956, which abolishes both polygamy and the husband's right of *talaq*. In Pakistan the Muslim Family Laws of 1961 made reforms in the law, custom, and usage governing succession, marriage, and divorce. Voting and political rights have been granted to women in Mauritania, Pakistan, and Syria. In thus adapting the texts of divine revelation to the needs of modern society, the reformers avoid, at least formally, the secularization of the law and preserve the Islamic ideal of a way of life based upon the command of Allah.

**JINNI** [*jĭn'ē*] **or GENIE** [*jē'nē*], in Muslim literature and Arabic folklore, a supernatural creature having magical powers. In most instances he is formed like a man, but among his magical powers is the ability to alter his size and shape. He can also influence mortal affairs either for good or for evil. Occasionally, the jinni is depicted as a slave in temporary bondage to a human master.

**KAABA** [*kä'ə-bə*] **or KABA** [*kä'bə*], a roughly cubical building (about 40 ft. each way) in the central courtyard of the Haram, or mosque of Mecca. Muslims throughout the world turn to it in worship. During the pilgrimage Muslims kiss the Black Stone built into one corner, and walk around the Kaaba seven times.

**KARBALA** [kär′bə-lə], city of central Iraq, capital of Karbala Province, situated at the eastern edge of the Syrian Desert, on a canal joining it to a tributary of the Euphrates River 20 mi. east. Lying at the end of a spur line of the Baghdad–Basra railway, it is 28 mi. northwest of Hillah and 60 mi. southwest of Baghdad.

Next to Mecca and to Najaf 50 mi. south, Karbala is the third-holiest city of the Shiite Muslim sect, and is visited annually by thousands of pilgrims bringing their dead for burial. Here, in 680 A.D., while trying to reclaim the caliphate, the Shiite Saint Husayn, grandson of the Prophet Mohammed, and his half-brother Abbas were killed by the Umayyad Caliph Yazid. Husayn's tomb, crowned by a gilded dome and among the most sacred Shiite shrines, and the tomb of Abbas dominate the city. Pilgrims to Mecca and to the tomb of Ali, father of Husayn, at Najaf, pass through Karbala. Nearby are ruins of ancient Babylon. Pop., 71,163.

**KHILAFAT** [ĸнĭ-lä′fət] **MOVEMENT,** expression of protest by Indian Muslims after World War I against the Treaty of Sèvres, because the treaty destroyed the Ottoman Empire, whose ruler was recognized by many Muslims as Khalifa (Caliph), or spiritual leader. Under the leadership of the brothers Muhammad and Shaukat Ali, the movement appealed to Indian Muslims to unite against the apparent disregard by the British of the religious sentiments of their Indian subjects and to demand the restoration of the Khalifa to power. It also proclaimed that it was the duty of all true Muslims to leave India for countries where Islam was respected. This notion led to disaster when, as a result, thousands of Muslims departed for Afghanistan only to be denied admission and to perish near the border.

The Khilafat movement had considerable impact upon India. It enabled Gandhi to create a common front for Hindus and Muslims and thus to further the cause of nationalism, which up to that time had received little support from Indian Muslims. The combined agitation of the two communities contributed to the success of the non-co-operation movement (1920–21) and to the moplah outbreak (1921–22). The establishment of a strong secular government in Turkey and the exiling of the last Khalifa in 1924 made continuance of the movement pointless, but it had served to create a new political awareness among Indian Muslims.

**KORAN** [kô-rän′] (Arab. Quran; formerly written Alcoran in the West), the holiest book of Islam. It is the collection of revelations in Arabic which Muslims believe God made to the Prophet Mohammed. Together with the several books of hadith, which are the reports of Mohammed's sayings and doings, it forms what may be called the scriptures of Islam. But whereas the hadith reports what Mohammed said in his own person, the Koran contains those utterances of Mohammed which were believed to have been dictated to him by the angel Gabriel from time to time as the very words of God. The Koran corresponds in form to the portions of the prophetic books of the Bible which are introduced by "thus says the Lord." Accordingly, "you" in the Koran refers to Mohammed and his followers, and "we" refers to God Himself.

Whenever Mohammed felt that Gabriel had visited him with a message, he uttered it to his companions, whereupon it was written down by secretaries and memorized by his followers. The messages, many of them brief, were then arranged in suras, or chapters, most of which include messages revealed on several different occasions. To some degree they were arranged by Mohammed himself, but the whole collection as it now stands in the Koran was put together by his followers a few years after his death in 632 A.D. The suras were arranged chiefly in order of length, the longest coming first. Under the third Caliph, Uthman (reigned 644–56), a standard edition was published. This did not quite eliminate variations; Muslims recognize seven slightly differing recensions as equally authoritative. Yet there is no doubt that the Koran of today is substantially as it came from Mohammed.

The Koran is not designed to be read as a continuous narrative or exposition, nor are most of the single suras. One who tries to read the Koran from beginning to end without preparation is likely to be confused and disappointed. Rather, as in the prophetic books of the Bible, the message of each Koranic passage is usually more or less independent of the passages next to it, having been revealed independently. A pious Muslim, therefore, meditates on each passage for its own sake as he comes to it. Throughout the Koran, whatever other subject is being treated, there are exhortations to godliness, sonorous praises of God and warnings against unbelief and wickedness. These give the book a unity of moral and emotional tone.

Framed by these often rather repetitive exhortations are the more substantive matters: descriptions of God's power and providence, of the delights of the righteous in Paradise, and of the misery of the wicked in Hell; and appeals to the evidence furnished by nature and history that the wicked are destroyed and that life can be resurrected out of death. The portions of the book written first, forming for the most part the shorter suras now placed at the end, often set forth appeals to faith and warnings of God's judgment in lyrically beautiful imagery. Somewhat later portions tell the stories of past prophets, chiefly Biblical figures (especially Moses, and also Jesus). These stories underline the stubbornness of men's resistance to God's messages as delivered to these prophets, as well as God's power in punishing the stubborn peoples.

The last portions to be written, usually placed toward the beginning of the Koran, deal more often with the life of the growing Muslim community of Mohammed's last years. They condemn the errors of the Christians (above all, the doctrine of the Trinity, as Mohammed conceived it) and especially the errors of the Jews, reassuring the Muslims in the face of the prestige of these older faiths; they deal with current crises, urging the believers to serve in the community expeditions and settling moral problems that arose; and, more generally, they provide rulings as to proper behavior, legal rights, and social obligations.

The word *quran* originally referred to recitation in worship. The original use of the Koran was in such recitation, and this has remained its most important use, whether the worship is in groups or individually. The Koran is felt as an eloquent and inexhaustible reminder of men's duties to God. Every Muslim is expected to memorize at least some words of it for use in his daily devotions; many memorize the whole. Unbelievers have traditionally been discouraged from handling the holy book, lest they defile it. Preferably, the Koran should be recited in the original Arabic in a prescribed manner, with each syllable musically intoned and with proper pauses, having an effect of great beauty. Professional Koran reciters (sometimes called "Koran readers"), often blind, may be called on to recite part or all of the Koran at special solemnities, such as weddings or funerals or in modern times over the radio. Popular thought has attributed powers of protection and healing to the recitation of the Koran, especially of certain parts, and even written copies of Koranic passages have been used as charms and amulets.

In addition to being a constantly recited reminder of God's providence and His judgment, the Koran serves, together with the hadith, as a primary source of sacred law in matters both of ritual and of social practice. Relatively few points of law are clearly expounded in the Koran—most of the law is derived from hadith—but such Koranic prescriptions as are explicit hold a privileged position in the Muslim law, though they are sometimes held in abeyance if they seem inappropriate to modern life. The Koran has also served in the past as the starting point not only of legal but of all learning, a touchstone for such fields as history and even astronomy and medicine among the very pious. It is, of course, the foundation of all Muslim theological studies. Though it presents no developed theological system itself, all the diverse Muslim theological systems claim to be derived from it and make use of Koranic words and phrases as their technical terms. Exhaustive commentaries on the Koran have been written by Muslims of many generations, from as many points of view. Some have conscientiously preserved important details about the circumstances in which individual passages were revealed, and how, therefore, they are to be understood; such commentaries are essential for the modern scholar as well as for the believer.

Muslims believe that the original of the Koran is eternally laid up with God; that indeed, as the very speech of God, it is an inseparable attribute of God. The beauty of the Koran's language in the original is very impressive and, being of God's authorship, is regarded as supernatural. Mohammed himself claimed no greater miracle than the inimitability of the Koran, which is still regarded as a standing miracle to prove Mohammed's prophethood. The original Arabic is rhymed and has a dignity of phrasing which has never been captured in translation.

There are many English renderings but none is yet fully satisfactory. That by A. J. Arberry suggests some of the music of the Koran, but the language is awkwardly anachronistic. Richard Bell's is more accurate, but is not arranged for reading. M. M. Prickthall's is tendentious and clumsy in style. N. J. Dawood's is readable but inaccurate. Of the older translations, E. H. Palmer's and J. M. Rodwell's (which later arranges the chapters chronologically) are still useful.

**MAHDI** [mä'dē], title of a figure many Muslims expect to appear at the end of history. He is to wage holy war till the world is filled with justice as it is now filled with injustice, ruling with the support of Jesus (returned to earth) till the Last Judgment. Many reformers throughout Islamic history have claimed to be the Mahdi and risen against corrupt Muslim governments of their day. A number have founded important dynasties, and some have founded new Muslim sects. Several Shiite Muslim groups have expected one of the imams (spiritual leaders) descended from Mohammed to take power as the Mahdi; the hidden final imam of the Imami sect of Shiite Islam is given this title.

**MAHOUND** [mə-hound', mə-hōōnd'], a medieval corruption of the name of the Prophet of Islam, Mohammed. Mahound was sometimes thought to be a false god, an idol, even the devil.

**MAMELUKE** [măm'ə-lōōk] **SULTANATE** (1250–1517), regime established by the Mameluke caste which usurped control over Egypt during the period of a military crisis following an invasion by the Crusaders. Originally slaves, mostly of central Asian Turkish origin, the Mamelukes were specially trained for military purposes and were first used extensively by the Abbasid Caliph Mutasim (833–42). The progressive militarization of the Near East led to the formation of a privileged Mameluke caste whose leaders asserted themselves politically. Their growing influence on the affairs of the state culminated in the establishment in 1250 of the Mameluke Sultanate in Egypt.

The succession to the Mameluke throne was usually determined by the outcome of a violent rivalry between the leading contenders of the ruling élite. The continuity of their regime was effected by fresh importations of slaves, mostly of Kipchak and Caucasian origin. The Mamelukes were successful in wars against the Crusaders and the Mongols. Internally, they oppressed the population with a predatory feudal system. The strength of their regime was gradually reduced by the Black Death ravages, by the spread of corruption, and by the overreliance on cavalry troops to the detriment of naval and artillery units. The Mameluke Sultanate was destroyed in 1517 by the Ottoman army of Selim I, which was equipped with superior firearms.

**MECCA** [měk'ə], holy city of Saudi Arabia and capital of Hejaz, located in a barren valley 46 mi. east of Jiddah.

A pilgrimage to Mecca, the most sacred city of Islam, is one of the five obligations of every Muslim. The chief shrine of the pilgrimage is the Kaaba, the great Black

Pilgrims at one of the gates of the great mosque in Mecca, the holiest city of Islam. The Muslim in the foreground has a waterpot used in washing himself before prayer, as is customary. (ALPHA PHOTO ASSOCIATES)

Stone before which Mohammed destroyed the idols of the polytheists on his triumphal return to Mecca from Medina. The Kaaba is housed within the vast courtyard of a great mosque, dating from 1570 A.D., the main architectural feature of the city. The mosque, surmounted by a huge dome, is in the shape of a parallelogram and the courtyard is enclosed by triple rows of columns. Thousands of pilgrims come to Mecca every year. The city is forbidden to non-Muslims, though a few have entered in disguise. Mohammed was born in Mecca in 570 A.D. He announced his early revelations here and left Mecca for Medina in 622.

**MEDINA** [mə-dē'nə], (Arab. **AL-MADINAH**), also known as Medinat en-Nabi, "the city of the Prophet," city of Saudi Arabia, the second holiest city of Islam and the burial place of Mohammed. The tomb of Mohammed and his daughter Fatima are inside the spacious Mosque of the Prophet, under a green dome. Originally built by Mohammed, the mosque was burned twice, then restored and enlarged several times, most recently in 1955.

Although pilgrims come to Medina, it is not obligatory for Muslims as is Mecca. Non-Muslims may not enter Medina at all. Mohammed lived in Medina for 10 years after his flight (hegira) from Mecca (622). Before his death (632), he had captured Mecca and laid the foundations of the Islamic state. Medina was the seat of caliphate until 661. It became part of Saudi Arabia in 1924.

**MOGUL** [mō'gəl] **or MUGHAL** [moŏ'gəl] (1526–1857), Muslim dynasty and empire of India. Although Babur, a descendant of Tamerlane and Genghis Khan, established the dynasty after he defeated (1526) Sultan Ibrahim's army of 100,000 at Panipat, Mogul rule did not flourish in India until the reign of Akbar the Great (reigned 1556–1605). He built the empire on two solid foundations, a sound revenue system and civil administration and religious toleration. Rather than parcel out his possessions among fief holders, Akbar employed salaried officials. His religious toleration won him the support of the brave Rajput generals, capable Hindu ministers and officials, and a contented peasantry. The religious policy, however, set into motion a conflict between the liberal Muslim school and the orthodox. Akbar left such a strong administrative system that the empire survived 22 years of the effete rule of his son, Jahangir. Under the succeeding two rulers, Shah Jahan (reigned 1628–58) and Aurangzeb (reigned 1659–1707), the religious controversy was resolved in favor of the orthodox school. Intolerance eventually resulted in the alienation of the Rajputs and opposition from the Sikhs and the Marathas. State expenditure was increased beyond the limits of financial prudence by Shah Jahan's construction of grandiose mosques and tombs, and Aurangzeb's endless military campaigns brought the empire to bankruptcy.

The death of Aurangzeb, who had extended the empire to the whole of India, was followed by a scramble for succession among his sons. Prince Muazzam emerged triumphant and was enthroned with the title of Bahadur Shah, but his rule lasted only until 1712. During the next 50 years the nobles and provincial governors, witnessing the obvious disintegration of the empire, declared themselves independent of Mogul power and India experienced a period of total anarchy. In 1739 Nadir Shah, the King of Persia, sacked and plundered Delhi, carrying away an enormous booty. From then on, the Mogul emperors were mere phantoms of their former selves. Nevertheless, for political reasons, succeeding powers such as the Marathas and the British were anxious to acknowledge the nominal sovereignty of the Moguls. In 1765 the Moguls were forced to hand over the administration of Bengal, Bihar, and Orissa to the British. The Emperor became a puppet in the hands of the Marathas as well. In 1804 the British defeated the Marathas and took the Emperor under their protection. During the Sepoy Mutiny of 1857 the rebels proclaimed the aged Bahadur Shah II as the Emperor of India. When the British regained power he was put on trial for rebellion. His deposal in 1857 formally ended the Mogul dynasty.

In the realm of the arts the Mogul Empire has seldom been equaled in Indian history. Akbar attracted poets, philosophers, and religious leaders to his court and encouraged the translation of Hindu works in philosophy and religion. The Taj Mahal, built by Shah Jahan as a monument to his wife, survives today as a work of incomparable beauty. Mogul painting, at first influenced by Persian art, emancipated itself and merged with that of the Rajput.

**MOSQUE** [mŏsk], Muslim house of worship. Lacking a native architecture, the early Muslims adopted the styles of conquered peoples, so that mosque designs vary widely in different lands. Certain elements essential to the cult nevertheless appear in even primitive mosques and remain fairly constant. First is the prayer hall (*maqsurah*), a wide but shallow rectangular structure walled on three sides, with its long front open to a court. Centered in the long rear wall is the prayer niche (*mihrab*), oriented toward Mecca; flanking it to the right stands the pulpit (*minbar*), approached by steep steps and covered by a high pyramidal roof or dome. Nearby in later mosques is a large elevated platform (*dikka*), from which prayers are read by the imam. Fronting the *maqsurah* is a spacious rectangular court, surrounded on three sides by arcaded porticoes. This court has a central fountain for ceremonial ablutions, and sometimes includes the tomb (*turbeh*) of the mosque's founder. The four corners or other points in the general plan are marked by slender towers (minarets), from which sounds the call to prayer.

The early structures of Syria and Egypt follow this typical form, as in the mosques of Amr (7th century) and Ibn

Tulun (9th century) at Cairo. The great mosque of Sultan Hasan (14th century), at Cairo, has four arms with pointed vaults arranged in cruciform plan about a central court. Moorish mosques, in Africa and Spain, follow the primitive type, for example, the one at Córdoba, whose *maqsurah*, with 16 rows of columns, occupies an area larger than any church; it became a cathedral in 1238. Persian structures are characterized by pointed bulbous domes, lofty portals, and magnificent polychrome tile both inside and out. Celebrated examples are the Blue Mosque at Tabriz (15th century) and the Imperial Mosque at Isfahan (16th–17th century). When Constantinople fell in 1453, the Turks converted the Byzantine Hagia Sophia into a mosque, and later employed its domical scheme in their Süleymaniye (16th century) and Ahmediye (17th century) mosques there. Indian mosques, which show Persian influence in their pointed bulbous domes, round minarets, and huge pointed doorways, are solidly built of colored stone with brilliant marble inlays. The finest specimens are the Great Mosque at Fatehpur Sikri (16th–17th century), the three-domed Pearl Mosque at Agra (17th century), and the Jama Masjid at Delhi (17th century).

**MUEZZIN** [mū-ĕz'ĭn], in Muslim worship, the man who utters the call to prayer, often from a minaret (the tower of a mosque).

**MUFTI** [mŭf'tē], Muslim legal scholar qualified to give advice in the form of a *fatwa*, or ruling on Sacred Law, by applying the relevant principles of the authoritative texts to actual cases. Because of the wide scope of the Islamic religious law (Sharia), these cases might range from private matters of religious practice to public and political questions. Although essentially a private office exercised by those qualified by general repute, official muftis were publicly appointed in the Ottoman Empire, the chief mufti being known as the Shaykh al Islam.

**MULLAH** [mŭl'ə, mōōl'ə], title derived from the Arabic *mawla* ("master"), used in the Indian subcontinent to denote a qualified exponent of the Islamic religious law.

**MUSLIM CALENDAR,** a lunar calendar used by Muslims for religious and often for civil purposes. It consists of yearly cycles of 12 lunar months (reckoned from new moon to new moon), numbered from the year of Mohammed's flight to Medina, which began July 15, 622 A.D. This is called the *hijri* era, from the Arabic *hijra*, "flight" (Lat. *hegira*). Since 12 lunar months are about 11 days short of a true solar year, each new Muslim year begins that much earlier in the round of the natural seasons. Hence any given Muslim date may recur at any season, and does not answer to any given date in other calendars. Accordingly,

The Jama Masjid, a 17th-century mosque in Delhi, India.
Francis O'Neil—Pictorial Parade

a special formula must be used for rendering dates from the Muslim into the Gregorian calendar; the simplest for most purposes is that the Gregorian year is 622 plus the *hijri* year, minus one thirty-third of the *hijri* year.

The Muslim day is reckoned from sunset to sunset, and the month begins (in orthodox doctrine and old popular practice) at sunset when the new moon is seen. Hence the length of a given month has varied, sometimes even from place to place according to visibility. For official purposes, however, 30 days have usually been assigned to odd-, 29 to even-numbered months, the 12th month also receiving a 30th day in certain years, for determining which several systems have been used. The names of the months are, in order: Muharram, Safar, Rabi I, Rabi II, Jumada I, Jumada II, Rajab, Shaaban, Ramadan, Shawwal, Dhu-l-Qaada, Dhu-l-Hijja. The Muslims use the same week as do the Jews and Christians.

In addition to this religious calendar, used for literary and historical purposes, Muslims have almost always used solar calendars, especially for fiscal purposes, some of them of great mathematical accuracy. At present, the Gregorian calendar is in official use in most Islamic states.

**OTTOMAN** [ŏt'ō-man] **EMPIRE,** the greatest of the Muslim states. Its 600-year history extends from 1299 through World War I. Under Osman (d.1326), considered the founder of the dynasty, the Ottoman Turks began their westward expansion at the expense of the Byzantines. By 1400 Osman's successors controlled the greater part of Serbia, Bulgaria, and Walachia. In their most significant victory over the Christians, the Muslim forces captured Constantinople (1453). Soon afterward the khanate of the Crimea became part of the Empire, as did Egypt, the Red Sea shore of the Arabian Peninsula, and the Mediterranean shore of Palestine and Syria.

Under Suleyman I (reigned 1520–66) the Ottomans reached the zenith of their power and civilization. The Empire lost both territory and prestige during the 17th and 18th centuries. The 19th century saw superficial reform efforts, followed, in the 20th century, by the founding of the Turkish republic.

**RAMADAN** [răm-ə-dän'], also Ramazan, the ninth month of the Muslim calendar, during which Muslims are to fast (if in good health), taking neither food nor water from earliest dawning to sunset. As a lunar month, it may occur at any season of the solar year. The month is to be devoted to prayer. During the daytime work is reduced to minimum essentials. After sunset food is taken. During the nights pious Muslims attend special services in the mosques, while the more frivolous have sometimes created a carnival atmosphere. The end of Ramadan is marked by the lesser bairam, one of the chief festivals of the Muslim year.

**SAYYID or SAYID** [sĭ'yĭd], an Arabic term for "chief." It is above all applied to the descendants of Mohammed, especially through his grandson Husayn. Honoring the sayyids is regarded among Muslims as a religious obligation. In some lands they are distinguished by green turbans.

**SELJUK or SALJUQ** [sĕl-jook'] **DYNASTIES.** In the 11th and 12th centuries these dynasties arose as the result of an invasion of the Near East by the Turkish Oghuz tribes under the leadership of the Seljuk family. According to Turkish tribal customs, conquered territories belonged to the leading family whose senior member exercised over-all political supremacy. Thus, though several Seljuk petty dynasties were established to rule various parts of the Seljuk Empire, they ruled under the sovereign power of the dynasty of the Great Seljuks (1038–1157).

The founder of the Great Seljuk Dynasty, Tughril Bey, was formally recognized in 1055 by the head of the Abbasid caliphate as Sultan of the Muslim Empire. The power of this dynasty extended over the eastern provinces of the Abbasid caliphate (with the exception of Kerman in Iran) and continued under Tughril's two successors, Alp Arslan (d.1072) and Malik Shah (d.1092). A subsequent series of weak rulers and the rise of rival Seljuk dynasties undermined the position of the Great Seljuks, whose line ended in 1157 with the death of its last Sultan, Sanjar. The main achievement of the Great Seljuks was destruction of the Buyid (Buwayhid) regime and their reinvigoration of the orthodox (Sunnite) form of Islam.

Under the over-all sovereignty of the Great Sultans, other members of the Seljuk family succeeded in founding their own dynasties. Thus Mahmud, son of the Great Sultan Muhammad, originated in 1118 a branch known as the Seljuks of Iraq. Its history was characterized by fratricidal struggles, skillfully exploited by ambitious local leaders in Iraq. The political weakness of the Seljuks of Iraq prevented them from helping to defend Islam against the Crusaders.

The Seljuks of Kerman (1041–1186) originated with Kawurd Kara Arslan Bey (d.1074), who had occupied Kerman during the early phase of the Oghuz invasion. Except for a brief period immediately after the death of Alp Arslan in 1072, the rulers of this dynasty accepted the sovereignty of the Great Seljuks.

The branch of the Seljuks of Syria started with Tutush, son of Alp Arslan, who occupied Damascus in 1078 and was killed in 1095 during a war against the Great Seljuks. His sons Ridwan (d.1114) and Dukak (d.1104) founded ephemeral dynasties in Aleppo and Damascus, respectively. The rivalry between these two branches of the Seljuks of Syria was one of the causes of the success of the First Crusade (1095–99).

Another important Seljuk dynasty came into being through the achievements of Suleyman ibn Kutulmish (d.1086) after the battle of Manzikert (1071). His successors established the powerful sultanate of Rum.

**ULEMA or ULAMA** [o͞o-lə-mä'], the body of men learned in the Muslim law and faith. (An individual learned man is called *alim*.) The ulema are not properly called priests, for they are not ordained to any special role in ritual. Their sole qualification is their degree of learning. Yet in each Muslim land they have recognized leaders and often act as a group in the name of Islam.

**UMAYYAD** [o͞o-mī'yăd], also spelled Umaiyad, Omayyad, and, incorrectly, Ummayad, Ommiad, two dynasties of Arab caliphs.

**The Umayyads of Damascus (661–750 A.D.).** The Umayyads were the first dynasty of caliphs in Islam. Before them the four "upright," or Patriarchal, caliphs had ruled (632–61) by right of election or designation to the caliphate. The third of these, Uthman (reigned 644–56), was of the Umayyad family, which had been powerful in ancient Mecca. After Uthman's assassination in 656, his relatives led by Muawiya, the Governor of Syria, demanded vengeance on the murderers of Uthman from the fourth Caliph, Ali (reigned 656–61), but did not receive satisfaction. An inconclusive civil war resulted, but when Ali was assassinated by a former follower, Muawiya assumed the caliphate without challenge. He made Damascus his capital.

Muawiya I (reigned 661–80) was a masterly politician who governed the Islamic Empire by opportune use of conciliation and force. He set up a dynasty in his family, an action which stabilized the state but was later criticized as un-Islamic. Ruling an empire stretching from Libya to Iran and from northern Syria to the south of Arabia, he renewed the Arab attacks against the Byzantine Empire. He long threatened Constantinope itself by sea (674–78), but made no headway on this front.

Muawiya's son Yazid I (reigned 680–83) easily suppressed a brief insurrection by Husayn, the son of Ali, but the death of Husayn in 680 aroused strong and enduring emotions among his followers, the Shiites. Next the Empire was torn by war with a rival Caliph, Ibn al-Zubayr of Medina. Peace was restored by the victory of another Umayyad Caliph, Abd al-Malik (reigned 685–705). Under Abd al-Malik and his sons who succeeded him the expansion of Islam was resumed. To the west, Arab armies conquered northwest Africa and most of Spain, while to the east other Arab forces conquered the lower Indus valley and western Turkestan (now Uzbekistan). Constantinople was attacked again (717–18), but once more it held out.

*The Decline of the Dynasty.* This entire, vast Empire was held under one government until the end of the dynasty, but it was subject to severe stresses. There were the rivalries of Arab tribal groups, the smoldering hostility of the Shiites, widespread disapproval of the dynasty in Muslim religious circles, and the national hatred of the Persians for their Arab conquerors. After the reign (724–43) of Hisham, the weakness of the Umayyad caliphs gave an occasion for revolt to all of these discontented groups. They were cleverly combined in a single insurrection by the Abbasid family, descendants of the Prophet Mohammed's uncle, Abbas. Raising a rebellion first in northeast

Iran, the Abbasids soon sent an army to Iraq, defeated the royal forces, and in 750 had the Umayyads slaughtered.

*Contributions of the Umayyads.* The Umayyads of Damascus founded the system of administration developed by later Muslim caliphs and sultans, adapting the autocratic and centralized institutions of the old Byzantine and Sasanid empires to the needs and outlook of an Islamic state. In the same period the doctrines and law of Islam itself were being molded into their distinctive Islamic forms out of the diverse heritages of the Arabic revelation and traditions of the Prophet, and of the Greek and Syriac learning of the conquered Christians. Architecture and the decorative arts lacked an Arabic tradition, but Byzantine and Iranian traditions were rapidly developed in characteristic Islamic ways. The grandest surviving Umayyad monuments are the Dome of the Rock in Jerusalem, the Umayyad Mosque of Damascus, and the ruins of several royal palaces in or bordering on the Syrian Desert. Arabic poetry alone seemed to resist the influences of the conquered nations.

**The Umayyads of Córdoba (756–1031 A.D.).** A young grandson of the Caliph Hisham, Abd al-Rahman, escaped the massacre of his kinsmen in 750 and made his way to Spain. Gathering followers, he overcame the Arab Governor at Córdoba and re-established the Umayyad Dynasty there, as the Amir Abd al-Rahman I (reigned 756–88). By withdrawing homage from the Abbasid Caliph in Baghdad, he became the first Muslim ruler to maintain a state independent of the caliphate.

The dynasty thus founded ruled al-Andalus (Muslim Spain and Portugal) from Córdoba for nearly three centuries. The kingdom at most times included the whole peninsula south of Coimbra in the west and the Ebro River in the east. During these centuries the Christian kingdoms of the north made little progress in the reconquest of Spain. The only important city recaptured by them was Barcelona in 801. The reign (822–52) of Abd al-Rahman II was notable as a period of prosperity. Andalusian culture now became more responsive to influences from Baghdad and eastern Islam. But by 900 al-Andalus was suffering from its recurrent anarchy, with Arabs fighting Berbers and other Arabs and with rebellions by the Mozarabes (Arabic-speaking Christians). The dynasty barely survived, until the reign (912–61) of the great monarch Abd al-Rahman III. He restored unity and prosperity after many struggles and made Córdoba a capital of world renown. He assumed the title of caliph in 929, when the Abbasid caliphs had lost real power and the Sunnite world was threatened by Shiite caliphs, the Fatimids, who were expanding their empire from Tunisia. The kingdom's well-being continued under al-Hakam II (reigned 961–76), a booklover who collected a vast royal library.

In the following reigns power was usurped by a minister of great ambition and ability, the chamberlain al-Mansur (Almanzor), the terror of the Christian kingdoms, who raided them almost annually until his death in 1002. But al-Mansur had undermined the prestige and education of the ruling dynasty, and after his death neither his sons nor the Umayyad caliphs could prevent Muslim Spain from falling into anarchy. Córdoba was sacked by Berber troops in 1013. Umayyad rule ended officially in 1031, and the country fell apart into a number of small kingdoms.

*Monuments*. The outstanding monument of the Umayyads in Spain is the Great Mosque of Córdoba. Founded by Abd al-Rahman I, it was successively enlarged down to the time of al-Mansur, and became one of the largest and most splendid mosques in the world. The palace of Abd al-Rahman III at Madinat al-Zahra, outside Córdoba, has left impressive ruins. The art of Umayyad Spain has distinctive features, such as the horseshoe arch, which became part of the tradition of later western Islamic (Moorish) art. Arabic literature and philosophy did not reach their bloom here until a later period.

Right, ornate Dravidian temple over-tops the everyday traffic on a street in Srirangam, southern India.

Left, Nataraja, or a dancing representation of the Hindu god Shiva. This Indian figurine dates from the 12th or 13th century.

*Information Service of India*

*Government of India Tourist Office*

# 5 · HINDUISM

**HINDUISM** [hǐn′dōō-ǐz-əm], indigenous religion of India and the faith of the large majority of the inhabitants of the Indian Republic, as well as of many people in East Pakistan and Ceylon, and those of Indian descent in parts of tropical and subtropical Asia, Africa, and America.

Superficially, the most striking features of Hinduism are polytheism, mysticism, asceticism, belief in the transmigration of souls, the sanctity of certain animals, and a rigid social order of classes and castes under the leadership of the priesthood. Some of these features are disappearing, however, and it should be remembered that the apparent polytheism of the Hindus is explained by their theologians as basically monotheistic, the many lesser divinities being aspects or emanations of a single diety.

### History

Hinduism is the result of a fusion between the fertility religions of the more primitive inhabitants of India and the sacrificial cult of celestial divinities introduced by the Aryan invaders c.1500 B.C. The earliest traces of it are found in the remains of the prehistoric cities of the Indus Valley, evidencing the worship of sacred animals and trees and divinities resembling the later god Shiva and the Mother Goddess. The hymns of the invaders are preserved in the Rig-Veda, the oldest and most sacred of the Hindu scriptures. The main feature of the religion of the Aryans was the large-scale sacrifice of animals. Another striking feature was the drinking of the sacred liquor, soma, which induced divine ecstasy. At this stage there is no evidence of belief in transmigration.

As the Aryans spread over northern India, their sacrifices became more complicated and the influence of the Brahmans, the priests who alone could perform them, increased correspondingly. With this there developed a growing tendency to asceticism and mystical gnosis, as a better means than the sacrifices of achieving lasting spiritual results. This later Vedic period, from c.900 to 500 B.C., saw the composition of three later Vedas—the Yajur, the Sama, and the Atharva; lengthy appendices to the Vedas called Brahmanas and Aranyakas, describing the symbolism of the sacrificial ceremonies; and the earliest Upanishads, containing fine mystical passages teaching the unity of the individual soul (atman) and the cosmic soul (Brahman), which can be realized by meditation and mystical gnosis. These Upanishads contain the first clear formulation of the doctrine of transmigration, typical of all later Indian religion. In the 6th century there emerged several heterodox teachers who completely rejected the Vedas and the sacrificial cult. Chief of these were Siddhartha Gautama, the founder of Buddhism, and Vardhamana Mahavira, who reorganized earlier heterodox ascetics into the order of Jains. These teachers emphatically rejected animal sacrifice as inconsistent with their doctrine of noninjury to life (ahimsa) and as useless for spiritual progress. Their teachings influenced orthodoxy, and were largely responsible for the disappearance of the great Vedic sacrifices.

**Literature.** Now, Hinduism, as distinct from the religion of the Vedas, began to appear in something like its present form. With the decline of interest in sacrifice, many of the Vedic gods lost prestige, and others came to the forefront. The popularity of mysticism and the respect paid to it led to the formulation of philosophical and theological systems explaining the cosmic process and the relation of the individual to the world spirit. Chief among the new gods were Vishnu and Shiva. The former plays a small part in the Rig-Veda, as a divinity connected with the sun and the sacrificial ritual. Well before the Christian era, however, Vishnu was being worshiped as the creator and sustainer of the universe. At the same time, other religious groups were beginning to ascribe the same importance to Shiva, who combined the attributes of non-Aryan fertility divinities with those of Rudra, a minor god of the Vedas. The most outstanding literary product of the period was the Bhagavad-Gita containing much fine ethical teaching, perhaps the most influential sacred text of Hinduism in the 20th century. In it the hero Krishna declares himself to be an avatar, or full incarnation, of Vishnu, who should be worshiped with sincere love and devotion rather than with sacrifice. From this time devotional worship (puja) replaced sacrifice (yajna) in most branches of Hinduism.

During the early centuries of the Christian Era, a new body of sacred literature appeared, which, though theoretically less sacred than that associated with the Vedas, is now much more important. These writings include the two great epics, Ramayana and Mahabharata; lengthy verse treatises on cosmology and religious legend called puranas; and texts on law and human conduct, known as dharmashastras. At this time the social order grew more rigid and the rules of class and caste were tightened. Toward the end of the Gupta period (c.500 A.D.) new features emerged, including the worship of the Mother Goddess, sometimes with animal sacrifice of a type different from that of the Vedas, and barbaric customs such as widow burning and ritual suicide, which had little or no justification in earlier religious literature.

The main developments in Hinduism during the medieval period came from south India. The philosophical speculation of the Upanishads had developed into six orthodox schools of philosophy. In the Vedanta school certain teachers appeared in the peninsula who had a very enduring influence on later Hinduism. Chief among these were Shankara, Ramanuja, and Madhva. It was in the south also that the earliest surviving religious literature in the modern languages of India was produced by Tamil hymnodists, who were devotees of Shiva or Vishnu; their songs encouraged an intense love of God and of one's fellow men, the spiritual attitude known as bhakti. Similar teachers, spreading their doctrines through hymns sung in the local languages, later appeared in all the main regions of India, and every important Indian language has a large body of medieval devotional literature of this type.

**Islam.** A new factor appeared at the end of the 12th century. Islamic Turks from Afghanistan became rulers of northern India and gradually spread their power in the Deccan. In most of its chief features Islam is diametrically opposed to Hinduism. Islam, strictly monotheistic, rejects transmigration, has no true priesthood, abhors the worship of images, and maintains, at least in theory, the religious equality of all Muslims. It is not surprising that there was occasional friction between the two religions, but a harmonious relationship was more usual, and some mutual influence occurred. In the 15th century, for instance, Kabir, a weaver of Benares, opposed image worship and pilgrimage and taught brotherly love in beautiful hymns still sung all over northern India; his chief inspiration was certainly the earlier teachings of bhakti, but some Islamic influence is quite evident. A more significant example of eclecticism is found in the work of Nanak (c.1469–c.1538), founder of the religion of the Sikhs, which contains elements of both Hinduism and Islam.

**Reform.** By the 18th century the main force of the devotional movement was spent. Hinduism, thrown back upon itself by the domination of Muslims, seemed ossified, a degenerate system of complex rituals and taboos, with little of ethical value in its teachings and with great truths of its past largely forgotten in a plethora of stultifying, and often positively harmful, superstition. The ability of Hinduism to resist the propaganda of both Christianity and scientific humanism has been due partly to the conservatism of Indian social life and custom, but largely to the work of a number of 19th-century reformers. Realizing the weakness of Hinduism in the face of Western culture, they restated its message in forms more appropriate to changed conditions and to advances in human knowledge.

The first of these reformers was Ram Mohan Roy, a Brahman of Calcutta, who founded a reformed Hindu church, the Brahmo Samaj. Much influenced by Unitarian Christianity, he rejected image worship, polytheism, and objectionable social customs such as widow burning and polygamy. In western India, Dayananda Sarasvati founded a similar reformed Hindu church, the Arya Samaj. Dayananda was somewhat closer to tradition than Ram Mohan Roy, and by fantastic interpretations he claimed to find in the Vedas nothing but pure monotheism, devoid of all objectionable elements such as animal sacrifice. He rejected all later Hindu religious literature as corrupt. Another most important force in the revival of Hinduism was the Bengali, Narendranath Datta, who took the religious name of Vivekananda. On the basis of the teaching of a famous and saintly mystic, Ramakrishna Paramahamsa, Vivekananda founded the Ramakrishna Mission, which adopted the Christian missionary practices of vigorous preaching and active social service, and is perhaps the most vital force in 20th-century Hinduism.

These and other reformers had opposed the rigidity of caste, and, ignoring, or liberally interpreting, sacred texts to the contrary, had proclaimed the brotherhood of all men. Their influence was felt by educated Hindus, but it had little effect upon the masses. With the great civil disobedience movement led by Mahatma Gandhi, however, the new ideas began to exert a far wider influence, since they formed the ideology of the movement which he led. Gandhi must, therefore, be considered one of the most important influences in the modernization of Hinduism. In many circles arid ritualism, effete social customs, and priestly obscurantism may still remain, but the religion of India has displayed a surprising vitality in the face of difficulties, and shows no sign of disappearing.

### The Gods

The Hindu conception of divinity is somewhat different from that of the religions of the West, and this must be borne in mind in any study of Hinduism. Western theology has generally emphasized a transcendent and unique divinity, who created the universe as something apart from himself. For the Hindu, God evolved the cosmos from his own being. Divinity, therefore, inheres in every portion of the universe. God manifests himself in an infinite number of forms, all of which are, in a mystical sense, essentially unreal reflections of the single glory pervading all things. Whatever god a man worships, his prayer reaches the same divinity. On this theological basis, the cults of a multifarious collection of great and small divinities are fitted into an essentially monotheistic system.

**Three Groups.** Most Hindus fall into one of three groups, based on the divinity which by family tradition they look on as the highest manifestation of the Universal Spirit. The Shaivas maintain that Shiva is the chief god and that all others are subordinate manifestations of him. He created the world, maintains it through his divine asceticism, and will destroy it at the end of this age. For the Vaishnavas, the world appears when the god Vishnu awakes at the end of the cosmic night, and creation is the work of Brahma, the first being to emanate from Vishnu. Vishnu preserves the universe throughout the cosmic day, occasionally incarnating himself as an avatar in order to save it from the attacks of demons. When the night begins, the ultimate god will once more withdraw, and the universe will be destroyed and merged into his being, until he wakes again at the next cosmic dawn. The Shaktas, on the other hand, have for their chief object of worship a goddess, the wife of Shiva, called by many names. The god is transcendent, withdrawn, inaccessible, and therefore insignificant; it is the goddess, personifying Mother Nature, who produces the world, who sustains it with loving care for the righteous and terror for the sinner, and who will ultimately destroy it. She is the Shakti, the personified power, of the supreme divinity.

To the Westerner it may seem strange that these three great divisions of Hinduism survive without serious friction. Occasional cases of mild persecution have occurred, but in general the three have existed side by side in friendliness. The devotees of one sect will often take part in the worship of another and visit the other's temples. No Hindu would claim that systems not his own are completely without validity; and the theologian will admit that other doctrines also reflect the truth, but less fully and accurately than his own.

Of the three great divinities, Shiva is often worshiped in the form of an upright post with rounded top, the linga, a phallic symbol showing his original character as a fertility god. He often appears as the divine dancer, one of the most beautiful conceptions of Hindu religious art, and is also portrayed in many other forms. His worship is particularly popular in south India. Vishnu is less often worshiped in his supreme form than in that of one of his incarnations, especially Rama and Krishna. As the latter,

Shiva as the incarnation of the forces of Creation, Preservation, and Destruction, from the cave temple at Elephanta (8th century).   (PICTORIAL PARADE)

he often appears as a handsome young man playing a flute and symbolizing the call of God to the human soul to draw near and rejoice in his presence. In her gentler forms, as Parvati or Uma, the Mother Goddess is portrayed as a beautiful woman, still young, but very matronly in appearance; in her fiercer aspects she appears as Kali, a terrible ogress, and Durga, a stern-faced beautiful girl riding a lion.

**Other Gods.** As well as the three great divinities, there are many others worshiped by Hindus. These include Ganesha, the son of Shiva and Parvati, a quaint figure with an elephant's head. He is the patron of all practical enterprises and is reverenced at their commencement; he also takes a special interest in learning and literature. Skanda, or Karttikeya, another son of Shiva, is especially popular in south India, where he has assumed some of the functions and character of an old Tamil fertility god, Murugan. According to tradition, he is the captain of the army of gods, leading them in battle against the demons, and he is depicted as having six faces and twelve hands.

A very popular folk divinity in many parts of India is Hanuman, the monkey helper of Rama, the seventh incarnation of Vishnu. He symbolizes the active power of God in the world, always ready to help his worshipers in trouble. The most popular goddesses, after the Mother Goddess, are Lakshmi, the wife of Vishnu and the bestower of wealth and prosperity, and the beautiful Sarasvati, goddess of music, art, and learning. In eastern India the tutelary deity of snakes, Manasa, who is also thought of as a daughter of Shiva, is worshiped for protection against snakes. Similarly, Shitala, the goddess of smallpox, is worshiped both to avoid this disease and to cure it when it occurs.

Other very ancient gods have lost their popularity, and though they are often referred to in legend, play but a small part in religious life. Among these, Brahma, considered the chief god at the time of the Buddha, has degenerated. As creator, he is little more than the deputy of Vishnu, and is rarely worshiped. Indra, the war-god of the

Aryan invaders, is now largely neglected, and Varuna, the great sky-god of the Rig-Veda, has become the god of the sea, and receives little attention. Surya, the old sun-god, to whom splendid temples were erected less than 1,000 years ago, is still sometimes worshiped, but his status is comparatively low, whereas Agni, the fire-god of the Vedas and intermediary between gods and men, has lost much of his importance since the abandonment of the larger fire sacrifices. He is, however, still remembered when ceremonies, such as weddings, involving the use of a sacred fire are performed, and by a few old-fashioned Brahmans who continue to perform ancient domestic fire rituals, without, of course, making animal offerings.

There are also numerous lesser gods. For the peasant the hills, woods, and streams around his village all have their tutelary deities; all rivers and mountains are sacred, notably the river Ganges. Cattle, monkeys, snakes, and to a lesser extent, certain other animals are sacred, and to an orthodox Hindu their lives are inviolate. If it is absolutely necessary to kill a snake in self-defense, the orthodox will perform a penance. Certain trees and plants are specially holy, notably the banyan and pipal trees and the tulsi plant, a species of wild basil. There is also a kind of relative divinity inherent in great and important people—parents are gods to their children, husbands to their wives, teachers to their pupils, masters to their servants, Brahmans to the lower classes, kings to their subjects. At a special annual festival, a carpenter worships the divinity inherent in his saw, a peasant that in his plow. In some measure, divinity dwells in all things.

### Transmigration and Salvation

The orthodox Western conception of immortality, in which the soul is incarnate in a body once only, is foreign to indigenous Indian religion. In Hinduism it is universally believed that the soul passes from one body to another over a period of immense duration, its new body and its fortunes in each successive life being conditioned by its former behavior. This doctrine of karma needs no divine intervention or judgment after death, but is simply a matter of natural law. The universe is so made that evil and selfish acts inevitably bring unhappiness for the agent, either in this life or the next. Most Hindu theists, however, have maintained that God by his grace can set aside the effects of karma for those who truly turn to him.

Again in contrast with Western religions, Hinduism holds that all animals have souls, fundamentally similar to those of human beings. Owing to sins in earlier lives, these souls must inhabit such bodies until the effects of their evil deeds are fully reaped, when they will be reborn in happier circumstances. Similarly, souls now suffering in the seven hells will ultimately be purged of their sins and obtain reincarnation on earth. On the other hand, however, those now enjoying bliss in one of the heavens, as the result of their former virtue, will sooner or later be reborn, and may in the future fall to a lower level in the scale of being.

The ultimate aim of the pious Hindu is to escape from samsara, the continual round of birth and death, and to obtain final release; all religious activity is theoretically directed to this end. The six systems of orthodox Hindu philosophy are looked on as means of obtaining release (mukti, or moksha), and constitute alternative systems of salvation. Of the six, five are now of little importance except to scholars: the Nyaya, a school specializing in logic; Vaisheshika, which propounded a system of atomism; Sankhya, a dualist school maintaining that salvation is to be obtained by the complete separation of soul and matter; Yoga, a school concerned chiefly with mystical praxis, the doctrines of which have become virtually the common property of all branches of Hinduism; and Mimamsa, which was specially devoted to the exegesis of the Vedas. The Vedanta school, in its numerous subdivisions, has for the past millennium and a half provided the chief intellectual background of Hinduism.

Following the Upanishadic sages, all the schools originally maintained that salvation was to be obtained through knowledge—not mere intellectual knowledge, but full and absolute realization. From the point of view of the older Vedanta of the school of Shankara, the realization needed was of the ultimate unreality of the phenomenal world (maya), and of the oneness of the human soul and the single impersonal world spirit, which underlies all things, even God himself, who is the primary manifestation of the unmanifest. This realization is only to be gained after a long course of meditation and spiritual exercise, for which it is necessary to give up all family and other ties and to lead the life of an ascetic (sannyasi). The system of Shankara is often known as Advaita, or monism.

In opposition to Shankara, Ramanuja maintained that salvation was to be obtained by devotion to God, rather than by spiritual exercises. For him the ultimate and Absolute was not an impersonal entity, but the god Vishnu, and the soul, even in the state of salvation, never completely lost its individuality. His system, known as *Vishishtadvaita*, qualified monism, has probably had greater influence on popular Hinduism than that of Shankara, though the latter has always gained greater support from the learned. There are numerous lesser schools of Vedanta, most of them deviating in some measure from the strict monism of Shankara. Of these perhaps the most interesting is that of Madhva, which maintains a doctrine of dualism (dvaita), holding that the soul is always completely distinct from God.

### Rites and Ceremonies

Hinduism, unlike Western faiths, is not a congregational religion, though congregational services have been introduced by some of the reformed sects. The temple is a comparative innovation in Hinduism, not certainly attested before about the beginning of the Christian Era. In the temple the god is treated in the manner of a great king. He is reverenced with offerings of flowers and food, songs are sung in his honor, and dances are performed before him. He gives audience to his subjects, who may approach him singly or in groups, make their offerings to him, lay their petitions before him, and depart. Although pilgrimages to famous temples and sacred spots are exceedingly meritorious and popular, they are not essential to the religious life. The most important rites are performed in the home; every Hindu residence contains at least one sacred image or picture, which is the center of the religious feeling of the household and in larger homes is kept in a special chapel.

Thus Hinduism is essentially a family religion, and its domestic rites are designed to establish and maintain family solidarity. In the literature on dharma, the right conduct of the Hindu in all aspects of his life, there are long instructions on the domestic sacraments and rituals, which mark the stages in the life of a man from before birth to death. Some orthodox families still attempt to keep all these rituals, but today the less important rites are neglected in many homes. The ancient initiation ceremony (upanayana), by which boys approaching puberty were brought into the Aryan fold and invested with the sacred thread worn constantly over the right shoulder, is now rarely performed except in orthodox Brahman families. The complicated marriage ceremony, however, is still general, even with those Hindus who claim to be emancipated from the ritualism of tradition. Containing elements going back to the remote Indo-European past, it has as its central rite the circumambulation of a sacred fire by the couple, with their garments tied together. The marriage ritual binds the couple together indissolubly, even when the marriage is not consummated. Until child marriage was forbidden by law, weddings often took place before puberty, the bride remaining in her parents' home after the ceremony. This resulted in numerous child widows, who had never known their husbands. Orthodox Hinduism prohibited the remarriage of widows and condemned these women to very unhappy lives as inauspicious encumbrances to their families. Until prohibited by law, polygamy was permitted in Hinduism, but was not looked on with favor for ordinary Hindus unless the first marriage failed to produce sons.

Normally the Hindus cremate their dead. The funeral rites, among the most potent factors in maintaining family feeling, involve the daily offering of balls of rice (pinda) for the welfare of the soul of the departed, for a period now usually of 12 days after the cremation, and at less frequent intervals later. Without these offerings, the soul is thought to be unable to find rebirth and to remain a dangerous and miserable ghost, likely to harm the surviving family members. With the due performance of these sraddha ceremonies, however, those virtuous ancestors who have achieved rebirth in heaven will use their power for the welfare of the household. It is thought that seven generations of ancestors, as well as the dead man for whom the ceremony is performed, benefit from sraddha, which can only be effectively carried out by a son. For this reason the orthodox Hindu craves sons, and the wife who produces only daughters or no children at all is liable to be displaced by a co-wife.

As "the wife is half the man," it is to be expected that the Hindu widow should wish to join her husband in the other world. The orthodox widow leads a life of great austerity, engaged constantly in prayers for the welfare of her

A durbar, or meeting of Indian princes, in the private temple of the maharaja in the city of Bharatpur. The meeting commences Holi, a three-day spring festival honoring the Hindu deity Krishna. Among the rites conducted in the temple is the throwing of a red powder upon the participants. The bright color of the powder connotes happiness, and casting it expresses joy.

husband in his new life; she is inauspicious and can take no part in family festivities. Often, she burned herself on her husband's funeral pyre. This practice, prohibited in 1829, was rare or nonexistent in early Hinduism, but was commended in later lawbooks and formerly was quite common in high-caste families; for by it the wife was thought to purify herself and her husband from their sins and ensure a very lengthy period of rebirth for both of them in heaven. The practice of widow burning is often wrongly called suttee, or sati, a word which actually means "a virtuous woman," and refers to the widow herself, not to her self-immolation.

### Class and Caste

Traditionally, Hindu society is hierarchically stratified, and the ethics of older Hinduism are centered around the preservation of the divine social order, without whose smooth and orderly functioning it is impossible for men to find salvation. Hindu society is divided by class (varna) and by caste (jati). These two divisions, though traditionally linked, seem to have arisen independently.

The efforts of reformers and the influence of modern Western ideas and 20th-century technological advances militate against the Hindu social order, which is rapidly weakening in the cities, and more slowly in the countryside. Though traditional Hinduism is very closely linked with the hierarchical social order, it has in the past shown remarkable adaptability, and it is likely that it will succeed in adapting itself to the changed social patterns of an equalitarian society.

## Denominations

**ARYA SAMAJ** [ärʹyə sə-mäjʹ], Hindu reform organization founded in 1875 by Dayananda Sarasvati, a Brahman from northern Bombay. The association sought to revive Vedism and advocated the abolition of caste, since it maintained that the Vedas, the ancient sacred literature of the Hindus, which it held to be infallible, did not recognize caste. The society favored mass education, the emancipation of women, and the remarriage of widows. It opposed child marriage and image worship. Righteousness and service to humanity were recommended as guides to proper conduct. Acting as a check upon both Christianity and Islam, the movement attracted many followers and achieved its greatest strength in North India.

**BRAHMO SAMAJ** [bräʹmō sə-mäjʹ], Hindu religious reform society founded in 1828 by Ram Mohan Roy, a Brahman of Bengal. Dedicated to nonsectarian worship of the Eternal, the sect promulgated a reformed theistic Hinduism. After the death of the founder in 1833, leadership passed to Debendra Nath Tagore. In 1865 the rival teachings of Keshub Chunder Sen divided the sect. Influenced by Christianity and Western ideas, the movement advocated abolition of the caste system and child marriage and favored emancipation of women and remarriage of widows. The society, although small in numbers, had a wide influence among Hindu intellectuals, especially those educated in Europe.

**SHAIVAS or ŚAIVAS** [shiʹvəz], members of that branch of Hinduism which looks on the god Shiva (Śiva) as ultimate and accepts him as the chief object of worship. With the Vaishnavas and the Shaktas the Shaivas form one of the three main divisions of Hinduism. They are divided into several sects, and their temples are found all over India, but they are strongest in the peninsula, especially in Madras State and in Kashmir.

**SHAKTI** [shäkʹtē] **or SAKTI** [sakʹtē], in Hinduism, general name for the consort of the god Shiva (Śiva). Shakti is the mother goddess and manifests herself in many different forms. Her cult is widespread in India, although she is worshiped at various places and times under different names, such as Kālī, Durgā, Devī, Mariamma, and Caṇḍī.

Theologically, Shakti is conceived as the active, powerful component of the universe, while her husband, Shiva, who holds the power of universal destruction, rests in deep contemplation. Thus, the cults of Shiva and Shakti are closely related. They stand in sharp contrast to the cults of the god Vishnu (Viṣṇu). The former cult demands blood sacrifices and a religious attitude of childlike surrender, as opposed to an attitude of love and offerings of devotion given to the incarnations of Vishnu. The many forms and characteristics of Shakti probably represent a gradual accretion of local and tribal goddesses into general Hindu belief. Procedures for worshiping the Shakti and invoking her power are contained in the relatively late Sanskrit texts called Tantras.

**VAISHNAVAS,** followers of the Hindu god Vishnu, forming one of the main branches of Hinduism. Vaishnava sects and their temples are found in all parts of India. Most Vaishnavas are especially devoted to one of the 10 incarnations of Vishnu, now usually to Rama or Krishna.

## *Personalities*

**DAYANANDA SARASVATI** [də-yä-nŭn′də sŭ′rəs-vŭ′tē] (1824–1883), founder of the Arya Samaj, a Hindu reform society. Born in India of a brahmin family, he mastered Sanskrit in early youth and became an ardent student of the *Vedas*, the most ancient Hindu scriptures. His faith in image worship was shaken by the sight of mice crawling over and defiling an image of the god Shiva. At 25 he renounced the world, began practicing Yoga, and undertook a devoted study of the Vedanta, a philosophical system based on the *Vedas*. Preaching that the *Vedas* contained all spiritual truth, he opposed image worship and popular religious traditions which he considered distortions of pure Hinduism. His attacks on the caste system brought him into conflict with the teachings of Brahmanism.

**GANDHI** [gän′dē], **MOHANDAS KARAMCHAND** (1869–1948), pre-eminent nationalist leader of India, and saintly world figure known everywhere by his informal title of Mahatma ("Great Soul"). Born in the small princely state of Porbandar on the Kathiawar Peninsula of western India, Gandhi came from an orthodox *vaishya*

Information Service of India
Mohandas Karamchand Gandhi, Indian nationalist leader.

(merchant) caste family. His father, as chief minister of Porbandar, provided Gandhi with a disciplined elementary education and arranged for his marriage at the age of 13. Kasturba, his wife, who bore Gandhi four sons, died in 1944.

Gandhi went to London when he was 18 for legal training and was called to the bar at the Inner Temple in 1891. His life in England included time spent on intensive reading of the *Bhagavad-Gita*, the New Testament, and other religious texts, as well as close study of the social philosophies of Leo Tolstoy, John Ruskin, and Henry David Thoreau—all of whose influences are to be seen in his own personal and political creeds.

Upon returning to India he practiced law for a time in Bombay, but in 1893 he went to South Africa to join an Indian law firm. Although he conducted a successful professional business there, the racial discriminations to which Indians and colored South Africans were subjected so disturbed Gandhi that he relinquished most of his legal practice and devoted himself to the cause of securing social, civil, and political rights for the Indian community in South Africa. Suffering arrest and bodily assault on several occasions, Gandhi nevertheless perfected techniques for nonviolent resistance to South African repressive measures which he called *Satyagraha*, literally, "holding fast to truth."

He was a persistent and effective foe of British and Boer policies which segregated white and nonwhite communities in South Africa. But during times of national conflict, such as the Boer War of 1899–1902, the Zulu Rebellion of 1906, and the early phase of World War I, Gandhi helped organize and recruit personnel for British ambulance corps units. In 1914, after years of bitter dispute, Gen. Jan Christiaan Smuts of the Union of South Africa signed an amicable agreement with Gandhi removing some of the restrictions on the Indian community. It was a matter of deep regret to Gandhi in later years that the 1914 pact proved to have little lasting benefit. But the resistance techniques of *Satyagraha*, developed in South Africa, were to provide Gandhi with a dramatic and persuasive political and moral method for reducing the effectiveness of British power in India.

Gandhi returned to India in 1915. His mentor, Gopal Krishna Gokhale of Bombay, a leader of the moderate forces in the All-India National Congress, drew Gandhi into politics. Gandhi did not immediately make his influence felt, despite his celebrated South African reputation. He proved to be a poor speaker when compared with senior colleagues, and his ideas on nonviolence appeared defeatist to the more radical members of the Congress.

At his *ashram* (religious retreat) established near Ahmadabad, and in talks and articles, Gandhi advocated *swaraj* ("self-rule," or "home rule"). Deeply concerned by disturbances in the Punjab, by the massacre at Jalianwalla Bagh, and by the passage of the Rowlatt Acts in 1919 which ordered severe penalties for sedition, Gandhi persuaded the Congress to undertake a campaign of civil disobedience in protest against the government on a mass basis. Members of the Congress were ordered to give up governmental appointments and titles, to form national schools, to boycott British goods, to use Indian-made articles exclusively, and to participate in disciplined, nonviolent demonstrations. Although the movement was remarkably nonviolent, considering the numbers involved, some violence did occur. Gandhi called off the mass campaign when he learned of violence in the town of Chauri Chaura instigated by a group of Congress resistors. Gandhi was arrested in 1922 and sentenced to six years' imprisonment, but was released in 1924 following an operation. In the same year he was elected president of the Congress. He was imprisoned often in the years that followed.

Until his death Gandhi remained the undisputed leader of the Indian nationalist movement. He led the India-wide boycott of the Sir John Simon Commission in 1927—a mission sent to India to determine the next stage for constitutional advance. He also led the famous march to Dandi in 1930 for the purpose of making salt from the sea in defiance of the government's tax on salt. He attended the second Round Table Conference in London in 1931. When the London conference failed to move India rapidly toward self-rule, he returned to India and organized a new civil disobedience campaign. During World War II he encouraged non-co-operation with the Allied forces because freedom was not guaranteed for India. Gandhi similarly rejected the constitutional solutions, first offered by Sir Stafford Cripps in 1942, and later by Lord Wavell, as inadequate, partial measures.

Concurrently with his fight for independence, Gandhi also fought for the betterment of the status of noncaste Hindus (untouchables), whom he called *Harijans* ("children of God"), and worked for closer relations between the Hindus and the many minorities of India, especially the Muslims. But he was unable to quell the rising tide of the Pakistan movement. In 1946 riots between Hindus and Muslims broke out first in Calcutta, and then spread throughout India. Gandhi spent his last months in sorrow; even though India became free on Aug. 15, 1947, it was partitioned, and Pakistan was founded as a separate state.

From the 1930's Gandhi shared leadership with a selected group of nationalists whom he especially encouraged and advised, such as Vallabhbhai Patel, Maulana Abul Kalam Azad, and Jawaharlal Nehru. Gandhi had the authority to control Congress policy with a dictator's hand, but he sought consensus in his dealings with colleagues by means of discussion and persuasion in the interests of truth—as he saw it. Gandhi's political activity was intimately tied to his exploration of ultimate truth, which to him was a religious experience. "The little voice within," his moral appraisal of right action, gave him a conviction of correctness of interpretation in debate that to others often appeared to be unshakeable resistance to any point of view other than Gandhi's own.

The full measure of Gandhi's political greatness may lie in the leaders of eminence he left behind to guide the Republic of India in its years of nation building. More likely, he will be remembered for his saintly qualities that transcend the political moment and attach Gandhi to the ancient spiritual heritage of his country.

Mahatma Gandhi was shot to death on Jan. 30, 1948, in Birla House, New Delhi, by an extremist Hindu who blamed Gandhi for the partition of India. He died with the words "Ram! Ram!"—an invocation to God—on his lips.

**GHOSE** [gōs], **AUROBINDO** (1872–1950), Indian scholar and patriot, Yoga philosopher, and mystic teacher. He was born in Calcutta and educated at King's College, Cambridge. In 1893 he returned to India and devoted himself to the study of Indian culture. After a period of political activity in support of Indian *swaraj*, or self-rule, he was arrested as a revolutionary and imprisoned. During his prison term, he felt that he received a message from God directing him to work for the spiritual regeneration of India and the world. In 1910 he retired to Pondicherry, French India, where he studied Yoga and attracted a community of disciples. Through his writings, he taught the Integral Yoga, an all-inclusive spiritual discipline recognizing the supremacy of the spirit without denying the reality of matter. According to Aurobindo, matter, life, and mind are different levels in the evolution of "Supermind," which transcends reason. The final perfection is achieved when Supermind descends and spiritualizes the lower levels.

**RAMAKRISHNA** [rä′mə-krĭsh′nə] (1836–86), Hindu mystic and leader of the modern revival of Hinduism. He was born of a Brahman family in Bengal and even in childhood showed an intense longing for realization of God and an indifference to study and worldly affairs. At the age of 16 he became a priest in the Kali temple at Dakshineswar near Calcutta. He spent the next 12 years in virtually uninterrupted prayer and meditation, and his whole-souled worship strengthened his desire for a vision of Kali, the Divine Mother. After attaining such a vision, he practiced the disciplines of various Hindu sects and saw visions of Rama, Krishna, and Shiva. He married, but his wife remained a disciple and a nun. Ramakrishna became a monk and followed the teachings of Vedanta, a Hindu philosophical system, through which he experienced Advaita (nonduality) and realized his oneness with the Supreme Spirit and the creation.

Ramakrishna then devoted himself to a study of Islam and had a vision of God as Allah. Turning to the study of Christianity, he attained a vision of Jesus and realized the essential unity of all religions. Shortly before his death, Ramakrishna initiated some of his disciples into a monastic order led by the saintly Vivekananda to carry his message through the world.

**SHANKARACHARYA** [shŭng′kə-rä-chär-yə], **or THE MASTER SHANKARA** (c.788–820), Indian philosopher, saint, mystic, poet, and religious reformer. Born of a scholarly Nambudri subcaste of a Malabar Brahman family, Shankara was a prodigious student of the Vedas, the oldest writings of the Indo-Aryan people. To reconcile the standards of knowledge and the socioreligious beliefs of his time with ancient traditions, Shankara reinterpreted the Vedic literature. He composed commentaries on the Bhagavad-Gita, the Upanishads, and the Brahmasutra. He also propounded the philosophical system known as Pedanta, based upon his commentaries.

In the Vedanta, the ultimate real is One, and so Shankara's philosophy is known as Advaita, nondual, or monism. Moksha, liberation, or salvation, can be attained by the individual by discarding ignorance, or avidya. Knowing the true nature of reality leads to realization of the identity of the individual soul, atman, with Brahman, the cosmic soul.

A monk adept in yogic practices, Shankara founded four monastic orders, and established four mathas, or monasteries, in the four directions of India. Shringeri is in the south, Badrinath in the north, Puri in the east, and Dvarika in the west. He opposed the atheistic philosophy of Buddhism, which was prevalent in India at that time. Among intellectual traditional Hindus, Shankara's Vedantic philosophy has remained in vogue.

**VIVEKANANDA** [wē-wē-kä-nŭn'də] (1863–1902), Hindu saint and religious teacher. Born in Calcutta as Narendranath Datta, he received a thorough Western education at the University of Calcutta. Dissatisfied with the superstitions of orthodox Hinduism, Vivekananda sought religious inspiration first in the Brahmo Samaj and later from the great mystic and Vedantist Ramakrishna Paramahamsa. After Ramakrishna's death Vivekananda, as his chief disciple and spiritual successor, traveled throughout India as an austere monk. He believed that Hinduism was the great strength of India and should be its religious mission to the world. Shocked by the misery of the Indian masses, he saw that the remedy lay in wider education and in the acceptance of Western science and technology.

In 1893 Vivekananda represented Hinduism at the Parliament of Religions in Chicago, where he preached Hinduism to large and receptive audiences. In 1894 he founded the Vedanta Society in New York. Three years later he returned to India, and was acclaimed a national hero. Taking up the task of regenerating India, he established the Belur Math monastery, organized the Ramakrishna Mission, and exhorted the young to pursue the ideals of renunciation and social service, especially among the poor. His great spiritual power and personal magnetism inspired other great Indian national leaders, such as Mahatma Gandhi, to develop further the theme of social service as a religious duty.

# Terms

**AVATAR** [ăv-ə-tär'], the incarnation or "descent" of a deity to earth and his embodiment as man or animal, usually to save the world from impending destruction. In Hinduism, the phenomenon is associated with the god Vishnu.

**BRAHMA** [brä'mə], creator-god of the Hindu pantheon. In the Gupta period (c. 4th-5th century A.D.) a Hindu *Trimurti*, or trinity, evolved, consisting of Brahma the creator, Vishnu the preserver, and Shiva the destroyer. Brahma, the masculine form of, and agent for, the neuter Brahman, or world spirit, was himself created. After the 5th century A.D. his worship declined and today only a single temple dedicated to him remains, near Ajmer.

**BRAHMAN** [brä'mən], one of the four large hereditary groups into which the social organization of the Hindus of India is divided. They enjoy the highest status in the varna system, popularly called the caste system, and their traditional calling is to act as the priests and religious leaders of the society. Actually, in modern India many Brahmans do not carry on religious work but enter other professions. However, no one who is not born a Brahman may perform Brahmanical religious functions.

According to Hindu belief the Brahmans descended from seven great seers or Rishis, who were so pious and learned that they acquired supernatural power. There are a great many Brahman subdivisions. There is a primary partition along geographical lines and further groupings under these.

The religious functions of the Brahmans are of different kinds. Some Brahmans, called Purohits, officiate at familiar rites such as marriage. Others act as temple priests. Those who minister to pilgrims at important shrines are the Pandas. Those who give religious instruction to persons seeking it are known as Gurus.

Because of his high social position and his religious role, the Brahman is treated with decided deference. It is considered meritorious to feast and give religious alms to a Brahman and extremely sinful to subject a Brahman to physical violence.

**BRAHMANISM,** Western term having no Sanskrit equivalent, applied to the system of religious doctrines and institutions of the Brahman caste in Hinduism. Originating in the Vedas (compiled c.1500–900 B.C.), the tradition later developed into a pantheistic conception involving the search for, and discovery of, a unifying principle or single spiritual reality, *Brahman*. Salvation meant transcending the illusion of duality and passing through stages of bliss until *Atman*, human soul, attained union with *Brahman*.

The great social institution of Brahmanism, the caste system, was dominated by the Brahmans, who controlled the ritual sacrifices, which were the means of achieving salvation.

**CASTE** [kăst]. The word caste combines the meanings of the Hindi terms *varna* and *jati* and refers to large Indian social groups. The *varnas* are the four great divisions of the Indian population: Brahmans, Kshatriyas, Vaishyas, and Sudras, with the Brahmans in the superior position and the Sudras at the bottom. In Hindu belief these distinctions are divinely ordained. The division into hierarchically arranged groups, or castes, is correlated with occupational functions. The Brahmans are the traditional priests of the society, the Kshatriyas form the military and governing group, the Vaishya, originally agriculturalists and herders, became the traders and businessmen, and the Sudras were the servants of the others. Today most of the artisan groups and agricultural laborers are drawn from Sudra ranks. Each Sudra group is known as a *jati*.

*Varnas* are endogamous and hereditary—a person must marry within his *varna*, and he and his children remain members throughout life. The Sudras are further divided into two sections, sometimes known as "clean" and "unclean." The unclean Sudras are the "Untouchables" whom Gandhi called Harijans, or "children of God," in an effort to arouse the national conscience to their plight. The traditional work of the Untouchables is often something considered religiously polluting to other castes, such as working in leather or disposing of the carcasses of dead animals. Untouchables were often denied the priestly services of Brahmans and access to temples, drinking wells used by higher castes were closed to them, and they were forced to live in separate hamlets. Even the "clean" Sudras have suffered considerable disabilities in the past, since the greatest gap in the caste system has been between the three upper *varnas* and the Sudras.

Public discrimination against "Untouchables" was made illegal in India by a new constitution, effective in 1950, which emphasized the equality of all citizens before the law. The political power of the "Untouchables" has made them privileged regarding government employment and admission to institutions of higher learning. The caste organization remains, but it is constantly being modified.

The three upper *varnas* are called "the twice-born" because their boys pass through an initiation ceremony after which a sacred thread is worn which is symbolic of a second, or intellectual and religious, birth. This rite involves social and religious prerogatives and has not been available to the Sudras.

Each Hindu *varna* has many subdivisions, particularly the Sudras whose smaller segments are known as *jati*, a word that has become synonymous with caste in many contexts. Thus, such groups as gardeners, potters, and carpenters, even though they are all Sudras, are recognized as separate *jatis* or castes. Each group is governed in caste matters by its own caste assembly, and each has strict rules controlling dining and social relations with other *jatis* and *varnas*. Violation of the regulations may result in fines or other penalties. Although marriage must be within the caste, marriage partners ordinarily come from different sections of the *varna* or *jati*.

**DHARMA** [där'mə], the conduct of life in Hinduism. By birth into a family, every person inherits and is obliged to follow the dharma of a class. Dharma is based directly on tradition rather than on revelation; but ultimately it is centered on religion. It is one of the four ends of man, the others being kama, or pleasure; artha, or material prosperity; and moksa, or release. In modern India dharma may be regarded as right or proper conduct regardless of one's birth.

**DURGA,** Hindu goddess usually regarded as the wife of Shiva. The name is one of many used to represent the female or active aspect of the godhead. As Durga, the goddess is recognized in both destructive and beneficent forms. In Hindu iconography she is depicted as a ten-armed goddess in battle against the forces of evil. Today she is worshiped mainly in her beneficent form. The festival of Durga (*puja*), held annually in September or October, is the occasion for family reunions and celebrations.

Indian painting (18th century) depicts Durga, one of the aspects of the Shakti, killing the Buffalo demon. (PHILADELPHIA MUSEUM OF ART)

**GANGES** [găn'jēz] **RIVER** of northern India, known as the great holy river. It rises on the southern slopes of the Himalayas and, penetrating the mountains, flows southwest and emerges onto its extensive delta at Hardwar,

where the Upper Ganges Canal irrigation system begins. It then flows southeast to Allahabad where it receives its great tributary river, the Jumna, and finally into the Meghna estuary of the Bay of Bengal.

**GUPTA** [gōop'tə], northern Indian dynasty (320–544) which was marked by the golden age of classical Sanskrit, and the development of a universal Hinduism. The founder of the Gupta house was Chandra Gupta I who was styled the "supreme King of great Kings." Thereafter, all Gupta Kings ruled by divine right. The dynasty succeeded to the domain of the Andhra kingdom and also included all of northern India and Gujarat. The second ruler of the line, Samudra Gupta, is portrayed in the ancient Allahabad Pillar inscription as being the incarnation of justice and Vishnu's mortal representative. He was praised as charitable, intelligent, well-versed in the scriptures, and a gifted musician and poet. Perhaps more important was his talent as a warrior who led his troops to successful conquest. The dynasty was blessed with other outstanding leaders including Chandra Gupta II.

The rule of the Guptas brought all persons, regardless of caste, property, or status, under the supreme law of the King, which was detailed in the Lawbook of Yajnavalkya. As such, it was the full expression of Hindu culture and law, and led to a universal religion not reserved exclusively for the Brahmans but extending to all castes. Thus, it created a single culture, polity, and law. Although language was the great cultural contribution of the Guptas, art and architecture also flowered, and a spacious and naturalistic character emerged, marked by pillars in the style of a pot base with an ornate foliage-carved staff.

The empire began to disintegrate as the western provinces were lost to the Huns in the 2d half of the 5th century. By 465 the Gupta dominions were overrun except in Bengal, where their rule endured until 544.

**GURU** [gōo'rōo], traditionally, a spiritual preceptor who indoctrinates his students in the basic tenets of the Hindu faith and instructs them in the proper execution of various ritual performances. As the belief in a more personalized deity developed during India's Middle Ages, gurus were often revered no longer as simply spiritual guides but as avatars of the deities themselves. In more recent times, especially among the Sikhs, the guru has assumed a political significance.

**KALI** [kä'lē] ("the Black One"), Hindu deity usually represented as the wife of Shiva. The goddess, known by many names, is regarded as the female, or active, aspect of the godhead. As Kali she is associated with death and destruction. She is depicted in Hindu iconography as a grotesque creature wearing a garland of skulls and dancing on the inert body of Shiva. The festival of Kali is celebrated annually in India in October and November.

Hindu pilgrims bathing in the muddy waters of the sacred Ganges River at Varanasi (Benares). To Hindus the Ganges' waters can cleanse, purify, and cure.

**KARMA** [kär'mə] (Skr., "work" or "deed"), in Indian religious thought, the inescapable law of cause and effect governing physical and moral actions. Enjoyment or suffering in this life results from deeds or thoughts in one's past lives, while present thoughts and actions will determine the character of future lives. Rightly understood, the doctrine of karma means that man is master of his destiny, since every good act ultimately results in happiness and every evil deed brings sorrow.

**KRISHNA,** the eighth incarnation of the god Vishnu. He is

adored in various forms in India today: as a child-god with miraculous powers; as a joyous, attractive, mischievous young man who woos and wins thousands of milkmaids by the entrancing music of his flute and the beauty of his person; as a hero-king; and as the Lord himself who counsels Arjuna in the Bhagavad-Gita and thus gives expression to the essence of Hinduism. The Krishna story doubtless combines several traditions: pastoral, erotic, heroic, and religious—some indigenous to south India, and some taken from the mythology of the Aryan invaders from the northwest.

Krishna and his beloved Radha, in an 18th-century Indian painting.
(INFORMATION SERVICE OF INDIA)

**KSHATRIYA** [kshăt'rē-yə], second of four hereditary castes into which the Hindus of India are grouped, ranking immediately below the Brahmans. Traditionally the Kshatriyas are the soldiers and rulers of the society. They are organized into a large number of graded clans. In parts of north India, the Kshatriyas are called Rajputs.

**RAMA,** in Hindu mythology, hero of the Sanskrit epic Ramayana. He represents for millions of Hindus the noblest ideals of Hinduism: he is the kind husband, brave hero, and just king. His wife, Sita, and he together personify conjugal fidelity and devotion. His brothers and he, and his faithful associate, Hanuman, the monkey demigod, similarly portray unswerving dedication to an ideal. Rama is the seventh incarnation of the god Vishnu and therefore is divine as well as ideally human.

**SHIVA or ŚIVA** [shē'və], one of the chief gods of Hinduism, looked on by the Shaivas (Śaivas) as the ultimate divinity. Worship of a god with some of his characteristics can be traced back to the prehistoric Indus civilization, and his cult absorbed that of the Vedic god Rudra.

In popular Shaivism he is an ambivalent diety, with both mild and destructive aspects. He is often represented as an ascetic, meditating on Mount Kailas, attended by his spouse Parvati, his bull Nandi, and his two sons, the six-faced Skanda and the elephant-headed Ganesha. In South India he is popularly thought of as the divine dancer, and certain medieval icons of the dancing Shiva are among the best-known works of Indian art. But he is most widely worshiped in the form of the linga, a stylized phallus, the emblem of his creative power.

Despite primitive elements in some aspects of Shaivism, medieval Shaiva theologians in Kashmir and the Tamil country produced works of great subtlety and high ethical value. In these texts Shiva appears as the highest godhead and is wholly beneficent.

**SUDRA,** hereditary caste having the lowest status in the fourfold social system of the Hindus of India. Most of the artisans and laborers are Sudras.

**SUTTEE** [su-te'], rite practiced by certain Hindu castes in India, notably the Rajputs, in which the living widow was cremated along with the corpse of her dead husband or buried alive with him in his grave. The term derives from the Sanskrit word *sati,* meaning "a good woman," "a true wife," and thus denotes the wife who performed the supreme act of fidelity by sacrificing herself. The proper Sanskrit term for the act itself rather than the person performing the act is *sahagamana,* "keeping company." It was probably introduced into southern India with the Brahman civilization. The act was not compulsory, but there were religious sanctions in the form of a belief that a woman who chose to remain a widow rather than sacrifice herself would never be emancipated from the status of woman to a higher status in the cycle of reincarnation. Herodotus reports that the rite was practiced by the Thracians, and it has also been reported as being practiced by early non-Christian peoples living in the Volga region of Russia. Suttee was legally abolished in India in 1829, but sporadic cases continued into the 20th century.

**VAISHYA or VAIŚYA,** third of the four hereditary and honorifically graded social divisions of the Hindus of India. The traditional calling of the Vaishyas is business and trade.

**VISHNU** [vĭsh'nōō], one of the chief gods of Hinduism. In the earliest literature he appears as a solar deity and is connected with the Vedic sacrifice. Vishnu's importance gradually increased, and other gods were identified with him until, by the beginning of the Christian Era, he was widely worshiped as the ultimate divinity.

In classical Hindu mythology Vishnu is the sustainer of the universe, which comes into existence when he wakes at the end of the cosmic night, through the mediation of the demiurge Brahma. When he sleeps at the end of the cosmic day the universe is destroyed. Vishnu reigns with his consort Lakshmi, the goddess of wealth, in his heavenly palace, Vaikuntha.

From time to time Vishnu takes material form and descends to earth to preserve creation from threatened catastrophe and to uproot evil. Nine such divine incarnations (avatars) have occurred during the present world cycle, at the end of which a tenth is expected.

**The ten incarnations** of Vishnu, according to the usual formulation, are the following.

*Matsya,* the fish. Vishnu became a great fish to save Manu, the progenitor of the human race, from destruction by a deluge. He rescued Manu with a boat, which was made fast to a horn on the head of the fish. In this legend Mesopotamian influence is probable.

*Kurma,* the tortoise. Vishnu became an enormous tortoise to recover certain divine treasures which had been lost in the deluge. The ocean was churned by the gods, using Mount Mandara, pivoted on the back of the Tortoise, as a churning pole. The treasures emerged from the waters like butter in a churn.

*Varaha,* the boar. A demon dragged the earth down into the depths of the ocean. Vishnu, taking the form of a mighty boar, killed the demon and raised the earth on his tusk.

*Narasimha,* the man-lion. Vishnu became a monster, half man and half lion, to destroy a powerful demon who was impervious to the attacks of god, man, and beast.

*Vamana,* the dwarf. To regain the world from the clutches of another demon, Bali, Vishnu became a dwarf. He begged of Bali as much land as he could cover in three paces, and when the request was granted he assumed his true form and bestrode heaven and earth in two paces, leaving only the infernal regions to the demon.

*Parashurama.* To free the world from the oppressions of the Kshatriya, or warrior class, Vishnu was born as Parashurama, the son of Jamadagni, a Brahman. He destroyed the Kshatriyas in 21 great battles.

*Rama,* one of the most famous legendary heroes of India. A prince of Ayodhya, Rama saved the world from the afflictions of the demon Ravana, from whom he rescued his beloved wife Sita, who had fallen into the demon's clutches. Rama forms the model of the ideal Hindu son, husband, and ruler.

*Krishna,* a legendary prince who is the subject of much popular tradition. Born of the royal family of the rulers of Mathura, as a child he was smuggled out of the city to avoid murder at the hands of his wicked cousin Kamsa, who had usurped the throne. He grew up incognito among the herdsmen of Vrindavana (Brindaban), near Mathura, and his youthful amours with the milkmaids (*gopi*) form the subject matter of much Indian art and poetry. Later Krishna killed Kamsa and gained the throne, but transferred his seat of power to Dwarka in Gujarat. He appears as a conqueror and destroyer of demons, but his main role in Indian tradition, after that of the divine lover, is as the friend and mentor of the five Pandava brothers in the Mahabharata. He is reputed to have preached the Bhagavad-Gita before the great battle of Kurukshetra.

*Buddha.* Siddhartha Gautama, the founder of Buddhism, was accepted as an incarnation of Vishnu by the 12th century. The god descended to earth in this form to put an end to the sacrifice of animals or, according to some sources, to ensure the damnation of the wicked by persuading them to reject the Vedas.

*Kalki,* the incarnation yet to come, who, at the end of the present cycle of cosmic time, will destroy evil and restore the golden age (Krita Yuga). Zoroastrian and possibly Christian ideas may have influenced the doctrine.

Today Vishnu is chiefly worshiped in the forms of Rama and Krishna, who are probably the most popular objects of religious devotion in India. The other incarnations now play little part in the religion of the ordinary Hindu, though the evidence of images and inscriptions shows that the boar incarnation was quite widely worshiped in the Gupta period (4th–6th centuries A.D.)

**YAMA** [yä′mə], Hindu god of death. In the Vedas, the ancient sacred writings, he appears as the guardian of the blessed dead and the ruler of paradise. Later, in Indian medieval writings, he is depicted as judge of the dead and lord of the infernal regions, where the wicked await rebirth. Yama is usually dressed in red.

Julian Press, Inc.

One of the eight states of Yoga, the "Lotus Posture."

**YOGA** [yō′gə], one of the principal systems of salvation in Hinduism. The word "yoga" describes the disciplines for self-development, primarily for the realization of God by direct experience. But yoga may also be used for such lesser ends as the control of natural forces and physiological processes. "Yoga" comes from the Sanskrit root *yuj,* meaning "to yoke"—the individual self with the Divine. The classic text by the teacher Patanjali (300 B.C.) describes raja yoga, or royal yoga. One who practices yoga is called a yogi. The Yogasutras are brief statements to be memorized for the purpose of mastering a much larger body of knowledge.

Life itself is considered a yoga, but, more specifically, there are types of yoga which are suitable to the individual's development and nature. A spiritual director, or guru, is necessary in order to practice yoga, especially in the later stages of development. The classifications of yoga and their emphases are bhakti, love and devotion; karma, selfless action; jnana, knowledge and wisdom; hatha, physical and vital (known to the West as breathing and posture exercises); and integral, a modern development by the 20th-century mystical teacher and theologian Aurobindo Ghose.

Although these yogas appear separate, their essence is one. Breathing exercises are primary in hatha yoga, but they are a part of other yogas. Bhakti yoga emphasizes intense love and devotion to God (Ishvara), yet devotion is also an aspect of raja yoga. The Ishvara concept is defined as that which possesses divine attributes or qualities and offers grace to man. The summit of yoga, however, goes beyond to that which is indefinable, or Brahman, the world spirit.

**The States of Yoga.** The eight successive steps of yoga are given in Sanskrit to emphasize that there are no exact English equivalents to the deeper meanings of these terms—the meaning is discovered in experience. (1) Yama is the exclusion of evil actions, that is, self-control. (2) Niyama is the regular and complete observance of moral rules. (3) Asana means postures; the most famous of these is padmasana, the "Lotus Posture," in which the worshiper sits with the feet placed soles up on the opposite thighs. (4) Pranayama is the practice of controlled breathing. (5) Pratyahara is the restraint of the senses. (6) Dharana refers to steadying the mind by intense concentration on a single object. (7) Dhyana is deep meditation. (8) Samadhi is the attainment of pure consciousness at the highest level of one's being. The samadhi experience is overwhelming and not definable.

The purpose of this process of yoga is to realize the ultimate reality. Its end is mukti, release or salvation.

## *Literature*

**BHAGAVAD-GITA** [bŭg'ə-vəd-gētə] (Skr. "Song of the Lord"), world-famous religious classic interpolated in the epic, the *Mahabharata*, and reputed to embody the essence of Hindu religious experience. A philosophical dialogue between Arjuna, the hero of the epic, and Krishna, the avatar of Vishnu, the poem is of composite authorship and consists of 700 Sanskrit couplets in 18 chapters. In it Krishna discourses on God, the soul, and the ethical and spiritual disciplines by which men of different castes may achieve salvation. The central theme is the necessity for action and devotion in all circumstances. There are actions which are intrinsically right, and man fulfills his function in society, and attains union with the deity, by executing his allotted duties with devotion to God and without concern for the immediate results.

**BRAHMANAS** [brä'mə-nəs], ritualistic interpretations of the Hindu Vedas in Sanskrit prose. Composed in the pre-Upanishadic period (c.9th century B.C.), the principal ones are the *Aitareya* and the *Satapatha*. Containing elaborate liturgical instructions for sacrifices, they are the source of many myths and legends, and of some of the Hindu social practices relegating women and low-caste persons to inferior positions.

**MAHABHARATA** [mə-hä'bä'rə-tə], the most comprehensive Hindu epic, compiled, according to legend, by the poet-sage Vyasa. A compendium of religion, philosophy, and politics, the Mahabharata epitomizes popular Hinduism. The main story revolves around the strife of two related royal families, the Pandavas and the Kauravas, which exploded into a disastrous civil war involving the whole Indian nation. What was probably once a comparatively short epic celebrating the battles of the early years of the Aryan conquest of India drew to itself many legends and wonder tales of all India. With its hundred thousand Sanskrit couplets, the Mahabharata is easily the longest epic of man. Among all its heroic men and women the most prominent is the luminous figure of Krishna delivering his sermon, the Bhagavad-Gita.

**MANU** [män'oo], **LAWS OF** (Skr. *Manu-Smrti*, "Code of Manu"), codification of Hindu law made c.100 A.D. by the historical Manu, a sage and lawgiver. Based on the Vedas, the code depicts a society ruled by a feudal king advised by three learned priests. The laws, which established a system of penalties ranging from gentle admonition to capital punishment, were partial to the higher castes and discriminated against women and the lower castes.

**PURANAS** [poo-rä'nəz] (Skr., "tales of antiquity"), holy books of post-Vedic Hinduism, written in simple Sanskrit verse and relating the myths concerning the origins and early history of the world and of the popular deities. There are several minor works and 18 major texts; the most popular of these is the Bhagavata Purana, telling of Vishnu's incarnation as Krishna. The names of the different Puranas involve the proper names of the gods or sages with whom the particular Purana is concerned or the name of the principal narrator who reputedly related or revealed the Purana to men.

Meaningful dating of the Puranas is difficult because they are often miscellaneous compilations loosely assembled within a series of enclosing dialogue frames. Probable dates of compilation range from the 3d to the 16th century A.D., and some of the material may be much older.

**RAMAYANA** [rä-mä'yə-nə], Hindu epic recounting the story of the hero Rama, an incarnation of Vishnu. The traditional author of the poem was the sage Valmiki, a contemporary of the historical Rama, a Prince of the 8th or 7th century B.C. Written with consummate poetic and dramatic skill, the tale narrates Rama's early life, his marriage, and his adventures, including the battle with the demon King Ravana to recover his abducted wife, Sita. Rama is depicted as the ideal husband, brave leader, and just, benevolent King. Sita, the personification of wifely devotion, stands as the ideal of Hindu womanhood. Like the other great epic, the Mahabharata, the Ramayana illustrates abstruse Vedic truths in a popular style and has been a source of ethical values and religious inspiration for all Hindus.

**SANSKRIT** [săn'skrĭt], the ancient literary and sacred language of India. It is no longer spoken except as a liturgical language. Sanskrit is the oldest of the Indic (or Aryan, or Indo-Aryan) languages.

The word "Sanskrit" itself means "refined," "elaborated," or "well formed." The language is distinct from the generally later languages, called Prakrits ("Prakrit" means "natural" or "common"), which constitute the second stage of development of the Indic languages. Although there undoubtedly were a number of dialects of Sanskrit, only two have come down to us. These two represent chronological stages rather than contemporaneous regional variants of the same language. The oldest form of the language is called Vedic Sanskrit, or simply Vedic, after its principal (and oldest) literary documents, the monumental Vedas. The Vedas are in the language of a people who called themselves Aryans and who were the earliest Indo-Europeans to enter the Indian subcontinent. The later stage of the language is called Classical Sanskrit.

The literature in Sanskrit is almost staggering in quantity and is extensive in scope. Practically every genre, covering almost every area of human activity, is represented. The oldest literary documents, dating from about the middle of the 2d millennium B.C., are the Vedas already alluded to. The word "Veda" means "(sacred) knowledge" or "(sacred) lore," and the Vedas are held to be divine revelation. They form the core of the religious system called Brahmanism. They are metrical or poetic

## महाभारतसारः

### आदिपर्व

#### मङ्गलाचरणम्

॥ श्रीगणेशाय नमः ॥

नारायणं नमस्कृत्य नरं चैव नरोत्तमम् ।
देवीं सरस्वतीं चैव ततो जयमुदीरयेत् ॥ १ ॥

ॐ नमो भगवते वासुदेवाय । ॐ नमः कृष्णद्वैपायनाय ।

#### अथ भारतोपक्रमः

(अ.१) लोमहर्षणपुत्र उग्रश्रवाः सौतिः पौराणिको
नैमिषारण्ये शौनकस्य कुलपतेर्द्वादशवार्षिके सत्रे ॥ १ ॥
सुखासीनानभ्यगच्छद्ब्रह्मर्षीन्संशितव्रतान् ।
अथापृच्छदृषिस्तत्र कश्चित्प्रस्तावयन्कथाः ॥ २ ॥
कुत आगम्यते सौते क्वार्यं चिह्नतत्स्वया ।
कालः कमलपत्राक्ष हंसैतत्पृच्छतो मम ॥ ३ ॥

Part of a page in Sanskrit, from the Mahabharata (Great Tale of the Descendants of Bharata). The Mahabharata, one of the oldest and most important Indian epics, was composed in Classical Sanskrit.

in form. The Brahmanas, which, along with other types of theological writings, are attached to the Vedas, explain the relation of the ceremonial sacrifices of Brahmanism to the dogma expounded in the Vedas. The Brahmanas are notable for being the first prose to be found in any Indo-European language. Much of the literature in Classical Sanskrit is profane, as opposed to the sacred character of the Vedas.

Apart from the Vedas and the philosophical literature (the Upanishads), the most significant early Sanskrit literature is epical: the massive Mahabharata and the Ramayana. While not divorced from religion, these two great works have a unique and majestic literary quality of their own.

**SUTRAS** [soo'trəz] (Skr. *sutra*, "thread," "pithy wise saying"), basic texts of the six systems of Hindu philosophy. Composed between the 5th century B.C. and the 5th century A.D., some of the texts have legendary origins, and some have varying editions. The most important sutras are the Brahmasutra by Badarayana, the Yogasutra of Patanjali, the Sankhyasutra by Kapila, the Nyayasutra of Aksapada Gautama, and the Vaisheshikasutra by Kanada.

**UPANISHADS** [oo-păn'ə-shădz] (Skr. *upanisad*, "to sit near [the master]"), a series of 108 mystical texts which are the basis of the six systems of Hindu philosophy. The Upanishads form the concluding portion of the Vedas, the sacred texts of Hinduism. According to tradition, the earliest sections of the Upanishads were composed in the 8th century B.C., but the later parts are of much more recent date. The principal theme of the texts is an inquiry into the nature of the individual self or soul (atman) and its identity with the universal self or world soul (Brahman).

**VEDAS** [vā'dəz] (Skr., "knowledge," "sacred lore," "sacred book"), the earliest religious texts of India, composed c.1500–900 B.C. in the Indo-Aryan language known as old or Vedic Sanskrit. The Vedas comprise four books, or collections, of sacrificial formulas and hymns to the gods and demigods of the Aryan peoples whose civilization flourished in India during the 2d millennium B.C.

The earliest, the Rig-Veda, is a compilation of 1,028 hymns of praise to the nature gods Indra (thunder), Varuna (rain), Surya (sun), and Agni (fire). The Sama-Veda, a collection of over 1,000 chanted songs, contains only 75 new songs. Most of the songs are rearrangements of hymns from the Rig-Veda. The Yajur-Veda, written about a century after the Rig-Veda, comprises sacrificial hymns containing specific instructions for the use of priests in conducting sacrifices. The Atharva-Veda, the latest book, is composed of spells, incantations, and songs.

The Vedas have been kept intact through a long tradition of oral transmission. Many Hindu reformers have advocated a return to the religion of the Vedas, in which there is no reference to caste.

Philip Gendreau

The Badri Das Temple in Calcutta, capital of West Bengal and the leading port in India. One of the marvels of Calcutta, the temple is the center of Jainism, a religion that separated from Hinduism c.6th century B.C.

# 6 · OTHER RELIGIONS

**BABI** [bä′bē], known also as Ahl-e Bayan, a sect founded in 1844 by Sayyid Ali Mohammed of Shiraz, Iran, who was called the Bab (Gate to the Truth). Though the original intent of the movement was to purify the branch of Islam called Shiite Islam, it soon developed into an independent faith, the followers of which called for social reforms. A successor of the Babs, Bahaullah (1817–92), expanded the original doctrine into one of pacifism and humanitarianism. The movement, known as the Bahai faith, spread to both Eastern and Western countries, including the United States, during the 20th century. The main group in the United States established itself in Wilmette, Ill.

**ETHICAL CULTURE, SOCIETY OF,** an organization founded in New York City in 1876 by Felix Adler, on the basis of his conviction of the changeless character and absolute sovereignty of the moral law and the need of instruction in ethical principles. Societies were later founded in Chicago, Philadelphia, Boston, and other cities, each separate and autonomous, but with like aims. In 1889 the existing groups formed the American Ethical Union with the purpose of establishing new societies, the furtherance of the Ethical Culture Movement abroad, and the publication of literature interpreting the movement's principles and aims. Societies were established in England, Austria, and Germany.

The membership has never been large, but has included persons of great influence. The society allows the utmost freedom of theological thought, but always affirms its basically ethical nature. Ethical Culture meetings are conducted very much as church services, with music, meditation, the reading of Scripture or some other inspirational literature, and an address on some pertinent religious, philosophical, or moral theme. The movement has been quite active in practical efforts through education and social action to improve the level of social and individual life. Headquarters of the Ethical Union are in New York City, where the bimonthly periodical, *The Ethical Outlook*, is published.

**JAINISM** [jīn'ĭz-əm], an Indian religion founded by a Kshatriya, Vardhamana Mahavira ("the Great Hero"), in the 6th century B.C. partly as a protest against the sacrificial cult of Brahmanic Hinduism. Jainism at one time was very popular, but it lost ground with the spread of the Hindu devotional movement, and is now chiefly confined to mercantile castes in Gujarat and parts of Mysore.

Jainism is an atheistic religion. The universe goes through a process of advance and decline according to natural law. It consists of an infinite number of souls, naturally omniscient and blissful, enmeshed in matter. Suffering results from this, and the aim of the soul should be to escape from matter, and the concomitant round of transmigration, and to regain its pristine glory. Matter is drawn to the soul chiefly by deeds of selfishness and violence, and hence salvation is to be obtained by strict nonviolence (ahimsa). Jainism attributes life not only to men and animals, but also to plants, fire, air, earth, and water. In fact, the whole world is packed with souls, tightly bound by matter, which causes them continual suffering. Since injury to these souls can be avoided only by living the severely self-disciplined life of an ascetic, Mahavira established an order of monks, which still survives.

Jains, monks and laymen, must avoid all taking of life, and are therefore vegetarians. The monks take elaborate precautions so as not to injure the minute living things believed to inhabit natural objects. The layman is precluded not only from professions necessitating the killing of men and animals, but also from others, such as pottery making and metalwork, which involve injury to these minute forms of life. Hence most Jains have become merchants and bankers; and, as their ethics encourage frugality, they are among the wealthiest communities of India.

Jainism is divided into two chief sections: the *Digambaras* ("space-clad"), mainly in Mysore, who hold that the monk should live in a state of complete nudity, according to the teachings of Mahavira, though today *Digambara* monks normally wear robes; and the *Svetambaras* ("white-clad") of Gujarat, who maintain that the rule of Mahavira is not applicable to the present degenerate conditions of the world, and that monks should wear white robes. The two branches of Jainism have different scriptures, though their fundamental doctrines do not differ greatly.

The Jains have produced a great body of sacred literature, in various languages, and their philosophers have developed a distinctive relativistic epistemological system of great subtlety. Jain thought had some influence on Mahatma Gandhi, especially in respect of his insistence on complete nonviolence.

**SHINTO** [shĭn'tō] (Jap., "way of the gods" or "*kami* way"), the indigenous religion of Japan.

**Primitive Shinto.** In the main, primitive Shinto may be characterized as a simple cosmic religion. The early Japanese never thought of themselves as in any way separated from cosmic existence and the rhythm of nature. They did not draw a sharp line of distinction between the heavenly and earthly domains, and they had only a vague notion about the life to come. Central to their religion was the belief in *kami*, which is usually translated as "god" or "gods" but also means "above," "superior," or "divine," signifying any thing sacred or extraordinary that arouses man's respect and reverence. The ancient Shinto myths mention 800 myriads of *kami*, manifested in mountains, trees, plants, beasts, birds, rivers, and human beings—implying that the entire universe is a community of living beings, all sharing the *kami* nature.

The cosmological myths of primitive Shinto depict a three-dimensional universe. In the highest level (plain of the high sky) male and female *kami* reside, in the lowest level (nether world) unclean and malevolent spirits reside, and in the middle domain (manifested world) humans and other beings reside. However, in actual practice the early Japanese paid little attention to the myths of the three-dimensional universe. Rather, they envisaged both the domain of *kami* and the nether region as being in the other world, which was frequently associated with certain mountains or with islands. At any rate, the Shinto myths trace the origin of heaven and earth to the marriage of Izanagi ("he who invites") and Izanami ("she who is invited"), whose union also resulted in the birth of the sun goddess Amaterasu O-mikami. The sun goddess in turn sent her grandchild, Ninigi, and other *kami* into the human domain, and Ninigi's descendant, Jimmu, is said to have been the first legendary Emperor of Japan.

The sociopolitical unit of the early Yamato kingdom was the clan (*uji* and *kabane*), ruled by its head, who also acted as the chief priest. Each clan was united by the cult of its clan *kami*, to whom the whole clan turned in time of need. Among all clans, the most powerful was the imperial (*Tenno*) clan, whose head, the emperor, claimed political as well as religious authority over all other clans within the kingdom. The emperor ruled the nation, presumably following the instructions of the heavenly *kami*, communicated to him through divination and other religious practices. In so doing, the emperor and his priests took seriously the magical power of spoken language. Beautifully phrased and correctly uttered words were believed to bring about good results, while carelessly phrased and incorrectly pronounced words were believed to bring about bad results. Hence great importance was attributed to the priest's ablution and to the careful recitation of the *norito* (supplications to the *kami*), which usually contained words of praise, lists of offerings, and words identifying the persons offering the prayers.

The simple faith and practice of primitive Shinto were destined to undergo changes under the influence of Sino-Korean civilization, especially Confucianism and Buddhism, in the 5th and 6th centuries A.D. In spite of the initial resistance of Shinto priestly families to the introduction of Buddhism, Shinto came to be overshadowed by Mahayana Buddhism in the 8th century. It was also during this period that the two historical writings regarded as the semisacred scriptures of Shinto were compiled. The Kojiki (The Records of Ancient Matters), completed in 712 A.D., was written in Chinese characters used phonetically to approximate Japanese sounds. The Nihongi, or Nihon-shoki (The Written Chronicle of Japan), composed entirely in Chinese, was completed in 720 A.D. In the 9th century Buddhist leaders interpreted the Shinto *kami* as manifestations of the Buddha and thus developed the pattern of Shinto and Buddhist coexistence, known as *ryobu Shinto*, that lasted until the 19th century.

**Shinto Revival.** Although there were sporadic attempts to restore the power and influence of Shinto, its revival did not take place until the 18th century. In 1798 the Japanese scholar and poet Motoori Norinaga completed a 49-volume work entitled the *Kojiki-den* (The Annotation of the Kojiki), which has remained the most authoritative interpretation of Shinto doctrines. With the decline of the Tokugawa feudal regime in 1867 the Meiji government dissolved the pattern of Shinto and Buddhist coexistence. It promoted Shinto as a patriotic national cult above all other religious systems by supporting Shinto shrines and priests with government funds.

**Sect Shinto.** Meanwhile the social upheaval, caused largely by the transition from a feudal regime to imperial rule, resulted in the development of messianic movements, mostly among the peasants. The Meiji government classified these movements, 13 in number, as Sect Shinto (*Kyoha Shinto*), even though some of them had no connection with Shinto in origin or in ethos. The largest among them, Tenri-kyo, has numerous parishes in all parts of Japan today and also maintains active missions in some parts of North and South America.

**State Shinto.** In retrospect it becomes evident that extreme nationalists and militarists utilized Shinto by identifying it with the emperor cult in order to mobilize the nation from the time of the Sino-Japanese War (1894–95) until the end of World War II. Immediately after Japan's surrender to the Allied Powers, the occupation authority instructed the Japanese government to terminate the sponsorship, support, perpetuation, control, and dissemination of Shinto on any level—national, prefectural, or local. The authority also persuaded the Emperor to declare publicly that he was not divine.

**Shrine Shinto.** Although State Shinto was thus disestablished after World War II, Shinto as a religion continues to exist in various forms. There are about 80,000 Shinto shrines today. Many of them have joined a voluntary organization called the Association of Shrine Shinto (Jinja Honcho) that co-ordinates their activities. Imperial Household Shinto is carried on in the three shrines inside the imperial palace. It also preserves a special relationship to the Grand Shrine of Ise dedicated to the sun goddess who was originally the tutelary *kami* of the imperial clan. Furthermore, Domestic Shinto has been preserved by many families, centering around the household *kami* shelf (*kami-dana*), which is dedicated to the tutelary *kami* of the family.

**Shinto Worship.** Pious Shintoists aim at communion with the *kami* in their daily life by observing household rituals as well as by participating in shrine cults on festive occasions. In the main, Shinto emphasizes worship at the expense of doctrinal teaching. The four main elements of Shinto worship are purification (*harai*), offering (*shinsen*), supplication (*norito*), and a symbolic feast (*naorai*). Shinto, although not lacking in transcendental elements, tends to stress simple, this-worldly virtues, such as joy, gratitude, a harmonious life, and sincerity (*makoto*). It is to be noted that many Japanese find no conflict in adhering simultaneously to Shinto and Buddhism.

**AMATERASU O-MIKAMI** [ä-mä-tä-rä-soo  ō-mē-kä-mē] ("The Great *Kami* Shining in Heaven"), commonly known as the Sun Goddess, is the central deity of the Shinto pantheon. Originally she was the tutelary *kami* and the ancestor of the imperial clan; as such her influence increased with the expansion of imperial power, so that the notion of the solar ancestry of the imperial family became widely accepted by the 8th century. Her *shin-tai* (literally "*kami* body," an object in which the spirit of the *kami* lives) is the sacred mirror that resides in the Inner Shrine of Ise, while its replica has been placed in the central shrine (Kashiko-dokoro) of the imperial palace in Tokyo.

A camphor-wood torii, or doorless gate of a Shinto holy place, built 1875, on the sacred island of Itsukushima, Japan.

George Holton—Photo Researchers

**SIKHS** [sēks], members of an Indian religion founded in its original form by the Punjabi teacher Nanak (1469–1538), the first of the 10 gurus (teachers) of Sikhism. The Sikhs were at first a pacific sect, not sharply distinguished from the Hindus. As a result of persecution by the Mogul government, however, the 10th guru, Govind Singh (became guru 1675, d.1708), reorganized the Sikhs into a martial order. At his death he gave orders that the Granth, the Sikh sacred book, should henceforth be the guru, and the line of teachers came to an end. The Sikhs rapidly gained converts and increased their military strength. By the early 19th century the Sikh empire reached its widest extent under Maharaja Ranjit Singh (1780–1839), who at the end of his rule controlled much of present-day West Pakistan, Kashmir, and Indian Punjab. The Sikh state was conquered by the British East India Company in 1849 after two hard-fought wars.

Despite the loss of its independence, the Sikh community flourished under British rule, and in the 20th century it has increased considerably in number and influence. As a result of the partition of India in 1947, there are now hardly any Sikhs in Pakistan. They are very numerous in Indian Punjab, and there are Sikh colonies in all the chief cities of India. Throughout India the Sikhs have a reputation for courage, honesty, and trustworthiness, but they are also unjustly noted for their obtuseness, and many popular humorous proverbs and jokes are told at their expense.

**Characteristics of Sikhism.** The Sikh religion developed out of Hinduism under the influence of Islam, and it also contains features perhaps showing Christian influence. Sikhs are more strictly monotheistic than Hindus, referring to God as Ram, the Hindu name, as Akal ("the Timeless"), and as Wahguru ("the Great Master"). Like the Hindus they believe in the transmigration of souls, but like the Muslims they object to the worship of images. In their gurdwaras, or temples, the sacred image is replaced by a large copy of the Sikh scriptures, referred to as Granth Sahib (Lord Book). This is a lengthy collection of hymns in Punjabi and Hindi, composed by the Sikh gurus and various Hindu hymnodists.

Again like the Muslims the Sikhs believe in the complete equality of all members of the faith. A ritual meal taken in common, perhaps influenced by the Christian Eucharist, was inaugurated by Govind Singh to break down vestiges of caste feeling among his followers. A further possible borrowing from Christianity is a form of baptism, in which the young Sikh is sprinkled with sweetened water stirred by a sword. After this he becomes a full member of the faith and is entitled to take the title Singh ("Lion").

Certain regulations of Govind Singh have given the Sikhs their distinctive appearance. The orthodox male Sikh must always wear certain articles, known as the "five k's" (*kakar*), because in Punjabi their names begin with that letter. These are long hair (*kes*), which, including the beard, must never be cut; a pair of sewn underpants (*kachh*), replacing the Hindu dhoti; an iron bangle (*kara*); a comb (*kangha*) to keep the hair in place; and a short sword or dagger (*kripan*). The hair is always worn under a turban in public. Orthodox Sikhs rigidly avoid alcoholic drinks and tobacco, but they are permitted to hunt and eat meat.

The chief religious center of Sikhism is the Golden Temple of Amritsar in Indian Punjab. This was established at the end of the 16th century under the patronage of the Mogul Emperor Akbar.

Certain branches of Sikhism did not adopt the reforms of guru Govind Singh, and their members are not always easily distinguishable from the Hindus. In the 20th century the orthodox Akali sect has been gaining ground at the expense of the others. The Akalis are a powerful force in contemporary Indian political life, especially in Indian Punjab.

**AMRITSAR** [ŭm-rĭt'sər], city of northern India, in the state of Punjab, and the principal religious center of the Sikhs. It is located on the border between India and West Pakistan in the middle of the Bari Doab, between the Ravi and Beas rivers. The city was founded in the 16th century by the fourth Sikh Guru (high priest), Ramdas, on a piece of land granted by Emperor Akbar. The name derives from the pool called Amrita Saras ("pool of immortality") in which Guru Arjan later built the celebrated Golden Temple on a little island. The temple, surrounded on all sides by the pool and having marble walls and a copper-gilded dome, does not possess much artistic beauty, but it is annually visited by a large number of Sikhs. One of the richest temples in India, it is managed by a committee elected by the Sikh community, and its officers exercise an important influence upon the politics of East Punjab.

During the first half of the 19th century, under Ranjit Singh and his successors, Amritsar became the greatest commercial center in the Sikh kingdom, and it continues to be a major center of trade and traditional industries.

**TAOISM** [dou'ĭz-əm, tou'ĭz-əm], system of Chinese philosophy and religion.

**Philosophy.** Philosophical Taoism is known as the system of the hermit philosophers, and it can best be described as a philosophy of "live and let live." Lao-tzu (c.575–c.485 B.C.) is traditionally regarded as its founder, and Chuang-tzu (c.369–c.286 B.C.) its chief exponent. The *Tao Te Ching* (attributed to Lao-tzu) and the *Chuang-tzu* (by Chuang-tzu) are its basic texts. The central theme of this system of thought is the "Tao." Not unlike the English word "way," which is often used to translate it, Tao means literally "the path" or "the road," but in the philosophical context it has come to signify the basic principle that pervades man and the universe. Thus the Tao is eternal and absolute, infinite and immutable. Hence Taoism expounds the doctrine of inaction, or *wu-wei*. "The Tao does nothing and yet there is nothing left undone," says the *Tao Te Ching*. The final goal of this system of naturalistic mysticism is the complete union and identity of the individual with the whole of nature. In this mundane world everything is relative, whereas only in the world of Tao is there absolute freedom and complete equality.

**Religion.** The beginnings of Taoism as a religion go back to the latter half of the 2d century A.D. Amidst widespread political and social unrest a scholar named Chang Ling became the leader of a fast-growing politico-religious community. Eventually the sect became known as the Taoist religion, and the leadership of the religion remained in the Chang family until 1927. The Taoist religion claimed Lao-tzu as its founder, absorbed the folk religion of nature worship, and borrowed heavily from Buddhism. For example, it is not always easy to tell a Taoist temple from a Buddhist temple. A notable feature of the Taoist religion is its stress on various rituals which would result in long life. Taoism is ranked with Confucianism and Buddhism as one of the three "religions" of China.

On the whole, Taoism as a religion is popular only among the uneducated. But as a system of philosophy and a way of life, Taoism has challenged and attracted the best of Chinese minds throughout the ages. The importance of Taoism is only second to Confucianism in setting the pattern for Chinese life and culture. The stamp of its charm of serenity and detachment is unmistakable in such expressions as Chinese landscape painting, nature poetry, and the development of the branch of Buddhism now internationally known as Zen.

**CHUANG-TZU** [jwäng'dzŭ'], **or CHUANG CHOU** (c.369–c.286 B.C.), ancient Chinese philosopher, poet, and mystic. He is best known as a founder with Lao-tzu, who lived two centuries earlier, of the important system of Taoism. Born in the district of Meng, in what is now Honan Province in Central China, Chuang-tzu briefly held a minor local government post. He soon lost all interest in fame and fortune and became a recluse. His teachings consisted mainly of the relativity of knowledge, equality of things, and absolute truth and freedom in the *Tao*. He presented his ideas through imagery, anecdote, and parable, as well as the allegory and parody of the *Chuang-tzu*. Written in poetic prose, several of the 33 chapters of this work are considered to be literary masterpieces. The characteristic humor, charm, and detachment of the work are evident. For example, in the well-known piece, the "Butterfly Dream," on waking, Chuang-tzu wondered "whether it was Chuang Chou dreaming that he was the butterfly or the butterfly dreaming that it was Chuang Chou," and concluded dryly, "between Chuang Chou and the butterfly presumably there is a difference."

**LAO-TZU** [lou'dzŭ'] **or LAO-TSE** (c.575–c.485 B.C.), philosopher of ancient China and founder of Taoism. The life of Lao-tzu is enshrouded in greater obscurity than that of most of his contemporaries, partly because of his own preference for anonymity. According to tradition, Lao-tzu was a man of Ch'u (now Honan Province), which at the time was regarded as South China. His family name was Li and his given name, Erh; "Lao-tzu" was an affectionate epithet, equivalent to the phrase "elderly master." It is said that he served the Chou court as the keeper of the imperial archives. A legend relates that Lao-tzu, who believed that forms and ceremonies were practically useless, advised the ambitious young Confucius to forget his grandiose plans for world order. Evidently, Lao-tzu did not take students nor did he leave a record of his doings and sayings, as was the custom with thinkers of the day.

The traditional story of Lao-tzu in his old age riding to the Western Pass and into oblivion beyond the pale of civilization gave rise to the popular pictorial representation of his riding on the back of an ox. It is told that when Lao-tzu stopped at the pass, the keeper implored the Old Master to write down his teachings for the keeper's benefit. If tradition is to be believed, "Thereupon Lao-tzu wrote a book in two parts consisting of some five thousand words, in which he discussed the meaning of the *tao* and the *te*." The book which actually came to be written bore his name, the Lao-tzu. It was subsequently also called the *Tao Te Ching* (Classic of the Way and Power), and is the all-important text of Taoism. Consisting of 81 brief chapters, this small classic is not only the shortest, but also one of the most provocative and inspired works in all Chinese literature. Much speculation has been directed to its authenticity, literary style, and date of composition, as well as to related information concerning its purported author. Presumably the book was completed in the 4th and possibly even 3d century B.C., but some of the ideas and teachings, held perhaps by the hermit philosopher himself, might well have been of an earlier origin.

Lao-tzu and the *Tao Te Ching* advocated the importance and supremacy of the *tao*, an over-all principle pervading nature and man, which could be grasped better through intuition than understood through the intellect. This element of mysticism in Taoism was later seized upon by occultists, and Lao-tzu was made a saint of the Taoist religion and the *Tao Te Ching* its primary scripture.

**ZOROASTRIANISM** [zō-rō-ăs'trē-ən-ĭz-əm], Persian religion founded by the reformer Zoroaster (q.v.) in the late 7th or early 6th century B.C. The official religion of the Achaemenid dynasty, it was revived by the Sassanid rulers. As a state religion, Zoroastrianism was abolished after the Islamic conquest in the 7th century A.D. It is still practised by the Ghebers of Iran and Parsis of India, in somewhat modified form. The sacred books of Zoroastrianism, known collectively as the Zend Avesta, were not written down until the early Christian era. The Avesta represents a confused and sometimes contradictory compilation of the teachings of Zoroaster and the doctrinal accretions of subsequent centuries.

Zoroastrianism was a monotheistic faith with a strong ethical emphasis centering about the dualistic concept of the conflict between Good and Evil. Good was manifest in the creator-god of light and truth, Ahura Mazda, the great, beneficent Wise Lord. His evil opponent was Angra, Mainyu, or Ahriman, the spirit of darkness. The ultimate triumph of Ahura Mazda was assured. But during the struggle, men could aid the cause of Ahura Mazda by making free ethical choices and judgments in their daily lives. These were made with reference to the Amesha Spentas, moral entities created by Ahura Mazda. They were Justice, or Truth, Good Thought, Dominion, Piety, Prosperity, Immortality, and Obedience. It was believed by some that Zoroaster would return to prepare the coming of the final judgment.

The belief in a future life and in immortality is revealed in the concept of the Last Judgment. On that day, Ahura Mazda was to assign the upright to Heaven (immortality) and consign the followers of Ahriman to the regions of eternal darkness. Pride, sloth, and gluttony were among the sins, while representative virtues were tilling the soil, obedience to authority, fulfilling contracts, and showing mercy. Traditional Zoroastrianism was opposed to excessive fasting or grief, animal sacrifice, idol worship, or asceticism. Zoroastrianism influenced Christianity indirectly through other religions to which it gave birth, such as Mithraism and Manichaeism.

**AVESTA** [ə-vĕs'tə], canonical literature of Zoroastrianism, still used by the Parsis as their holy book. The oldest part of the text was composed, in part, by Zoroaster, and added to over the centuries. Comprising 21 books of prayers, songs, doctrines, laws, and moral precepts, the Avesta was supposedly destroyed when Alexander burned Persepolis. Remnants were collected by the Sassanian Persians in the 3d and 4th centuries, and the remains reassembled in the 13th–14th centuries, after Islamic destruction. *Zend* denotes the commentary on the Avestan text.

**MAGI**, originally a Median priestly fraternity of Iran. After the Persian conquest of Media, the Magi became priests of the Iranian nature religion, possessing special privileges. Accepted by the Achaemenid kings, the Magi adopted the near monotheistic Zoroastrian religion, which, under their influence, became increasingly diluted by the introduction of old Aryan gods and Magian ceremonies.

Later, the Magi spread this modified Zoroastrianism throughout the Near East. The word "magic" derives from the supposed power of the Magi over demons. A group of Magi is reported to have come to Bethlehem shortly after Jesus' birth because they had seen an unusually bright star (Matt. 2:1–12). Later tradition makes them kings.

**PARSIS or PARSEES** [pär'sēz, pär-sēz'], Zoroastrian religious minority of India and Pakistan, numbering over 117,000. They are concentrated chiefly in Bombay Province, particularly in the city of Bombay. They speak Gujarati and are of Iranian origin.

After the Muslim conquest of Iran (641), faithful Zoroastrians gathered in Kuhistan, migrating a century later to India, first to Kathiawar (766), then to Gujarat (785), where they built a fire temple. In 1090 their descendants dispersed to various Indian settlements, chiefly in Bombay and Baroda, each group carrying with it sacred fire, the focus of worship, from its old temple. At the end of the 15th century Changah Asa led a religious revival.

The modern Parsi has become a monotheist, retaining the Zoroastrian Great God, Ahura Mazda, as the One God, his major attributes being personified by the seven ancient divine beings, the Amesha Spentas. Fire itself is not worshiped, but is a medium of worshiping Ahura Mazda, though the place of worship is still called a fire temple; that is, fire is the immediate focus, and doubtless a terrestrial medium of the Power. The Parsis expose their dead on iron gratings in "towers of silence" set in gardens, usually atop a hill, where vultures consume the flesh; the bones, dropping down through the grating, are sufficiently exposed to disintegrate fairly rapidly. The priesthood constitutes a distinct class, and only those born therein can function as priests. A male member of this caste can, however, choose to become a layman.

The declared community aims are unity, power, peace, and justice. The principle of benevolence is emphasized. Though the Parsis were originally primarily agriculturists, they have long played a leading mercantile role, and in the 19th century many acquired vast fortunes, especially in the cotton and steel industries. They have provided expanding educational facilities, so that by the turn of the 19th century the Parsis had the highest literacy rate in India. Their cultural and economic importance is far out of proportion to their small numbers.

**ZOROASTER** [zô'rō-ă-stər], Persian name Zarathushtra (c.660–583 B.C.), ancient Persian religious reformer. According to one interpretation, he was born in Azerbaijan, near Lake Urmia; according to more recent theory, in Media, on the central plateau. At the age of 30 Zoroaster received a revelation of a new religion, which he proceeded to preach. At length he converted King Vishtaspa of eastern Iran, and thereafter the religion spread rapidly. Zoroaster was slain by the Turanians during their invasion of Bactria. The psalms, hymns, and songs of Zoroaster are contained in the Gathas, probably the oldest section of the Avesta.

# 7 · RELIGION: A SUMMARY

**RELIGION** [rĭ-lĭj'ən]. Modern scholars have frequently argued that religion is derived from magic. But magic is a man-centered business and seeks to control the actions of the Sacred in the interests of man. Religion, on the contrary, is mainly God-centered and aims at bringing the human element under the control of the Sacred. Nevertheless religion is often intertwined with magic and is seldom entirely pure. Religion proper is of a number of types, for example:

Various aspects of primitive religions are sometimes referred to as *pre-animistic* and *animistic*.

The *monotheistic* faiths hold that there is only one Supreme Being, while the *pluralistic* religions say there are several or many gods.

The *ethnic* religions confine themselves to a single group of people, which may number millions. The *universal* religions seek to carry their beliefs to all mankind.

The *revealed* religions hold that God at some particular time, or times, revealed Himself, sometimes in a miraculous way, to men.

The *prophetic* religions believed that God showed His purposes to men through great spiritual leaders called prophets.

The *founded* religions are those established by one person, as opposed to such faiths as Hinduism that recognize no single great leader.

**Period of Advance.** There was a period in history when there was a breakaway from traditional types of sacrificial and ritual religion. This period, extending roughly from about 500 B.C. to 300 A.D., arrived in some countries early and in others much later. Until this time religion was largely, if not entirely, concerned with the due and correct performance of external rites and ceremonies. To secure favorable relations with the Sacred, these rites had to be correctly performed, at the proper time, in the proper place, and by the proper person.

Such rites, it was believed, would bring the worshiper into harmony with the Sacred, but it is seldom that one can be sure that the hope of influencing, if not of controlling, the behavior of the Sacred was entirely absent from their performance. It was also believed that the course of events, although determined by powers beyond the control of men, could be predicted by the observation of certain phenomena such as the flight of birds, the position of the heavenly bodies in the sky on a given occasion, or the condition of the entrails of sacrificed victims. All of these phenomena, in a prescientific age, were thought to be in some way linked with the activities of supernatural beings. Religion of this kind persists still in many parts of the world, and even educated people often find it hard to detach themselves from it. In a somewhat softened form it may actually be discerned within various sorts of institutional Christianity and in Islam.

But it is certain that during this new period in history (sometimes called axial), there arose prophets, sages, and apostles who challenged this system of observances, of ritual, and of divination, and questioned its validity. Fresh types of religion emerged: prophetic, mystical, strongly ethical, and often without priests. We have the best-known examples in the preserved utterances of the Hebrew prophets, though similar sayings, in different contexts, are to be found in other parts of the world. In spite of these protests, the old forms of religion went on as before, sometimes side by side with the new, and each untouched by the other. But at other times the old was modified by reinterpretation so as to be given an altered significance.

Various classifications of religions have been suggested, such as natural or revealed, local or universal, world-affirming, world-renouncing, or world-transforming. Some critics have maintained that all religion is bad, or at least belongs to a stage in human development which has now been superseded. Others have said that there is both good and bad religion, and that the good belongs to the axial and postaxial varieties. Sometimes a philosophy develops into a religion. At other times a religion develops a philosophy, or is even succeeded by a philosophy, either rationalist or with a rationalist tinge.

**Ethnic and local religions** are represented by orthodox Hinduism, by Japanese State Shinto, by the ancestral religions of Mesopotamia, Egypt, Greece, Rome, and Celtic and Nordic Europe, as well as by the more primitive types occurring throughout Africa, the South Pacific, and the American continent before its occupation by European colonists.

Zoroastrianism, which began in Iran about 500 B.C., sprang from the teaching of the prophet Zoroaster, who proclaimed a fine, world-affirming moral monotheism. He recognized the existence of an evil power, however, with which the good would be in conflict until it finally gained the victory. So he declared it the duty of all true believers to fight on the side of the good. This religion had very little direct world influence, however. In the face of advancing Islam its followers fled to western India, where they became known as Parsis (Persians). They are mostly concentrated in Bombay. Some are liberal and progressive, though they refrain from propaganda and the admission of converts. But Zoroastrianism exerted a profound influence on Judaism, and through Judaism on Christianity.

Efforts have been made to convert Hinduism from an ethnic, or local, into a universal religion. So far they have been unsuccessful, partly because Hinduism is not only a religion but a vast social system confined within the borders of the subcontinent of India.

Buddhism began as a world-renouncing humanistic philosophy in India and has only gradually grown into a religion. This is due perhaps to some covert influence traveling from the Middle East, under which the original Gautama has come to be regarded as one of many recurrent incarnations of the Cosmic Spirit. In some countries where Buddhism prevails, the original ethnic religion is retained by the peasantry, with the recognition that for monks and educated people there is a higher system in which the original Buddhist philosophy has developed into a sort of paradoxical mysticism.

Judaism, strictly speaking, is an ethnic religion, though with the dispersion of the Jews it became almost worldwide. There have been times when it has sought to proselytize, but these efforts have not been general or sustained. In spite of its geographical expansion, Judaism has remained the religion of the descendants of Abraham.

**Universalist Religions.** Strangely enough, though, the offspring of Judaism, Christianity, seems to have developed into the only actual universalist religion in both its claim and scope. The Christian assertion is that the Deity has nowhere left Himself without a witness, and the Divine Logos lightens everyone who comes into the world. Nevertheless only the historical Jesus, as the supreme and perfect expression of the activity of the Divine Logos, has in His teaching and life initiated the full and perfect revelation of the character and action of the Deity. So the Christian claim is that in some form or other Christianity is destined to supersede all other religions, absorbing and preserving whatever is good in them and rejecting and discarding all that is bad or inferior. And it is significant that Christianity in its missionary efforts has gone into every part of the world and has converts on every continent and in every clime.

Islam, later in origin than Christianity, has made similar universalist claims and has drawn a large amount of its inspiration from Christianity and from Talmudic Judaism. But it has nevertheless remained mainly a religion of the heat belt and principally either of people who are Arabic in origin or of Semitic peoples related to the Arabs. It has made converts in Indonesia and among some African peoples, however, with its stark and simple monotheism.

Bahaism is a 19th-century development of Iranian Islam, which Islam rejected as heretical. It now claims to be a separate religion and with the aid of Western money is seeking to become the world faith of the future. It lays great stress upon the oneness of mankind, but adds nothing substantially new to what has already been said in this respect by Christ and Mohammed.

Sikhism is a hybrid religion of considerable beauty, springing from contact between bhakti Hinduism and Islam, and therefore indirectly influenced by Judaism and Christianity. Its adherents, coming from north India, have spread widely, as far apart as Great Britain and Kenya. They tend to form a separate social, as well as religious, community, but always with a strong military interest.

In Japan a great many hybrid sects are now springing up, based in some measure on the traditional synthesis of Shinto and Buddhism. Zen, an early example of a pure and reformed type of Buddhism, seems to be attracting considerable interest even in the West.

Much cross-fertilization has taken place in the past between Judaism and Christianity, on the one hand, and the ethnic and founded religions, on the other. Still more is now going on. Consequently, it is not easy to distinguish today between the specific tenets of any given religion and what may be due to external influences acting upon it. It is unwise to regard the shrinkage which has taken place in some religions as inevitably permanent. Changing circumstances, political and otherwise, may lead to a revival and re-expansion of religions like Parsiism, Judaism, and Sikhism, which now show some evidences of revival and propaganda, perhaps, in their more liberal forms.

**RELIGION, PRIMITIVE,** the beliefs, practices, and institutions of a religious nature among peoples without writing. Such peoples include all of mankind from its earliest beginnings, about 1,000,000 years ago, until the dawn of history, that is, until the invention of writing, as well as the numerous groups still without written languages and traditions in Asia, Africa, the South Seas, Australia, and the Americas. It is these varied groups that we refer to as primitive or tribal peoples. From their great diversity in time and space and manner of living it follows that we should more correctly speak of "primitive religions" than of "primitive religion," as if there were only one to be compared with one of the great world religions.

**Characteristics.** Tribal peoples of both the distant past and of the present do, however, have certain features in common. In the religious domain, illiteracy means the absence of a body of sacred scriptures, as well as the lack of a formal, written body of theological accounts—both common characteristics of the great world religions. Tribal groups, furthermore, being without true history, since they are without writing, usually believe that their institutions have existed since the beginning of time. Consequently their religions lack a tradition of a founder or prophet, another characteristic of the world religions. As a rule, the universe, however it is thought to be organized, is believed to have included, in its original formation, the people and their practices and institutions.

Because tribal peoples live either by hunting, gathering, and fishing or by the raising of a few crops, they generally have little economic surplus. Every individual must work hard and contribute his share of labor in the constant effort to obtain food. Consequently, as a rule there are no full-time specialists in religious activities. It takes the wealth of cities to support priests and priesthoods, temples, and other religious institutions, such as those which developed for the first time in the early cities of the Near East. The absence of an organized priesthood, then, is also related to the absence of a formal, organized theology.

Since tribal groups are relatively small in numbers and are generally isolated from other groups, there is often considerable difference in the way of life practiced by groups living in relative proximity. Their religious traditions also tend to be distinct. In other words, religion is an integral part of the unique culture of such groups, and religious practices are closely tied to beliefs held about the origin of the group and its way of life. Another feature of the great world religions—the missionary spirit—is notably absent. Most tribal peoples feel no need to convert others. This is especially true when practice and belief are concerned with the group's ancestors. One's own ancestors cannot work for someone else and would indeed have no reason to do so.

**Religion in Everyday Life.** Perhaps the most indisputable generalization that can be made about primitive religions is that what we separate and refer to as "religion" interpenetrates all aspects of everyday life, often from the most humdrum daily tasks to the most exalted and esoteric rituals. It is usually possible for the observer to isolate aspects of activities as dealing with the practical, or secular, concerns of life and to assign others to the religious sphere. To the participants, however, both of these aspects appear necessary for the accomplishment of the task at hand.

Thus among the Ojibwa Indians of the Eastern Woodlands region of North America hunting was a highly skilled activity. Yet it was also a sacred occupation. Success in hunting was attributed not only to the skill of the individual—although that skill was indispensable—but also to the co-operation of the spirit bosses of the particular animal species. Similar religious significance has been attributed to the cave paintings of game animals of the Upper Paleolithic Age. For example, the sacred act of representing the animals in effigy was perhaps thought to strengthen the effort of the hunters. Similar observations may be made concerning peoples who plant and harvest and whose rituals are directed toward the fertility of their fields. Nowhere do tribal peoples believe that rituals are sufficient in and of themselves. But hard work alone is often unable to bring about the desired results, and religious activity may help.

It is clear, then, that religious belief and activity are concerned with those spheres of life which are of crucial importance to the survival of the group. Each group has a series of beliefs which interpret the significant aspects of the universe, which create order out of chaos, and, most importantly, which hold definite implications for action to influence or control the flow of events. The Trobriand Islanders of Melanesia, for instance, believe that, in addition to careful gardening practices, certain incantations are necessary for the growth of their yams. They have specialists who know just how to recite these incantations in the appropriate manner. Tribal man is no philosopher and no scientist—at least in the modern sense of these terms. His concerns are with the economic and social crises of life. His world view provides him with explanations and with rules of behavior to deal not only with the chase or the control of crops, but also with such events as birth, illness, and death.

**Primitive Religion and Experience.** There undoubtedly exist individual differences in all societies in the degree of interest in and knowledge of traditions and ritual practices. Yet when belief interpenetrates all aspects of life, and when alternative explanations of any specific phenomenon would involve a total revision of one's world view, it is evident that religious skepticism is unthinkable. This is not to say that skepticism with reference to specific practitioners or even specific practices may not be frequent. However, it is manifestly impossible for any one individual to reject the total fabric of explanation and beliefs without prior acquaintance with other, alternative modes of interpretation.

Furthermore it must be remembered that our beliefs and attitudes organize our experience for us. Thus once we hold certain expectations our experiences can always be interpreted to fit these expectations. People who believe in the capacity of some of their fellows to harm them through magical or supernatural means may actually sicken or die when they suppose they have reason to suspect others of wishing them harm. Beliefs are a powerful force not only in our behavior but also in our interpretation of, and reaction to, the behavior of others and the phenomena of the external world. As a result, all beliefs contain sufficient reference to observable events to receive support from the very observation and interpretation of empirical phenomena, as well as from personal, subjective experiences such as dreams and visions.

Thus missionaries of the world religions often find that their teachings are interpreted in the light of previously held local beliefs, a phenomenon which leads to the development of religious syncretism, the reconciliation of conflicting beliefs. For instance, in Haiti, African gods are often identified with Christian saints. In cases in which local religions are driven underground, this leads to the distinction between "approved belief" and "superstition." European beliefs in trolls, gnomes, fairies, and vampires, as well as the use of Christmas trees and yule logs, derive from just such pre-Christian beliefs. The former remain superstition, while the latter are incorporated into the body of approved religious customs.

**Origins of Religion.** Contemporary anthropologists are impressed by the great variety of primitive world views and attempt to understand each in the context of a particular culture. In the 19th century, however, students of tribal man, extending the theory of evolution to culture, were interested in discovering the origin of religion. They attempted to trace the development of religion from these presumed origins to their own day in a series of stages, or levels. To this end they considered contemporary tribal groups as remnants of various distinct, earlier stages of human development. Sir Edward Tylor held that animism, man's attribution of spiritual qualities to all aspects of the world around him, was the earliest form of religion. According to Tylor, early man's psychic experiences, dreams, and visions led him to believe in the separate existence of body and soul. When the discovery was made of the widespread belief in mana, that impersonal force to which many peoples attribute strength, skill, and luck, as well as the powers of nonhuman beings and materials, R. R. Marett posited a preanimist stage, or animatism, the belief in mana. Today we hold such a search for origins to be speculative and useless. We can never hope to go back to the precise moment at the dawn of human consciousness which led to the "origin" of religion.

Yet even before the advent of our own species, we find, in the caves of Neanderthal man, evidence of burials and of what may have been altars to the bear. These physical remains are subject to many interpretations; yet it is evident that the first steps in religion were taken by men prior to those of our own species. However, we cannot hope to ferret out the steps of religious development in which the Victorian writers were interested. The archeological record has preserved for us only physical remains of what may have been ritual activities. It is hazardous to interpret these in the light of later and diverse systems of belief.

Futhermore we have no reason to believe that contemporary hunting and gathering groups, such as the Bushmen of the Kalahari desert or the Eskimo of the Arctic Regions of North America, represent the way of life of our own extinct ancestors of Upper Paleolithic or Mesolithic times in Europe or Asia. Bushmen and Eskimo have developed very specific and highly ingenious adaptations to specific, marginal environments. While their tools are simple, there is no reason to believe that their world views and religious practices have remained unchanged for some 20,000 years. Indeed, we know that they have moved into their present environments in relatively recent times.

The existing hunting and gathering groups, furthermore, present two additional obstacles to our search for origins and simple evolutionary schemes. (1) They represent a great deal of variation in beliefs and practices. We may generalize to say that game animals are usually of importance in the beliefs of hunting peoples, while fertility of plants and animals is of importance to horticultural and agricultural peoples. But these generalizations are very broad and must be amended considerably for any specific case. (2) Some of the groups with the simplest technology and least control over their environment exhibit what has been called a primitive form of monotheism, a belief in a single creator deity, which may or may not be surrounded by a host of lesser spirits. This contradicts the evolutionary theories according to which monotheism was a late development. One scholar, Wilhelm Schmidt, developed the theory of a universal primitive monotheism—traces of which are to be found among the most primitive peoples extant today—which was obscured by later developments.

**Magic and Religion.** Some writers, particularly Sir James Frazer, have attempted to distinguish between "magic" and "religion." Frazer claimed that religion was animistic, thus demanding the propitiation of superior powers, whereas magic was mechanistic and concerned with direct cause-effect relations and was indeed primitive man's science. Others, such as Bronisław Malinowski, have shown that both magic and religion deal with areas outside of primitive man's empirical knowledge. Malinowski did, however, contrast magic and religion. He asserted that magic deals with areas of individual concern, such as health and fertility, whereas religion deals with areas of group concern, such as the irreparable disruption of the group as a result of death.

**Continuity of Religion.** The great variety of magico-religious phenomena must be stressed, and simple, unitary systems of explanation are to be avoided. While certain differences between the world religions and primitive religions have been mentioned above, distinctions should not make us overlook the important factors of continuity. All human groups find it necessary to develop explanatory systems with implications for action. Primitive religions are the systems of this type which tribal societies have developed in the course of their long histories. Their specific beliefs and rituals may at times appear strange to us. However, they can be understood in terms of their own histories and cultures and the functions which these practices play in the maintenance of the individual societies as going concerns. Nor must we believe that primitive religions lack ethical content. Indeed, the force that belief and religious institutions exert as social sanctions often makes other formal sanctions like law unnecessary.

We must also recall that while we know a great deal about the formal theological positions held by various representatives of the world religions, we know, on the whole, very little of the actual beliefs of those in the great civilizations who are *not* religious specialists. There is reason to think that there is much continuity in our civilization with the animistic and magical beliefs of tribal peoples, often in the guise of science itself.

**AGNOSTICISM** [ăg-nŏs'tĭ-sĭz-əm], from the Greek *a*, "not," and *gignoskos*, "knowing," a term coined by Thomas Henry Huxley to denote his skeptical view of religion, and now used generally to refer to the attitude and tenets of those who believe that the existence of God cannot be known or proved, and who urge, therefore, a suspension of belief.

**ANIMISM** [ăn'ə-mĭz-əm], term introduced into anthropological writings by Sir Edward B. Tylor in 1871, defined as "the general belief in spiritual beings," which constituted for him the minimum definition of religion. People lacking such a belief were from his standpoint without religion. On the other hand, all religions from the lowliest to the highest represented in his theory forms of animism. He held that primitive man developed the idea of spirits from a belief in immaterial souls which survive the body. This idea he further held to have been derived from such experiences as dreams, trance states, and the awareness of death. He accumulated a vast body of materials from a broad range of different societies to substantiate his generalizations. He found that among primitive peoples the idea of soul easily expanded to include souls of animals and even of inanimate objects, as well as of men. Ingeniously, he derived the idea of sacrifice from animism.

Tylor's aim was not only to describe the existing beliefs of mankind, but also to find in the wide distribution of certain beliefs evidence for the evolution of culture, especially religion. Together with many of his contemporaries, he held that existing primitive peoples—that is, peoples without written traditions—were to be equated with the early types of man, who left only scant evidence of their beliefs in the archeological record. He thought that beliefs and practices of diverse peoples were strictly comparable, without consideration of the particular history or culture of the groups in question. He believed, further, that it was possible to discover in the practices of contemporary peoples those which were survivals of the past and could therefore reveal the path of evolutionary progress.

Tylor's evolutionary doctrines and his comparative method have been largely superseded. His theory of the origin of "the belief in spiritual beings" has been criticized as too rational, and various other forms of primitive religion have been suggested as earlier, such as totemism, animatism, and ancestor worship. Yet his view that the belief in souls derives from such human experiences as dreams and trances still has adherents.

The term "animism" is also frequently used to characterize the assumption that all, or most, things in the universe are, or are potentially, animate, and have such personal characteristics as volition. It is often stated that primitive peoples are animistic in this sense, and that animism represents the childhood of mankind. It is similarly also often stated that there is an animistic phase in the development of children. But both these propositions have been challenged.

The term is also used to designate the general religious beliefs of tribal groups who are not adherents of such world religions as Christianity, Buddhism, and Islam. Thus in African census reports animists are distinguished from Christians and Muslims.

**ASCETICISM** [ə-sĕt′ə-sĭz-əm] (Gr. *asketes*, "one who practices virtue"), a discipline of self-denial, renunciation, and detachment, known to all higher religions. It is found to a marked degree in some Eastern religions, especially in Hinduism and Buddhism, and was practiced also by some of the schools of Greek philosophy, particularly by the Stoics and Cynics. In the Hellenistic period of the Roman Empire, it characterized certain Gnostic sects, where it was based on the doctrine that matter is evil and only spirit is good. The purpose of Gnostic, like the later Manichaean, ascetic practices, therefore, was to liberate the spirit from matter and unite it with the divine.

Asceticism in the Judaeo-Christian tradition is derived from the doctrine that God is the creator of everything, and that man is created in His image. The purpose of this asceticism, therefore, is not to deny the body, but to achieve peace with God through discipline of the body.

The main characteristics of Christian asceticism in the early years were detachment from the world, the practice of continence and virginity, and the renunciation of personal property. The early ascetics found the source and inspiration for this life in the New Testament "asceticism of the Cross."

In the 3d century in Alexandria, a theology of asceticism was developed, defining the aim of ascetic practice as the vision of God. Fasting, continence, and virginity were not ends in themselves, but preparation for the contemplative life, which required some measure of solitude. Thus the most dramatic expression of asceticism in the late 3d and early 4th centuries was the life of Christian hermits like St. Antony, who sought the solitude of the desert, and ironically found themselves surrounded by a community of admiring disciples. As a result Christian asceticism eventually found its most accepted expression in monasticism.

Asceticism dramatizes the basic tension between the revealed and the temporal order, between the world to come and this world. It affirms that man's purpose is to know, love, and be united with God. Therefore ascetics have consistently fought the tendency to reduce religion to a matter of ritual observances.

**ATHEISM** [ā′thē-ĭz-əm], the doctrine that there is no God. The word is often applied loosely, as a term of abuse, to anyone whose definition of God disagrees with that of the speaker. It is in this sense that Spinoza was called an atheist, despite the fact that one of the main tenets of his philosophy asserts that only God has substantial existence.

Atheism must be distinguished from agnosticism, for the latter doctrine does not deny that God exists, but rather denies that we can know whether or not there is a God. Arguments for agnosticism tend to consist, for the most part, of criticisms of theistic attempts to prove the existence of God. They are appropriately negative in seeking to destroy grounds for believing that there is a God without attempting to prove that the theistic conclusion is false. Atheism, on the other hand, affirms that we can know that there is no God, and is therefore inconsistent with agnosticism.

The traditional atheist argument is the argument from

evil. One formulation of this is as follows: If there were a God then He would, by definition, be both good and powerful. If there were a good and powerful God, then there could be no evil in the world. But there is evil. Therefore there is no God.

Although formally unobjectionable, the argument from evil can be criticized on material grounds, and theists have urged that one or more of its premises are in fact false. Thus, it has been argued that God is not "good" in the sense of the word that applies to familiar, mundane virtue; that God need not be sufficiently powerful to prevent evil; and even that there is really no evil in the world. It is interesting to note that the most significant argument offered in defense of atheism is a moral argument.

**DEISM** [dē′ĭz-əm], religious belief in a God who has created the world and then has no further concern with it. The term is used specifically to describe a particular philosophical movement of the 17th and 18th centuries. Influenced by the writings of Herbert of Cherbury and, particularly, by John Locke's *Reasonableness of Christianity* (1695), the Deists attempted to establish religious belief based upon reason alone. They believed in God, but rejected the uniqueness of the Christian Scriptures. Some accepted the Christian notion of immortality, while others rejected it.

The movement found greatest expression in England, led by such men as Matthew Tindal (1657–1733), whose *Christianity as Old as the Creation* (1730) was considered the Deists' bible, and Henry St. John, Viscount Bolingbroke (1678–1751). In France the movement was represented by Voltaire and the Encyclopedists, and in Germany by Hermann Samuel Reimarus (1694–1768). Later, Deism became influential in America, particularly through Thomas Paine's *Age of Reason* (1794), which was the American classic on the subject. Other adherents were Ethan Allen, Benjamin Franklin, and to a lesser extent, Thomas Jefferson.

**GNOSTICISM** [nŏs′tə-sĭz-əm], group of religious movements of the first two centuries of the Christian Era which offered salvation on the basis of a secret wisdom (Gr. *gnosis*) more complex and exciting than the relatively simple beliefs of Jews and Christians. Gnosticism has been considered as a Hellenic influence on Christianity, but Oriental strains, including eccentric forms of Judaism, seem more conspicuous. Our chief information has come from Christian writers who described Gnosticism as they attacked it; in recent years this has been amplified by the discovery of Gnostic writings in various languages. Most Gnostic systems are based on some form of dualism—either a dualism of finite and infinite, connected by a series of emanations, or a dualism of good and evil, explained as the struggle of rival divine powers. The two greatest Gnostic systems, representing these two ideas respectively, are those of Valentinus of Alexandria and Marcion of Pontus, who flourished in the mid-2d century. Both of these claimed to present a superior form of Christianity; but some other Gnostics were pagans who merely introduced Jewish or Christian names and ideas into their systems, which had contacts with philosophy, on one hand, and magic, on the other. After the 2d century Gnosticism as such was moribund, though its influence lingered in such diverse movements as Neoplatonism and Manichaeism, and later in some of the medieval heresies.

notions borrowed from Buddhism, Gnosticism, and orthodox Christianity. The Manichaeans were thought of by some people, including some of their own followers, as heretic Christians. Mani had in fact declared that his message superseded that of Jesus. Despite persecution, Manichaeism spread widely in the East and the West, and traces of it were still found in Asia in the 17th century.

**HENOTHEISM** [hĕn'ō-thē-ĭz-əm] (Gr. *hen*, "one"; *theos*, "god"), term applied to two different forms of worship of a supreme being. One form is somewhat like monotheism; the other is closer to polytheism. The form encountered by the Hebrews in the eastern Mediterranean during the 2d and 1st millennia B.C. was a variant on monotheism: each tribe or culture had its own deity, who was supreme among that people, but not, or not necessarily, supreme among neighboring peoples. The henotheism of the Hindus of the Vedic period (also 2d and 1st millennia B.C.) was a variant on polytheism, the worship of many gods. The vedic worship recognized one member of a pantheon as the supreme being at a given time, succeeded in turn by another member of the pantheon.

**MANA** [mä'nä], inanimate power believed by Polynesians and other peoples to reside in objects or persons and to account for their skills, achievements, or special qualities. Thus an ax has mana to cut and a singer has it to sing. In Polynesia, where this belief is traditional, mana increases with each generation and with birth order, so that a firstborn son has greater mana than his parents. The term "mana" originated in Melanesia, but similar beliefs have almost world-wide distribution. Among American Indians, the concepts of manitou, orenda, and wakanda are similar in nature. Robert R. Marrett, an English anthropologist, held that belief in mana was the earliest form of religion.

**MANICHAEISM** [măn-ə-kē'ĭz-əm], a religion founded by the fanatic Persian mystic Mani (c.242 A.D.). Manichaeism was dualistic, holding that there are two major conflicting forces in the world. There is the good, spiritual power of Light and the evil, material power of Darkness. Man, a creation of Evil, but compounded in part of Light, was to strive to release the Light within himself in order to bring about the ultimate triumph of Light over Darkness. Members of this secretive sect who rejected the material in favor of austerity became "elect" or perfect, assured that death would mean immediate entry into eternal bliss. Adherents of lesser purity, known as auditors—St. Augustine was an auditor for a decade prior to his conversion to Christianity—could be reborn to try to perfect themselves and become "elect." Those who rejected the Manichaean revelation were doomed to eternal darkness.

Manichaeism was a blending of Zoroastrianism, with

**MONISM** [mŏn'ĭz-əm, mō'nĭz-əm], any philosophical theory attempting to explain complex phenomena by postulating one basic kind of entity or cause. In metaphysics there are several kinds of monism. (1) Materialistic: the entire universe is explicable in terms of matter; all theories of mind or spirit are unnecessary (Lucretius, Karl Marx). (2) Idealistic: the entire universe is explicable entirely in terms of mind or spirit; the hypothesis of dead or nonliving matter is inconsistent and unnecessary (George Berkeley, J. G. Fichte). (3) Neutral: there is a basic stuff in the universe which is neither mind nor matter, but appears sometimes as one and sometimes as the other (William James, Bertrand Russell). (4) Pantheistic: the basic stuff of the universe is God or the One, appearing in different forms under two general attributes, thought and extension (Spinoza; some Neo-Platonists). Monism is contrasted with dualism and pluralism, which postulate two or more basic explanatory factors in the universe.

**MONOTHEISM** [mŏn-ō-thē'ĭz-əm] (Gr. *monos*, "one"; *theos*, "god"), belief in one God as the Creator and Governor of the universe. Monotheism must first be distinguished from polytheism and henotheism. In polytheism there may be a hierarchy of gods of whom one is the supreme deity, as Zeus was among the Olympians, and Odin among the Norse gods in Asgard. In henotheism, the tribe or nation may worship only one god, to whom they feel the debt of absolute allegiance, without denying the existence of the gods of other tribes and nations.

Next monotheism must be distinguished from pantheism, on the one hand, and deism, on the other. In pantheism God is not the Creator of the universe, but the universe itself. In deism, while he may have been the Creator of the universe, he is not its perpetual Governor.

In the strict sense, Judaism, Christianity, and Islam are probably the only monotheistic religions, and they all stem from the one tradition: Hebrew monotheism.

Historically the question regarding monotheism is: Did monotheism develop from these conflicting views of deity, or are these conflicting views retrogressions from a once universal monotheism? As far as history is concerned, the Egyptian King Ikhnaton (14th century B.C.) was the first national figure to have formulated a monotheistic belief and worship, and Hebrew monotheism was an 8th-century B.C. development of the great Hebrew prophets.

But what about prehistoric man? According to Sir Edward Burnett Tylor (1832–1917), the first professor of anthropology at Oxford, the most primitive religion was some form of animism. Later Sir James G. Frazer, of Cambridge, presented the view that prehistoric man at first had no religion at all, his life being dominated by magic. Then Gilbert Murray, of Oxford, showed how in Greek religion Olympian polytheism had developed from magic and a more primitive nature worship. However, the Austrian anthropologist Wilhelm Schmidt (1868–1954), a Roman Catholic priest, has advanced the thesis of a monotheistic high god concept among primitive men, in his *Ursprung der Gottesidee* (Origin of the Idea of God), 1912, a view also held by others. An example of the high god concept cited is that of Manitou, the supreme being of the Algonkian and other Indian tribes of North America. But the American anthropologist D. G. Brinton (1837–99), in his *Myths of the New World* (1868), and the American ethnologist H. R. Schoolcraft (1793–1864), in *Notes on the Iroquois* (1847), held a different opinion. They believed that the concept of a supreme being, Manitou, among these North American Indians was a creature of European acculturation through the early missionary work of the Jesuits. The issue is still debated.

**MYSTICISM** [mĭs'tə-sĭz-əm] (from Gr. *mystes*, "one who is initiated"), practice of communion or union with the supernatural. It is commonly associated with a rite of initiation which causes the initiate to transcend earthly experience and feel a oneness with the extra-earthly.

According to William James in his *Varieties of Religious Experience* (1902), the mystical is actually or potentially an aspect of all religious systems and is world-wide in its distribution but varies in significance in different times and cultures. The shamans of northern Asia evoke a trance state, in the course of which communication with the spirit world is presumably effected and healing acts and divination are performed. Yoga in Hinduism and nirvana in Buddhism are mystical states of sensory transcendence, which form the subject of a highly developed speculative literature in Asian thought.

The mystical state played only a minor part in the ancient Hebrew religion, but the medieval cabalistic tradition was strongly mystical, and the later 18th-century Hasidic sect based upon the cabala was primarily concerned with the achievement of spiritual ecstasy. In ancient Greece the Orphic and Dionysian cults were essentially mystical, and when Christianity emerged it soon found itself in competition with these Greek mystery cults and with Persian Mithraism. Through the centuries Christianity has developed its own great mystics: Meister Eckhart (13th and 14th centuries), St. Catherine of Siena (14th century), St. Teresa of Avila and St. John of the Cross (16th century), and Jakob Boehme (17th century). And in Islam the Sufic cult particularly has developed a doctrine and ritual of mysticism.

**ORTHODOXY** [ôr'thə-dŏk-sē], conformity to an official, accepted body of doctrine, especially with reference to religion. Deviation from such doctrine is heterodoxy, and

opposition to it, heresy. Since several differing "orthodox" groups may exist within a religion, it is probably impossible to determine which holds the "right," or official, belief. For such distinction, a widely accepted standard by which to judge the conflicting "orthodoxies" would be necessary, but this criterion seldom exists. Hence, orthodoxy at any particular time is usually the result of historical circumstances rather than of an absolute, rational decision.

Early Christian orthodoxy was centered about faith in Christ and faith in the power of His Church to guide man toward salvation. The Eastern branch, influenced by the Greek emphasis on reason, supplemented faith with theology (which included the concept of the Trinity). The Western branch was influenced by Roman Stoicism (and hence emphasized man's moral life) and by Rome's acquisition of empire (and hence stressed church organization and expansion). In later years, the Western Church (Roman Catholic) also accepted reason as a necessary adjunct to faith. Faith, however, still remains the foundation of Roman orthodoxy.

Protestant orthodoxy began in the mid-16th century with the Reformation confessions of faith—statements based on the teachings of Luther and Calvin (for example, the Augsburg Confession, 1530, and the Belgic Confession, 1561). In the 17th and 18th centuries Protestant orthodoxy laid down rigid formulations, particularly the inerrancy of the Bible, a view still accepted by fundamentalists. Liberalism and modernism, however, have tended in the 20th century to ease the strict orthodoxies of the past.

In Judaism orthodoxy is usually judged by the strictness of conformity to the Torah (the five books of Moses) and the Talmud (additional laws). The more liberal branches of Judaism (Conservative and Reform) may be considered heterodox, or even heretical, by the Orthodox, depending on how far they diverge from "right" belief.

**PANTHEISM** [păn'thē-ĭz-əm], religious doctrine that sees God in all existence, either from the point of view that God is the universe or that the universe in its totality is God. The Jewish and Christian religions accept a transcendent God, and thus reject pantheism. Some other religions, notably Hinduism, are based on a pantheistic concept. The term "pantheism" is also used to refer to the worship of various gods of different cults, or to the toleration of the worship of various gods.

**POLYTHEISM** [pŏl'ĭ-thē-ĭz-əm] (Gr. *poly*, "many"; *theos*, "god"), belief in and worship of more than one deity, in contrast to henotheism and monotheism. The term is of Greek origin and referred to the plurality of gods in the Greek pantheon. Polytheistic worship is found among many peoples. Polynesians, for instance, worshiped gods of the sky, peace, war, and a supreme, or primary, creator. The Algonkins of North America had many manitous (gods), relating to various natural forces and objects in the sky and on earth. The Buryats and other peoples of North Asia had the practice of worshiping not only gods but lesser spirits as well. The distinction between the worship of a deity and the veneration of spirits is not always hard and fast.

**THEOSOPHY** [thē-ŏs'ə-fē] (from Gr. *theos*, "god"; *sophos*, "wise"), literally "divine wisdom," or "knowledge of the divine," arrived at by direct intuition or philosophical speculation sometimes supplemented by historic revelation. Early examples of theosophy are Gnosticism and Neoplatonism. Specifically, the word today refers to a modern movement of religio-philosophical character founded by Helen P. Blavatsky and organized in New York City in 1875 with the help of Col. Henry S. Olcott as The Theosophical Society. Madame Blavatsky and Col. Olcott settled later in India and established world headquarters for the movement at Adyar, near Madras.

Theosophy represents a combination of religious and philosophical ideas drawn from Christianity, Hinduism, Buddhism, and Egyptian Hermeticism. The writings of Madame Blavatsky, purporting to be an ancient wisdom received by her chiefly from "the Masters," serve as its principal basis. Annie Besant succeeded Olcott as world president and was perhaps the foremost writer and exponent of Theosophy's teachings. Like other movements, it soon developed divisions. In America one branch has its headquarters on the West Coast, while the Theosophical Society in America has its center at Wheaton, Ill. Through the teachings of Theosophy some knowledge of Hinduism and Hindu influence has penetrated Western culture.

# INDEX